GIALLO MELTDOWN:
A Moviethon Diary

Richard Glenn Schmidt

Copyright © 2015 Richard Glenn Schmidt

All rights reserved.

ISBN: 150783912X
ISBN-13: 978-1507839126

DEDICATION

Like everything else, this is for the killer.

CONTENTS

Thank Yous

Introduction   1

The First Giallo Meltdown   3

13 More Kills for the Killer   22

La miasma della morte   36

Red, Yellow, and Black Forever   60

Black Glove Outlet Mall   80

The Murderess Kills Her Victims to Death   98

The Case of the Bleeding Eyeholes   114

Rusty Straight Razor Dance Party   134

Planet Giallo   158

Laughter in a Glass Coffin   175

You Should Have Killed Me When You Had the Chance   192

Penultimate Radiation   220

The Last Dead Body (is Mine)   242

Index   261

THANK YOUS

To my mom, Darlyn, who has always said that she knew that my writing would make me rich and famous one day. And now that day has come. Oh wait, what? I guess I better keep at it. To my wife LeEtta, who has seen more gialli than any seemingly normal woman should ever see. She supported me while working on this book in the hopes that we would eventually get back to British period pieces. To my mother-in-law, Margie, who saw quite a few obscure gialli with us during all this craziness. This kind woman was relentlessly supportive of all of my projects and funded more than a few purchases of some great giallo DVDs. Lady, you will be missed greatly. To my friend Brad Hogue (and his wife Elizabeth), who, despite living several states away, is my brother-in-arms in all things gialli. He's a true blue duder and his enthusiasm for genre cinema knows no bounds. To my friend Shelly Freauf, who has attended more moviethons and has sat through more crappy movies with us than any of our other friends. To my friend Eric Grubbs, who has encouraged and advised me on my book projects. Go find his books now! To all my friends who stopped by to attend a moviethon: Nafa Fa'alogo, Richie Saldivar, Matt Torrence, Stephanie Pincus, Zac Tomlinson, Kat Horace, Sam Higgins, Kathleen & Mackenzie. And last but not least, I have to thank some of my Internet pals that encouraged, lent a hand, and/or inspired me along the way: Ryan Clark, Jeffrey Canino, Shrub G Haus, Justin Kosch, Joseph A. Ziemba, Scott MacDonald, Troy Howarth, Chris Baker, Davo, Aaron Duenas, Martin-Luther Presley, Simon Wright, Jose Cruz, Jeff Chaffee, Matt Farley & The Shockmarathons crew, The Giallo Ciao Ciao Crew, Robert Harrison, Jacob Gustafson, K H Brown.

INTRODUCTION

I like to pretend that there is a tiny little country filled with both tacky ultra-modern and beautiful classic architecture existing alongside one another in equal measure, lit in garish, sometimes psychedelic colored lights at all times. Its population is made up of 3 types of people: beautiful women, red herrings, and killers. On every street corner, in every cruddy apartment, mansion, lunatic asylum, rundown theater, or castle, someone is being killed with a straight razor, a knife, an axe, a meat cleaver, a garrote, or a shallow bathtub. Everyone starts out more or less happy in this little country. Each citizen is issued oversized sunglasses and bottles of J&B Scotch Whiskey. But then they inherit a fortune, spurn the advances of a psychotic lesbian, or witness a terrible crime. This is when their slick polyester duds become stained with fluorescent and impossibly red blood. Priests, hookers, wealthy jetsetters, artists, musicians, police detectives, hobos, hippies, blackmailers, and especially fashion models are all dropping like flies while a million black-gloved murderers are working around the clock, making sure that the murders never, ever stop.

Welcome to Giallo Meltdown, my friends. For the uninitiated, giallo (or gialli in plural form) is a somewhat obscure subgenre of thriller films. It first generated in Italy where the pulp mystery novels had yellow (or 'giallo' in Italian) spines. The heyday of this genre was in the 1960s and 1970s and the films are primarily Italian though Spain, England, the US, and a few other countries got caught up in the act. In the 1980s and 1990s, the giallo fell out of favor thanks in part to its bastard child, the slasher film. But these yellow films never really died and some filmmakers are still letting its bloody influence seep into their work to this day.

I got into giallo in the same way that I think a lot of its fans did: through Italian horror. Thanks to Joe D'Amato's Absurd, Dario Argento's Phenomena, Michele Soavi's The Church, and Lamberto Bava's Demons, the groundwork had been laid in my youth for my Italian horror awakening. In 2002, after a long break from horror movies, something snapped in my brain and I became a diehard fan of the genre. It wasn't long before I found out about the giallo genre and I was hooked from the start. This book is the diary that I kept while I obsessively watched as many gialli in a row as my mind and body could handle.

The miracle of DVD, Blu-ray, awesome bootleg companies, and The Internet brought me a staggering number of titles and I never stop feeling like the luckiest son of a gun in the world. For all you genre cinema purists out there, this book may annoy you. I am very liberal with the definition of what is and isn't a giallo so there are bound to be some controversial titles stuck in these pages. It's been my intention from the very beginning to see every giallo ever made and to see how far the blood-soaked tendrils of this subgenre continue to reach to this day. If I feel like the genre influenced a film in a profound way, it's here. I hope you will approach Giallo Meltdown with an open mind and not be too harsh on my choices. No one is going to mistake this book for the 'Definitive Guide to the Giallo' and I never set out to do that. This is my journey through my favorite Italian-born brand of trash cinema and I hope you have fun with it.

I documented each of these moviethons in real time and let the writing happen as I experienced these films, many of them for the first time. Sometimes, in my cinematic stupor, things got really weird and confused and in my editing, I have done little to fix anything. The more surreal moments and the stream-of-consciousness ramblings are some of my fondest memories, even if they are very blurry.

Most importantly, I want you to know that if I could stage each of these moviethons all over again and invite you along for the ride, I would. If you've ever devoted an entire weekend (or longer) to the consumption of movie after movie after movie then you know what I'm talking about. Even if you don't know, I wish you could have been there! I hope this is enough.

Before I forget, I must mention that I did my best not to ruin the endings of the films I've written about in this book. Yes, some plot details are spoiled in my ramblings but I never reveal the killer's identity or give the whole thing away.

THE FIRST GIALLO MELTDOWN

I've been wanting to do a giallo moviethon for about 4 years now but I had so few titles that it was impossible to put one together. Well, the tide has turned and now I have too many to fit them all into just one movie marathon. In order to bring down the numbers, I decided to eliminate the masters, Dario Argento, Mario Bava, and Lucio Fulci, from the playlist. Sorry boys but I figured it was time to examine the best of the rest of the Italian genre directors. Besides, I've got a hankerin' for some Umberto Lenzi, Aldo Lado, and Sergio Martino.

I narrowed my selection down to 28 titles, printed them up, cut them into little strips of paper, and then stuffed the strips into a black glove (actually one of my wife's mittens) so that they can be selected at random throughout the moviethon. The entire event was scheduled to begin on Friday night and end around 60 hours later on Sunday night. To make sure that I had enough time to recover, I took the following Monday off of work. My wife LeEtta did the same so that she could take part. I also invited several friends over to come and get giallofied.

Little did I know that two and half days later, I would be mentally and physically whipped, slashed, and bludgeoned by only 21 of those 28 titles. There was nothing that could have prepared me for the cackling madness and alarming physical breakdown in store for me. The combination of junk food and an ocean of caffeinated beverages did their damage as well. Dear readers, this is the story of the very first Giallo Meltdown and I swear that all of it is true.

FRIDAY

LeEtta and I get off work and head immediately for ABC Liquor where she can get some Admiral Nelson's spiced rum. I already have some J&B at the apartment so I'm all good. We hit up Cigar Castle so that I can stock up on some smokes. The Macanudo Bus is there and we finagle some free cigars along with my three purchased cigars: Top Cigars, Oliva, and Tatuaje. We then run by Wendy's (it's on the way home) and pick up an easy dinner.

I say a few opening remarks to LeEtta, the cats, and our bird since no one else has arrived yet. I then take a big swig of J&B to christen the beginning of the marathon. I give LeEtta the honor of picking the first movie and she chooses one I've never seen: The Iguana with the Tongue of Fire. Ladies and gentleman, this yellowest of yellow Moviethons has begun!

"Well now, my fleet-footed filly, are we going to have it off in the bushes or on the bike?"

6:45 PM
The Iguana with the Tongue of Fire (1971)

Whoa, acid in the face! And we're off to a good start. LeEtta refers to Luigi Pistilli as 'the Italian Jeremy Irons' and I'm not going to argue with that. His voice actor is awful and the scriptwriters think that Irish people say "well now" at the beginning of every sentence. Hilarious. More dialogue malfeasance occurs when Inspector Lawrence tries to explain the iguana metaphor behind the title of the movie. LeEtta and I are dumbstruck by that one.

Hey look, Renato Romano (of Seven Blood-Stained Orchids) playing a shifty-eyed limo driver. Wait, what is going on with the plot? No worries, the presence of a young Dagmar Lassander helps me to forget all of my cares. There's an Agatha Christie reference but before I can remark on its significance in this giallo, Anton Diffring erupts in an awesome freakout!

Director Riccardo Freda may not be at the top of his game with this one but dang, he's sure not afraid of the gore effects. Oh grandma, put on your glasses so you can hear what people are saying! This is definitely a great giallo to start with thanks to a black-gloved killer, red herrings every 5 minutes, and it's even shot with some style. The final reveal is pretty lame if I think about it too much but the bloody climax makes up for it. The first film of this moviethon is complete.

"She reminds me of a werewolf."

8:25 PM
Naked You Die (1968)

LeEtta reaches into the black glove and draws out this 1968 Antonio Margheriti film. The mod soundtrack and that amazing "Nightmare" song were probably out of fashion the moment this film hit theatres. It already reminds me of a German Krimi rather than a Giallo. The movie is so light and fun that I keep expecting Dinah Shore to show up. Instead, the frighteningly expressive Marc Damon (of Johnny Yuma) is here to creep me out with that freaky smile and a hankerin' for the student body.

Speaking of creepy, just look at Jill. She looks like Jerri Blank! Isn't she just so much fun with her walkie talkies?! Eleonora Brown makes everything sweet as the romantic Lucille. And Luciano Pigozzi (Baron Blood) makes a fine groundskeeper but an even better pervert. However, it's the scenery and the cinematography that really steals the film. Where the hell was this filmed? Ugh, that scuba gear bit was pretty much the most awful thing I've ever seen.

This film is starting to lose me. My friend Richie arrives (with two 32oz bottles of Miller High Life (for him not for me)) just in time to witness me begging Naked You Die to end. I can't really put my finger on why this film is pissing me off so much. The lack of blood and gratuitous nudity isn't really the problem. I can handle a tame flick. It's just that all of the fun of the first half has just drained away. I suspect that if I give this film another shot at a later date, I'll probably end up loving it. (Author's note: I was right, I totally love Naked You Die now.)

CIGAR BREAK

Richie and I retreat to the patio so that I can complain some more about the retardulous (that's retarded and ridiculous) Naked You Die. The weather is cool but not nearly enough for December. The Christmas lights I put up are twinkling very nicely. I light up an Oliva cigar (a new favorite of mine ever since the Argentophobia Moviethon) and crack open a Monster energy drink. We discuss the films to come and my plans to keep watching them until the dawn of Monday morning. After I've smoked the cigar down to the nub and talked Richie's ear off, we head back inside.

"The past and your fate are linked with death."

11:25 PM
The Bloodstained Shadow (1978)

Richie pulls Antonio Bido's The Bloodstained Shadow from the black glove and I'm pretty psyched. This was one of those flicks that I outright hated upon first viewing it but I've come around to it. It's still a slow burn but it is an intelligent and a visually stunning giallo. There's a really creepy inbred vibe coming from the small-minded townsfolk. Take that and combine it with some sacrilegious imagery and you've got one of them there artistic statements, I think.

Much like Dario Argento's Bird with the Crystal Plumage, a piece of art and a recurring memory hold the key to solving the case. Oh snap, there's a séance! I really do have an indiscriminate love for séances in horror movies! I love the scenes with Lino Capolicchio and Craig Hill shouting at each other. Hmm, I think I needs me some gourmet cheese. I open the package of Cotswold that LeEtta's mom sent us and it is some mighty fine stuff.

Speaking of cheesy, what is with that gay boat ride? We are all alarmed by Sandra's (Stefania Casini) lack of grief over her mother's death. For God's sake, someone stuffed mommy's friggin' head into a lit fireplace.

Well, at least she's painting her way through her pain. This movie's soundtrack is brought to you by not only Stelvio Cipriani but Goblin as well. Now there's a fuckin' power team! Their music fits together perfectly with the chilling atmosphere Bido brings to the film.

"Too many books never did a woman any good."

1:15 AM
Seven Deaths in the Cat's Eye (1973)

I pull the strip of paper out of the black glove and I'm a little disappointed. Seven Deaths in the Cat's Eye is good but I was hoping for Richie's benefit that it would be something more typical for the genre. The gothic overtones and quasi-supernatural moments nearly disqualify this as a giallo. However, a black-gloved killer, a slew of murders, and a totally insane plot manage to stabilize its genre status. Holy shit, some rats just ate that duder's face off. Could Luciano Pigozzi be the killer? Nope, he's dead.

Hey Corringa (Jane Birkin), nice job setting your dang bible on fire. That's two films filled with blasphemy in a row! And that ape. That's just filmic blasphemy. I hate monkeys. With that, LeEtta says she's going to bed. We bid her goodnight and I realize that I'm talking my head off which Richie finds amusing. No wonder nobody comes to these things. Oh, sweet bisexual Suzanne, you're as hot as Hiram Keller is a badass.

There is a sweet dream sequence with some very outlandish imagery that just kicks my ass all over town. Is this giallo fantastico? There is no question that the camerawork, the editing, and the lighting are all excellent in Seven Deaths. Oh great, another horribly fake Irish accent thanks to the voice actor dubbing over evil French composer/songwriter Serge Gainsbourg who plays the police inspector. My God, the lighting in this film is outstanding. Antonio Margheriti, I forgive you for Naked You Die.

FINAL THOUGHTS (FRIDAY)

Okay, so we had a shaky start. Fate wasn't cruel but she wasn't on my side either. What was with the two moderately-paced (SLOW!) gialli in a row for Richie? That's just cruel. And Naked You Die? What a huge disappointment. I can't remember the last time I was begging for a giallo to end. Oh wait, yeah I do. French Sex Murders, anyone? That shit is banned from the Moviethon. Richie takes his leave but wishes me luck on his way out. Well, I'm going to bed now. The easy part is over.

SATURDAY

It takes a helluva long time to get moving this morning. I'm tired as hell plus I was dreaming about gialli half the night. I kid you not, people, Joe Dellasandro was in my dreams! Hey, that's not gay at all. LeEtta and I go to breakfast at Einstein's for some bagel sammiches and then we go to the grocery store which turns out to be the longest event of our lives. A packed grocery store with three cashier's lanes open. Back home, we gamble with our scratch-off tickets and lose. Oh well, no luck there. LeEtta chooses Your Vice is a Locked Room and Only I Have the Key from the black glove. Hey, things are looking up.

> *"You see, murder has a habit of involving all sorts of people for no reason."*

11:00 AM
Your Vice is a Locked Room and Only I Have the Key (1972)

The giallo with the longest title I've ever seen also happens to be a favorite of mine. Director Sergio Martino cold rocks the genre with this one. Bruno Nicolai's score is fantabulous and gets stuck in my head instantly. This decadent film has the most sleaze, violence, nudity, and J&B than any of the films so far. Where was this one when Richie was here? Well, he did miss the hippies singing that "Daughter-Daughter" song. Fuck was that about?

It's about time that the bewitching Edwige Fenech showed up. More eye candy includes the very severe Anita Strindberg in one of her finest roles as the painfully mistreated Irina. Her well-written character sparks some debates between LeEtta and I about her motivations. Hey look, it's Luigi Pistilli once again. I have a tough time separating the actor from the drunken and criminally abusive Oliviero character in this movie. The guy is such a bastard. I like the underused actor, Franco Nebbia, as Inspector Faola. Did I mention the J&B?

Everything can be summed up by Ivan Rassimov's amazing gray hair. Or maybe it can be summed up in those lesbian scenes or a bag of sheep eyes. Woops, that was some (thankfully) unconvincing cat violence. I feel really bad about their poor maid Brenda. She probably should have quit a long time ago. Oh well, too late now. Hey, look more J&B!

I'm not saying you shouldn't name your cat Satan but be prepared for the worst when you do. Man, this film is as perverse as they come. It definitely lives up to its title. Folks at home, be sure to check out the equally awesome The Strange Vice of Mrs. Wardh, also featuring Fenech and Rassimov. All I can say now is that the next film is going to have to be pretty awesome to even come close to this one. Too bad there wasn't any J&B in Your Vice. (Wink.)

LUNCH

LeEtta escapes the moviethon to go to one of her friend Allison's baby shower. I go on a Taco Bell run to grab myself some completely unhealthy food; a Crunchwrap Supreme, a Chicken Quesadilla, and a Mountain Dew will do the trick. I'm starting to think that I should eat more healthy for the next Moviethon. Hmm... yeah. Anyway, before she left, LeEtta reached in the black glove and pulled out All the Colors of the Dark.

"Now you're one of us, Jane."

1:20PM
All the Colors of the Dark (1972)

Sergio Martino returns with a vengeance. The opening dream sequence is really nuts. Ivan Rassimov returns without the gray hair this time but with these odious blue contacts (that look quite painful). The way out soundtrack can't be ignored and nor can the luscious Edwige Fenech. George Hilton makes his first appearance in the Moviethon. Oh yes, we'll be seeing him again later. Hell, even the sweet and lovely Susan Scott is in this one.

This film borders on the giallo fantastico with its nightmarish visions, Satanic cult, and hints of ESP. I notice that the cats are sleeping through this one but not me, I'm all wound up. Besides, the whole issue of whether or not Jane (Fenech) is taking her weird blue pills has me in a tizzy. Well, I'll be damned. There's Luciano Pigozzi again! The duder gets around.

Here's another weird Giallo that gets better with multiple viewings though it does have a few problems. The plot gets so wound up with the conspiratorial angle that it just starts falling apart by the end. Jane's confession at the end is completely baffling. Oh well, the camerawork and the presence of the lovely Marina Malfatti make up for all of this. At the end of this film, I reach into the glove to find another Sergio Martino classic in my hands... Torso.

"Look at all those knockers."

2:57 PM
Torso (1973)

I can't believe my luck. A Sergio Martino trilogy? Sweet! It took me a while to acquire Torso on DVD but once I did, it was a revelation. This sleazy and reprehensible flick is loaded with hot chicks, gore, dirty hippies, and sex. This is a classic giallo custom made for the discerning Eurotrash connoisseur. Don't believe me? Just watch that priceless stalking sequence in the swamp. Or could you be convinced by the nudity in the first 18 seconds? The Italian title translates roughly to "The Body Bears Evidence of Carnal Violence". You're damn right it does!

The soundtrack by Guido and Maurizio De Angelis is so perfect for the material. I'm starting to get pretty sick of Suzy Kendall; can't really put my finger on it. However, I am still head over heels with Carla Brait though. She's awesome in The Case of the Bloody Iris but she doesn't get nearly enough to do here. Well, she gets to be a lesbian but I think that's the most character development she gets. Ernesto Colli, that painfully ugly guy from Autopsy, plays the ill-fated scarf seller. John Richardson of Eyeball is all up in my grill.

One of the best moments comes from the dumbfounded delivery boy: "Milk, bread, and eggs." The gore isn't very convincing but there certainly is enough of it to beat me into submission. Speaking of beatings, the dreamy Luc Merenda gets to pull off the most amazing drop kick I've ever seen during the climactic fight sequence. Torso ends and I'm completely satisfied yet I must reach into the black glove again. Oh hell yeah, it's time for Strip Nude for Your Killer. Edwige, I'll be with you soon.

> *"Don't get any ideas in that pretty little head,*
> *my sweet. You'll be sorry."*

4:32 PM
Strip Nude for Your Killer (1975)

When it comes to sleaze, forget Torso, this one will leave you feeling so very dirty. Even the funktastic theme song has an undeniable seediness to it. I'm just glad we finally get to my favorite giallo fodder: fashion models! Did someone say 'genital mutilation'? Okay! Where do I sign? As if Edwige Fenech and Femi Benussi weren't enough of a draw. Despite its grimy near-porno vibe, Strip Nude for Your Killer is shot and edited with style.

This movie would be nothing without its totally unlikeable "hero": Carlo. This prick is played by Nino Castelnuovo (Massacre Time) and the guy outdoes himself womanizing and choking Edwige Fenech. It's hard to convince someone of your innocence with your fingers wrapped around their throat. Well, unless you're a macho piece of shit, I guess. Carlo's bizarre ideas about milk are just totally astounding: "Milk is good for you. It gets your corpsuckles [sic] going. Especially after a strenuous evening."

Andrea Bianichi, you magnificent bastard, what have you done? I don't know who's more dangerous, the horrible fat man with the blow-up doll or the motorcycle jumpsuit-clad killer. What I do know is that this sex-obsessed flick lives up to its title and the final wrap-up is one of the greatest moments ever committed to film. Sorry about the butt sex threat, duder.

CIGAR BREAK, ETC.

LeEtta returns from her social engagement and we both run outside for some fresh evening air. While we are in front of our apartment building stretching, I start singing and dancing to the theme song of Strip Nude for Your Killer. Just as we're about to go back inside, our friend Shelly arrives with her own bottle of J&B and some smokes. We retreat to the patio where I light up an amazing Tatuaje cigar. After that, we order some Chinese food (that takes nearly two hours to arrive!) and Shelly picks Eyeball from the black glove.

"It's a personal tragedy to realize that I'm not immortal."

8:21 PM
Eyeball (1975)

Finally, we get to some Umberto Lenzi. Eyeball is certainly an appropriate title but the Italian one (which I prefer) roughly translates to "Red Cats in a Glass Maze". Even more odd is that my copy has the opening titles referring to the film as "The Secret Killer". Here we find yet another sweet score from Bruno Nicolai. The theme of which bores into your skull, finds a warm and squishy spot, and never leaves.

This entertaining little gem has got it all: J&B, ridiculous lesbian stereotypes, an entire cast of nutty red herrings (until they get killed), and even George Rigaud as a priest. Rigaud showed up in about 7 or 8 gialli during his career. Mmm, Martine Brochard. I have a huge crush on this chick but LeEtta and Shelly are sickened by how pasty and skinny she is. I agree that she needs a sammich especially since her boobs are about to roll off her ribcage. We're all intrigued by the lovely Naiba.

It's no Seven Blood-Stained Orchids (my favorite) that's for sure but Eyeball is one of Umberto Lenzi's most entertaining gialli. There's a plethora of eye violence and one victim's body is devoured by pigs! Okay, the movie suggests that her body was eaten by oinks but you don't really get to see that unfortunately. It's just another moment of confusion in this very convoluted plot that I love every minute of. LeEtta reaches into the glove and randomly selects A Blade in the Dark.

*"Listen to me, music man. Nothing will help.
I'm going to kill you."*

10:03 PM
A Blade in the Dark (1983)

While the credits are rolling, Shelly says, "Hey, I thought we weren't watching any Bava!" I tell her it's okay because it's Mario's son, Lamberto, behind the camera on this one. Mario Bava? Sorry but that's a whole other Moviethon for a whole different weekend. I'm digging on this cast: Andrea Occhipinti of New York Ripper, the great Michele Soavi, and of course, Stanko Molnar of Bava's Macabre. When I go on the lamb, I'll be using the name Stanko Molnar to keep the cops off my trail.

The first death scene puts Shelly into hysterics and I realize I'm in trouble. You see, what folks don't understand is that after you have watched hundreds of Italian horror films, you start failing to notice how silly these things are. Moments that would cause most folks to eject the DVD immediately just don't faze me anymore. But I digress…

Watch as I sing the praises of the male cast of A Blade in the Dark (or as I like to call it: "Desperately Seeking Julia"). The women, on the other hand, are pretty silly. Their characters just aren't written very well and the voice acting just blows. One particularly awkward line of dialogue causes Shelly and me to go nuts. When Sandra asks, "This is all the whiskey you possess?"; we pretty much lose it completely.

This painfully 80s film is definitely easy to heckle but I still love it. The claustrophobic atmosphere, the soundtrack by De Angelis, and the setting are all very cool. Plus, the kill scene in the bathroom has to be one of the most brutal in the genre. Before this movie can get too good though, we have goofy ass garbage like this: "That's not a spider, that's a cockroach!" one character yells as what is clearly a spider crawls across the floor.

SHORT BREAK

LeEtta did not survive the (mental and physical) carnage of A Blade in the Dark and went to bed some time ago. Shelly hits the road still in shock from the film. With "This is all the whiskey you possess?" still ringing in my ears, I reach into the black glove and pull out one of the finest examples of giallo: Seven Blood-Stained Orchids. Stupid randomness, why am I alone when this classic is drawn?

"Naturally, that's one thing you can be sure of, killers are out of their minds."

12:01 AM
Seven Blood-Stained Orchids (1972)

Antonio Sabato, you're my hero. Actually, Umberto Lenzi is my hero for directing this stylish and pitch perfect giallo. This was one of my first non-Argento and non-Fulci gialli that I'd seen when I had first gotten into this stuff and it still ranks way up there at the top of the heap for me. I find the story in this one to be the least clunky in the genre and the ending is suspenseful as hell.

I don't really like German actress Uschi Glas as a heroine but I suppose she'll do. Some of the supporting ladies in this flick are to die for. There's the severe Rosella Falk and the always gorgeous Marina Malfatti. Be sure to look out for Marisa Mell (Lucio Fulci's Perversion Story) in dual roles. Though he's not nearly as hot as the ladies, he's still a great character actor with a ton of personality; I'm talking about Renato Romano!

Everyone should watch this movie. It's got hippies, sexy women, and a nasty death scene involving a power drill. What more could anyone ever want? Okay, so maybe Uschi Glas has redeemed herself at least a little bit. The climactic stalking scene with her where she's being pursued by the killer around the grounds of her house is just amazing. And with that, it's time to pick the last film for the night from the black glove. Despite the dull ache that has settled in my eyes, I'm happy to see that I've chosen What Have You Done to Solange?

"Real screwing? No way. Not after what happened to Solange."

1:35 AM
What Have You Done to Solange? (1972)

Who has the greatest name of all time? Well, it's Fabio Testi. Wow. Fabio. Testi. Anyway, the guy is a great actor and his character in this film, Enrico, is such a dick. Somehow, I end up liking him despite what a bastard he is. His love affair with high school girl Elizabeth (played by Cristina Galbó) is hard to forgive when his wife is played by the stunning Karin Baal (who tries to look ugly in the first half of the film).

Oh my God. Look at that little lost kitten. Who will come along and rescue that little lost kitten? And what about that other little lost kitten? You know, the one inside of all of us? Aren't we all just little lost kittens? Who will rescue us?

I'm thinking that this film is trying to be provocative with its rampant nudity and genital mutilation but it's betrayed by the old fashioned morality in some of the characters' attitudes. Is a girl's life really worth less than her virginity? What the fuck is that about? Okay, so maybe the film is criticizing these beliefs, not supporting them. Meh, I'm too tired for analyzing. Director Massimo Dallamano's choice to expose the parents' and educators' naivety of the world of teenage girls works quite well.

There is a great moment with a priest lineup that totally goofs on the giallo genre. That's about all the fun we get here what with the violence being both brutal and depressing. Overall, Solange is very grim but actually quite smart for the genre. Its message may be as clear as mud but it is a great film with some stark and memorable images. Well, that concludes Saturday's films.

FINAL THOUGHTS (SATURDAY)

I'm trapped inside a maze of Italian architecture and razor-wielding murderers in terrible 70s fashions around every corner. There's lots and lots of corpses piling up almost too quickly to count and my only instinct is to watch more films. I'm really not looking forward to waking up tomorrow. I suspect that I'll feel like death warmed over. Wow, everything ended on a real downer with Solange. Yup. Goodnight.

SUNDAY

Somehow I manage to wake up and start getting ready for the final day of the Moviethon. Everything is a blur until my breakfast sandwich and a Coke at Bob Evans. This sandwich is composed of sausage, an egg, two kinds of cheese, and mustard (that's my addition) on a bun. I'm totally spaced out and my head and eyes are still sore from yesterday. In order to get me back on track, LeEtta and I go to 7-11 where I get a Java Monster Big Black energy drink for my troubles.

"I'm back, Kitty... And I'm going to kill you!"

10:26 AM
The Red Queen Kills 7 Times (1972)

LeEtta chooses very, very well from the black glove as The Red Queen Kills 7 Times is a classic. Everyone should run out and by the NoShame DVD immediately. Bruno Nicolai's soundtrack is haunting and infectious. Any film with Barbara Bouchet and Marina Malfatti playing sisters is priceless in my book. Unfortunately, the lead in this one leaves a lot to be desired. Ugo Pagliai is Martin, our bland hero, and let me tell you, this guy is no George Hilton.

Ah yes, our fashion models. And I also like that Freddie Mercury took a break from Queen in order to play the police inspector. I'm just kidding, the guy under that unfortunate mustache is Marino Masé and he can't protect you. That's what I love about this film. It just feels as though nowhere is safe. The Red Queen could strike at any time, even in broad daylight. Sorry kids, your unholy apartment décor and your giant sunglasses will not save you this time.

Beware the minor spoilers in this paragraph. I swear I'm not trying to spoil the film for you. Oh man, what is with that freaky junkie dude? Oops, he's dead. Although Martin's wife gets the best death scene in the movie, our rapist blackmailer junkie definitely tries to show her up with his exit. Model turned B-movie queen, Sybil Danning, is scorchingly hot in this one even though she has some sexy competition from Bouchet and Malfatti.

What I want to know is how in the hell they pulled off that watery dungeon bit for the climax? I think that is the most expensive setpiece I've ever seen in a giallo. The gothic setting in the German castle is one thing but that flooding sequence must have set the production company back a few bones. The only thing more elaborate is the nutty denouement with about 49 different twists. Geez, that's a great ending. I start dancing to the closing credit music and then reach into the black glove to find that I've chosen The Night Evelyn Came Out of Her Grave. YES!

"A lot of men like strange games."

12:14 PM
The Night Evelyn Came Out of the Grave (1971)

Chalk it up to happy coincidence or to my poor shuffling skills but the next film comes in the same double DVD set as The Red Queen Kills 7 Times. Emilio Miraglia, you retired (or died) much too soon. To give you an idea how much I love this film, this is my third time owning a copy of it. First, I bought it on a whim on one of those bargain horror collections. I loved it and after I discovered it was blatantly censored, I bought it again when the Eclectic DVD came out. That turned out to be a disaster so I jumped at the chance to get the NoShame DVD.

Anthony Steffen is pretty fearless in this film. His character, Lord Alan Cunningham, is such a piece of shit. It took me a couple of times before it really sunk in that the guy is a dang serial killer. Well, with friends like Dr. Timberlane (Giacomo Rossi-Stuart) and Cousin George (Enzo Tarascio), it's no wonder Lord Alan has gone off the deep end. Watch out, ladies, he's a hair puller. Ouch. Hey look, Erika Blanc is doing a strip tease in a coffin!

Classy. Marina Malfatti... AGAIN? Damn, she's all over this Moviethon.

This truly wacky flick has albino maids and the brutal death of the wheelchair-bound Aunt Agatha which is probably my favorite death scene in the entire giallo genre. My reheated Chinese food from last night hits the spot perfectly and I'm thinking that composer Bruno Nicolai must have gotten his first Echoplex when he was writing the music for this one. Uh oh, we're getting all twisty here.

There is a genre defining moment in this one. If I tell you what the hell's going on, it'll spoil the whole dang thing. You'll just have to see this one for yourselves, folks. The ending just leaves me shrugging my shoulders and going: "All's well that ends well, I guess." Knowing that life can't get much better than this, LeEtta chooses Killer Nun from the glove.

> *"Oh, come on. Look this way. Sister Gertrude is just dying to make love to you."*

1:56 PM
Killer Nun (1979)

It still surprises me that this is one of LeEtta's favorites. It certainly is a memorable and sacrilegious piece of trash that is as much of a nunsploitation film as it is a giallo. Anita Ekberg is really slumming it up this time but at least it's better than French Sex Murders. The denture smashing scene is probably the funniest/cruelest thing I've ever witnessed. Joe Dallesandro, the man of my dreams, is here and is (thankfully) dubbed but I swear I can still hear his horrendous voice in my head. Oh well, the super-hot Paola Morra is here to take the pain away.

Ekberg's performance as the troubled Sister Gertrude is pretty amazing. She commits more acts of nunly malfeasance than you can imagine. She goes from slutty nun to junky nun to lesbinun and I couldn't ask for more. My God, this movie teeters on the brink of destruction. I don't know how it manages to stay together. Luckily, there's a cast of weirdos to keep things from getting dull.

Woops, what was I just saying? LeEtta just woke me up. I think I missed about 15 minutes there. Instead of being pissed off about dozing off, I actually feel completely refreshed. Ah, look at that, I'm awake in time for an amazingly evil murder. Everything goes back to being really strange and laughable almost immediately. Now there's a potentially evil scene: a crippled man getting kicked to death. Too bad it is so poorly staged that it isn't the least bit effective. You know, LeEtta may be on to something. This definitely gets better with repeat viewings.

*"If you can't play ping pong,
don't get mixed up in politics!"*

3:25 PM
Who Saw Her Die? (1972)

I reach into the glove and pick this little gem. Who Saw Her Die? comes from director Aldo Lado, the guy who brought us the excellent Short Night of the Glass Dolls and the derivative Night Train Murders. This unsettling and atmospheric film is definitely his finest hour in genre cinema. The child murder angle of the film is sad and affective but this very unique film somehow remains entertaining.

Okay, let's not give Franco (played by George Lazenby) the father-of-the-year award. Franco's doomed daughter, Roberta, is played by the princess of Italian horror, Nicoletta Elmi. This little girl (who gives LeEtta the creeps) had roles in some major Italian horror classics like Argento's Deep Red and Mario Bava's Bay of Blood. Ah, it sure is nice to see Anita Strindberg again.

It's hard to keep track of all the eccentric and perverse characters in Who Saw Her Die? Although I have no trouble keeping track of Dominique Boschero. It seems that Venice is beautiful but it's also a terrible and dangerous place. Don't ever go there. Ennio Morricone puts together one of his finest scores here. The choral pieces are one of the most unique aspects of this film. A great ending is nearly ruined by the crappy last minute revelation.

CIGAR BREAK

LeEtta and I head out for some fresh air. Of course, my fresh air is tainted by an awful cigar. I picked up a Macanudo but it's really shitty. The flavor of the tobacco is ruined by the preservatives. Good thing it was free. We walk around the lake looking at the birds and the beginnings of dusk. I'm actually in a lot of pain tonight. My brain feels like a balloon rubbing against the inside of my skull and my eyes are starting to recede. Something has gone wrong.

*"Don't thank me just yet. Wait until I try and make it
with you and you find out what a bastard I am."*

5:51 PM
The Case of the Bloody Iris (1972)

LeEtta picks this out of the black glove and my spirits are uplifted. If you're thinking of getting into these films then start right here. The thing is, if you don't like The Case of the Bloody Iris then something is very wrong with you. This is my favorite giallo of all time. It's cool, garish, silly, and totally irresponsible entertainment. This was my first encounter with the power team: Edwige Fenech (in a chic sailor suit) and George Hilton.

This film has the gayest of gay stereotypes and the dumbest of cops. It also has the loveliest of ladies with the goofy Marilyn and the bewitching Mizar (played by Carla Brait). Hell, the cast even includes Luciano Pigozzi and Maria Tedeschi. The Case of the Bloody Iris is completely guiltless trash and even features a hippie sex cult. I'm amazed by how much I love this film. I'm barely ready for the next one when LeEtta randomly picks Nothing Underneath.

"Okay, okay. If you're not having fun, I've got another idea. How about a little roulette?"

7:29 PM
Nothing Underneath (1985)

This title is totally alien to me. This film appeared pretty late on the scene. There weren't many gialli being produced by 1985 so I'm surprised that this one is as good as it is. Perhaps, my rock bottom expectations are helping. Whoa, these actors... It seems as though the director went for Z grade American actors instead of B grade Europeans. Our hero, Bob, is played by Tom Schanley. He's okay but pretty stiff. Well, we've got Donald Pleasence at a Wendy's salad bar. That's something!

The camerawork is very good and there is quite a bit of panache to be found in this low budget production. There are plenty of fashion models to keep things interesting. Director Carlo Vanzina knows enough to put the classic imagery into the film but neglects to hold back on the cheese. Watch out for that scissors-wielding maniac. Holy shit, that ending is perfect. Haunting and brutal. Too bad the setup was lacking.

"For a murderer, he sure has a great face."

9:11 PM
The Case of the Scorpion's Tail (1971)

Another one from Sergio Martino? I sure hope that some of the money I've spent on these DVDs makes it to his great grandkids' college fund or something. I'm starting to feel oddly elated like maybe things are picking up. Oops, never mind what I just said. That pathetic fake ass airplane just blew up. George Hilton is back with us but his voice actor sucks. Evelyn

Stewart is back with a vengeance (for a little while anyway). Surprise, surprise! Anita Strindberg is our heroine.

This plot is running circles around me. That weird woman looks familiar to me. Oh wait, it's Janine Reynaud of Jess Franco's Succubus (among other things). Bless you, sweet Internet. There's Luigi Pistilli yet again as another police inspector. And Alberto de Mendoza (from The Strange Vice of Mrs. Wardh) plays Interpol agent John Stanley, my secret hero.

I'm starting to have serious doubts about The Case of the Scorpion's Tail. It's not that the movie is bad it's just that its timing in the Moviethon could not have been worse. I can't get a hold on this one. My belief in the powers of Anita Strindberg is getting me through. There's also some beautiful lighting, a couple scenes of grisly violence, and a pair of bad sunglasses helping me along. I don't think I'll ever leave a movie playlist up to chance ever again. Having said that, I ask LeEtta to pick the next film from the black glove.

"And you up there? You think you're dancing?
You're a herd of elephants!"

10:45 PM
The Dead Are Alive (1972)

The film starts and complete chaos breaks out. LeEtta and I have seen a lot of things in this Moviethon but never has a film taken us to this point: we don't have a fucking clue what is going on! Sitting through this Eurovista DVD is going to be a challenge. It feels like there are scenes missing and that isn't helping us get a grip on things. Plus, the plot seems to be meandering or purposefully trying to screw us up. An obtuse giallo?

The Dead are Alive or The Etruscan Kills Again comes from Armando Crispino, the man who directed one of my favorite guilty pleasure gialli: Autopsy. This film... well, this might be genius or idiocy, I can't tell. During a POV stalking sequence, LeEtta says, "That is one KILLER point of view." And I realize that Giallo Meltdown has driven her completely insane. For some reason, I'm starting to get chills and a general good feeling about The Dead are Alive.

I'm asking you, the Gods of the DVD underworld, to restore this film. And you, dear reader, if you have a better copy of The Dead are Alive, then hook me up. Aw, look, they were too cheap for a man-sized J&B bottle. They must have been on a really tight budget.

Ugh, our leading man is Alex Cord? This guy is awful. Plus, I've never liked John Marley. He does have Irene, his hot secretary. Wait, we're gonna be okay because Enzo Tarascio is here as the detective. That's right, it's Cousin George from The Night Evelyn Came Out of Her Grave. If I'm not mistaken, there's a familiar face among those dancers. Hell, I think that it's an uncredited Carla Brait from The Case of the Bloody Iris.

I was right, it's starting to work. I'm nostalgic for this film and I've never seen it before. This is one of those 4 in the morning half-forgotten memory movies that have always haunted me, yet it's totally new. There's something important going on here. This movie, despite being shoddily plotted, is still beautiful enough and odd enough so that everything just works. I can't do it. I can't sit through another movie. My brain is throbbing and I'm just so nauseous right now.

FINAL THOUGHTS (SORT OF) & THE END (KIND OF)

I feel like I'm going to die. I cannot look at the TV anymore. Everything is so funny now. I go outside to unplug the Christmas lights and it strikes me how hilarious the sky is. It is cool out tonight and the crisp air is almost tricking me into thinking I've got a couple more hours left in me. The moon is up and all of the sidewalks are brimming with invisible murderers. I hold onto the railing of my patio and just laugh and laugh. Why won't Luciano Pigozzi make a cameo in my life?

My cackling brings tears to my eyes and all I want is to solve a mystery. I'm sure there's a killer with a straight razor out there, somewhere, who is just trying to work an inheritance scam by slaughtering a bunch of seemingly random people and he/she needs to be caught before it's too late. I'm sure there's a rooftop chase with George Hilton or maybe someone is manhandling Edwige Fenech. For God's sake, someone get through to Anita Strindberg, she doesn't know that the killer is none other than-

> *"No, I want to feel the trembling flesh in my hands as I squeeze the life out of the body."*

10:10 AM
The Fifth Cord (1971) & THE CONCLUSION (MONDAY)

I can't quite articulate how happy I am that we took the day off of work today. I've got a giallo hangover and we need a cooling off movie. In order to subvert our random system, I abandon the glove and choose The Fifth Chord. While not my favorite of all time or anything, this is probably the most perfect giallo ever made. Franco Nero, Renato Romano, Rosella Falk, and a bunch of other familiar faces come to bid farewell to this Giallo Moviethon.

Well, at least we get to see the most ridiculous sunglasses ever worn by a human being. Luigi Bazzoni's The Fifth Chord has more style than it knows what to do with and occasionally the world turns into this gorgeous blue-tinted nightmare. And just listen to that. Ennio Morricone provides us with such a great note to end on. God damn, that was amazing. This Moviethon is over, y'all.

I feel defeated, you know? I had 28 films I wanted to watch but only got to view 21. Hell, I can barely keep my eyes on The Fifth Cord right now. This is the longest Moviethon I've had so far and that's something, right? I even beat out Doomed Fulci-Thon which was 18 movies. Could there be a sequel? Giallo Meltdown 2? Giallocalypse? Oh, it's very likely. There are just so many more titles left. I really wanted to end on My Dear Killer (featuring George Hilton with a sweet mustache) or (the awkward and nasty Mimsy Farmer vehicle) Autopsy. The final body count for the first Giallo Meltdown is around 143. Eh, it could have been so many more. Mark my words: this ain't over.

GIALLO MELTDOWN 2:
13 MORE KILLS FOR THE KILLER

As I promised at the end of the first Giallo Meltdown, I am returning to the world of the giallo. While not as large in scope as the original, I've picked 13 titles for GM2 which promise to deliver the body count, the trashy thrills, and the god-awful fashions. I wanted to acquire several more titles before staging another one of these. Now that I have an international DVD player, the world of the giallo has gotten just a little smaller. When I noticed that the Region 1 DVD release of In the Folds of the Flesh had been pushed back yet another month, I gave up waiting and decided to get this party started.

It's hard for me to stay out of Italy. When life has got you down and you just need a little pick me up, I suggest watching a bunch of poorly dubbed fashion models get slaughtered for some boneheaded reveal at the end of a tasteless cinematic romp. When their neon red blood spurts across the screen, your troubles and cares will just melt away. Screw politics and screw the economy, I'm checking myself into Italy 1972 and I ain't comin' back until I'm covered in blood, velour, and J&B.

FRIDAY

I made sure to take care of some of the supply buying the night before. LeEtta and I picked her up some wine and I got myself a supply of Vitamin Water, Mountain Dew Code Red, and Sunkist orange soda. I really hope that Vitamin Water isn't complete garbage. This is me trying to be "healthy" for a change. No Taco Bell runs or greasy pizza deliveries. This is the moviethon where I don't get heartburn.

"I'm ready for anything... with the right person."

5:14 PM
Forbidden Photos of a Lady Above Suspicion (1970)

Those are some charming affirmations there, Minou (played by Dagmar Lassander). Oh good God, this soundtrack is hypnotic and candy-like. Okay, forget the affirmations, she's mixing tranquilizers and liquor. And suddenly, it's nighttime and our hot and sexy Little Miss Trouble is walking along the beach, alone. Bitch, are you crazy? Let the torment begin. This total creep (played by expert of creepitude: Simón Andreu) starts tearing her damn blouse.

And now it's time to tear some shit up at the disco. Fabulous! Dang, these are some seriously sexed up horny ladies. Susan Scott (as the slutty Dominique) is here and she is as painfully hot as usual. Say, you guys, that's a nice "decompression chamber" you got there. Show me some science, please. Hey, this guy wants to play with Minou's body... and her mind.

NO THROW CASSETTE IN OCEAN! FISH WILL DIE! I hope there isn't anymore blackmail in this movie, I just couldn't handle- What, more blackmail?!? Nooo! Meh, that's nothing compared to the tense pea soup eating scene. Minou is quite traumatized by this point; probably by that awful jacket her husband is wearing. My nerves are on edge, I tells ya. Geez, Dominique isn't too supportive either.

Minou explaining that Peter is her husband AND her father figure is a little revealing about her character. Nothing fucked up about that. And now she's a pill-poppin' freak as well. Zoinks! They done pulled the old apartment switcheroo! Everything that implicated the bad guy (as well as confirmed his existence) has mysteriously disappeared from that room.

Yes, listen to your doctor; women always invent mysterious blackmailers just to get attention. It's just something they like to do. Ah, another scary wig! The ending of this film is nicely put together and very tense. However, this is not the most exciting example of the genre. Damn it, Dominique, you are a raging slut! "Personal demonstrations", really? Chicks, man.

"What I want looks like a big string of sausages."

6:57 PM
Puzzle (1974)

Friends, Romans, duders... I present to you: Luc Merenda! He plays Edward, a guy with some serious memory issues. We just spotted some J&B, y'all. Puzzle wastes no time dumping us into the thick of it. After some very ewww-inducing footage of boys swimming at the local YMCA, we are introduced to Luca, the creepy little sassy-pants bastard. This kid is such a pimp. Next we meet Sara, played by Austrian hottie, Senta Berger.

Hmm, so Sara plans to leave that chainsaw in the kitchen? I highly doubt that will come up again later. Hey, it's Bruno Corazzari (from Seven Bloodstained Orchids) as George, the snotty (literally) psycho who leaves a trail of tissues behind him everywhere he goes. Shelly says that the CDC is going to come after this guy. Edward is afraid of his memories and was traumatized by violence; his character is actually written very well.

Luca, you stupid fuck, don't lose the dog! Now look what happened! Anita Strindberg makes a cameo but the only thing memorable about it is her awful, awful hair. The climax is approaching and all of the pieces start to fit together. When the bad guy is revealed, he is a really badass dude. We get a very tense finale with some awesomely gratuitous slow motion. Too bad that closing song is so heinous that it almost spoils everything.

CIGAR BREAK

I light up my delightfully awesome Chateau Real cigar. This is a light cigar with a lot of flavor. Of course, it is complimented perfectly by a Sunkist orange soda. You see, Sunkist is one of the few orange sodas with caffeine. It's like more addictive than like crack and meth put together (probably). From my vantage point on the porch, I see that LeEtta is watching the first McCain/Obama debates. Isn't that interesting?

More importantly, fall has finally come! The air smells so good. Living in Florida really makes you appreciate even the slightest weather changes. The sky is both cloudless and moonless tonight. All of this is made perfectly eerie by my giallo soundtrack mix spiked with helpings of 60s/70s era Rita Pavone. Once the cigar is done, LeEtta prepares a cheese platter for us and we snack ourselves silly.

"He's a typical Italian: lazy. Not like the Swedish."

9:29 PM
Death Carries a Cane (1973)

Now that's the kind of quality I've come to expect from a DVD. This glorified bootleg (from X-Rated Kult) looks murky as hell and features some great scratchy audio. It doesn't really matter because that opening music by Roberto Pregadio is goddamn lousy. Hey look, it's Susan Scott again. This time she plays Kitty, a chick who witnesses a murder. Man, Italy is friggin' scary. We are introduced to her jerk boyfriend, Alberto (played by Robert Hoffmann). He is suspect number one because he has a mustache and he's a fucking bastard. I hate him.

These two make a great couple. Kitty wears floppy hats and makes weird sculptures of mutilated bodies while Alberto likes to stab them repeatedly for, you know, art or something. Creepster Simón Andreu shows up again but this time as Marco, a composer who suffers from impotence. Hey, hold the phone! Marco's astoundingly sexy lady friend is Lidia (Anuska Borova), the hot reporter. And she has a twin sister? There is a God.

What giallo would be complete without indifferent and incompetent police? We have our man in the form of Inspector Merughi (but I call him "Inspector Asshead"). The cheesy zooms and close-ups of guilty faces are astounding. Okay, the composer has redeemed himself. The really freaky stalking music is all aces. This should be called Death Limps Along Slowly.

Go, stripper ballerina, go! Now look who decided to join us! It's Luciano Rossi and he is playing a suspicious looking guy named Richard. That's my name! The body count is climbing so let's dress up Kitty like a hooker and use her as bait for the killer. Death Carries a Cane has some wacky shit going on and it's funny as hell. And it's bloody and violent too!

How about some more red herrings? The genius of the writing comes when Kitty keeps having to go peepee (her words, not mine) during the climactic investigatory scene. The ending is pretty intense but it is all ruined when the killer's motives are explained. My jaw drops as some fucking incoherent psychobabble garbage comes out of my TV. Okay, that was lame. We switch the audio to the German track to see if LeEtta (who took the language in high school) can tell if the dialog is any better there. The results are inconclusive.

"But it's been said that no one is closer to God than a loony."

10:57 PM
Autopsy (1975)

SOLAR FLARES! THEY ARE TO KILL YOU! Now this is one of my favorites. A weird and unsettling music score by Ennio Morricone, stock footage of sun flares, and a rash of violent suicides. Mimsy Farmer (of Four Flies On Grey Velvet) plays Simona, our demented heroine with terrible hair. She is a morgue attendant who has visions of fornicating corpses. She is the cold fish girlfriend for her frustrated boyfriend Edgar (Ray Lovelock). Oh, now I get it. She's got daddy issues to go with her sex issues.

J&B will not save you. Death will destroy you as this is one ghoulish film. The morgue is especially clammy and freaky. After his sister supposedly kills herself, Father Paul Lenox (Barry Primus) shows up to prove that she was murdered. How is he going to find her killer if he drives like a dang maniac? Between the lousy priest, Father Paul (who was a racecar driver 'til he killed a bunch of fans in an accident), and her sex addict (and collector of vintage pornography) boyfriend, Edgar, Simona should just go ahead and become a lesbian.

The editing of Autopsy is top notch. A little dog abuse. Woops, that's not nice. Geez, I hope that dog bit the fuck out of his handlers that day. There is menace around every corner and something ugly everywhere you look in this grotesque entertainment. This movie is so friggin' loaded with craziness. Death is here and so are the show-stopping setpieces. What's up with that breakdancer mannequin?

Mimsy Farmer has had enough, y'all. She just took a fork to a guy

(Ernesto Colli). Whoa, this movie is getting a little kinky. And why not? Everything in this film is sweaty, ugly, and claustrophobic; so why not freaky nasty too? We've got wall to wall sex and sleaze. This is a guilty pleasure, for sure.

And there's a whole lotta pseudoscience too. They hook her paralyzed dad up to the talking machine. What? It's all total nonsense. Now this... THIS is the aesthetic I crave all the time. Italy is an alien landscape and I'm a friggin' astronaut, y'all. The slow motion birds mean that everything is going to be all right. Just ignore the brains splattered on the pavement. Bless you, director Armando Crispino, bless you.

SATURDAY

In bed last night after Autopsy, my mind was racing. I was trying to write my own giallo in my head but I couldn't get past the first killing, much less the plot. Screw it, the plot for my yellow film will have something to do with a wacky inheritance scheme. No one's ever done that before.

My dreams were equally erratic. I kept running around in various imaginary films trying to solve the mystery and expose the killer's identity. When the alarm started beeping at 8:45am, the phrase 'WE SELL DECORATIVE TILES' was echoing through my head as though someone had just screamed it into my ear. Perhaps that is the vital clue to figuring out who the killer is.

We get the usual breakfast at Einstein's. LeEtta gets a spinach and bacon Panini while I stick to my Asiago cheese bagel with plain cream cheese, lettuce, tomato, and bacon. We head straight for the liquor store for a bottle of J&B (WE WERE OUT!), a bottle of Jameson's, and some wine. I spotted a bottle of Mount Gay rum which amused me very much. Back at the apartment, I take a ceremonial shot of J&B which hits me like a punch in the face. How the fuck did people drink so much of this stuff in all these Italian movies?

"You have a great talent for simplifying everything, don't you?"

10:59 AM
The Designated Victim (1971)

Tomas Milian, you magnificent son of a bitch! Gah, that opening song is painful. Milian plays Stefano, a guy with big dreams. Big dreams of spending his shrewish wife's fortune, that is! And he wants to run away with his mistress. Wow, what a likeable guy. Enter the fruity Count Matteo Tiepolo (AKA Freddie Mercury) who is flamboyant beyond belief. Hey look, it's

Enzo Tarascio (from The Night Evelyn Came Out of Her Grave)!

After a chance encounter in Venice, he offers Stefano the whole Strangers on a Train thing. If Stefano will kill Matteo's abusive brother, then Matteo will take his wife out for him. Wait, that's totally unrealistic. How the hell did Matteo get that female slave of his? How did he get a slave at all? He seems like a bottom to me. Anyway…

Aside from that odious opening song, the soundtrack by Luis Enríquez Bacalov is superb. The scenes in the rotting Venice are gorgeous. Modern science cannot measure the amount of homoerotic overtones in Stefano and Matteo's relationship. I keep waiting (though not exactly hoping) for them to break the tension by making out or something. This movie is pretty dang awesome by the way.

This situation is getting sticky and Stefano's mistress's helmet hair is growing. Stefano never agreed to their little pact but he's just desperate enough (thanks to Matteo's manipulations) to go through with it. It's not that he isn't guilty as hell of trying to rob his wife blind but I kind of feel bad for the guy. Dang it, Tomas Milian is so cool it hurts. He makes me want to run out to a bar and get into a pushup contest. That sounds kind of gay too, actually. Maybe I won't do that.

"My frontal lobes are very developed."

12:38 PM
Plot of Fear (1976)

Nice apartment, duder. Is Oscar Wilde your decorator? My my, we're off to a kinky start. Feel your eardrums melt as the fucking awesome opening music pummels you to death! There is a very brutal bludgeoning with a monkey wrench. Our friendly neighborhood police inspector for this slick giallo is Inspector Gaspare Lomenzo (Michele Placido). This guy is neurotic, egotistical, and brilliant. He and his black girlfriend exchange some endearing racial slurs. Ain't that sweet? "You're the queen. So kiss your white slave!" Hey, awesome. John Steiner is in this!

Things get creepy as more info about the infamous "Fauna Lovers Club" is revealed. Rich creeps watching raunchy cartoons and playing sex games… nasty. With all these folks turning up dead, it's obvious that there's some shady shit going down at the Villa Hoffmann. I love how both Eli Wallach and Tom Skerrit are in this movie and both of them are dubbed by lame voice actors. The hottie of Plot of Fear is Jeanne (Corinne Clery) and oh yeah, she gets nekkid.

Hookers and tigers don't mix! Forget solving the case, Gaspare is so wound up, I think he's going to explode. There is some great misdirection with the killings. Where will the clever killer strike next? I sure hope he doesn't strike during the gratuitous sex scene. Wow, this film by director Paolo Cavara gets better with every viewing. Once again, I'm blessed by my international DVD player. LeEtta just made the best lunch: couscous, fresh asparagus, with a fried egg on top. This will give me the strength to survive.

Oops, we just got to the sped up fight scene. Okay, that really didn't need to happen. Why did the editor turn into a douche right there? The relentless detective is a mess in his personal life but is all aces in solving the case. There are some very evil and totally reprehensible characters in this movie. Plot of Fear seems to be trailing off at the end but comes together at the last minute. It might be just a little convoluted but it's still a classic.

"You have to regain consciousness or I get no pleasure."

2:12 PM
The Black Belly of the Tarantula (1971)

I'm making this a Paolo Cavara double feature so I'm turning back the clock to 1971. While not a favorite, Black Belly is still a grand giallo. Any film that starts with Barbara Bouchet getting a sensual massage is automatically good. Uh oh, the killer (wearing brown gloves, not black) means business. Geez Miss Bouchet, do you think your nightgown is friggin' complicated enough? Why don't people listen to their dogs? "BARK! BARK! Hey lady, the killer is in the house! BARK! BARK!"

Ennio Morricone does it again with another freaky and sultry score. In a rare appearance in a giallo, Giancarlo Giannini is awesome as Inspector Tellini, a flawed but very interesting character. He's constantly questioning himself and wondering if maybe he would be better suited for a different line of work. Another cool (though minor) character is "The Catapult", an eccentric private dick who always gets his man. Oh shit, roll out them creepy mannequins.

There are so many familiar giallo starlets in this movie that it's easy to get confused. Barbara Bach (of Short Night of Glass Dolls), Rosella Falk (of The Fifth Cord), and even Annabella Incontrera (of The Case of the Bloody Iris), are here to make me feel special and really, really nerdy. Detective Tellini's greatest accomplishment in this movie? Busting the spider/drug smuggling ring! It's all in a day's work our hero. And so is getting humiliated in front of the entire police force. God, give this guy a fucking break!

Tellini's wife, Anna (Stefania Sandrelli), is such a great character. I sure hope the killer doesn't go after her. I sure hope there aren't any gay stereotypes in this- OH SHIT! TOO LATE! Eugene Walter, the guy from The House with the Laughing Windows, plays the crazy waiter with his homoguts cranked up to 11. You better get home, Inspector, your lady friend is in trouble. Careful Mr. Killer, Tellini has had enough of your bullshit. Ah, I swoon at that final shot with our hero just disappearing into a crowd of people.

POWER NAP

I'm able to sneak in an hour long power nap in before LeEtta wakes me up to let me know that our friend Shelly has arrived. I didn't dream about gialli but I did wake up with a start. So maybe I had psychic revelations about the killer while I slept but I just haven't sorted them out yet.

"My specialty is courting women in front of their husbands."

5:16 PM
The Strange Vice of Mrs. Wardh (1971)

Director Sergio Martino (Torso) finally makes his appearance in this moviethon. Mmm, Julie Wardh (the loverly Edwige Fenech) likes it rough and she's haunted by the memories of the kinky and freaky sex her old boyfriend used to deliver by the truckload. The spectacular Ivan Rassimov makes any film he appears in very special and this one is no exception. No way! Is that the same lame ass wallpaper from The Red Queen Kills 7 Times? Or is that just the same dang apartment?

George Hilton (of My Dear Killer) is pretty damn smooth in this flick but that kind of goes without saying. Wow, swingin' party! So this is what people did before reality TV. Rassimov's character is such an amazing bastard. Hey baby, let's make love on a bed of shattered glass. That's what ladies really want. I love the oversaturated soundtrack with reverb and echo doubling up and threatening to explode my friggin' speakers.

There is a plethora of sex and nudity in Strange Vice. We also get the cute and vapid Carol (Conchita Airoldi). Poor Julie, why is her husband Neal, so vanilla? Doesn't he know he should beat on her once in a while to keep the spice in their marriage? Speaking of spice, check out George Hilton's fringe jacket. He may win the award for worst dressed man in this moviethon. And I don't even give out awards.

I think Julie has a propensity for bad relationships. Her old boyfriend is a sadist, her husband is a cold fish, and her new lover is going to get them both killed in a motorcycle accident by riding like a goddamned maniac! From this tawdry tale, I've learned two things: 1. when your husband is a diplomat, you have to cheat on him and 2. don't ever come between a woman and her bratwurst.

I think Julie has issues. She gets all upset when people try to kill her and stuff. Okay, so maybe that harpoon was meant for her but she should just chill. Woman down! Woman down! Hey doc, the fuck is with that bizarre archaic resuscitation technique? And I don't think that duct tape on a window makes it "hermetically sealed".

This is a top notch giallo. Why the hell didn't this get picked for the last Giallo Meltdown? Oh yeah, that's right, I left that playlist up to chance. Never doing that again! This flick even has the old ice in the latch trick (saw that in Autopsy). Very clever. One of the best things in this movie is the glee that the killers get from committing their 'perfect crime'.

CIGAR & DINNER BREAK

We retreat to the patio where I have a Mountain Dew and a Flor de Nicaragua cigar. LeEtta is drinking some Carlo Rossi Paisano wine while Shelly drinks Peroni Nastro Azzurro. That's right... Italian beer! Shelly has truly gotten into the spirit of things. We talk about God knows what until my cigar is gone. Then we head inside to order some Chinese food.

"You're trapped, shit-face!"

8:34 PM
Delirium (1972)

Mickey Hargitay (of Lady Frankenstein) grabs us by the hair and dunks our faces into the sleazy world he inhabits. He plays Herbert, a sex maniac. These pitiful day for night scenes are giving me the willies. I love Marcia (Rita Calderoni), Herert's sedated wife and their nearly comatose servant girl. This is supposed to be England? Who wrote this fucking thing? Eww, this movie is dirty. Stupid and dirty. Lick your shoulder, servant girl, lick!

Pseudoscience, psychobabble and a light whipping. Red panties, no panties, white panties! Now that is consistent filmmaking. Whose daydreams are these, anyway? Gah! We are being molested by ugly faux Tom Selleck. Oh, he's into young stuff. That's a shocker. Ha ha ha! His wife is still a virgin! He's an impotent dumb loser dumbass.

Speaking of impotence... Asian Wok brought me the wrong goddamned entrée. I ordered chicken with broccoli and instead I got shrimp with mixed vegetables. This is not a crisis situation but it is certainly a downer. My egg rolls will get me through this. Nothing will get me through this fucking movie though.

Joaquine, were you a hooker in another movie? And now we have what... poltergeist activity? Oh, it's just a tape recorder. What in the unholy fuck is going on here? Screaming, screaming, and more screaming. Miss

Marcia just keeps freaking out, calming down, and then starts up again. And again. Seriously, the last half hour is just her ranting and raving. This... oh... THIS WILL NOT END!

"In Italy, I feel... I'm in my underwear."

10:28 PM
Death Walks at Midnight (1972)

Oh Luciano Ercoli, only you can heal the damage brought on by Delirium. Hey there, Susan Scott, you're back! Thank you so much. Girl, you own this movie. Scott plays Valentina, a goofy broad who agrees to take a hallucinogenic drug so that she can be interviewed during her trip. Unfortunately, while under the influence, she witnesses a brutal murder in an apartment across from hers.

There are some strange duders in this movie. There's Peppito (the lady man with a beard) with some vital information, and the killer with the spiked glove who looks like somebody's grandma. Why don't we all go on a little trip to the funny farm? I think I need to go. This shit just gets crazier and crazier every second. Valentina sporting her tin foil wig! WTF? This here is some crazy craziness!

Luciano Rossi (my hero) turns in one of his most unnerving performances as the hired killer with the throwing knives and a childish laugh so shrill that it can strip paint. Good God, why can't all gialli be as good as Death Walks At Midnight? The badass fight scene at the end is the icing on this bloody cake.

SHORT BREAK

At great personal risk, I take an invigorating stroll to go and get some caffeine. The best thing about apartment living is that there's always a soda machine around for a late night boost. It's very quiet for a Saturday night (I keep my ears open for approaching footsteps). I breathe deep of the cool night air and I feel really good about the rest of the moviethon ahead of me. In the overly lit laundry room, I get a Mr. Pibb Extra from the machine. I get back home to find LeEtta and Shelly ready for the next flick.

"If I was a girl, I'd become a hooker."

12:25 AM
The Suspected Death of a Minor (1975)

We finally get to a flick I've been really wanting to see and judging by the funktastic Goblin-like music by Luciano Michelini, this is going to pretty awesome. Okay, since the great Sergio Martino (All The Colors of the Dark) is the director of Suspected Death, I might be a little biased already. Uh oh, pissed off Kevin Bacon-looking dude, what are you going to do? Why must you brutally stab the sexy lady?

Mmm hey, this movie is filled with pretty people. There are hookers and pimps and then there's our hero. Paolo (Claudio Cassinelli) is a detective but he sure as hell doesn't act like one. He knows the only way to catch criminals is to get down and dirty. When the rest of the force is too concerned with gambling on soccer than solving a few murders, it's up to Paolo (with the constantly broken glasses) to save the day. He even enlists some goofus to help him uncover a conspiracy.

Can I be the first to ask what the fuck is going on? This film is very entertaining, sleazy, action-packed, and fun but I'm totally lost. It just keeps pulling the rug out from under you? The slapstick scenes are priceless. And that nutty car chase. What is this, a Charlie Chaplin giallo? The soundtrack for this film is really out there. Was that a Deep Red parody I just saw?

Oh snap, Little Orphan Slutty just burned evil Kevin Bacon's face real good. The self-referential moment where the theater is playing a Sergio Martino movie is very pleasing to my nerdy brain. Hey look, Paolo finally got some new glasses and he's about to solve the mystery. What a strange friggin' movie: a comedy cop thriller with some giallo overtones and a couple of brutal death scenes. Awesome.

SHORT BREAK

Shelly takes her leave of the Moviethon and LeEtta has claimed that she is going to bed. However, she is in the kitchen making a lot of noise. I sneak in to get my other egg roll and I see that she is cleaning up. What a woman! I'm extremely sleepy right now but I'm thrilled at the opportunity to see another unseen giallo. It's a sequel of sorts to What Have You Done to Solange? Let's hope this one is really good or else I'm gonna be totally screwed. As the movie starts, LeEtta goes to bed, wishing me luck.

"It's a disgrace, Inspector. Lovers, drugs, double life- She was only a child!"

2:08 AM
What Have They Done to Your Daughters? (1974)

A young girl has been found hanging from the rafters in a trashy apartment. Um, that's not a very convincing setpiece there. They keep showing the body too and it's pretty fake. A female district attorney? Now that's progressive! She is Assistant DA Vittoria Stori played by Giovanna

Ralli (from Cold Eyes of Fear) and boy does she have a mess on her hands (other than her huge hair).

Hey look, it's Claudio Cassinelli. He was just in Suspected Death of A Minor. Now he's Detective Silvestri. So if you drop out of college one of your employment opportunities is "professional agitator". The suicide leads to another crime and another. This is going to be a very sad story, isn't it? SEX IS BAD AND DIRTY!

This mystery intrigues me. My brain feels like someone is strangling my brain. What? Oh, hell yeah. That dismembered corpse just made my day, oops, I mean my morning. It makes up for that not so great hanging corpse from earlier. Beware the scary motorcycle killer, he's got a big ass machete. The car/motorcycle chase is frickin' great! With its seedy characters, broken morals, and destroyed innocence, this film plays on the conservative fears of the time. The youth has gone wild!

There is much big violence. Much bleeding. Vice is a sickness at the core of it all and its corruption spreads all the way to the top in a conspiracy of sin. At least, that's the message of this movie, I guess. The crying and the melodrama make for a nice mix with the tense stalking scenes. Leave the little girls alone, please.

"We've got to go back to the start and begin again."

3:42 AM
My Dear Killer (1972)

My face feels hot. My Dear Killer is a classic and this moviethon must end with it. It's one of the first non-Argento gialli I ever purchased. It opens with one of the best death scenes ever. George Hilton plays the brilliant but flawed Detective Luca Peretti. Luca is an eccentric with a short fuse. His wife Anna (Marilù Tolo), a doctor, is so hot. They got marital issues and shit! Her ancient answering machine is pretty great.

Eurohorror super-starlet Helga Liné makes a nice though brief appearance. There's a 3 second strangulation (one of my cinematic pet peeves) but the scene is saved by the subjectivity of several unreliable witnesses. A child's drawing holds the key to the entire case. Now where have I seen that before? There's a super dark slab of depressing storyline in this film.

I love how the schoolteacher (Patty Shepard!) goes home after work and watches Django on TV shortly before being brutally murdered with an electric saw. Oops, was that a spoiler? Woe is me, I'm a detective with a pencil-thin mustache and I'm under so much pressure right now. This case makes me unable to pleasure my wife who happens to be mind-bendingly sexy!

My Italy looks like this. I'm finally at the point in this moviethon where I get that indescribable feeling I get while submerged in gialli. I can find my new perpetual home inside of one of these gorgeous scenes. There's just something about that 70s Italian cinematography. The shit is drugged, yo!

This is such a grim story but I know our awesome detective can save the day. Everyone who watches these movies knows that the best gialli always have some poor slob who gets murdered in his shack. You know, struck down in cold blood while trying to sleep in his shanty. I love the boxy Mercedes the cops cruise around in.

THE ENDING = PERFECTION. I'm not fucking joking around! Once all of the hoopla with the red herrings is finally put aside, we get to the nitty gritty. When Hilton confronts his group of suspects, the lights go out a la Agatha Christie and the tension just explodes.

CONCLUSION

Sometime around 5:30 in the morning, I'm singing in the shower. The lyrics go like this: "Giallo! Oh! Giallo! Oh! Aiuto! Aiutooo!" A very groggy LeEtta catches me in mid-song just to make sure I'm coming to bed. Next thing I know, I have flopped my weary body into bed and for a moment, I'm too tired to sleep. While trying to find some meaning to the clues and an ingenious way to ensnare the elusive black-gloved killer, I pass out.

Just before 10:00am, I wake up to one of our cats, Sparkles, stomping on us and meowing very insistently about food or something. I remember dreaming about lists and lists of gialli. There were pages and pages of titles that I was highlighting and getting all fired up about as I ogled the directors, actors, and composers of these imaginary flicks. How dull is that? I think that means the killer got away again.

LeEtta has understandably vetoed my mumblings about extending the moviethon into another day. Come on! We could watch The House with the Laughing Windows, Knife of Ice, Delirium: Photos of Gioia, and Crimes of the Black Cat. Shit, it looks like I'm building the playlist for Giallo Meltdown 3 already. The post-moviethon hangover is mixing with the euphoria of 13 giallos all so nicely.

Why do I have this compulsion with these films? The beautiful (and often naked) actresses are a bonus, the gallons of fluorescent blood are important, the delicious kitsch, the mouth-wateringly sumptuous soundtracks by mad Italian composers are essential, and, of course, there's also the presence of immeasurably cool duders like George Hilton and Ivan Rassimov. I just answered my own question.

I still can't formulate the right combination of words to describe the feeling that I get after a moviethon like this. All I know is that the real world becomes more beautiful and is sharpened into a razor's edge of tangibility. I know this is isn't Italy 1972 but it sure does feel like it. Prepare, mio amico, this is only part 2 in a trilogy. I can feel it in my yellow bones.

GIALLO MELTDOWN 3: LA MIASMA DELLA MORTE

I am possessed by a subgenre. The more of these films I watch, the deeper I get. I hope these Giallo Meltdowns help you, the reader, realize that these yellow films need to be avoided at all costs. You cannot watch just one giallo and be done with it. Next thing you know, you'll have at least two shelves of your DVD collection dedicated to this stuff. If it can happen to me...

FRIDAY NIGHT

It's hot outside. Florida in the springtime? That's not exactly a revelation. But it's also very weird out. The wind is blowing and the world feels unsettled like we need to get our asses back indoors before it's too late. Someone is out to get me. My wife LeEtta might also be in danger so time is of the essence.

Is this normal moviethon panic? Gee, I hope I don't catch a cold. Gosh, I hope the car (our 1978 Ford Thunderbird) doesn't break down coming back from the liquor store. Golly, I hope there isn't a tornado. These are the kinds of worries I get right before we get started. My biggest fear, of course, is me giving up in the middle of things which has happened before.

We go to the drugstore after work so LeEtta can get wine and I can get Arizona iced tea and Vitamin Water. Once we're home, I fry some asparagus in a pan while she boils a pot of couscous. We throw these things on a plate with a little parmesan cheese and oh yeah, it's an amazing meal. The asparagus is perfectly seared and I don't want the meal to end. Okay, enough grub, it's time to start this motherfucker.

> *"You cannot imagine the pleasure it gives me to watch a woman in the grip of fear."*

5:30 PM
The Frightened Woman (1969)

I want to begin with a title I've never seen before and The Frightened Woman will do just fine. This film has one of the most distinctive opening credits sequences I've ever seen. The whiny wah wah of the guitar of Stelvio Cipriani's score combined with the weird set designs (one of which is a giant woman with teeth in her vagina) is pretty far out. Is anyone else confused? This stylish and eccentric beast is just getting started and I have no idea what's going on.

Dagmar Lassander (of Forbidden Photos of a Lady Above Suspicion) is with us but she's all nerded out. She plays Maria and her feminist views challenge Dr. Sayer (Philippe Leroy). He invites her back to his place for some research materials. Silly woman, once the J&B starts flowing, you don't stand a chance. Hey, that's cheating! You can't drug J&B, it's already an aphrodisiac. Oh goody, Dr. Sayer is a kinky freak and he really, really, really hates artificial insemination. Then he makes Maria his captive. This is not going to end well.

Kiss him! Kiss him! You shall make love to my dummy which is an exact replica of me! Now Dr. Sayer wants a foot rub? Man oh man, this guy knows how to live. He reveals to Maria that he has captured many women before her and toyed with them until he got bored then killed them. In order to avoid being the next victim, she tries to seduce her captor. Wow, her new outfit is some strategically placed strips of gauze. She's seducing him but it's working on me! Duder's living room is insane!

And now our wacky couple is in love! They even have a wonderful montage of good times and sexy play. What could POSSIBLY go wrong? The scene at the railroad tracks with the not so subtle oral sex joke is pretty darn amazing. Ah yes, this is just the kind of psychosexual artsy (and surreal) trash that I needed. You smell that? It's irony, bitches. I really don't know what else to say. You have to see this one for yourselves, folks.

"This place is the Mecca of video poker."

7:03 PM
The Card Player (2004)

Dario Argento makes his first appearance in a Giallo Meltdown and it couldn't be with a more unspectacular film. Detective Anna Manni (played by Stefania Rocca) is challenged by a killer to a game of internet poker. The stakes of the game are this: if the killer wins, he kills his captive but if Sara wins, the killer will let the girl go. The idiot police chief makes a stupid call and the girl dies. And with that, we've got our first sighting of black gloves in the moviethon.

Gotta love that morgue worker; he's a kooky guy who refers to the cadavers in the freezers as his 'dolls'. Ew, nice corpse! Sergio Stivaletti went all out on this one with some disgusting dead body setpieces. Much of the violence happens off camera in The Card Player but Argento definitely doesn't shy away from the gruesome forensic work. They call in some drunken Irish detective (Liam Cunningham) to help out with the investigation. Okay, he's not drunk... yet.

There are some bad actors and some bad dubbers but they are all equally blessed with the chance to deliver some really bad dialogue. Luckily, the movie is shot gorgeously and the main characters are played quite competently by Rocca and Cunningham. The cops pick up this lucky kid named Remo (Silvio Muccino) with the "Midas Touch". They employ him to play against the killer and save the third victim before she gets diced up with a box cutter. Irish man makes love to Italian woman? What will their children's accents be like?

The standout scene in The Card Player comes when Sara spots the killer just outside her window. Just before the hour mark this film actually becomes quite frightening. It's a family affair when Fiore Argento shows up as one of the intended victims of the killer. Well, she makes out better here than in Phenomena Wait, does Fiore live through this movie? I'm watching it right now and I can't remember. Forget it, I'm not rewinding this shit.

The gimmick of this movie is, for my money, a dismal failure. I really despise card games and especially people who play card games. LeEtta says I'm biased and that she plays card games. Oops, I'm trapped. Okay, my wife is a cool chick so when she plays cards it's okay. But I just can't like The Card Player. How can a movie be so good and so bad at the same time? The biggest 'fuck you' to the viewer comes from the killer's motive. It's pretty pitiful but I won't reveal it to you. I have a strong urge to turn this off but I can't. I have to see this through. Don't listen to me, this is a pretty good movie, beautifully shot even, but it's just not my style.

"Calm down, Martha!"

8:46 PM
Knife of Ice (1972)

Umberto Lenzi, you fabulous bastard! I want to thank you for the graphic bullfighting footage but I'm not going to. And no, the quote from Edgar Allen Poe doesn't help. Carroll Baker plays Martha and she's got some major issues. She's on psychological mute due to some past trauma. Damn it, why am I so tired? Oh yeah, I stayed up late watching that stupid Metallica documentary which is impossible to turn off. Hey look, it's Evelyn Stewart as Martha's friend Jenny. Stewart's presence almost guarantees that you're in for a good time. Yikes, there's a man with spotty eyes watching the girls!

What is up with the staff in this house? Mrs. Briton is "irreplaceable" but Maria the maid is a useless piece of shit. And Marcos the driver (Eduardo Fajardo) is one freaky duder. Uncle Ralph (the guy with the bum ticker) is played by George Rigaud, who was in The Case of the Bloody Iris and about 15 other gialli. Jenny brings a piece of the past with her and it stirs up some painful memories for Martha. Her parents died in a railway accident, by the way. That's why her volume is turned all the way down.

Oh, I guess Evelyn Stewart won't be in the rest of the movie. A maniac, perhaps a SEX MANIAC, killed her. It seems that there is a killer on the loose and that cat looks like our cat, Crisco. These cops are pretty smart. They deduce that since two blond girls have died that means that Martha is next. The soundtrack by Marcello Giombini is pretty tight and the Spanish scenery is gorgeous. Mrs. Briton is no longer irreplaceable; she's just a dead non-living corpse who got murdered to death. The mark of the devil is left at the scene.

I think this junkie satanist hippie is to blame for all of this. The cops corner him in the graveyard with his stash of morphine. Some local mentally handicapped girl named Christina gives Martha the greatest gift of all, a Snoopy pendant. They're game of blindfold and go seek turns deadly when young Christina turns up dead. My wife is nodding off. Man, we are totally out of it tonight. Sleep deprivation is a bad way to prepare for a moviethon. LeEtta wakes up and decides to call it an early night.

The funniest thing about Knife of Ice is that Carroll Baker plays mute Martha like she's mildly retarded. Not a great performance but that's about the only thing I can complain about. The first time I watched this flick, I was very disappointed but now I'm diggin' on it. It's hard not to love a film with a cemetery as beautiful as the one here. Even though Lenzi's Seven Blood-Stained Orchids is still my favorite, Knife of Ice does have a kick ass ending and is worth tracking down.

"Well hold on to yourself, baby, I'm about to let this big mother fly."

10:16 PM
The Killer Must Kill Again (1975)

This time around, we know who the killer is right off the bat. He's an ugly bastard (Antoine Saint-John) and a dead booby squeezer. George Hilton is here as Mainardi, a complete sonofabitch. He witnesses the killer disposing of a body and sees an opportunity for blackmail so that he can finally rid himself of his rich wife Norma. The drone of the strings on the soundtrack by Nando De Luca is really intense.

Did I mention that the killer is ugly? Yeah, this guy looks like an anorexic cancer skull. And this Saint-John actor guy isn't just a pretty face either; he also happens to pull off an unnerving and relentlessly evil performance as our local assassin. Hey guys, don't sit next to each other in the darkened theater like that. No one thinks you're planning anything but man-love. Whoa, Mainardi's house is all giallo, all the time!

Luigi Cozzi, who went on to direct the abominable splatter sci-fi flick Contamination, likes to provide the juxtaposition of images with quick editing. For instance, showing Nora's murder while her asshole husband is yucking it up at a party is just one of his tricks. Later in The Killer Must Kill Again, a brutal rape is intercut with a steamy sex scene and it is really fucking annoying.

The perfect murder goes awry when two dumb thrill-seekers steal the killer's car with Norma's body stashed in the trunk. The wannabe criminal is Luca, played by Alessio Orano of Lisa and the Devil, and his girlfriend Laura is Cristina Galbó from What Have You Done to Solange?. Leaving a trail of idiocy in their wake, it is easy for the killer to find them and stay on their tail as they make their way to the beach. Aw, that is so sweet. They're going to the seaside so Luca can deflower his lady.

The cops pay a visit to George Hilton and the chief inspector on the case is Eduardo Fajardo (who was just in Knife of Ice). He thinks that George's wife has been kidnapped and doesn't immediately suspect the guy of being a complete fuckbag. Meanwhile, the kids go to a beautiful shack on the waterfront and Laura begins to sense that something bad is going to happen. She's right. Some bad shit is about to go down.

Luca goes out to pick up some food and leaves Laura alone. While he's out, scumbag Luca meets a stranded (and slutty) motorist (Femi Benussi) and they have sex in the car (which still has Norma's corpse in the trunk). Indirect necrophilia! At the same moment the hot sex is taking place, Laura is getting raped by the killer. Thanks, Luigi Cozzi, you're an asshole! Your attempt at being provocative is stupid and you pretty much ruin this movie with the whole sexy-rape bit.

SO ANYWAY, Luca comes back with his ditzy blond friend and the killer is there waiting for them. Wouldn't you know it, that little slice of roadside trash gets the best death scene in the movie. Ladies, pay attention, you should never sleep with Luca by the roadside because you will die. Things are heating up and I've already given away too much already.

Technically, The Killer Must Kill Again is very well made and there are some very cool moments but I wouldn't call it a classic. This movie has all the right elements for a great giallo including a palpably bleak atmosphere but I just can't connect with it. The exploitation bit just doesn't sit right with me. This is an odd flick to end the first night on but there are more great (and better) things to come tomorrow. Goodnight all.

SATURDAY

I don't know if other horror movie obsessives experience this phenomenon or not but I sure do. I call them bland nightmares. After thousands of hours of gore, zombies, death, blood, and mayhem on video, these things no longer haunt my dreams. Instead I have terrifyingly banal stress dreams about awkward social situations. I'll have work-related horrors in which a meeting I'm at turns into me getting put on the spot and fired for mild infractions like eating the last donut or not complimenting my boss's new shoes. Honestly, I wake up in a cold sweat from this dull garbage.

Long story short (too late), I did NOT dream about a razor-wielding maniac nor did I dream about Carol Baker's silent scream. I sure as hell didn't dream about that stupid rape sequence from The Killer Must Killer Again (thank God). That was a weird way to start this moviethon. Two great movies and two busts. Great scenes in both of the downers but not great films. So far, The Frightened Woman has been the best surprise.

LeEtta and I get up at a reasonable hour and go for breakfast at Einstein's. I know, I know. We are creatures of habit and the killer could easily find us and slash our bagel swallowing throats but that's just a risk I'm willing to take. I recently discovered their garlic and herb pizza bagel so you really can't blame me, right? We go to 7-11 afterwards where I get a Slurpee, some sweet tea, and various bagel and pretzel chips. It's getting late, I better get the first movie started.

"You slut! I knew I couldn't trust you."

10:44 AM
Liz & Helen (1969)

If I was smart I would have a Riccardo Freda moviethon. The guy was a major talent that slipped into obscurity while my other favorite directors were having their heyday. Holy crow, that opening car vs. train wreck is pretty amusing. The train is about to hit the car when the entire scene magically turns into a toy train set and a model car colliding with comedic violence. This DVD from Alfa Digital takes some getting used to. This glorified bootleg is a composite of two prints of the film, each with varying quality. As the movie plays, it switches back and forth between these versions which is pretty damn annoying. Waa, waa, I'm a big baby!

The magnificent Klaus Kinski plays John, a man who is concerned about his wife Helen (Margaret Lee) and her lesbian relationship with Liz (Annabella Incontrera). His heartbreak turns into an obsession and he is forced to let her go. Some mysterious black-gloved person plants a bomb in her car and Helen dies in a hilariously fake car wreck (more toys). John is grief stricken and can't believe that Helen is dead. However, he does have a really hot secretary to keep him company (but he brushes her off).

Lucio Fulci co-wrote this script (sort of) with Riccardo Freda. Riccardo Freda co-directed I Vampiri with Mario Bava. Mario Bava worked on Inferno with Dario Argento. Dario Argento was working with Lucio Fulci on the screenplay for Wax Mask when Fulci passed away. This is all very fascinating (and tenuously connected). I'm a super nerd by the way.

The pop song that Helen used to listen to begins playing one dark and stormy night in his mansion. Suddenly, we have a gothic scenario as John roams around with a candelabra to light his way. He discovers a hottie named Christine (Christiane Krüger) using his shower. John is such a pimp that he's all like 'Beyatch, I ain't got time for you. Now get out my castle!' Wait, that doesn't make him a pimp. That makes him an idiot!

John drives Christine to a hippie festival where there's rampant nudity, bad music, shaky camera, and unsafe motorcycling. In a back room, the filthy pervert hippies show a porno starring Christine and a woman who shares many similarities with dead Helen. John is disturbed but not because these filthy libertines are destroying everything moral and sacred in our great nation (this is England, right?). Instead, he's rather perturbed by the fact that Christine claims to have made this film AFTER Helen's death. Vertigo, anyone?

After some wheeling and dealing (and threatening Christine with a broken bottle), John obtains the film and even more clues point to the fact that Helen might just be alive. He tries to get his father-in-law to buy into his story, which is actually pretty amusing. 'Dad, you've got to believe me! Now come over here and watch this porno starring your daughter.' Oh shit, the film has been switched and now it looks like John is a crazy-pants. And the whole style of the film just took a turn towards film noir.

John's hot secretary returns for some lovin' and I have to say, 'Helen who?' How lame is this dude? I guess I'd be pretty distracted by The Case of the Returning Furs (and Dog) if I were John too. This movie does have some unfortunate padding. The climax is about start when John has to go to a bar and think about things. Lame. Oh snap, there's the twist! Deja vu? No, it's the same fake ass car/train accident AGAIN. Genius!

"I was right, you're a sweet, sweet whore."

12:21 PM

Spasmo (1974)

What initially repelled and attracted me to this film was its awful trailer. The not-so-spooky voice screaming 'Spasmo!' over and over again was hilarious but didn't exactly make me want to give this Umberto Lenzi flick a chance. When I finally did get around to it, Spasmo turned out to be an excellent flick. It is on the dry side with very little bloodshed and a slow pace. Plus, it's more of an arty mystery flick than a straight up giallo. But I ain't compainin'! Spasmo has just enough kink and twisted psychology to fit right into my collection and this moviethon.

Christian Bauman (played by Robert Hoffmann) and his lady friend Xenia (Maria Pia Conte) are strolling by the seaside talking about strangled dogs when they spot what they think is a dead body by the water. It turns out to be a living corpse named Barbara (Suzy Kendall). Barbara explains that she passed out from the heat but she sure is acting suspicious. She bolts but they run into her later at a yacht party. Xenia bluntly announces that she isn't pregnant because she just got her period. Though it should be joyous news, this revelation darkens the mood so Christian runs off with Barbara. This is all pretty stupid.

LeEtta notices something important. Christian and Barbara have now started a relationship. It's not just sex either. They've abandoned their significant others for a suddenly deep devotion for one another. This happens all the time in gialli. This "love" often propels the story along or at least makes things more shocking when one of the interested parties turns out to be the killer. I don't think Suzy Kendall is attractive, by the way. LeEtta says she looks like a dried up Sandra Dee who's been used up by one too many Dannys. Grease has been on TV a lot lately.

Ennio Morricone is a god by the way. His soundtrack for Spasmo is a leering, slithery, and atonal monster that freaks me out. While shaving off his beard (at Barbara's request), Christian is accosted by a duder with a gun in the bathroom. Christian accidentally kills him so he and Barbara go on the run. They break into Barbara's friend's castle by the beach and it just happens to be very creepy (and tacky) inside. Christian finds a pair of bloody garden shears in the yard but he just tosses them down the well. Nothing strange about that, right?

Two weirdos, Malcolm (Guido Alberti) and Clorinda (Monica Monet), show up and this movie becomes instantly hilarious. The dialog becomes so awkward and stilted that it is impossible to take any of it seriously. Line after line of baffling bullshit comes tumbling out of these characters' mouths and I can't help but fall in love with Spasmo even more. I haven't even mentioned the parade of mutilated mannequins and sex dolls on display in this film. It seems that someone really hates fake ladies.

And where the fuck is Ivan Rassimov? The credits promised me he was in this! I want my Rassimov! Christian hooks up with Clorinda (sort of rapes her actually) but it turns deadly or does it? Spasmo continually throws logic out the window. Whether it is on purpose or not, this movie is so dern confounding that it's impossible to figure what's going on. The most important thing is that Christian has an awesome car. I'm not a car person but his luscious BMW is making me drool.

Ivan Rassimov is FINALLY here as Fritz. He's Christian's brother who brings us his confusing plot revelations, I guess. The brothers have their showdown (sort of) and everything is explained. Everything except for the first two thirds of this fucking movie. But it ain't over yet, kids. The unintentional comedy just keep on coming. I can't help but love the ending even though the road to get there was a treacherous one. Spasmo is as Spasmo does.

"Dirty keeler!"

2:01 PM
7 Murders for Scotland Yard (1971)

This Spanish giallo is pretty half-assed but I just can't resist the chance to sneak Paul Naschy into a Giallo Meltdown. A man picks up a whore after she asks him that age old question: "You wanna make it?" They go to her room where she starts to undress but we are denied! The goofs who released this DVD have given us the "clothed" version. There will be no nudity in 7 Murders for Scotland Yard but that's okay. I'm more concerned about the terrible gore effects. The hooker gets stabbed and her skin resembles a leather handbag.

Paul Naschy plays Pedro, a drunken ex-circus performer who limps around getting into bar brawls. The blue-tinted flashback where we see Pedro's 'career-ending' injury is pretty priceless. He stumbles getting down from the net and then rolls around in pain for some reason. The police already suspect Pedro of being the killer because he is an unusual person. Then his wife gets murdered. Poor guy. Apparently, the killer is of the Jack the Ripper variety and keeps souvenirs of his crimes in jars in an old house that serves as his hideout.

Campbell, the detective on the case and Winston (played by Renzo Marignano), a school teacher (played by Andrés Resino of Werewolf Shadow), are buds and are casually discussing this rash of recent murders. Winston's ditzy wife Sandra (Orchidea de Santis) has some ideas about the perpetrator but no one listens to her. The next day at school, Winston makes a pass at one of his naughty girl students. What the hell kind of a boarding school is this? The post-modern concrete structure is just about the worst location in the world and the filmmakers even try to fake the height of the building by showing the girl going down the exact same flight of stairs twice.

Uh oh, the student Winston fancied just got murdered and now the cops are even more confused. Meanwhile, Pedro hooks up with another broad named Belinda. She gets plastered and makes an incredible speech about what bastards men are. In the next scene, Pedro wakes up to find Belinda murdered beside him and the cops banging on the door. Now he's kind of the prime suspect.

BREAK TIME

My in-laws arrive for a brief visit, which gives us a chance to take a break from this dang movie. We go out to Jimmy John's for some subs and they're delicious. Back home, we gab for a while. They make their exit and then it's back to the moviethon.

7 Murders for Scotland Yard (CONTINUED)

Oh shit. Winston's wife Sandra just got gotten by the killer. Now Pedro is hiding out in some new broad's apartment drinking up all of her Vat 69. Her name is Lulu and she can't be havin' any of his bullshit. She gets pissed off and kicks him out. Detective Campbell tells Winston that he knows about he and Sandra's marital problems. Winston admits to being impotent and blah blah blah. Now Pedro is fighting some dudes in the most awkwardly staged fight scene ever filmed. Shit, this flick is all over the damn place. At least the organ-driven lounge music is nice.

In order to convince us this film actually takes place in England (HOW EXOTIC!), we get some nice yet endless shots of London. One of the unpaid extras actually tries to duck out of the way of the camera while he's walking right towards it. Okay, the rest of 7 Murders may be a convoluted disaster but at least it looks amazing. I tip my hat to cinematographer Diego Úbeda. The bloody and tense climax of this one is actually pretty cool.

"Damn you, blind man!"

5:38 PM
The Crimes of the Black Cat (1972)

The opening music by composer is very seductive. Anthony Steffen plays Peter Oliver, a blind composer who overhears a conversation that he shouldn't have. His caretaker is Burton and he is played by the awesome Umberto Raho of Four Flies on Grey Velvet and so many other gialli. Victor Morgan (Giacomo Rossi-Stuart), the co-owner of a nearby fashion house is not too faithful with his wife Francoise (Sylva Koscina). Hey look, it's Annabella Incontrera, the rabid lesbian from The Case of the Bloody Iris, and she is as foxy as ever. She's playing Helga, yet another lesbian character. Nice work if you can get it.

A mysterious woman in a white cloak delivers death by one of the most bizarre methods I've ever seen. A very ornery kitty cat with poison on his claws delivers a fatal scratch to a fashion model! This giallo stereotype named Paola just happened to be lovers with Peter and since she had just dumped him, our bitter blind friend is now a suspect. Peter and Paola's friend Margot decide to try and figure out why she was killed.

We have another murder and so far everyone is a freakin' suspect! The mysterious woman in the white cape is Susan, a junkie who is under the control of someone else. And she owns a parrot! The cat has struck again and the lesbian is dead. Peter is composing a score for a giallo film and the clips are from Lucio Fulci's A Lizard in a Woman's Skin. LeEtta's friend Kat arrives in time to witness the freakin' junkie go through one of her unintentionally funny morphine withdrawal fits.

And then the mystery starts to bog down the movie. Peter demonstrates how the cat could be trained to kill someone and it is pretty unimpressive. Kat and LeEtta escape to get a bite to eat. Things start to pick up as the body count rises. With the junkie out of the way, the real mastermind behind the murders gets in on the action. The Crimes of the Black Cat really compensates for its brief slowness by going into overdrive for the last half hour. The plot goes nuts but before the big reveal, we are treated to a very nasty slashing in the shower. Peter is alone with the killer in his apartment for the showdown (with badass lighting) and we finally get to know what the fuss was all about in a typically rushed giallo ending.

"Listen, don't think so hard. Get undressed."

7:17 PM
Perversion Story (1969)

Lucio Fulci has officially entered into his first Giallo Meltdown. This DVD didn't come out until long after my Fulci-themed moviethon was over. I am very pleased that his 1969 giallo can finally make its moviethon debut. Perversion Story AKA One on Top of the Other opens with the shakiest helicopter shots I've ever seen. San Francisco has never been so bouncy. It turns out that the 'San Francisco treat' is Dramamine.

In our second Vertigo ripoff of the day, Dr. George Dumurrier (played by Jean Sorel) is the man behind a specialized clinic which is in danger of going under due to his many unpaid debts. George is married to Susan (Marisa Mell), a woman at death's door due to her chronic asthma. He takes a moment explaining to his wife's new nurse about her medications and how confusing them could cause SUFFOCATION and DEATH. Hey script, telegraph what's going to happen much?

Of course, George is a cheating bastard with a hot (though somewhat masculine) mistress named Jane (Elsa Martinelli) who wears see-through panties. She dumps him because he won't leave his wife for her. Oh no, not more bouncy helicopter shots! He and his Jane patch things up but while they're celebrating, George gets the call that his wife has dropped dead. Back at the house, we see just how morbid Fulci can be. Susan's corpse is laid out in black, hands clasped on a black bedspread and the whole scene is beautifully death-obsessed.

Apparently, Susan took out a 2 million dollar insurance policy on herself just before she died but George claims that he had no knowledge of it. With the investors backing out of his clinic and the insurance company breathing down his neck, George decides blow off some steam at a strip club. It is there that he sees a stripper named Monica (Marisa Mell again) who is a dead ringer for dead Susan. Her strip tease atop a big motorcycle is fifteen different varieties of hot.

George gets his chance to make love to Monica but he's haunted by visions of dead Susan which gives their affair a nice hint of necrophilia. Ain't that sweet? Wow, this big jazzy score by composer Riz Ortolani is the bomb. The cops haul in Monica for questioning. They suspect that she is Susan in disguise and that she and George are working an insurance scam. Pudgy-faced Fulci makes a director's cameo as a handwriting expert. In an odd scene, Jane tricks Monica into getting naked but I forget why.

We have a J&B sighting and Marisa Mell parading around in a very unflattering outfit. The cops flip flop after they prove that Monica and dead Susan are not the same person. Now they just think that George is a murderer and he's on death row awaiting the gas chamber. I'm leaving out huge chunks of this awesome story here because it gets pretty complicated and I don't want to totally ruin the movie for you.

CIGAR BREAK & DINNER

Out on the patio, I smoke a powerful and tasty Gurkha cigar (provided by my father-in-law) while downing a Vitamin Water (Sync flavor). My iPod is loaded with selections from giallo soundtracks. It is a cloudless night that is blessedly cooler than the day. My eyes feel like oversized pool balls that were stuffed into my eye sockets in a most unpleasant manner. The girls return from dinner at Tia's on Fowler Avenue with some delicious Tex-Mex leftovers for me: cheese flautas, guacamole, and refried beans which I devour like a starved animal.

"But I'm alive. You can't do this!"

10:00 PM
Short Night of Glass Dolls (1971)

I just accidentally made this a Jean Sorel double feature. I forgot that he stars in this Aldo Lado masterpiece. Sorel plays Gregory Moore, a man found unconscious in the park and brought to the hospital. He is pronounced dead on arrival and taken to the morgue. There's just one little problem, Gregory ain't dead. He can't move but he can hear, see, and feel everything around him.

In this paralyzed state, he is placed in the freezer with only his own thoughts screaming out even though no one can hear him. The rest of the movie bounces between flashbacks and the present while Gregory pieces together how he ended up in this terrifying predicament. Memories come floating back to him, sometimes out of order and each detail reveals clues to the mystery.

It took me a long time to warm up to Short Night of Glass Dolls. This movie bored me to tears the first few times I watched it. But tonight, something is different. Gregory, an American journalist in a politically unstable Prague, isn't afraid of uncovering corruption. Valinski (José Quaglio of Who Saw Her Die?) is his awesome Slovakian friend.

Gregory's girlfriend Mira shows up. She is played by the lovely Barbara Bach of (The Black Belly of the Tarantula) and their relationship is very sweet. But there is an aura of dread hanging around this young couple. Some diabolical trouble is brewing, yo.

Jessica (Ingrid Thulin), a fellow reporter, ex of Gregory, and wearer of terrible headscarves is very jealous of Mira. She tries to woo him back but he's faithful to his lady. Later that night, Gregory runs out to meet his colleague for some information on a story. When he returns, Mira is gone. She's disappeared without taking her passport, her money, or even her clothes. Thus begins the investigation to find a hottie.

Kat comments on Jean Sorel's shiny and luxurious hair. Who am I to deny its power? The tense soundtrack is masterfully composed by Ennio Morricone. Things get really strange, paranoid, and just plain trippy as neon red blood is spilled and we meet eccentric ephemeral characters who are more dead than alive scattered all over the city.

Gregory uncovers a conspiracy involving high society and members of the government involved in a satanic sex/death cult. We're all relieved when Jealous Jessica takes off her fucking headscarf and finally reveals that she is indeed a human being. When the going gets rough, Gregory sleeps with Jessica. Rebound much? After his guilt-sex with Jessica, Gregory decides to end it all. I'm just kidding.

There's a damn hippie singing about butterflies and a rain of blood. One of Gregory's friends, a doctor, notices that his body has not gone through the proper stages of rigor mortis nor has the temperature dropped as normally. Now Gregory is headed for his own autopsy. Will he make it? The tension is palpable. How will this end? I'm a total schmuck for not digging on this film until I'd watched it about 4 times. Duh.

GOODNIGHT

Kat bids us farewell and takes her leave. It's still a little early but I want to get some rest. There is a lot of ground to cover tomorrow in the yellow gloaming of Giallo Meltdown 3. What the hell am I talking about? Good night, y'all.

SUNDAY

Around 7:30am, our cat Sparkles decides that it is time for me to wake up. She crawls over my side and gets between LeEtta and me. She then proceeds to push herself into my stomach and bark at me. Yes, our cat barks. When her purr engine is going and she wants to get our attention, Sparkles will get our attention with quick bursts of meowing. To me this sounds like a very sick dog. I painfully come to the realization that I can't go back to sleep and I might as well get up.

After feeding our demonic cats, I wake up LeEtta. She feeds the demonic bird, we go to breakfast. It's Easter Sunday so Bob Evans is closed. We head up Fletcher and then to Bruce B. Downs where there's a godless Panera Bread. The place is practically deserted. I order a sausage, egg and cheese sandwich and LeEtta gets a spinach and artichoke soufflé. We also get a cinnamon bun to share. THIS IS A FEAST! We hit the drugstore for some crackers and so I can get some Vitamin Water. Then it is back home and the Easter Sunday giallo slaughter can begin.

"That lady's a mystery I'd rather not solve."

9:56 AM
Amuck! (1972)

Barbara Bouchet and Rosalba Neri. What more could you ask for? Well, how about some sleazy sex and a killer soundtrack by Teo Usuelli to tickle your fancy? Bouchet stars as Greta, a young lady who arrives in Venice to work for a writer named Richard Stewart played the freakin' awesome Farley Granger. He and his wife Eleonora (Neri) are a little strange and the moment they are alone, they exchange some suspicious glances. Police commissioner Antonelli (Nino Segurini) stops by, investigating the disappearance of Richard's previous secretary, Sally.

In town, Greta meets with the commissioner and reveals that she and Sally were friends and that she got the job working for Richard in order to find out why her friend disappeared. Next, the naked nudeness of Barbara Bouchet! Greta is surprised by Rocco, a mentally handicapped fisherman, hanging around her window. Richard explains that Rocco is harmless. Then

Eleonora soothes Greta to sleep with the help of a sedative and then molests her while she's doped up. Slow motion lesbian shenanigans! And to think it's only her second night at her new gig.

Clearly, Richard and Eleonora are two depraved freaks that throw sex parties and drink alcohol and take drugs. These degenerates watch porno films and grope each other in the dark. Greta loses her cool at the party when Richard plays a film starring her friend Sally. Richard notices her slipup and the games begin. He begins to outline a hammy who-dunit for her to dictate, which, of course, is the story of what happened to Sally.

Ah, sweet memories of Sally (Patrizia Viotti). In a flashback, we find out that she and Greta were more than friends. Their nudie frolicking in the waterfall turns to sexy experimentation. Back in the present, the malevolent butler (Umberto Raho) nearly catches Greta snooping around and ends up locking her in the creepy basement. The tension goes up when Richard and Eleonora return from a hunting trip and Greta narrowly escapes getting caught prowling around.

Later, Greta meets up with Rocco at his shanty. A proper host, he kills and flays an eel for her. There is some awkward sexual tension there that just should not be and Greta goes back to the house. A surprise supernatural moment comes when Eleonora (who, according to Richard, has ESP) goes into a trance and we get an impromptu séance. She channels Sally and warns Greta that she's in danger. This film is friggin' awesome.

The next morning, Greta joins the Stewarts on one of their hunting expeditions and it turns ugly. While running from a volley of 'friendly fire', Greta falls into quicksand but is saved by Antonelli who comes out of nowhere. While relating her side of things, Greta confuses 'complicated' with just plain stupid and the cop leaves without doing anything. Oh man, it is so fucking obvious that Richard and Eleonora are guilty as hell. Since when do Italian cops do things by the book?

Greta confronts Richard about what really happened to Sally and he relates a tale of sex, booze, and retardation. It seems that Eleonora encouraged Rocco to get it on with Sally and things went wrong, very wrong. This scene is very dark and disturbing but it lets you know that this movie is no longer messing around. Greta is put at ease now that she finally knows 'the truth'. Now Richard and Eleonora have Greta right where they want her. I'm a huge fan of this underrated little flick.

"Sometimes I think you have a professional sickness."

11:39 AM
Door Into Darkness (1973)

I had read about these hour long giallo films produced for Italian television by Dario Argento. I waited and waited for years for these to become available her in the US. When they did come out the consensus of most of the reviews I read was that this four hour anthology wasn't very good. Argento himself introduces the stories and even does a little acting as a hitchhiker picked up by the main characters of the first tale.

"The Neighbor"

Luigi Cozzi directs the first of these films. In it, Stefania and Luca (Laura Belli and Aldo Reggiani), move with their baby into a new place by the seaside. They arrive to their destination and what's the first thing they do? They manage to get their car stuck in the mud. Foreboding! There's no phone, it's a creepy place, and the place is filthy. They stay up late watching Abbot and Costello Meet Frankenstein. The main thing to note here is a stain on the ceiling that looks like a big vagina.

Stefania finally notices the stain on the wall and they decide to go upstairs and figure what the dang neighbors are up to. The tap was running in the bathroom and the whole apartment is flooded. They turn off the water but find a dead woman in the tub. This discovery is accompanied by an explosive burst of jazz and I discover that Sparkles the cat is totally passed out and not at all concerned with Stefania and Luca's situation. Crisco, however, is wide awake and ready to help save some lives.

The plot for this one is pretty weak as 'ugly Richard Gere' (their murderous neighbor, played by Mimmo Palmara) comes back and they try to distract him from figuring out they have discovered his secret. Aw, the poor killer is depressed. He mopes about the place dragging his shovel behind him. I feel for you, bro.

The pacing is way off and I'm relieved that this isn't a full length movie. Oh yes, I loves me some Italian architecture. Hey, the killer is really a nice dude. He thinks he's doing the couple a favor by killing them. I'm glad that's over. At least Cozzi didn't sneak any rape scenes into this one. My good friend Nafa calls to say he'll be coming over soon.

"The Tram"

While cleaning a tram, a bus station worker discovers the corpse of a woman stuffed under a seat. An eccentric detective named Giordani (Enzo Cerusico) gets frustrated when he can't figure out how the hell the girl was stabbed to death in a trolley full of passengers. Dude has this irritating affectation of snapping his fingers while he's thinking and yeah, he thinks a lot. The next day, the cops get a confession from a loony and it is a really funny scene.

They round up all the passengers who rode the train the night of the murder and it is a deluge of familiar faces. Even Maria Tedeschi, the old lady from The Case of the Bloody Iris, is in this one. After they recreate the events of that fateful night, the ticket collector looks very guilty. The guy gets 30 years but the detective knows something is wrong.

Giordani decides to recreate the events of that night one more time. He gets the bright idea to use his hot wife Giulia (Paola Tedesco) in place of the dead girl. This is probably not a good idea, duder. This story is world's better than the first. I hope they keep getting better.

"Eye Witness"

Nafa arrives right at the beginning of this episode. This one starts with Argento asking a detective for a good story. None of the lurid tales impress the master of horror until this one. Hey, it's Marilù Tolo, George Hilton's hot wife from My Dear Killer. Both Nafa and LeEtta question my proclamation of her hotness but damn it, the woman is gorgeous to me. She plays Roberta, a woman on her way home who nearly runs over a girl on a deserted road. It turns out the girl has been shot to death. When the killer comes after her, she bolts to a diner and calls the cops. She relates her story to the cop and wouldn't you know it, there isn't a body or even a bloodstain to be found.

Her husband Guido (Riccardo Salvino) shows up and he doesn't believe her either. The cop's advice: "Be with your husband. Don't expose yourself." Back at home, Roberta reads, smokes a lot and gets mysterious phone calls. Guido gives her a ring with an insect on it because it's their anniversary. There is some debate between Nafa, LeEtta and myself about which anniversary is the insect jewelry anniversary. They go out for a hot night of dancing and driving around. Roberta gets horny on the way home so they stop on the side of the road to make love (presumably).

The next day, the detective shows Roberta some photos of girls that have been missing. Instead of a book of photos, they have a machine the size of a house with two small monitors on it. The editor decides to show us important things that we'd have to be blind to miss by zooming in on them. There's lots of bad jazz in this one. The drummer gets many chances to solo (which almost makes up for it).

In order to catch and kill the killer, Guido comes up with the worst plan in the history of plans; the lynchpin of which involves Roberta hiding behind the couch. Trapped inside the house with the killer trying to get at her, Roberta is totally screwed. The reveal at the ending is incredibly stupid. Even the subtitles start to give way to complete nonsense and typos.

"The Doll"

Robert Hoffmann, Erika Blanc, and Umberto Raho? Yes! We got some POV action up in here, y'all. A person escapes from an insane asylum in broad daylight and then the plot just kind of shatters into a thousand pieces. We don't know what's going on but this reeks of Argento. Robert Hoffmann's character is very unfriendly. He checks into a hotel where a nosy old lady gets all up in his business. Could he be the escaped maniac?

The oddly pretty Erika Blanc shows up. She's a seamstress and she gets killed off pretty quickly. The scene is very atmospheric with a rather hyperactive camera. Nice. Hoffmann's on the run with the cops on his tail so he buys a scarf to disguise himself. He starts following a lady (played by the totally gorgeous Mara Venier) and they end up back at her place. Hmm, if I say any more about this one, I'll ruin it. This is just a really cool episode.

POWER NAP

Unfortunately, Nafa has to leave already due to his lady friend leaving her keys in Orlando or something. I decide to take a nap. I dream of a confusing giallo TV series with a kind female narrator who explains everything to me. The episodes get faster and faster as I fall more deeply asleep. Next thing I know, I'm in a sitcom trying to catch my roommate's hamster that has escaped in the house. I chase it all over the place trying to keep the cats away from it. When I finally do catch the thing it is some kind of super hamster with armor and super jumping legs. Then the hamster turns into Maggie on a black version of "The Simpsons".

The father says something witty, the canned laughter kicks in, and then the credits roll. That's when my alarm goes off and I look around the room. The afternoon sun is pouring in through the curtains, bathing the room in a soft yellow light. I feel very strange. I do NOT want to think about what any of those dreams symbols meant.

"I wasn't in jail for 13 years for nothing,
I'm a specialist!"

5:35 PM
In the Folds of the Flesh (1970)

In the Folds of the Flesh is an Italian/Spanish co-production that must be seen to be believed. After a nonsensical quote, the first thing we see is a severed head. So I just took a disorienting nap and this is what I wake up to? My head feels like it is filled with helium and I don't even notice that my mouth is hanging open for the first several minutes of the film. A fat man on a scooter is trying to get away from the police and a woman named Lucille (Eleonora Rossi Drago) is trying to cover up the beheading of her husband. These two meet by chance then we flash forward 13 years.

Nowadays, Lucille and her family have covered up the murder of the father all this time and it's driven them mad. Her son Collin is the man of the house and he doesn't like it when Michelle, a childhood friend shows up. The word 'titillating' comes up over and over again as Michelle brashly hits on Collin's lover Falesse (Pier Angeli), the lady of the house. Falesse is completely insane by the way. The special attention sets her off and she knifes the fool to death. Next, Michelle's jerky friend Alex (Víctor Alcázar) comes sniffing around and is an even bigger sleazeball. Hey you stupid asshole, don't spit on Collin's pet vultures!

Now Falesse hooks up with Alex and Collin is none too happy to see her in the arms with another man, another victim. This dang family sure knows how to entertain. Falesse strums the guitar while Collin talks about being a true artist. I feel like I'm going mad. Falesse and Collin start making out when some erotic poetry they recorded together starts playing on a tape recorder. Alex thinks he's in for a good time with Felesse but he shares the same fate as her father.

Pascal (the fat man of the scooter-riding variety) is fresh out of prison and has returned to blackmail Lucille and the family for what he witnessed 13 years ago. Pascal is played by Fernando Sancho who lent his enormous talents to a ton of spaghetti westerns. In this movie Sancho is a cigar-chomping pirate who drinks a ton of J&B. When the family refuses to dig up their father's body, Pascal kills one of Collin's precious vultures and they get to brawlin'.

This garishly colored gem of a film is definitely one of a kind. The music is a hodgepodge of library music. Every character is either a scumbag or a maniac. Pascal takes the family hostage, rapes the women, and makes Collin shine his shoes. He plans on extorting $200,000 out of them but Lucille plans to poison Pascal with dissolving poison cyanide tablets; the kind she learned all about when the Nazis killed her family.

The plan to kill Pascal actually works so Lucille and Collin dissolve his body with acid. Andre (Alfredo Mayo of My Dear Killer), the father who we thought was dead, returns and everyone (including myself) is totally confounded. The explanation is so overly complicated and idiotic that I'm not even going to go in to it. The plot is collapsing onto itself!

Holy shit! Andre just delivered a 360 degree bitch slap to Lucille. God help us all, this movie is a mad little adventure. In the Folds of the Flesh has even driven Baby, our bird, insane. She is screaming her little green head off while plot revelation upon plot revelation just keeps on a-comin'. There is no way to keep up or make sense of any of it. Who cares? I just know that I fucking love this movie.

"You are full of shit but I like you."

7:19 PM
Watch Me When I Kill (1977)

I finally got to ditch my shitty VCI DVD of Watch Me When I Kill when I obtained a good copy from Shameless. Not that this film was one of my favorites or anything but you know how it is when you get a restored edition, you just gotta see what's been right under your nose the whole time but didn't really appreciate because of a poor quality transfer, right? RIGHT!?!? Sorry about that but In the Folds of the Flesh drove me insane.

A pharmacist is murdered in a seemingly senseless crime. The guy gets bashed on the head with a blunt object and then one of the most half-assed throat-slashings I've ever seen takes place. The killer narrowly avoids being spotted by several witnesses including Mara (played by Paola Tedesco (didn't we see her earlier today?)), a performer at a nightclub who gets close enough to hear the voice of the murderer. Her mustachioed friend Lukas (Corrado Pani) shows up and he takes her home. Let me stress that this duder Lukas is one smooth bastard.

The killer comes snooping around in Mara's apartment (great scene, by the way) but flees when interrupted by a neighbor's dog. Fearing for her life, she crashes at Lukas's place. The next morning, they chill in the courtyard while he smokes cheap cigars and drinks J&B. Giovanni (Fernando Cerulli) is an old gay man who lives in Lukas's building. He receives and records a threatening phone call. The person doesn't speak but plays a series of odd sounds. He takes it to Lukas and they go to a sound studio to decipher the recording. I'm probably making this film sound really boring. Sorry, there's just a lot going on.

Esmerelda (Bianca Toccafondi), a friend of Giovanni's who is somehow connected to all of this, gets killed in an especially horrible way (head stuffed in oven). Then while helping Giovanni park his car, Mara is nearly murdered by an unseen assailant who is actually gunning for him. Instead of going to the police, Mara and Lukas decide to solve the mystery themselves. Holy shit, this progressive rock music is awesome but it's quite interruptive.

Whoa, second film in a row with a Nazi plot thread. Turns out some of the victims were former Nazis or something and the killer wants retribution from them all. Giovanni retreats to Padua where he thinks he will be 'safe' from the killer. Not true. While taking his pretty blue bath, he gets drowned to death. Lukas comes to meet him there, finds out he was murdered, and goes on investigating. The townsfolk are not too friendly, especially that subnormal vagabond who laughs at Lukas's misfortune.

Lukas finds Esmerelda's dad who talks about some cryptic shit. Damn it, this whole town needs to be destroyed. Everyone in Padua is a dang inbred freakazoid. The closer Lukas gets to solving the mystery, the more interesting this film becomes. This story is quite intriguing and the movie has a low budget grittiness to it that is actually charming.

SMOKE BREAK

LeEtta and I head outside. I load my pipe with Aslo Black tobacco. The package says it's "The Magnificent Dane". I can't argue with that. LeEtta smokes Djarum Blacks and drinks wine. I'm washing my pipe smoke down with Gold Peak sweet tea. The sky is thick with clouds and the breeze is blowing the trees around seemingly in slow motion. Planes fly overhead and their headlights light up the clouds in eerie streaks. I tell LeEtta that it is very strange outside and we should be very concerned.

"Hellooooo. You look good on television."

9:39 PM
Phantom of Death (1988)

Michael York, Edwige Fenech, Donald Pleasence, Ruggero Deodato, and a ninja. Fenech is looking good though just a little tired in this movie. Holy crow, this might just be the bloodiest one in the moviethon. A woman gets killed by a sword and she's a real gusher, I tells ya. Michael York plays Robert, a concert pianist whose girlfriend wants to get married. I am in awe of what I think might just be Edwige Fenech's real voice. She plays Elaine, the director of a fashion house (YES!) and is falling for Robert even though she thinks he's a bastard. But his music has a strange effect on her. Robert is learning the art of the ninja.

Donald Pleasence plays Inspector Datti. His assistant mentions that the victims "juggler vein" was cut. Robert's two timing girlfriend who is way too young for him decides to stop fucking a younger dude named David and come back to him. Oops, too late! She just got murdered in a lovely slow motion spurting blood fiesta. Very nice. Datti's daughter is really annoying. She plays the flute in her pink overalls. The killer calls him up to threaten him and promise that there will be more victims. Boy oh boy, this is a shit role for Pleasence and he lets it show.

Robert has a degenerative illness that making him crazy as a loon and extremely violent. The doctors say that it is hereditary but I suspect the real cause is Elaine's monstrous shoulder pads. Every outfit she wears, even her pajamas have shoulder pads. Was Bea Arthur her wardrobe assistant? Fenech is still hot as hell years after her days as a sexy movie starlet. Her sex scene is actually tasteful! Pino Donaggio, your composing skills are kind of annoying. Did you know that?

We go back to Venice just in time for Carnivale that way fugly Roert can wear a mask. The illness is making him age very rapidly and the makeup on York is actually really good with its insanely exaggerated liver spots, wrinkles and rotting teeth. It is quite nasty. Robert wants to get caught but the rage inside him is too great. He has to go on killing. Trust me, I know the feeling.

Datti catches Robert but lets him go because he looks too old to be the killer. I know I said as much before but clearly Donald Pleasence does not give a triple fuck about this role. Robert confronts Elaine and reveals his secret. Her revulsion when she realizes the truth is very convincing. Damn it, Fenech can freakin' act! Okay, Donaggio, that closing theme is pretty awesome. Dude pisses me off. How dare he get all good and stuff after I've been dogging him this whole time?

> *"It's been a long time since I've talked with anyone sane."*

11:14 PM
The House of the Laughing Windows (1976)

Talk about transcending the genre. We are at the last movie of Giallo Meltdown 3 and holy fuck, it's a true classic. Director Pupi Avati created this masterpiece in 1976, that magical year. Later he would go on to direct Zeder, one of the greatest Italian horror films of all time. But that's for another moviethon. This movie is an eccentric and legitimately frightening piece of work. I will not be able to do this one justice here. Don't go another day without watching this film.

Stefano (Lino Capolicchio of The Bloodstained Shadow) is hired to restore a disturbing fresco of St. Sebastian by Legnani, a mad painter. The town where the fresco is located is a dead place where everyone seems like they're in shock or heavily medicated. On his first day there, he is warned to go away by a frightening voice on the phone. Stefano's myopic friend Antonio (Giulio Pizzirani) tries to tell him what's up but is so paranoid that he can barely get through it.

Stefano hooks up with the town slut (who looks like a leftover Fellini character) for a lazy afternoon shag. Man, this movie is so dreamlike. Everything is quaint but very weird and pretty soon, this dream will turn into a nightmare. His buddy Antonio ends up dead but our hero doesn't get the hint and hightail it out of town like we know he should.

Stefano gets mixed up with Lidio (Pietro Brambilla), this sadistic little freak who acts as his guide around town. No one scares me more than him. The landlady gives away Stefano's room so he has to get a room in the an old spooky house just outside of town. The freaks in this shitbox town are harboring a terrible secret.

Dang, this is one creepy ass movie. There are always footsteps, voices, and odd things happening in the dark. While exploring his new digs, he finds the coolest tape recorder ever made. On the tape is the voice of the mad painter describing his colors and death. His colors. And death. And purity. Colors in his veins. Purity and- You get the idea. The feeling of dread grows more powerful with every scene.

Stefano meets the lovely Francesca (Francesca Marciano), the new teacher at school (the slut from earlier left town, by the way), and she shows him her refrigerator full of snails. The restoration of the painting reveals two murderous female figures torturing St. Sebastian but who were Legnani's models? No one knows shit. The kindly but tight-lipped priest is played by Eugene Walter, who was the ludicrously gay waiter in The Black Belly of the Tarantula.

A sweet romance between Stefano and Francesca blossoms. After they make love, they come to their senses and plan to leave this crazy town forever but Stefano is obsessed just can't leave the mystery alone. LeEtta has gone off to bed but not without expressing her desire to watch Laughing Windows again sometime. Now it's just me, the cats, and the killer. We are fucking doomed. Coppola (Gianni Cavina), the town drunk, is the only one willing to help Stefano but there is much danger ahead.

Just like a nightmare, things change and you can never go back to the same place twice. People disappear, clues disappear. Stefano discovers that the two figures in the painting were the mad painter's sisters. In order for him to paint death more realistically, they killed for Legnani. The evil bitches spurred him on and he became more and more insane. It culminated with the painter setting himself on fire and running off into the woods, never to be seen again. Which is actually a pretty funny scene. How did the townspeople lose him? He was on fire in the middle of the night!

Stefano is completely possessed by the mystery of Legnani now. He can't just walk away now. He's too close to it now. Francesca is scared so he agrees to leave with her. Before they catch the morning train out of town, Stefano has to check one more thing. JUST ONE MORE THING! What could possibly go wrong? Despite being threatened by townspeople to keep his mouth shut, Coppola leads Stefano to where the bodies are buried.

The House with the Laughing Windows finally reveals itself and I'm getting freaked out. I can't tell you how many times I've watched this film and it still makes me uneasy and depressed. I adore it! Once the veil is lifted and Stefano sees things the way they really are, it is even worse than he suspected. He calls in the authorities but it's too late, the evidence is gone. Now it is just Stefano, the killers, and a town full of cowardly people who have turned their backs on the past. I am now eternally unsettled.

CONCLUSION

The day I watched my first official giallo (Deep Red), I ceased being normal (which is arguable since I can't really say how 'normal' I was to begin with). Now I'm an even weirder duder because this is easily the most bizarre of the Giallo Meltdowns so far. Days off? Some people take them to catch up on "Battlestar Galactica" and some go Boogie boarding. Me? I use them to recover from moviethon hangovers.

The best outcome of this moviethon was the yellow reverie I was in for days and days afterwards. Some moviethons end very depressingly (like BAVADOOM) and some end in painful madness (the first Giallo Meltdown) but the effects of Giallo Meltdown 3 were different. For at least a week after I woke up on Monday morning, I felt as though I had done something really important. The world looked good and suspicious and my heart was light even with all the straight razors lodged in the ventricles. This will happen again, by God, I promise you, this will happen again.

GIALLO MELTDOWN 4:
RED, YELLOW, AND BLACK FOREVER

Every time I start prepping for a Giallo Meltdown, I think: "This is it. This is going to be the last one." It's a frightening thought but it's never true. Fact is, I'll probably never run out of gialli. While compiling my playlist this time, I realized I had too many once again. Unfortunately, I have to sleep and eat sometime so there are always titles that get cut and are thus reserved for the next Meltdown. DVD companies in the US have been slackers lately and haven't been churning out the giallo titles like they were a few years ago so I am resorting to bootleggers and the Internet. Sorry folks, there ain't no way I'm missing out on the good shit. No sir, uh uh.

It's strange but I just do all of this just to disappear for a few days. I go to this yellow place where the world looks faded, the film is all scratched up, and the dubbing is off. I know the killer is still out there, running amuck, and taking the lives of fashion models and people who are about to inherit large sums of money. Death is on its way and I hope that it is fabulous. Oh, I wonder what the body count will be?

FRIDAY

Today was pretty strange, even by moviethon standards. I actually ended up working late for the library on a video shoot which almost never happens. It was an exhausting day. That definitely never happens at my freakin' desk job! I get home around 6:30 and munch on some ground beef, black eyed peas, and green beans that my mother-in-law Margie had whipped up for she and LeEtta. She hadn't expected me home in time for dinner but Margie's meals almost always leave leftovers. I don't like peas or most things bean-related but I was starving so I just enjoyed it. We're late, late, late for the start of this moviethon, damn it.

"I'll make you piss your blood."

7:06 PM
Deadly Sweet (1967)

The movie starts and we get our first corpse! The lovely Ewa Aulin graces us with her beauteous presence and Margie comments on her Goldie Hawn-esqueness. I spout off some nonsense about exterials [sic] being shot in England and interials [double sic] being shot in Rome studios which may or may not be true. Bernard (Jean-Louis Trintignant) is our gumshoe friend and hero. Jane (Aulin) is our lady and she just lost her father. She and her whole dang family go to the disco after identifying his body at the morgue. Bernard pursues her and finds Jane hiding in a room with a freshly murdered man. "I didn't do it," she says and they immediately start making out WITH THE BODY IN THE ROOM.

Deadly Sweet keeps switching from black and white to color. It also has lots of artsy transitions, comic book sound effects, and mad cap comedic nonsense. I don't think Tinto Brass wanted to make a straight up giallo but I don't mind. Bernard runs into some thugs looking for the same diary he's after but he gets the jump on them. Wait, why are they all looking for that diary? I think it's Jane's. Shit, I have no idea but I'm amused. We get our first J&B sighting of the moviethon around 19 minutes. It won't be the last.

Maybe I'm just distracted or overly tired but this mystery is completely confusing right now. Bernard and Jane are prancing around in the park and don't seem to give two shits about solving the mystery so I guess I shouldn't either. Whoa, Bernard just got beat up by a dwarf and Jane got kidnapped. Bernard goes and harasses Jane's brother Jerome for some info. Now they're both out looking for Jane. Damn, Jerome has got one hot girlfriend. Did I mention how groovetastic and perfect this soundtrack is? Uh oh, the dwarf is molesting Jane. Ask any tall chick and she'll tell you, this is her ultimate fantasy.

In spite of its ponderous moments, I still dig this flick. The two lovers hide out at Bernard's buddy's place. He's a fashion photographer so they trash the place during their spirited lovemaking session. Me Tarzan. You Jane. Oh my God. These two should try being self-involved for a change. There are multiple references to Michelangelo Antonioni. Then the baddy guys rip out Bernard's eyelashes and everything goes all screwy. Where the hell is this all going? Oh fuck, the ending is awesome. Roberto Bisacco is in this; he played that impotent hothead Stefano in Torso.

"It's been a long time, Alice."

8:53 PM
Footprints on the Moon (1975)

And now for something even weirder. Here is another film to subvert the typcal giallo plot. We start off with a spaceman dragging another spaceman along the moon's surface. Then he takes off in the ship leaving the duder there to die. Next we see the lovely Florinda Bolkan (with a Mimsy Farmer haircut) as Alice, waking up in her drab, colorless apartment. The visions of the spaceman are from a dream she keeps having. Alice goes to her job as a translator to turn in her work but her boss tells her that she missed three days of work. Something definitely isn't right. All that she has to account for her lost time is a postcard from a place called Garma. Evelyn Stewart makes a brief cameo but she looks like crap. The director is trying to make Bolkan look like crap too.

The first half of Footprints AKA Footprints on the Moon is a study in beige and pale yellow; all is very cold, impersonal, and ultra-modern. When Alice finally gets to Garma, the world becomes colorful, vibrant. She arrives and oh my God, this movie is so beautiful. She meets a little girl named Paola, played by the odd-looking Nicoletta Elmi (of Deep Red and Baron Blood). She tells Alice that she met her in Garma a few days before and that she told her that her name was Nicole, not Alice. A mystery is brewing in this hypnotic film. The soundtrack by Nicola Piovani (The Perfume of the Lady in Black) is willowy and enigmatic.

Everything in this movie is so strange and then Klaus Kinski shows up as a scientist named Blackman. Nothing weird about that! Little details deepen the mystery because the more Alice learns, the more perplexing things become. Nicole. Who is Nicole? All of the scenery in this Garma place is astounding. She gets more answers from the wig guy at the hairdresser than from anybody else! Memories start to slowly rise to the surface. She finds the boy from her youth: Harry (played by Peter McEnery). He's all grown up and he tells Alice the truth. Aw, did someone just lose their marbles?

SATURDAY

Wow, that was a shaky, shaky start for a moviethon. The movies were great but I was a mess. I guess work really zapped me out yesterday. I'm looking at my pages of notes and they deteriorated pretty badly. One would think that I was at the end of a moviethon, not the beginning. This morning, we got up around 8:15am and started the morning chores. Then LeEtta, Margie, and I walked over to 7-11 for breakfast sandwiches. I get Mountain Dew, a sausage, egg, and cheese croissant, and a root beer for later. I'm trying to remember my dreams from last night. There were lots of bland running around and stressful disappointments (kind of like Alice's life before she went to Garma). Nothing even remotely giallo-related.

The weather this morning is a blessing. It is breezy and gorgeous. I'm sure the sun will be out later to wreck everything. I pick the Love and Death CD from the Luciano Ercoli double DVD set of Death Walks at Midnight and Death Walks in High Heels. The silky sounds of Stelvio Cipriani are perfect for cruising around Dale Mabry. We end up at Target (which eats up the rest of our morning) and on the way home, I decide to give Casa Tobaco a try. The selection is good there and it seems laid back enough. I might have to come back sometime to sit and smoke. I get two cigars. One for today and one for tomorrow. (Please note: This place sucks! I went back recently to smoke a cigar and they turned me away. Their smoking lounge is private! Members only. WHAT? This is fucking Carrolwood, morons! Anyway, I'll never give those fuckers money again.)

"My reputation is 100%."

11:28 AM
The Killer is on the Phone (1972)

Oh, I love that Lightning Video logo! I converted my VHS of this film to DVD-R with mediocre results but seeing it on Margie's widescreen TV makes me realize that it came out better than I remembered it. Oh shit, I forgot that Joe D'Amato is the director of photography for this one. This fact pleases me. The elegant Anne Heywood plays Eleanor, an actress who faints when she sees a hitman (Telly Savalas) on the street. She goes home to find that her house has been torn down. Hmm, chicks with memory problems; seems kind of familiar. Eleanor calls her sister looking for her husband Peter but he's been dead for 5 years. Savalas decides to follow Eleanor because he knows she knows who he is. Damn, this is way better than I remembered and the soundtrack by Stelvio Cipriani is great.

Jeez, Eleanor has really gone off the deep end. Her poor husband of the last 3 years is all like 'hey honey' and she's all like 'who the fuck are you?' Her hot sister Dorothy (Willeke van Ammelrooy) is trying to help her but to no avail. The look of pity on their stupid faces is pretty priceless. The dialogue is equally hilarious, especially when the doctor talks about giving her a shot of (gasp!) pentothal to help her recover her memories. The flashback to the time she spent with her first husband look like an Abba video until the hitman shows up and attempts to menace her with a knife. Now that her memory of the last 5 years has been wiped, she can't even remember Telly Savalas or why she should be afraid of him. This confuses the hitman and he becomes obsessed with her. Next, Eleanor gets on stage and starts performing as Lady Macbeth but the rest of the troupe is doing Lady Godiva. Woops!

Oh snap! Rosella Falk is in this one looking severe and lovely as always. She plays Margaret, Peter's sister, patron of the arts, and all around beyatch. Eleanor and Thomas (Osvaldo Ruggieri) start up an affair and it's just pathetic; partly because she is insane but mostly it's because Thomas is a complete pussy. Later, her husband (not the dead one) tries to drug her J&B and she splits the scene armed with a pistol. This should be fun. I think Telly Savalas is too cool for this movie. He frightens me and he's not even sucking on lollipops. He kicks the shit out of a couple of goons who try to remind him of another hit he's supposed to be working on.

The plot takes a turn for the strange when Eleanor tries to get Thomas to murder her husband (not the dead one) but- Oh wait, play within a play, y'all. This movie totally got me! Hardy har har! Now that Eleanor is back to the 'real world', she is just kind of a jerk to everyone. Telly Savalas finally kills someone but he got the wrong dang chick. Woops! For lunch, I eat my leftover chicken-fried steak and mashed potatoes from Mimi's Cafe while LeEtta and Margie eat yesterday's green beans, black-eyed peas, and meat. There's an awesome showdown at the theater and we finally find out who hired Telly Savalas to kill Peter and why. We get more wild overacting from Anne Heywood and we're done. Holy shit, that ending is pretty awesome.

"For an insurance man, you're not
behaving too well."

1:09 PM
A Black Veil for Lisa (1968)

Here's one from the download pile. Did you see that? Finally! A black-gloved killer is waiting to strike. He/she kills someone named Willy who the cops were after. Everyone is after Willy these days. It seems that someone is bumping off suspects before they can be brought in for questioning. Inspector Franz Bulon (John Mills) comes home to his bitchy wife Lisa (the smokin' hot Luciana Paluzzi). Franz's boss is a jerk and he talks like Boris from "Rocky and Bullwinkle". There's some kind of a drug ring in Hamburg and our goodly inspector is going to take it down. Whoa, someone keeps whispering "Lisa" over the music score so that we can remember Lisa's name (which is not easy).

Franz starts grilling poor Marianne (Renate Kasche) and his razor-sharp techniques get her to give up the goods on her friend Ursula. The cops and some thugs are looking for a loser named Kurt Muller. Muller likes to hide under the bed while people beat the crap out of his girlfriend. Robert Hoffmann (of Spasmo) shows up as Max Lindt and he's as smooth as ever. Someone is paying him to go after Muller as well. Someone mentions something about tulips and Max swears that this is his last job. He wants out! Yawn. So do I.

Max meets up with a hottie at a nightclub but the dance floor is too crowded for him (meaning there is one other couple dancing). Jeez, this movie is drab as fuck. I can't believe this is from the director of What Have You Done to Solange?; not that that's a wildly colorful piece of eye candy or anything but damn it, where's the style in Lisa? I spot a bottle of J&B and that brightens things up. Uh oh, Max lost his lucky dollar. That's a bad omen. Franz sure is obsessed with Lisa. Is she cheating on him? He barely has time to notice Max's silver dollar next to the body of one of the victims.

Franz picks up Max and is about to arrest him but he can't focus on his work because he thinks Lisa is out there somewhere bangin' some dude. He asks Max to kill Lisa. Max shows up to talk with Lisa about insurance but ha ha, she is too clever for him! Max is supposed to kill her but he's conflicted for some reason. Great scene where we think Lisa is dead. Shit! Who cares? I'm bored and sleepy. Sorry Massimo Dallamano, you have directed much better than this. Shadow, the official dog of Doomed Moviethon, gets to bark at some of the police dogs in the movie so at least one of us is entertained.

CIGAR BREAK

Oh my goodness, it is freakin' hot out here. The breeze from this morning has died and now the sun is doing just what I thought it would. This is only April. I can't imagine what summer is going to be like this year. Anyway, I've got a very dark and very flavorful Santa Luis Rey cigar and an A&W root beer made with "Aged Vanilla" (much better than their "Prepubescent Vanilla" days). I love this patio. It's so nice to finally be screened in for a change. Apparently, wasps are attracted to cigar smoke. I don't know if that's true. My research team are all on vacation. You look it up. Looking over my broken notes from last night once again, it's no wonder I called it quits so early. The only thing that kept me going was the awesomeness of Footprints. Hopefully, I'll be more lucid for the rest of Giallo Meltdown 4.

"Maybe you shouldn't have married a clairvoyant."

3:49 PM
The Psychic (1977)

This next one goes out to my homey: Death Rattle Aaron. Oh no, that little psychic girl's mummy just jumped off a cliff and her face exploded against the rocks on the way down. Fulci, you so crazy! Flash forward to the girl all grown up (Jennifer O'Neill) seeing her man Francesco (Gianni Garko) off on a business trip. Her name is Virginia and her theme song is the totally perfect fake Abba song "With You". On her way back home, Virginia has some disturbing visions while driving through a tunnel. She wakes up on the side of the road with a concerned cop shaking her awake. Luca, her psychiatrist (Marc Porel of Don't Torture a Duckling), says he believes that she does indeed have visions but you can totally tell that he secretly thinks that she's a nutbar.

While her husband is away, Virginia opens up his old house. Hmm, that nervous groundskeeper sure looks familiar. Could it be Gianpaolo Saccarola (of The Beyond and Tenebre)? He's not listed in the credits. WTF? One person that is definitely listed in the credits of this movie is Evelyn Stewart. She plays Francesco's sassy sister but more importantly, this is her second appearance in this moviethon. And once again, she looks friggin' awful. Poor thing. Fire the stylist! This is a beauty we have here.

Lucio Fulci is the fucking king by the way. This movie is so full of menace and foreboding. Tiny details are meticulously explored and something just ain't right. Oh yeah, this soundtrack is so perfect (it even inspired Quentin Tarantino to use it in Kill Bill). Virginia knocks down a wall based on her visions and she finds a skeleton there. Then the dead woman from her visions turns up very much alive.

The beautiful scenery is totally beautiful. Darn it, where's my thesaurus? Francesco admits to having an affair with the girl whose corpse they found in the wall (while she was still alive, apparently). The cops take him in for questioning and unfortunately for him, Virginia is trying to help clear him of any suspicion because she sounds like a dang lunatic! The pieces start coming together but it's the wrong puzzle. Suddenly, everything gets tense and insane as her visions start to come true. This is one eerie little film. Lucio Fulci, you're the coolest! I prefer this film's alternate title, Seven Notes in Black.

"I wonder what you think about... in that instant when you know you're going to die."

5:34 PM
The Fourth Victim (1971)

Hmm, I don't remember this one at all. I remember downloading it just to get another title for my Marina Malfatti collection and I think it has Greek subtitles. First of all, what is up with that distribution company's logo? Disco He-Man, anyone? We are first introduced to composer Piero Umiliani's ostentatious soundtrack and then we meet Arthur Anderson (Michael Craig) and his maid pulling a woman's body out of a swimming pool. Is she dead? Yes. Is she hot? Yes. They strip her, dry her off, and try to make it look like she didn't drown. Um, huh? Dang it, that is one hot corpse. We are cheated out of a peek at her dead boobs. Weak! Let me guess: I have the censored version? At the woman's funeral, a silly ass detective rushes in and asks the gravediggers to unbury her.

Arthur Anderson is accused of killing his third wife and for collecting a third life insurance policy. Motherfucker looks guilty as fuck. They haul his ass into court and we're treated to an intense (not really) trial scene. Arthur gets acquitted and goes for a walk in the park accompanied by some jaunty music. I guess he's out looking for a new wife. While we're watching this,

Margie springs dinner on LeEtta and me. It is a fine one too: baked haddock, couscous, broccoli, and cauliflower. It's wonderful and the first moviethon fish that wasn't sushi. Wait a second, this might be the first moviethon fish ever! Milestone!

So anyway, while Arthur is trying to get over his dead wife, he catches a woman swimming in his pool. Oh, it's Carroll Baker as Julie Spencer. Sorry folks, but I just really can't stand Carroll Baker. She is just kind of annoying at the best of times. But my spirits are still up because Marina Malfatti (of The Red Queen Kills 7 Times) is snooping around on the grounds of the mansion. That's always a good sign. Oh shit, for some reason, Arthur just married Julie. Hopefully, this one will end up dead too. According to The Internet, this is from director Eugenio Martin, the guy who directed the horror movie classic, Horror Express. Thanks, The Internet.

Julie is definitely up to some sneaky shit. On their wedding night, she starts tearing through his attic, looking for clues. She is obsessed with his previous wife, Gladys. Anderson discovers some disturbing skeletons in Julie's past including, but not limited to, the murder of her first husband. This is one of those flicks that I had a bad first impression with and I'm glad I'm giving it another spin. Okay, this Irish cop is almost totally incomprehensible. Will the real Julie please stand up? Or sit down? Some freaky shit is going on, yo.

> *"A naked woman doesn't have to go into explanations, especially when she is as young and as beautiful as you."*

7:29 PM
Eye in the Labyrinth (1972)

Bootleg Saturday continues with a very beat up copy Eye in the Labyrinth with Dutch subtitles that I downloaded. I'm watching this on my computer because it looks terrible on the TV. A creepy jazz band plays on while a man is chased by a knife-wielding maniac in a -you guessed it- labyrinth. After a gory stabbing and some weird camera angles, Julie (Rosemary Dexter), the hot girl dreaming all of this, wakes up screaming. I like where this is going. While looking for her missing husband named Lucas (Horst Frank), she gets bitch-slapped by a mysterious character in sunglasses. She calls bullshit on that, jumps into her convertible, and goes cruising to a small village where her husband was said to be going. The place is filled with suspicious characters including Adolfo Celi (of Who Saw Her Die?) as Frank, a strange character hanging about town.

Crisco has decided to join me (on my desk) for this viewing. It feels like anything could happen in this movie! This is what scrounging around in the cult film dumpster is all about, kids. Someone just tried to kill this gorgeous broad. Julie ends up staying in this weird house with some very odd freakazoids. The soundtrack by Roberto Nicolosi is just a lurid jazz fart festival that is probably going to get really annoying after a while. Julie goes skinny dipping (big mistake) and some local perverts steal her clothes. Good God, look at these plebes, they look like Metallica! Alida Valli (of Suspiria) is in this one and her performance is creepy (as usual).

So Julie is now staying at the compound of weirdos where people take pictures of her feet and act like complete assholes. This is definitely one bizarre friggin' movie. There's this weird little dude who keeps popping up. He's voiced by a woman and it cracks me up. Oh look, some J&B. I knew this movie wouldn't let me down. Everyone keeps lying to Julie about where Lucas is. One of the women tells Julie that Lucas raped her and then disappeared shortly afterward. People are on drugs here or is it just their personalities? Nope, there's a syringe.

Uh oh, she finds Lucas's car in the garage and she gets locked in there with the engine running. Before she dies, the least likely person rescues her. The flashbacks make Lucas look like a real jerk. Maybe Julie should stop looking for this sociopathic rapist jerkoff. We get cheesy acting and cheesy dubbing in this worthless yet perfect sleaze-gem. I sure hope someone rescues this flick from oblivion. I'm looking at you, legitimate DVD companies. Whoa, Julie just took some hits of acid. This is nuts! Eye in the Labyrinth is better than any other film ever made. The body of Lucas just washed up on the beach and all hell is breaking loose. Alida Valli's gonna wash her troubles down with some J&B. Now Julie is trapped with the killer! This one is going to be hard to beat, y'all.

9:32 PM
The Weekend Murders (1970)

Why the hell are Italians so obsessed with England? Here's a goofy little flick. We follow a British cop as he rides a bike and drinks some milk. Now we're on a golf course. Soothing music and quiet scenes explode into noise and classical music at the discovery of the first body. Hey, I didn't know that Evelyn Stewart is in this one. Bonus! Other bonuses include skewed camera angles by Guglielmo Mancori (Umberto Lenzi's Paranoia) and an amazing score by Francesco De Masi (The Hanging Woman). Plus, there's a will to be read, some fun murders, and everyone is a suspect. This parody of British murder mysteries is just a whole lotta fun and it gives me 'The Vibe'. You know what? All I have left to say about The Weekend Murders is that everyone should watch it. Goodnight.

SUNDAY

So, could you tell that my notes on The Weekend Murders were complete gibberish and I had almost nothing to write up? Here's the most sensical sentence: "the bumbling detective is the one who is the real detective". I guess I don't know my own strength. Anyway, I really wanted to sleep in today but our cats were very insistent on us waking up early (around 8am). Crisco worked especially hard by knocking over a plant on our dresser. Thanks, fucker! I did get to dream about an inheritance scheme and a bunch of wacky characters trying to evade a black gloved killer. That was great! Of course, the killer got away again. I take out the trash and discover that it's even more windy and sinister out than it was yesterday. It's also muggier and there's supposed to be a big storm heading our way.

I can't stop thinking about Eye in the Labyrinth. That nearly unwatchable bootleg was worth fighting through just so I could watch one of the most unfairly obscure gialli that I've ever seen. Margie, LeEtta, and I go to Panera Bread for breakfast. The soundtrack for the drive is an Italian pop mix I made with lots of Rita Pavone and Raffaella Carra. When we get there, I order sausage, egg and cheese on an Asiago cheese bagel. And hey look, they have Mountain Dew on tap!

> *"Sorry, baby. I hate to interrupt a professional at her job. And you are a winner; very nice work."*

11:09 AM
Cold Eyes of Fear (1971)

God damn this stupid Redemption DVD intro. What the fuck were they thinking with this intro? There are painful looking silicone boobers, white contact lenses, and corn syrup dripping out my TV. Thankfully, my wife and mother-in-law aren't in the room while this shit is playing. When the movie finally starts, the speakers explode with Ennio Morricone and Bruno Nicolai. These dudes kill my face with their 100% pure jazz-rock assault. I sure hope this movie is better than I remember it. My first impression was very negative. After the badass music, we see a woman (Karin Schubert) menaced by a duder with a knife. He cuts her clothes off and they make love. Then she stabs him, the lights come on, and everyone applauds. It was all a put-on! Oh Enzo G. Casterllari, you magnificent bastard!

Peter (Gianni Garko) steals Anna (Giovanna Ralli) from her boorish date at the nightclub so he can take her out on the town. They go back to his uncle's house for a late night of getting it on but there's a duder in gay boots lurking around the place. Peter and Anna start mackin' on the kitchen table but then the dead butler falls out of the pantry. I'm a little surprised something like that could ruin their sexy mood. Now Gay Boots (Julian Mateos) takes them hostage. Peter's Uncle Jerk (Fernando Rey) calls and is a total jerk as well as a judge. Uncle Jerk sends a cop over to deliver a letter. Will this cop be the hero and rescue our two annoying friends? I think that the music makes this film or maybe it's the J&B.

When the cop shows up and punches Peter in the face, I kind of figure out that something is up. This ain't no cop, this is a crook named Arthur (Frank Wolff of Death Walks on High Heels). Anna is so gorgeous but that damn fro she's sporting just ain't doing it for me. The hostage situation continues. There's lots of screaming and back and forth. It seems as though our two criminal masterminds have a special relationship. Is Gay Boots actually gay? Arthur tells Peter about a bomb he's planted at Uncle Jerk's office which will go off if he leaves his office. Ugh, this is some silly shit. The stupid judge just sits in his office, pontificating on the Latin phrase Peter told him over the phone. For the record, I'm enjoying this movie a million times more than the first time around but that's still not very much.

Now there's a biker gang stirring up trouble at a shopping mall. Huh? We find out that Arthur's motivation for this lame-brained scheme is that Uncle Jerk screwed him over. Peter is so stupid and naive that he can't believe it. When no one is looking, Peter cuts the lights and everyone in the house goes totally bonkers. We are treated to a tense showdown (way too long in the making) in the dark. There is some more nonsense with the bomb squad rescuing the judge and poopy poopy poopy poopy. Cold Eyes of Fear, what the fuck are you doing? I am glad I gave this film another chance but it still doesn't hold up all that well the second time around.

CIGAR BREAK

Out on the patio, I count my blessings once again. This closed in patio makes for an ideal place to smoke when the wind is picking up. Wind is a cigar smoker's worst enemy. Next to the wasp, I guess. Didn't I already talk about this yesterday? No wait, I've got it. The cigar smoker's worst enemy is mouth cancer. Anyway, I've got my Cain cigar and a couple of Vitamin Waters to go with my giallo music mix. I have a long way to go today. There's a headache brewing in the back of my skull but I keep on smoking.

It doesn't matter, the soothing sounds of Morricone's score for Forbidden Photos of a Lady Above Suspicion takes all of my cares away when I close my eyes. Through the sliding glass door I see that Margie is knitting while she patiently waits for stupid public television to go back to playing Victor Borge concerts instead of just talking about them and asking for money. The bastards want a donation before they'll finally release their famous hostage.

*"I don't know much at this point. But I know
the killer is a psychopath."*

2:00 PM
You'll Die at Midnight (1986)

I jump back on the computer for this mid-80s giallo from Lamberto Bava. The soundtrack is already cheesetastic. Oh, Claudio Simonetti, you are a genius. Some pervert is spying on a woman trying on lingerie in a shop. His dumb face is stuck in a horrible sneer. Maybe he was born like that. His name is Nicola (Leonardo Treviglio) and he's a detective. A man joins the woman in the dressing room and his sneer fades. Nicola gets pissed off and goes home to his shitty and ugly apartment. Oh, I see. That lady in the changing room was his wife. She comes home and we got some serious domestic violence going on here. Damn! She stabs him with an icepick and he tries to drown her in the dishwater. This is not how you treat your spouses, my friends. Haven't these people ever tried kissing or snuggling? Nicola runs off and his wife is soon stabbed to death by a mysterious killer with her own icepick.

Next we meet Anna (Valeria D'Obici), a psychiatrist. Nicola shows up at her place and tells her everything that's happened. He seems to have no idea that his wife is dead. Do we trust his stupid face? The cops show up and things don't look too good for the guy. The killer goes to the psychiatric hospital where Anna works and dicks around with some files on a computer. It looks like our killer, named Franco Tribbo, hasn't been active since the 70s. That guy, Paolo Malco (from House by the Cemetery and New York Ripper), is Inspector Terzi, our hero detective.

Anna is an expert on Franco Tribbo and we find out that he supposedly died in a fire. Even though I can't stand how this movie is awkwardly dribbling out the plot, I have to admit that this is actually a decent late 80s giallo. There's an awesome stalking sequence in an empty opera house. Lamberto Bava certainly knows how to deliver (once in a while). Hey look, it's Gianpaolo Saccarola from The Beyond. Later, Anna sees Franco in her house but Terzi doesn't believe her.

The killer is after this chick named Carol (Lara Wendel of Tenebre), who just happens to be Terzi's daughter. Nicola attacks Anna out of the blue and gets gunned down by the cops. Man, is any of this making sense? Of course, the killer who ain't dead yet strikes again so Carol and her 'cute' friends (annoying psychology students) leave the city so they'll be safe. They stay in an empty hotel by the beach. It's called 'Hotel Progresso'. Apparently, the word 'progresso' doesn't mean 'soup' in Italian. Whoa!

Next we meet Alberto, a Peeping Tom who is watching some chick work on her Flashdance routine. Hey, what the fuck? I just noticed something. How come none of the murders occur on or anywhere near midnight? It's in the dang title! When one of Carol's friends is threatened by the killer, she reaches for a mixer. This gives the killer a very nasty idea for her death scene (which takes place off camera (thank God)). You'll Die at Midnight is a pretty goofy movie but I dig it. We get a foggy finale and some of the least graphic genital mutilations ever filmed. It's fun and even mildly diverting but by no means a classic.

"Don't think about it. You must drink without thinking. It's only poison."

3:41 PM
Naked Girl Killed in the Park (1972)

I go back out to the living room to share this unseen-by-me giallo with Margie and LeEtta. I pop in the DVD from Euro Trash Cinema and it begins. Berlin. 1945. A Nazi and a dead teenage girl leave a mother and her son in a house with a bomb. That seems a tad elaborate. Flash forward to present day Madrid where some old duder is murdered on a haunted house ride. Holy crap, this Spanish/Italian co-production has my attention! It's Robert Hoffmann again. And there's Adolfo Celi again. Hoffmann is Chris, an insurance investigator who is looking into the case of the dead duder. The beneficiary of the corpse's will, Catherine (Pilar Velazquez), just happens to be a hot chick. She's getting obscene phone calls and she's really scared. Thank God, a giallo that isn't set in England.

Next up, we get some lovely, romantic interludes while Chris tries to get to the bottom of the case. Catherine's sister Barbara (Patrizia Aiutori of Torso) is hot for Chris's body. The family butler is played by Franco Ressel (who was in at least 6 gialli including Eye in the Labyrinth). We got some melodrama, y'all. An attempted rape that turns into a consensual sex scene (BOO!) as the farmhand has his way with Barbara. Must be a European thing. Chris is about to put the moves on Catherine but her mom (Irina Demick of Tragic Ceremony) totally cock-blocks him. So he does the next rational thing: he goes down to the barn and gets it on with Barbara.

Later, of course, Barbara is found with her throat slit, naked, and dead. Totally dead, naked, and IN THE PARK. Jeez, mom has snapped and we see how hung up she is on her dead husband. She stares at his portrait, rubs her martini glass on her face, and twirls around in her dress. This is an average thriller because sometimes (most of the time) average is all I need. Now a little gothic horror just got thrown in the mix. (Geez Catherine, why don't you try fainting some more?) And look, an obligatory bottle of J&B.

Margie and I are having a ball with this flick while LeEtta is confused but hasn't given up on it yet. None of us have any of the answers.

Catherine's and Barbara's mom sure is one cryptic lady. I think she just admitted to being the killer or maybe she didn't. She just told Chris to enjoy his drink because it is poisoned. Now mom and Chris are drunkenly making out. Scandalous! Oh shit, nothing is as it seems. This is a pretty awesome film (rape scene notwithstanding) and that ending is rad.

SHORT BREAK

While Margie is making dinner, I take Shadow for a walk. He's a kickass dog; part Blue Heeler and part Border Collie. He's cute, he's smart, and luckily, I didn't have to be the one who trained him. Bonus! Even with the wind whipping around us, it is still oppressively muggy outside. The clouds look threatening. Something ominous approaches. Back home, the feast begins. Margie brings out a delicious roast, potatoes, and fresh spinach. Sooooo damn good.

"Don't rely on appearances. Me? I'm a specialist in what's been discarded."

6:10 PM
Deadly Inheritance (1968)

The music for this film is already totally amazing. Fuzz guitar and a macho trumpet. Some duder in France gets hit by a train but he's only barely mutilated. He's left behind three daughters and a son (who will receive the money when he turns 21). One of the daughters, Simone (played by the super fine Femi Benussi) has a boyfriend but he's someone else's husband. Tramp! 15 minutes into the movie and she already gets a shower scene. Nice. Her crippled brother Janot (is played by character actor Ernesto Colli) and he tells Simone that he is going to fix everything with the will. So he jumps in front of an oncoming train!

This colorful film is searing itself on my brain. Why can't all gialli be this pretty? This is like a garish bitch-slap to the face. Just so you know, my brain is falling apart like a mush-like mess running through my fingers. This whole family is a bunch of scumbags. My favorite moment in the whole movie: Someone says, "The police will be here soon!" and without missing a beat, dad says, "Why? What did we do?" Um, I guess you had to be there. LeEtta is quite amused by their trashy antics. Deadly Inheritance is too much to bear. It's pretty, ugly, bright, dumb, shrill, and awesome. There's a slick nightclub called Les Cigales where all the cool kids hang out.

Simone's lover AKA Dickhead Duder (one of the many jerks in this movie) ends up dead in the shower with a bag over his head. Good riddance. Guess his little scheme of getting in on Simone's inheritance ain't gonna happen now. Wow, French people are jerks. They find the corpse of one sister in someone else's grave and Leon goes on the run. Boat chase! Man, this Leon (Ivo Garrani of Black Sunday) on the run bit is going on too long. He eats some sardines in a castle. That is pretty fun. Who is Leon you ask? He's somebody's slob husband. Pretty cool, huh? This reminds me of Naked You Die (which came out the same year). Hey Colette (Valeria Ciangottini), you better stay away from the business end of that golf club.

Oh crap, the power just went out! Not in the movie, IN REAL LIFE! This thunderstorm is really freaking Shadow out. Poor doggie don't like the thunder. Okay, we're back. I spend a solid 5 minutes trying to get the DVD player to stop fucking with me and go back to where we were before the lights went out. This movie just knocked my block off with the big reveal. Nice. It's convoluted but oh so grand and that ending is just odd. Why can't they all be like this? Thank you very much, Euro Trash Cinema!

"We aren't the castle type."

7:42 PM

The Bloodsucker Leads the Dance (1975)

I decide it is time that I ruin the night. Set in Ireland in 1902, this movie is so goddamn terrible, you'll have to see it (don't see it) to believe it (don't believe it). Miss Evelyn (Patrizia Webley) and her actor buds are invited by Count Richard (Giacomo Rossi-Stuart) to his castle to party, I guess. Garbled dialogue, totally inept acting, silly music, and a dreary, drowsy plot make for some shitty shit. Everyone teases Samuel (Leo Valeriano). They say he's half a man. But keep an eye on this guy, he pulls some totally insane faces later. These people make redonkulous sounds with their mouths that I think someone actually wrote. Giacomo Rossi-Stuart, what the fuck were you thinking? Your voice actor sounds drunk!

I've never seen anything quite this bad. Femi Benussi (the maid) and Luciano Pigozzi (the groundskeeper) just had a rape scene? How? Why? What does it signify? I guess it signifies that Pigozzi was pretty down and out. The 'Irish' castle is blowing LeEtta's and Margie's minds. They may never recover from the half-assed set design. I feel totally spaced out right now. These films are going by too fast. I can't get a grip on this shit. The Bloodsucker Leads the Dance is a romance for the ages. Holy shit. This Richard guy is totally okay if Evelyn is or is not his dead wife. Whatever! It's all the same to him.

There are lots of lukewarm sex scenes and lesbian ridiculousness. The actresses look really bored. Throw us a lifeboat and let it crush our soft skulls; we are drowning in a sea of terribleness. There are moments of priceless melodrama in the home of Pigozzi between him and his family as he chews them out and then gets chewed out by his wife. A storm is whipping up so the editor rolls out some black and white stock footage of a hurricane. This is a color film, you dick! Not you, dear reader, I was talking to the editor.

We finally get a murder and a poorly executed severed head effect. Oh no, another severed head. The lesbians are gone now. I might as well turn this off! Strangely enough, this movie isn't boring. The maids are trying to figure out who the killer is. A policeman shows up and explains everything which actually makes things even more inexplicable. They just went for the twisty fliparoo! Femi Benussi just did a 100 year long monologue. Fin.

"I may be homosexual but I'm not homicidal."

9:43 PM
So Sweet, So Dead (1972)

I put on another bootleg with Greek subtitles. This copy of So Sweet, So Dead is a little on the shaky side but watchable for sure. LeEtta takes her leave of us as she has to work in the morning. Margie and I wish her a goodnight. Farley Granger plays Inspector Capuana and I think he's dubbed. That is really annoying because Granger has a crazy awesome voice. I forgive the film because we've got Luciano Rossi (of Death Walks at Midnight) as a sicko morgue worker. And that is one naked dead lady. She's an upper class lady corpse!

Femi Benussi is here for a third film in a row! She gets just what the doctor ordered: a slow motion death scene. Wow, that may been the most giallo moment in a giallo ever. Hey duder, don't get all bent out of shape just because your lover just got mutilated to death. Rossi is so disturbing in this film. More corpses! And the ladies! There are so many wonderful giallo ladies in this movie. There's Benussi, Sylva Koscina (of Lisa and the Devil), Annabella Incontrera (The Case of the Bloody Iris), Krista Nell (The Red Headed Corpse), Angela Covello (Torso), and Susan Scott (Death Walks at Midnight). Gee, no wonder I had to have this one. Thanks again to Euro Trash Cinema, I owe you my (nerdy) life.

I can't believe how cheap and tawdry this flick is. I can't believe I'm watching this with my mother-in-law! Thank God she hasn't kicked me out of the house yet. There are lots of crazy theories by the clueless police force as to who the killer might be. They seem torn as to whether the killer is a sex criminal or a maniac. I just saw J&B and a very long sex scene. Wow. Thanks. What's his face's daughter just witnessed a murder so she is sure that the killer will be coming for her. That's a safe bet, missy.

I am paralyzed by a horrible case of hiccups but at least they are keeping me awake. I would be pissed if I missed any of this movie with its bloody death scenes, nudity, and sex sex SEX! Okay folks, we got an overkill on the sex here. No one seems really all that upset about these women being murdered. Events just happens in this cold and clinical fashion. The cop takes a chance by arresting the wrong man on purpose and a bizarre grandfather clock holds a key to the mystery. Wow, I like this movie a whole lot. Sylva Koscina actually had to choose between the big bottle of J&B and the very large bottle of J&B. What a woman! The ending of this film is so awesome. It's morally bankrupt and bleak in the best way.

GOODNIGHT

I'm fairly coherent when I say goodnight to Margie but my eyes are aching. It seems like I'm watching less films during these things but suffering more. I think it may be time to reinstate the Doomed Moviethon fitness program. In the shower, the water hits the back of my neck and it feels like I'm having a happy earthquake inside my brain. After I get out, I find that there's another big thunderstorm passing over the apartment. The lightning is flashing with an alarming regularity and there is rumbling aplenty. I know the killer is using the storm to cover his movements. The poor dog is pacing around and following me while I get ready for bed. Shadow is a big dog but the storms make him quiver like a cold puppy. Or perhaps, he knows there's something else out there, some other danger.

MONDAY

Well, I have the day off today and I usually use this freedom to recover from a Moviethon. But you know what? Fuck it! I've got more gialli than I know what to do with. I feed the cats and walk over to 7-11. It's bright out! The ground is wet from last night's storm and the world is alive. I get Mountain Dew from the fountain and a breakfast sandwich from the fridge. I also pick up Margie a large coffee and head back. I'm about to start the next movie and there's something stirring in my brain. My body is warning me not to go on, to take it easy. I say, "Eat black gloves, sucker!"

"I kill you again and again! I'll kill you a thousand times if necessary! So you never come back! Again!"

9:58 AM
Blue Eyes of the Broken Doll (1974)

This film has one fatal flaw: animal violence. It's real, not staged, and that's why I'm watching it alone. This is a damn shame too because I love

Blue Eyes of the Broken Doll. The late, great Paul Naschy introduces this Spanish giallo on the DVD. You sir, will be missed. The film starts with Naschy as a mysterious figure named Gilles, hitching a ride along a barren stretch of road. The soundtrack so far is deliciously loungy. The mountain scenery is beautiful and uh oh, the music by Juan Carlos Calderon just took a turn for the eerie. Gilles gets dropped off in a small village filled with jerks who are not very helpful at all.

After a glass of wine and a cheese sandwich, Gilles gets a lift from a woman with severe burns and a fake hand. She kills an injured bird along the way (staged, I hope) which causes him to have a flashback of strangling a woman to death. This woman with the fake hand is named Claude (Diana Lorys) and she informs him that she and her sisters need a man around the house. This scene is so full of foreboding. Gilles, duder, you need to get the fuck out of there. Go now! The other two hot sisters are everyone's favorite nympho Nicole (the wildly sexy Eva Leon) and wheelchair bound Ivette (Maria Perschy), who is clearly the craziest of the three.

I'm watching the awesome English dub of this film because it's hilarious. Something strange about Nicole: she never changes her clothes. Michelle (Ines Morales), the hot nurse, shows up to take care of Ivette. Holy shit! Mr. Former Body Builder Paul Naschy is ripped in this one. I need to get up and do some push-ups immediately. (I don't.) Gilles wakes up from a dream (of strangling that woman again) just in time for Nicole to sneak into his room, ready for action. Awkward sex scene! What just happened? Impotence? Premature ejaculation? No idea. Claude peeks in on Gilles to see him in bed with her raging slut of a sister and she is pissed.

While Gilles is out doing some half-assed yard work, some fucking guy shows up and starts some shit. They fight and during the throwdown, Gilles gets stabbed. But the other guy gets his own knife in the guts and flees. Michelle treats Gilles's flesh wound and the whole scene is freakishly erotic. Suddenly, Claude finds Gilles completely irresistible. The plot keeps getting more and more complicated so pardon me if I don't spend the next 3,000 words trying to explain it all. Gilles starts to fall for Claude and the killer strikes and some random chick gets wacked with a meat cleaver.

And here it is. At the 48 minute mark, we get a brief but horrifyingly real slaughtering of a pig. Look, asshole director, I know where bacon comes from. Nice job ruining the movie, you lame shithead. Obviously, the perpetrators seem like professional butchers and not actors, so I'm guessing that the pig was used to feed people and not just tossed away after giving its life for 'entertainment'. But I have to ask: why in the world is this in the movie? This heinousness is followed by another murder and we see the killer make off with his prize: the girl's eyeballs. Everyone suspects Gilles of the crime but there are so many red herrings in this film, it is anybody's guess as to what is really going on.

The killer takes out yet another blue-eyed beauty with a mini-rake. Oh no, not Nicole too! I miss that raging slut already. When Gilles finds out that the village cop has discovered his ex-con status, he and Claude split. This is actually a pretty sad scene. There's one last sick surprise before the credits roll. The director, Carlos Aured, also did The Mummy's Revenge, Curse of the Devil, and my favorite Naschy movie: Horror Rises from the Tomb. With Blue Eyes, Aured achieved a near perfect giallo trash/beauty spectacle. It really is a shame about that poor pig. Those wacky Europeans and their animal violence.

LUNCH

After I vacuum the apartment, Margie and I walk to 7-11 for hot dogs. It's surprisingly nice outside. I thought it would be muggier out but the outside world is just kind of pretty. I get a Coke/Pepsi from the fountain and pour some grenadine in it when I get back home. I have to keep going, there are more gialli to watch, damn it!

> *"Up until tonight, I thought this room would be called the Room of Truth. I was wrong!"*

1:15 PM
Death Laid an Egg (1968)

Special thanks to Chris Baker for hooking me up with this film! The opening credits are complimented very well by Bruno Maderna's discordant freakout music score. This artsy mess is all ultramodern cities and strangeness. Come on, you obtuse bastards! I'm ready for you. Trintignant is back in the moviethon. He plays Marco and he hates chickens because his wife owns a chicken factory! Ewa Aulin is back too. She plays Gabrielle and she makes my life worth living. Marco's wife, Anna (Gina Lollobrigida (whose name looks like LOL BRIGADE to me)), is a little wound up. She's dealing with some disgruntled former employees of the chicken factory. She blames them for all the accidents that have been occurring at the factory since she laid everybody off.

This is some heavy shit, man. Anna casually comments about how she would love to "dismantle" Gabrielle and how she is obsessed with hurting her. So far, this is all very strange and lovely. And I'm loving the out of tune jazz band falling down a flight of stairs soundtrack. While Marco is snooping around the lab one night (while following Gabrielle), he screws up the scientist's radioactive chicken experiment. No, I'm not making that up. That really is what just happened.

Mmm, Ewa Aulin eating ice cream. I could watch that all day. We see a flashback of her parents dying in a car accident (best shot in the movie, by the way). Marco admits his love for Gabrielle. Shit just gets weirder when an ad exec shows up with ideas for a new, hipper chicken (marketing chickens as soldiers, etc.). At a fancy party, Marco and company play a sick party game of inducing tears and almost-raping women. Marco picks up some random woman and murders her and I thought he was just into chickens. Anna finds a letter Marco wrote describing his sado-perversions but she doesn't realize that he's killing the women he picks up.

Whoa! The dog just fell into the chicken processor. What the hell is going on here? At least that was staged animal violence. Man, I'm getting burned out. And things just got stranger. Anna finds some headless and wingless chickens, the result of Marco's tomfoolery with the experiment. This discovery makes the scientist happy? This is weirding me out and not in a good way. Marco thinks the new chickens are monsters (which he himself made) so he destroys them with an axe in a scene that is friggin' disgusting. Now everything just went to hell in an egg basket. Were all the murders fake? Fuck! Death Laid an Egg is a totally unlikeable film. I think I liked it. I just can't say for sure.

CONCLUSION

I get up from the computer and pace around the office for a while (this isn't easy to do because it's a small office). I want to watch more movies but I can't. Not after the malignant assault of Death Laid an Egg. Nothing can (not) top that. When is too much not enough? Oh, I'll tell you! It's when you start a moviethon with an artsy flick and then end with an even artier one. There are a stack of unwatched movies but my hand shakes ever so slightly when I pick them up. Only 16 movies this time? The body count is only at 79? Sorry folks, I'm just done.

There is no doubt in my mind that there will be a Giallo Meltdown 5 and a 6 and a 7 and a tenteen. I go out to the living room and see that Margie is watching NCIS. I settle onto the couch and I immediately smirk at DiNozzo's goofy antics. In this episode, a black-gloved killer is taking out naval wives who cheat on their spouses. Gibbs goes undercover as the ghost of Edwige Fenech's late husband in order to ensnare her in her own inheritance scam. Best episode ever.

GIALLO MELTDOWN 5: BLACK GLOVE OUTLET MALL

Anything that's worth doing is worth doing five fucking times. Giallo Meltdown 4 ended on such a sour note that I couldn't wait to start the next one. In the months between these two moviethons, I acquired so many new titles that I was itching to do this again. There was also a blog event I did with a month of Asian horror films and the whole time I felt like I was cheating on my dear gialli. These movies are just so hypnotic, so rewarding.

After work on Friday evening, LeEtta and I ran to the store to get moviethon supplies. We had this idea of cooking a beef or pork roast, ripping it a new one like cannibal pagans, and then making some crazy good tacos. We got everything we needed but forgot tomatoes, lettuce, and avocados. Yeah, duh. We had to make yet another trip to Publix for that stuff in the morning. I did manage to locate Chalula, my favorite hot sauce.

I was trying to get some last minute things done before the movies started and my computer took a huge dump. It put me in a foul mood. I was trying to copy Oasis of Fear onto a jump drive while simultaneously recording a little vlog about the Giallo Meltdown experience, so of course, my computer crapped out. You could say that this was 'my fault' but whatever. The only thing I hate more than physical objects is technology.

So I go out into the living room and I'm grumbling in my chair about how pissed off I am and how I should just cancel the moviethon. I'm not kidding, I was actually debating this when my mother-in-law Margie told me I was being silly. And she was right. I thought of the fun and madness to be had and of all the good food to be consumed. Jeez, I'm such a weirdo. With my attitude finally adjusted, I put in the first movie.

SATURDAY

"I'm only English from the waist up."

10:39 AM
Oasis of Fear (1971)

This Umberto Lenzi movie starts with our 'heroes', Ingrid and Richard (Ornella Muti and Ray Lovelock), running through the streets of London buying illegal pornography to sell in Rome. Shit, this opening song totally blows. It's some odious 60s garbage with meaningless lyrics sung by a guy with a plaintive, howling voice. Once these two hippie freaks make some cash they blow it all on fancy meals, nightclubbing, giving balloons to poor kids, and releasing doves in crowded restaurants. I already hate these two jerkwads. Now that the money is gone, they take photos of themselves getting it on to sell to people. They're classy types.

Of course, they get busted immediately and are ordered by the pigs to leave Rome within 24 hours. Next, they are robbed by the wimpiest biker gang in Italy and then they run out of gas in the middle of nowhere. They manage to find a big house where a high society lady named Barbara (Irene Papas of Don't Torture a Duckling) is acting very strangely. They introduce her to philosophical claptrap, belly-dancing stripteases, and sitar music.

Barbara and Richard hook up and suddenly all that free love bullshit goes out the window. Poor Ingrid -who pushed the two together in the first place- is suddenly jealous when Richard bones Barbara. She even considers killing them with a pair of toenail scissors. I'm not making that up.

Our good friend Kat has arrived. We fill her in on what's been going on so far in this flick. Jeez, I hate it when people manipulate hippies but it's so easy and so fun. While buying some paint for their stupid gaudy car to turn it into a getaway vehicle, Richard confronts those bikers and gets half of his money back. Only half? What a pussy!

When these lamebrains finally figure out what their seemingly benevolent hostess has been up to this whole time, the kid gloves come off. Richard decides to torture Barbara by burning her boob with a lit cigarette. Of course, he chickens out and I bet Irene Pappas's body double was relieved. Ingrid and Richard are in serious trouble now and pretty soon it's all over. Hey look the inspector is played by Umberto Raho of Amuck! and The Bird with the Crystal Plumage. So the big twist happens and-

Oops! The video file of Oasis of Fear ends abruptly with just five minutes left. It seems that my computer gets the last laugh and I have to tell the girls what happens at the very end of the movie. Maybe that should be how all moviethons are done from now on; in the oral tradition.

"Raul, wet his forehead."

12:09 PM
The Bloodstained Butterfly (1971)

This one opens with two awesome things: badass classic music and a butterfly frame over the credits. The soundtrack settles into one of my favorite pieces of music ever composed for a giallo. It's by composer Gianni Ferrio (with a little help from Tchaikovsky) and it's nice to finally get to see the movie that this music belongs to. After a cryptic message about the past and the future being one or some crap, we're introduced to all of the characters with text explaining who they are. Love it!

While some children are playing hide and seek, they hear a woman's scream and a body rolls down a hill. A mysterious figure crouches over the body and makes a break for it when he hears the cops coming. The 'scientific police' are called in to figure out who the murderer is.

The victim is a 17 year old girl named Franciose which is weird because I didn't think it was illegal to kill a French person in Italy. The inspector (Silvano Tranquilli) just wants a decent cup of coffee and everyone keeps bringing him cups that are either too bitter or too sweet. After some potential scenarios of what might have happened, the cops think they have a suspect. TV host, Alessandro Marchi (Giancarlo Sbragia), is arrested and the case goes to court. Evelyn Stewart is here (with her severe face) as Maria, Alessandro's wife and mother of the dead girl's foxy best friend, Sarah (Wendy D'Olive of The Dead Are Alive).

Giorgio (Helmet Berger) is a concert pianist and a very suspicious young man who is kind of sort of dating Sarah. The defense attorney (Günther Stoll of What Have You Done to Solange?) rips into the circumstantial evidence like a sharp thing that cuts into things which are easy to cut into. But then the evidence stacks up again and we're back to Alessandro looking really guilty again. I swear this is actually more interesting than it sounds.

We get some pretty crazy revelations. For instance, the defense attorney is totally banging Maria. Hmm, conflict of interest much? We also see that Giorgio is a total psycho in the bedroom. He was Franciose's secret lover and he isn't taking her death very well. I see someone reach for some Astor cigarettes, the only brand for a giallo. Another murder is committed with the same modus operandi as the previous crimes so the cops know there's another motherfucker out there killing some fucking bitches. Yo.

LeEtta knows all about the hooker bonfires which amuses our friend Kat very much. I can think of at least two or three gialli that have prostitutes warming their hands by a bonfire or over a fire barrel. Take a shot of J&B when you see a hooker bonfire.

And now the defense attorney is trying to rape Sarah. Maria catches him but her only complaint is she's jealous. We all think he's the killer but I wouldn't put it past old Giorgio. He's wrestling with some serious ass demons. Serious ass-demons? There's an awkward dinner scene where Alessandro and Maria are reunited but the defense attorney and nearly-raped Sarah are there too. It's very tense but also a little hilarious. This is high drama, people. If you can't stand the heat, stay out of the heat. I can't say a word about the finale without totally spoiling it so we'll just move right along. The Bloodstained Butterfly is very heavy on the police and court procedural stuff but it's still pretty good.

"There are other Eleonoras in the world."

1:53 PM
French Sex Murders (1972)

I warn everyone how awful this movie is going to be but I don't think they believe me. The detective is played by Robert Sacchi, a friggin' Humphrey Bogart impersonator. Some douchebag named Antoine (Pietro Martellanza) steals some junk jewelry and goes to a brothel. Renato Romano, the guy who played the priest in Seven Blood Stained Orchids, plays a writer studying prostitutes. Yeah... studying. Barbara Bouchet is here as a hooker named Francine. Antoine is in love with Francine and boy is she lucky. Anita Ekberg plays the madam of these dang hookers and she has huge, distracting hair!

Francine gets murdered and Antoine looks hella suspicious. Rosalba Neri is here too? She plays Marianne, Antoine's backup wife or something. The cops find him and the least impressive chase scene in cinematic history happens. The guy playing Antoine is a freakin' four alarm fire of comedy. Now Howard Vernon shows up as a weirdo doctor named Professor Waldemar. He has a hot daughter named Eleonora (Evelyne Kraft) and she's got a little love thang going with his assistant named Roget.

Antoine gets convicted of murder and vows to come back from the grave to make everyone who condemned him suffer. Marianne is the only one who has doubts that Antoine is guilty. Everyone else is just happy to see him go away. Antoine breaks free from jail and his escape is funny as hell thanks to some bad editing and a fake severed head.

At a nightclub, Marianne is singing her monotonous French song (which I love). This nightclub is owned by her lover, Pepi (Rolf Eden), who beats up a guy getting too fresh with a young lady. The fight scene is pathetic thanks to the guy holding completely still while Pepi beats on him. Howard Vernon and Roget get Antoine's severed head for examination. Roget swears he sees its eyes moving. I can't believe there's a mad science vibe thrown into this shit too. Incredible!

Back at the 'Massage Parlor', Anita Ekberg's hair is actually getting bigger as the movie goes along. Someone kills her with a lamp. Multi-colored filters can't make up for the fact that a lamp murder is boring but I appreciate the effort. Eww, eye dissection! Actually it's less like dissection and more like just random slicing. Nice work, Dr. Dicknuts.

There's more drama between Roget and Eleonora. She is really serious about her father not approving of their relationship. Holy crap, there are so many flubs in this movie, I can't even keep track of them all. This movie is kind of painful. You try to keep track of what's going on but it's hard to keep track of all these crappy plot threads and boring police procedural stuff. There's a scene with three freakin' murders in a row to boost our spirits a bit. Kat was right. She said that I secretly enjoy French Sex Murders. It's still terrible but at least it's endearing to me now. If you can handle the Humphrey Blowgart impersonator, you can handle anything.

DINNER BREAK

The beef roast is done so LeEtta tears it apart and we have awesome tacos. It is just so fabulously delicious. We eat while watching some HGTV. The longer you live in an apartment, the more appealing the shows on this friggin' channel become. You look at these freaks complaining but how small their 2000 square foot houses are and you just want to jump into the TV and throttle them. Those bastards don't how good they have it. As usual, I eat too much. Looks like I'll be up late tonight!

"THEY ASKED FOR IT! DEATH! THE BASTARDS!"

4:25 PM
Don't Torture a Duckling (1972)

Dear, sweet Lucio Fulci. I haven't seen this movie in quite a while. This is a classic and it might just be Fulci's best film. The church is an ominous presence here but not nearly as ominous as these horrible little children. Before I go on about how all children are the spawn of Satan, let me say that we've already seen a woman digging up the corpse of a fetus (with some very jarring orchestra stabs from the soundtrack) and some local yokels (there's a lot in this movie) getting some old fat whores to accompany them into a small shack.

A local simpleton by the name of Giuseppe (Vito Passeri) is trying to sneak a peek on the action when some kids start making fun of him and calling him a big baby. He threatens to kill the kids and at this point, I'm more than ready to help. Next we meet the beautiful Patrizia (Barbara Bouchet) and she's as naked as the day she was born. She is a bored and spoiled socialite hiding out in the sticks because she got into some trouble in the city. Right now she is trying to seduce a young boy because she is a terrible person. There are so many moments of malignant beauty and moments that are just plain wrong in this film that I love it.

Before you can say 'bad touch', one of the jerky kids gets beaten on the head with a metal rod. The parents of this shitty kid get a call from a kidnapper who wants some cash or else the little mongrel will die. The cops step in, Giuseppe the idiot is arrested, and we find out that the kid is actually dead having been beaten and strangled to death. Giuseppe claims that when he found the body, he buried it, and then asked for the ransom.

The small town erupts and its citizens nearly tear the village idiot to pieces. Giuseppe is in the clear when another young boy is murdered.

The only connection these kids have to one another is that they all play soccer after church with Don Alberto (Marc Porel), a priest with beautiful bone structure. Badass reporter and just all around badass, Andrea (Tomas Milian), shows up in town to get the scoop on the murders for his paper. A third kid gets whacked and since Patrizia is such a sketchy scumbag, the cops pull her in for questioning. It turns out that she is using her little vacation to get clean of the drugs but is she a killer? More suspects start coming out of the woodwork but two are particularly interesting: Francesco (Georges Wilson), 'the old magician', and his mentally unstable female companion named Maciara (Florinda Bolkan).

Give it up for Florinda Bolkan, y'all. One of the finest giallo actresses goes all out with her portrayal of Maciara, a very misunderstood (and loony) woman. After claiming to have killed the boys with black magic, the cops let her go, and she is murdered by villagers (who still think she is the killer). Some directors would cut away but not Fulci. In gruesome detail, we see Maciara whipped to death with chains to the melodious strains of Ornella Vanoni. Unforgettable, horrific, and brilliant.

The police chief of the town can do nothing but shake his head in bemused frustration at how utterly fucking ignorant these townspeople are. All the actors are great. Tomas Milian gives an understated performance. I'm used to him playing things way over the top. The murders continue and everyone seems pretty friggin' guilty by my estimation. Who is the killer? Nope, I won't say anymore. Rest assured, Don't Torture a Duckling is as dark and cynical as they come.

CIGAR BREAK

I head outside to smoke my Mederos cigar. It is quite nice outside though I'm glad I have a sweater on. I have the iPod loaded up with the giallo soundtracks again as usual. Oh yeah, this is the life. I'm drinking my Honest Tea half sweet tea, half lemonade. I come back inside to find out that Kat is leaving. She wishes us luck and I pick another film.

"Don't worry, you won't feel a thing."

7:31 PM
The Two Faces of Fear (1972)

All right! George Hilton is in this one as Dr. Roberto Carli. Hilton is essentially the King of Giallo. The first time we see him in this film, he's pointing a gun at his wife, Elena (Luciana Paluzzi). People are arguing over

Dr. Michele (Luis Davila), a renowned heart surgeon, getting a new job somewhere. Dr. Paola Lombari, Dr. Michele's wife is played by Anita frickin' Strindberg (one of my favorites). Elena needs a heart operation and her husband is going to assist in the operating room?!?! Let me guess, this is going to end badly.

Oh snap, Eduardo Fajardo is in this one. They all seem to be afraid of what Elena is going to say to Michele to make him change his mind about taking that job. That night, while his parrot (who is dubbed like an old lady) is murmuring in the dark, someone shoots Michele to death. Paola thinks that Roberto shot her husband. And while she's totally upset about her husband dying, she goes right in to perform heart surgery.

The audio quality on this bootleg is not so hot. It gets real hissy and there's this high pitched sound that is pretty annoying. But the picture quality is awesome and the dialog is perfectly clear so I can't complain (I just did). Raise your J&B glasses high, my friends, we've got ourselves an idiot cop trying to interrogate Michele's parrot. Not surprisingly, Paola and Roberto are lovers.

This inspector (Fernando Rey) is a little sensitive about smoking. He quit recently, so he chews out the doctors for smoking in front of him. His idiot partner is still interrogating the parrot and he says that he even tried massaging its prostate. You know, if it wasn't for all the cool people in this movie, I wonder if I'd be that into it. Hospital administration intrigue isn't all that interesting even with stylish camerawork.

I just remembered that Luciana Paluzzi is the chick from A Black Veil for Lisa. This is a much better film, thank God. Some guy follows Elena home and she gets so scared that she has a heart attack. Now only Roberto can operate on her. The surgery scene is getting pretty intense. Will she survive? Robin Cook must have seen this movie and gotten inspired.

There's some debate amongst us as to whether or not this real heart surgery footage. I think it's real, darn it. The inspector gets a vital clue while Elena is on the operating table. This shit just got real. There's too many shots of people's stupid eyeballs bugging out over their surgical masks. Even though Two Faces of Fear gets a little slow, it's definitely worth watching. The way the inspector ensnares the killer is too cool!

"Two of you is too much for one woman!"

9:01 PM
Blood Link (1982)

Okay, we jump into 1982 with some Michael Moriarty action. I got this one on tape a while back and converted it to DVD-R. Come on DVD studios, release Blood Link! This movie has the same cinematographer as

Dario Argento's Inferno and a score by Ennio Morricone. Now hop to it! The tape started to go bad near the climax and I had to do some magic to keep it playing without disrupting the playback. Yes, I'm that good.

The opening scene: two people dancing in a ballroom. The man guides the woman into the next room and kills her quietly without anyone noticing. Michael Moriarty (one of the craziest actors ever) plays Dr. Craig Mannings and he keeps having visions through someone else's eyes. That someone is a murderer who looks just like him. His assistant/girlfriend Julie (Penelope Milford) is so amazing. Her acting style is very 1950s (in a good way) and she looks a little like Lina Romay. What a rack!

Dr. Craig is using himself as a guinea pig for some bizarre therapy which is drawing out these strange visions and ugly memories. He goes to Cleveland to visit his foster mother in an institution and she reveals that Craig's (formerly Siamese) twin brother Keith is out in the world somewhere. He becomes obsessed with finding him and gets a clue from one of his visions that Keith is in Germany.

It turns out that Keith actually is in Germany and just happens to be a serial killer, preying upon unsuspecting women. I totally forgot Cameron Mitchell is in this one and he's as blustery and corny as ever. He's harassing Keith because he thinks he's Craig and uh oh, now he's dead. The chick playing Cameron's daughter is a really terrible actress. She delivers her lines like she's passing a gall stone but what a rack! I think I know how they chose actresses for this movie.

Dr. Craig confronts his psycho brother and it's so bizarre. He threatens to turn Keith in for his crimes and that's when the shit hits the fan. Keith blackmails him for a murder but not to worry, Julie has arrived in Germany to save his ass. They are going to try and follow Keith through Craig's connection with him. I have to hand it to Alberto De Martino, the guy knows how to deliver a decent giallo. And he did it in the 80s! There's a thick layer of sleaze on this one. If any film could be called a psychosexual thriller, it is Blood Link. And I love the dark, enigmatic ending too.

"No, this time you have to pay more.
Necrophilia is an expensive vice, professor."

10:46 PM
A Dragonfly for Each Corpse (1974)

Okay, Paul Naschy, thrill me. A goofy looking hippie duder buys some dope off of a guy and then gets hacked to death with a sword by a mystery killer in a black jacket, black gloves, and bright red pants (that's a new one). The killer's trademark? Little dragonfly pins left next to the body. Detective Paul Naschy is a hothead. When we first see him he's about to beat the shit out of some random old man for some reason. And then there's another murder. This time the killer stabs a hooker with an umbrella with a knife on the end.

Erica Blanc plays Naschy's wife? This is truly awesome. There is a scene where she is washing his back while he smokes a friggin' cigar! Now more people are getting whacked by the killer. They are all pimps and drug dealers -the scum of society- and Naschy has no problem with who the killer is targeting. Next, we see a fancy party with some fashion designers in which Naschy's wife is one. At this particular party, there is a flaming gay stereotype and another duder whose chest hair is so thick you can see it through his shirt. Now an exotic dancer who hooks on the side gets offed.

I'm not sure which is more ridiculous: Paul Naschy's constant cigar chomping or his totally fake mustache. These sets are atrocious and they are helping to make this movie look so fucking ugly. Naschy vs. Nazi hippie gang? Wow, that's awesome. A man will only go so far in search of Muhammad Kaburi, you know what I mean? This movie is staged very badly and the pace is awkward to say the least. Maybe director León Klimovsky just wasn't into this one. Wait a second. Hold the phone! Naschy gets a severed head in the mail and Erica Blanc's reaction is priceless. Okay, this rocks. This is way better than 7 Murders for Scotland Yard, another Paul Naschy giallo.

Too many characters! Some dumbass professor (Eduardo Calvo of Blue Eyes of the Broken Doll) decides to attempt to blackmail the killer. We all know where this is going. No, we don't! The killer dresses up like a gorilla and strangles the dumb son of a bitch. What is so frustrating here is this bland as shit cinematography. There has been one cool shot so far but I'm starting to dig this bloody and hilarious movie.

Ha! The soundtrack has pieces of music lifted from Blood and Black Lace. If you feel like checking out A Dragonfly for Each Corpse, do it. Make sure you take your lactose tolerance medicine before you watch this cheesy flick. It features a priceless scene where a transvestite has a shootout with the cops while riding a roller coaster.

THE END OF SATURDAY

It's around 1:00 in the morning and our upstairs neighbor is drunk (presumably) and singing at the top of his lungs. It's either Neil Diamond or Jesus Christ Superstar or whatever. The point is, this guy is really belting it out. He sounds like a dying opera moose channeling the vocal prowess of Scott Stapp but in a bad way. It's funny and I'd probably try to record these sounds for later enjoyment but damn it, my head feels like a tube of toothpaste. Squeeze me. Good friggin' night.

SUNDAY

I woke up at 9 this morning. I get dressed and walk the dog. I think my dreams were primarily apocalyptic. Trust me, I'd rather face the killer wielding any sort of weapon than face my actual fears of the end of the world. Back at home, Margie is crocheting and LeEtta is making pancakes for the first time EVER. I run to 7-11 for a Vitamin Water and an Arizona Southern Style Sweet Tea. The Mountain Dew is very tempting but I must resist. When I get back, the pancakes are ready and they are delicious.

"Yellow carpets carry an ancient curse."

10:35 AM
The House of the Yellow Carpet (1983)

My homey-bro, Brad, sent me a copy of this film. Thanks Brad! It's from 1983 and we hear strange sounds coming from the movie. We see an apartment complex that is so creepy it reminds Margie of the one in Hideo Nakata's Dark Water. A woman named Franca (Beatrice Romand) lies dreaming of her lover named Ernesto. She cries out his name. The problem is her husband is named Antonio (Vittorio Mezzogiorno) and he's lying awake next to her like WTF?

The couple is trying to sell this big ugly roll of yellow carpet. While the husband is away dealing with his towed car, this creepy old guy (Erland Josephson) shows up to buy the carpet and starts harassing Franca. Okay, this is like the worst Craigslist meetup ever. The tension is almost unbearable. The creepy guy reenacts the murder of his wife for Franca's amusement or something. Mr. Creepy knows something about Franca's past. He gets her into such a frantic state that she breaks down and reveals that she was in love with her stepdad named Ernesto.

When her captor is distracted for a moment, Franca grabs the guy's knife and stabs him to death. She cleans herself up just in time to hear that someone is at the door. It is a woman (Milena Vukotic of Blood for Dracula) claiming to be the creepy guy's wife. She says that he is an actor and likes to practice his craft in unsuspecting people's homes. Franca throws this crazy ho out and then- Well, I'm not going to spoil it for you. The film just gets weirder and weirder but is actually a decent early 80s effort with lots of atmosphere and psychosexual craziness. I have a question: Why don't more junkies shoot drugs into their eye sockets?

RICHARD GLENN SCHMIDT

"Not in front of the cops, Little Boffo!"

12:10 PM
Death Steps in the Dark (1977)

This film has a lava lamp credit sequence and perfect opening music by Riz Ortolani. A bunch of knuckleheads are on a train in Istanbul and it isn't long before a black-gloved killer knocks out the lights, waits for a tunnel, and then offs some chick with a letter opener. When the lights come back on, things don't look too good for Luciano (Leonard Mann), an Italian photographer, because it was his friggin' letter opener. Dumbass! Who uses letter openers? I open my letters with my teeth and my feet like a real man. The detective on this case (Robert Webber) has stomach problems and makes weird sounds when he guzzles down Alka Seltzer. I can relate.

There is some Kenny Loggins-lookin' guy in this movie. He thinks he knows who the killer is plus he has one of the killer's gloves. HEY NOW! We get some insane close-ups of lesbian lovemaking. These characters are amazing and the script is a treasure trove of inanities. But the film is competently made, that's for sure. Kenny Loggins Clone decides to attempt to blackmail the killer. This is probably not a good idea.

Fearing that there is too much evidence stacked up against him, Luciano goes on the run. And he does it dressed like a lady. Hilarity ensues. Thanks to his pal Omar (Antonio Maimone), he is able to hide out in a tiny fishing shack next to some train tracks. More hilarity ensues. Luciano's model girlfriend Ingrid (Vera Krouska) shows up with some sardines for the poor guy. They take a shower together and the scene is actually sexy. Weird. Now for some trivia: J&B is more than prominently featured in this flick.

So Ulla, the black chick (Marie Liz Eugene), decides it's her turn to blackmail the killer. What the fuck? Did she not learn a damn thing from what happened to Kenny Loggins Clone? Now her lesbian lover is in danger. Oh damn, the murders are getting bloodier and nastier. By the way, Ulla's song that she sings at the nightclub is totally awesome. It's this schmaltzy disco garbage bomb that makes my teeth fall out.

Omar, could you please explain what the hell is going on? This movie is very goofy and genuinely funny in parts. Damn, I'm really lost now. Luciano and his gang are trying to break into someone's house for some reason. Oh yeah, they're after a golden bust of Ulla. I forget why. Okay, that ending was tight. Y'all need to check this one out. It's a great late-70s giallo with a cool ending and bonus: it's all totally ridiculous.

LUNCH BREAK

Margie and I go to 7-11 for some hotdogs. The world looks vibrant but it doesn't feel real. It's definitely too bright out. I feel like I'm high on something. Duh, it's the giallo vibe! Back at the apartment, LeEtta is digging into her leftover Mexican food (from our date on Thursday night). Once I have consumed my tube of mystery meat, it's time to start another film. What to watch? What to watch? Aha, here's one!

> *"My boyfriend, Mario, had a wild idea that we should make love in a whorehouse."*

2:19 PM
Psychout for Murder (1969)

The opening of this movie is an attention grabber, that's for sure. It feels like S.F. Brownrigg dropped some acid and said "Okay, let's make a movie in Italy!" A chick named Licia (played by Adrienne Larussa (who looks like Anne Hathaway)) is lying in a hospital bed while some crazy people are harassing her. Now they're threatening her with a syringe and having a threesome in front of her. Next, Licia is in therapy and her overacting is delightful. Hey, these people aren't dubbed. Italians always dub! By that fact alone, this is already one of the most unique gialli I've ever seen.

Her boyfriend, Mario (Nino Castelnuovo (the douchebag from Strip Nude for Your Killer)), tricks her into going to a whorehouse so he can call the paparazzi and blackmail her famous family. Wow, these sets are cheap. In order to cover up the scandal, her family sends her off to an asylum. The crazy editing, the silly acting, and the strident music make me fall in love with this one. This feels like two different movies slapped together.

Psychout for Murder just keeps surprising me. Now all of a sudden it has a really cool atmosphere. It's like Persona or something (but not really). Licia's sister Giovanna (Paola Pitagora) brings her some flowers and Licia takes them outside to stomp on them. I could watch that scene all day. Oh cool, Alberto de Mendoza (of The Strange Vice of Mrs. Wardh) is in this. He plays Francesco, Giovanna's husband. Licia is out of the loony bin and she's behaving very strangely. She doesn't seem bitter at all about being put away. That was sarcasm, by the way. Oh wait, now everyone is dubbed?

Now even her sister is acting a little batty. Licia is totally nuts and I am in love this movie! I'm ready to watch Psychout for Murder again and it's not even over yet. Aw, poor baby; she's having trouble with her transition back into normal society and her family is ready to put her right back in the nuthouse. She shows up in Mario's apartment with her father's gun and enlists him to wage a war on her father who is played by Rossano Brazzi of Frankenstein's Castle of Freaks. He also directed this.

My God, anything can happen! Hey, what is she doing with that shower nozzle? What the hell are those weird lights all about? Why is she setting up an elaborate trap? Adding to all this awesomeness is how washed out my copy of this film is. Licia's father's mistress throws a press conference and a bunch of kids turn it into a hippie happening with some rock and roll and crazy frivolity. Do not adjust your TV, this is the 1960s and this shit happens all the time. Then Margie wakes me up. I had no idea that I was sleeping. I only missed about 5 or 10 minutes. This movie is so perfect that you can sleep through it and it's still good. (Author's Note: The Italian version (Salvare la faccia) has a totally different opening than this cut.)

> *"Run towards the black shadow;*
> *death will come to meet you."*

4:14 PM
Enigma Rosso (1978)

And now we have yet another late 70s giallo with a totally funky music score by Riz Ortolani. That's twice today, Riz. My man, you are where it's at! Enigma Rosso opens with a corpse in a plastic sheet being thrown into the water. Fabio Testi (the greatest name ever bestowed upon a human being) is here mackin' on some klepto chick. Testi is a detective in this one and he's called in to work on the case. I keep hearing the phrase: "She's dead, wrapped in plastic." reverberating around in my head. This film is the end of the loose What Have You Done to Solange? trilogy; so it's no surprise that the first victim died from genital mutilation.

The car that was used to dump the body got dropped off at a chop shop so that bit of evidence is long gone now. The victim went to a prestigious girls' school and Testi goes in to investigate. This movie is kind of a remake of Solange and it's sparking discussions in our living room about nudity in movies and trashy entertainment. We're munching on cheese, crackers, pickles, and olives so huge parts of the plot are flying by unnoticed. A black glove wearing killer is targeting girls at the school that belong to a certain clique. Fabio's partner is named 'Starsky'? What, seriously?

Somebody tries to burn down Testi's trailer with him inside it and a motorcycle driving red herring dies and gets blamed for the murders. That's it. Case solved. Movie over. Uh uh, bitches, this shit ain't over. Now one of the girls is off to get an abortion and the trauma unearths some memories of an orgy that she and her buds attended. Whoa! That dildo is way too big! Jeez! This is beyond trashy. Next, one of the girls is killed with a dresser drawer. Is that the weirdest death in a giallo?

Fabio Testi interrogates a witness (Jack Taylor of Dr. Jekyll vs. the Wolfman) by scaring him on a roller coaster. This is the second time that a roller coaster has been part of the plot in this moviethon. Somehow all of these clues lead back to a forged art case from 3 years ago. I was about to say how obvious this plot is but then the movie just jumps the shark like a mofo. This is completely insane. What the hell just happened? I'm left totally speechless and yet, I'm still talking.

CIGAR BREAK

I head outside with my Arizona tea and a Carrillo cigar. Hot damn, this cigar is totally fantastic. From the moment I light it up, it is instantly tasty and wonderful. While I smoke and listen to giallo music, I'm texting like mad with Brad. He's many miles away (Kentucky to be exact) and having a moviethon of his own. I smoke and smoke but this cigar just never seems to get any smaller. People on loud motorcycles are going by and I laugh at their misery. They probably don't even know what a giallo is. Fools! Only I am truly living my life to its fullest. Hee hee!

"This is the first time that a man has rejected me!"

7:05 PM
Trumpets of the Apcalypse (1969)

I'm taking this little flick back into the office to watch on my computer because my copy is almost unwatchable. The smaller I can resize the window, the easier it'll be to watch. Oddly enough, I found this bootleg at my library on VHS years ago. The movie starts with some insane organ music and then a duder jumps out a window. Next we see some dang hippies at a nightclub. This film needs a proper release someday. And now another person has jumped to their death, a girl this time. Now the trippy ass credit sequence just kicked it. Wild, man, wild!

The chick who jumped to her death was Katherine. Her friend Ellen (played by the angelic Marilù Tolo) doesn't believe that it was a suicide. Catherine's bro Richard (Brett Halsey) shows up from the Navy and is understandably upset. He and Ellen go sightseeing in merry olde England. Why did Italians have such a hard-on for frickin' England? It turns out that Catherine was dating some total dickhead druggy hippie douche but had just broken up with him right before her death. Richard decides to do some more digging into his dead sister's life and he finds... MORE HIPPIES!

Richard scraps with some biker-hippies (including Boris, Catherine's ex-boyfriend) and beats their asses. Ellen looks into the suicide of her professor, the one who croaked similarly the day before Catherine died. Have I mentioned the sinister organ grinder yet? He gives this movie a sinister and surreal vibe and all gialli should have their own sinister organ grinder. Naw, that'd be too expensive. There are more hippies though; dirty, filthy, and stinking dope-smoking hippies!

Richard gets harassed yet again by Boris and the two boys start fighting. During this brawl, there's some sweet far out jazz that is screaming through my headphones. When he beats Boris's ass, Richard whips out a pistol and just starts shooting at Boris's crew. This is so badass that I think I might die. He gets away from the ruffians thanks to Boris's new lady friend. She tries to seduce him and he's not going for it. This whole movie feels like a "Rowan & Martin's Laugh-In" after party. Next, the black gloved killer knocks out Ellen and steals some files.

We finally find out about the "Trumpets of the Apocalypse", a piece of music so insidiously evil that if you listen to it, you'll kill yourself. I think that Brian Wilson wrote something similar but he called it "Smile". Oh and there is some weird Mesopotamian drug involved. I don't want to say anymore because I might ruin the movie for you. The whole thing wraps up very nicely and it's all just strange and fun. Remember kids, music plus drugs equals death.

"He's just an idiot drugged up to the eyeballs
but I don't think he's a murderer."

8:53 PM
The Killer Reserved Nine Seats (1974)

A gang of bitchy theatre frenemies go out to Patrick's (Chris Avram) theater. His family owns it but it's been closed for years. Oh wow, this theater is really beautiful. It inspires the actors among them to start spouting a bunch of Shakespeare. In fact, these are some really annoying and unlikable characters and this dialog is terrible! So yeah, I like this movie already. Whoa, Patrick's daughter Lynn (Paola Senatore) just started kissing him in a very un-daughterly way.

Everyone goes out exploring and some freaky shit happens. I'm not just talking about all the crazy bedfellows either. There's people dropping heavy objects from the rafters and there are mannequins turning into real people. Now everyone is sitting around talking about how they are glad that Patrick wasn't killed just now. What a bunch of lying two-faced peckerheads. My copy of this movie keeps jumping back and forth rather jarringly between the Italian version and the English dub.

Oh goodie, now they're performing Romeo and Juliet. When Kim (Janet Agren) dies as Juliet, she dies for real with a friggin' knife jabbed in her back. That's kind of hilarious. The keys to the front door have disappeared and the phones are dead. We're in for the long haul here, my friends. Gotta hand it to the director of this one, it's got some eerie moments. There's a mysterious voice reciting even more Shakespeare but the voice can't be recorded. God, I love supernatural gialli.

Whoa, the killer's mask is CREEPY and just plain wrong. And who is that woman playing Vivian, Patrick's ex-wife? It's Rosanna Schiaffino The Witch (1966)! Trust me, I did not pull that out of my brain. Bless you, sweet Internet. One of the lesbian chicks is being stalked below the stage and it reminds me of something I would've seen on TV in the middle of the night as a kid. Even the way she dies is so bizarre that it would have stuck in my memory. Ah, I love being nostalgic for a film I'm seeing for the first time. Trash movie regulars, Howard Ross and Lucretia Love are in this too?

I think someone in this movie is named Rutabaga or Rebecca. The killer in this is working too hard. First, he tries to slaughter these boneheads and now he's trying to drive them mad. Overachiever! The other lesbian (Eva Czemerys), the one I thought was named Rutabaga, dies horribly. The killer stabs her in the groin (presumably) and then nails her hand to a plank of wood. Nice going, you dang jerk! Jesus was not a lesbian!

Despite the danger, these jokers are still talking shit instead of working together to get the fuck out of this mess. LeEtta says that she can't find the entertainment value of this one. I still like it because it reminds me so much of nothing I've ever seen and/or something very familiar to me. Lynn just dropped acid or something because she's disco dancing in a see-through negligee. She's totally naked when her dad walks in and things get awkward. Damn, there's an odd tangent at the end of Nine Seats, what the hell?

QUICK BREAK

I take my shower early to wake myself up. My eyes feel like hard-boiled eggs and my butt is getting sore from sitting on it all dang day. Wait, don't I do that all day anywayI must say that if I decided to stop the moviethon now, I would be happy. Despite its flaws, The Killer has Reserved Nine Seats had moments that perfectly capture what I look for in a giallo. The mood is perfect. Why take a chance at fucking it up with another unseen movie? Fuck it. I'm armed with some peanut butter on toast and a glass of iced tea, I am ready. Margie and LeEtta have gone to bed.

"I suppose my mother would have been more polite but I wouldn't know because she's dead!"

11:01 PM
Paranoia (1970)

In Umberto Lenzi's Paranoia, Caroll Baker (an actress I still haven't warmed up to) plays a lady racecar driver named Helen. She gets into a wreck while she's thinking about Jean Sorel. Can't say I blame her, he makes me crash too. Helen is rushed into surgery and after she recovers, her doctor warns her to stay away from stress, especially racecar driving.

She gets an invitation from Maurice (Sorel), her ex-husband to visit him by the sea. This letter prompts her to steal her manager's car and drive off to the seaside. What a jerk! At Maurice's villa, she meets his new wife, Constance (Anna Proclemer) and um, she's kind of old. The sight of Maurice brings back the memory of when Helen tried to shoot him. Everyone in this movie says snotty things to each other and then they laugh about it. Between the gaudy fashions and the ornate sets, this movie is a feast for the eyes. We can also thank cinematographer Joe D'Amato as well. Whatta guy! There's a gratuitous Carroll Baker shower scene and I'm sorry, I just don't find this woman at all attractive. She's a little dumpy.

At dinner, Maurice is hitting on Helen and so is his wife Constance. We find out that Constance has a daughter from a previous marriage. Her name is Susan and Constance is trying in vain to control her. After paying off all of Helen's debts, Constance suggests that they team up in the fight to control Maurice because he's such a powerful drug. Damn you, Maurice, you're such a bastard. Constance suggests that they kill Maurice so that they can both be free of him forever.

While Constance is away and she is supposed to be thinking about whether or not she is going to help murder her ex-husband, Helen totally jumps in the sack with the guy. Then they go nightclubbing first and there's some swingin' good times. After their little weekend tryst is done, Helen decides that she hates Maurice because he won't leave his wife for her.

On a scuba outing, Helen and Constance try to kill Maurice but they totally fuck it up and Constance is stabbed to death. They ditch her body at sea, make the whole thing look like an accident, and now Helen and Maurice are together. Constance's daughter Susan (Marina Coffa) shows up and Helen starts to freak out. This might get complicated but I'm sure that bottle of J&B will smooth things over. Nope, Susan is just too curious and too bitchy.

It turns out that their idiot friend was filming their little boat ride and may have caught their crime with his camera. The twists just keep on comin'. Why are relationships so darn complicated? Why did Umberto Lenzi make so many movies with Carroll frickin' Baker? There is a scene where Jean Sorel is wearing a black and red plaid jacket with a blue and pink polka dotted ascot and our TV almost melts.

THE END

During Paranoia's entire running time, I was debating if it was the last movie or not. I was watching the 14th movie, out of the 18 or 19 I had picked for this moviethon, and I was totally wiped out. It felt like quitting but I was also very satisfied. Sunday had been one of the most satisfying days in the history of moviethons. Even with the huge dildo waving around in our faces during Enigma Rosso, it had been a fine, fine day. So around 1 in the morning, I decided to call it quits. Had I gone on the next film would have been Slaughter Hotel which, depending on your opinion, could have been the perfect final film or the worst fucking idea in the world. Expect to see that on the lineup for next time.

I slept very deeply and dreamed, not of the black gloved killer, but of zombies and then later, of rummaging through VHS tapes at a crappy old thrift store. I got up around 9am and it was pouring outside. Shadow was scared of the lightning and the thunder and very unhappy about the cold rain but I walked him anyway. I felt like the world was in anamorphic widescreen and that somewhere out there, some maniac was watching my every move from the comfort of a Mercedes Benz, black gloves squeaking quietly while he or she clenched the steering wheel. The straight razor shining, even in the darkness of their trench coat pocket. The weather was miserable but I loved it.

I like how I started and ended the moviethon with Umberto Lenzi. The guy could make a movie, damn it. Even though Paranoia was just a little disappointing, I still enjoyed the time I spent watching it. As always with these Giallo Meltdowns, I end up planning the next one in my head. Giallo Meltdown 6 will be friggin' awesome. Man, I just love these films so much. The act of watching a film (even a terrible one) from this bizarre subgenre makes me feel good inside. It makes me feel like I'm alive (which I assure you, I'm not). Keep your bungee cord and your ATVs, I've got hooker bonfires and a black glove with a million fingers.

GIALLO MELTDOWN 6:
THE MURDERESS KILLS HER VICTIMS TO DEATH

Hello friends! This is the first moviethon that is officially intended for the book you hold in your hands. You can thank the encouraging (and some rather threatening) words from friends and online acquaintances who wanted to see this project come together. It warms my heart to the boiling point knowing that folks out there appreciate these moviethons. Go ahead, imagine my heart boiling in my chest. I am.

My mother-in-law Margie has been battling cancer for the last two years with chemo, radiation, and the whole bit. She's been through a lot and LeEtta and I are right there, supporting her. The ride has been pretty wild too with ups and downs and miracles and bad news and run-on sentences. Because of this situation, escapist entertainment, having fun, and especially creative projects have become much more important to me. Aside from my normal obsession with this genre, I also need this book as a therapy tool.

FRIDAY NIGHT

LeEtta wakes me up from a very, very deep nap. I was having trouble keeping my eyes open at work so once I got home, I immediately went to sleep. Sitting on the edge of the bed, I try to calm my racing mind. I don't know what I was dreaming about but it must have been something intense. After I wash my face and walk into the living room, Margie offers me her leftover lasagna sitting in the fridge. I nuke the stuff in the microwave and cover it in a healthy layer of parmesan cheese. The lasagna is… perfect!

Once I've eaten, I head out to 7-11 for some drinks. It's a beautiful night and the air is dry and cold. The clouds are miles high and -what the fuck!?! Two idiots are making a ton of racket trying to kickstart a scooter. The air is full of their failure and they look like troglodytes. I pass Felix, a Puerto Rican gentleman with one foot, smoking a cigarette in the dark. He is a good guy, if a little nosy. At 7-11, I get 2 Arizona Southern Style sweet teas, a Mountain Dew, and a Coke from the fountain. Before my honorary shot of J&B (the liquor store only had the jumbo bottle), I make a ludicrously long and pointless toast. Okay, time for the first film.

"You see, I don't drink because I like it.
I drink to drown something."

7:37 PM
The Red Headed Corpse (1972)

No, this isn't a ginger-hate film, it's a sexy thriller with Erika Blanc and Farley friggin' Granger! And thankfully, he's dubbing his own voice! I wish I had Farley Granger's voice. I would record myself ordering pizza every day. In one, he plays John Ward, an alcoholic struggling artist who might be a little crazy. A hippie offers him some weed and he turns it down like a badass. The same hippie, who looks like George Harrison (except not hideously ugly), gives him a female mannequin. He explains to John that she's the best kind of woman; you know, mute and always skinny or something. Did I mention that there is some weirdo is snooping around his house at night? Well, there is. Nice score by Piero Piccioni, by the way.

At a trashy bar, a prostitute named Mala (Ivana Novak) hits on John but he turns her down like a badass. After he leaves, she follows and offers to do him for free which happens to Granger all the time. Mala offers to be a model for his paintings and John completely flips out. Now his mannequin turns into a real live, though mute woman (the luscious Krista Nell). Wait, what? Now that John is happy (and/or totally insane), he finally starts selling his nude paintings of Nell for decent money. Granger is bonkers in this, pulling all kinds of crazy faces for seemingly no reason.

John's cute and mute girlfriend/mannequin just turned into Erika Blanc! I beg LeEtta not to turn into Erika Blanc (or Kim Cattrall) because she scares me! This new sassy and talky version of John's lady friend earns him the big bucks for his art but things start to go awry. The moment she's left alone, Blanc bangs a hunter (Venantino Venantini of Seven Deaths in the Cat's Eye) who was just passing through. I hope he's shooting blanks! LeEtta looks up from drawing and says, "So I guess she isn't really a mannequin anymore, huh? I mean, now that other people are interacting with her." Good point!

Suddenly, Erika Blanc has yet another man in her life. Omar the sleazebag, who buys John's paintings, sets up a meeting between himself and Blanc. She flees his embrace and gets raped by the hunter. There's a couple of these rapey moments in this film. Yuck. The tension really becomes unbearable when John catches her blowing some teenage kid on the beach. To hide his pain and disguise himself for some snooping, Farley Granger dons the first pair of big sunglasses to grace the moviethon. He's becoming more and more enraged as his slutty mannequin lady flashes her goodies all over town. LeEtta says that she is ready for her to die now. Hmm... I wonder what's going to happen next.

"A girl like you, swanning around the world! It's unbelievable!"

9:05 PM
Crazy Desires of a Murderer (1977)

A man with bloodstained hands is wandering through a castle spooking an old wheelchair-bound man. Maybe now is a perfect time for a glass of chocolate milk. That's what I'm going to get for myself. You want one? I see that Piero Piccioni composed the awesome score for this film (that's two in a row). A swarthy gentleman named Bobby (Gaetano Russo of The Killer Reserved Nine Seats) is in trouble with some gangsters. He owes someone drugs or money or both. Next, a bunch of kooky kids show up at the castle and the suspicious glances start flying immediately.

Bleach Blonde #1, Ileana (the lovely Isabelle Marchall), is the daughter of the old man who owns the castle and her friends are using her to smuggle drugs into the country. The kids start partying and these fucking lushes run out of champagne. Ileana and her pal Gretel (the also lovely Adler Gray) go down to the creepy gothic wine cellar to get some more booze. They run into Ileana's freaky bro, Leandro (the bloody handed dude from the beginning of the film). He lives in the cellar and practices amateur taxidermy all day. His backstory: As a child, Leandro witnessed his mother killing a would-be rapist and he's never been the same.

When the party really gets underway, we get the first J&B sighting of the moviethon. I can't believe we had to wait so long! Shit, there are a lot of characters in this friggin' movie and there's a lot going on. Berta, the sexy maid (Annie Carol Edel) gets all sexy with Leandro when she gives him his medicine. Back at the party, both of the bleach blondes are groping each other in a rather uncreative game of charades. Next, the party splits into couples so that they can partake in some rancid lovemaking. There is some implied candle dildo action that warms my heart.

The killer strikes and claims the eyes (and nipples) of Bleach Blonde #2, Elsa (Patrizia Gori of Emanuelle's Revenge). The portly inspector (Corrado Gaipa) shows up and theorizes that the killer is a sex maniac. Classic! I should do a shot of J&B for that one. While the inspector interrogates all the suspects, I swear the guy is about to keel over. He does not look well but he's doing better than grumpy old wheelchair guy who had a heart attack after he saw the killer carrying a bag of eyeballs through the castle.

Bobby the scumbag has lost his stash and now he's fucked. He remembers a huge emerald that Leandro's mother was supposedly buried with so he breaks into her tomb. He's a classy bro. Bobby meets up with the gangsters at midnight and kills them both (in self-defense). He pushes their car over the cliff and it explodes before it even gets over the side.

Margie announces she is going to bed and we bid her goodnight.

Back at the castle, Ileana introduces the inspector to her psycho bro. In a flashback, we see Leandro killed his mother's lover. There was no rape at all; that was just a story to keep Leandro from being put away and to protect his mother's reputation. The cop decides to use Gretel as bait to lure the killer into a trap. This is an enjoyable (if somewhat sloppy) little flick. It reminds me of Sex of the Witch except it doesn't suck.

"You're a beautiful villainess."

10:58 PM
Death Falls Lightly (1972)

A rockin' soundtrack (can't get enough fuzz guitar!) and a killer stalking around an apartment in POV? I like this already! A smooth mofo named Giorgio (Stelio Candelli of Planet of the Vampires) discovers that his wife has been killed. His shady lawyer friend (Tom Felleghy) tries to help him establish an alibi and his hot blond mistress Liz (Patrizia Viotti of Amuck!) wants to help too. She helps me with her shower scene. The lawyer comes up with a plan: Giorgio and Liz will hide in an abandoned hotel until things cool down. In a very surreal and rather shocking moment, they drive past a car accident (with bodies in the road and everything) but don't stop to help. The lawyer hints that he and Giorgio have some dirty business together and it would bad for them both if he got arrested.

This film has some really wacko moments where we get to hear characters' thoughts and they are painfully obvious thoughts! Here's a big spoiler: everyone fucking hates Giorgio. I'm sorry if that ruins the movie for you. Anyway, Liz gets freaked out when Giorgio jokes about the hotel being haunted. Meanwhile, the cops investigate Giorgio's place and find a bloody crime scene. I was just about to say that this film doesn't have much style but then some fisheye lens awesomeness happened.

Giorgio's pals who arranged to hide him suspect that he may have actually killed his wife. While Giorgio and Liz are arguing, the film jump cuts to a scene of them smiling at each other. I'm not sure what just happened there. Okay, now every character is getting their own little internal monologue which is just freakin' stupid.

Liz and Giorgio are getting more than a little stir crazy in their ill-chosen hideout. After yet another shouting match, Liz goes completely berserk. Once she calms down, Giorgio admits that he is part of a big drug smuggling conspiracy that involves some very powerful politicians. In the middle of the night, someone stands over Liz while she's sleeping. These two lamebrains are not alone! If you hang with this one, Death Falls Lightly gets very special, especially if you like jump cuts and dream logic.

SATURDAY

Last night I dreamt that I was in a giallo. It was more of a crime drama but there was an old mansion and a killer roaming around. The details are fuzzy but it was enough to make me smile. The next dream was a rather promising sequel to From Beyond. (Stuart Gordon, call me!) After that I dreamed up my own version of Melancholia (which I haven't actually seen) and damn it, my version was pretty good. Women were drowning themselves in fountains and the sky and the earth were turning pink. I wake up feeling a little funky but very well rested.

At 7-11, I get LeEtta and I sausage biscuits for breakfast and a Coke from the fountain for me. The weather outside is lovely. The sun is fighting the clouds but a cool breeze is winning out. A dog runs after me happily on my way back. It belongs to the guy who owns Gino's, the Italian restaurant next to our apartment. It's a white Akita and the owner calls out to her: "Miska! Miska!" I walk with fluffy Miska back toward her owner so that she won't follow me home. One dog at home is enough.

Once inside, I eat breakfast and do some chores with the ladies. I cleaned the bathroom while LeEtta vacuumed. Margie cleaned the floors and then I start getting ready for another round of movies. My goal today is 7 films. I'm keeping this one real laid back though so if it's less, no big woop. Time for a shot of J&B. Ugh, it doesn't go down as easy as last night's shot.

"I should knock your block off?"

11:13 AM
Mozart is a Murderer (1999)

Okay, we get some late 90s made-for-TV Sergio Martino. Some obnoxious young people, Chiara and her fellow musicians, are partying in a bar. The next day, Chiara and company are performing some Mozart in a concert hall. Some creepy guy in a red leather jacket is stalking her. While they are performing, they stop playing right before the end of the piece, much to the chagrin of their music professor, Baraldi. He suspends them all after the performance even though exams are coming up. What a cock!

Chiara goes home and is immediately stabbed to death by a black gloved killer. A homeless lady gets nosy and the killer stabs her too. This movie looks promising if just a tad schlocky. Inspector Maccari (Enzo De Caro) finds some weird customized drug in Chiara's purse but he also finds clues implicating too many suspects.

At the funeral, the detective questions Chiara's friend who likes to play with snails. Oh yeah, Maccari is haunted by cheesy visions of his dead wife who had a huge rack. Apparently, someone wanted revenge on him and killed her instead. He feels kind of bad about that and stuff. Oh poor Arturo, he was in love with Chiara and couldn't bear to come to her funeral. The cops interrogate a fucking dork in a red leather jacket (I forget who he is) and it's the best scene since the murder. Very funny.

Eww, Baraldi can't keep his hands off the young male music students and I do mean young. What a pervo! Arturo gets naked and gets in his fancy spa tub. The killer strikes and Arturo is left floating dead and totally naked in his very fancy tub. Everyone thinks Baraldi is the killer. I know that I will never trust a music professor again. He and Arturo 'shared a moment' 8 years ago so Arturo and Chiara were blackmailing him. Margie and I are having a gay old time with these broken-English subtitles.

This movie just had the cheesiest 1970s-style storm cloud and hand-drawn lightning moment. It was heartwarming. The killer, who talks like Darth Vader, is coming after Maccari's girlfriend and his cat! When he finds his cat dead, his girlfriend comforts him. Apparently, the cat was his last reminder of his dead wife (other than photos and stuff). Another frickin' murder happens so Maccari is pulled off the case. I like how plot devices from the 70s are still perfectly fine in 1999. Despite some corny stuff and a pointlessly protracted ending, I was surprisingly entertained.

LUNCH

LeEtta and I run out for some food at Fresh Market. We kill their deli section getting all kinds of easy meals for the moviethon. I get a Buffalo chicken wrap but all the sauce was on one side of the wrap so I get a blast of heat from the meal. Otherwise, it's delicious. LeEtta gets some crazy big salad that she eats a third of and throws the rest in the fridge for later. Margie is enjoying some excellent mac and cheese. I call up my friend Brad in Kentucky so I can put him on speaker phone. This way we can watch the movie together. We are buds.

"I was only trying to make your toast edible."

2:16 PM
Hatchet for the Honeymomoon (1970)

The opening credits are tinted images projected on animated sand and they tell me all I need to know: Dagmar Lassander! The opening music is a cascade of lounge schmaltz trash on the rocks with a twist of psychedelia. This is Bava in late 1960s drive-in mode and this is one of his most underrated films. John Harrington (Stephen Forsyth), the main duder, is haunted by blurry memories and is quite in touch with his craziness. He knows he is a madman and is totally okay with that. John is compelled to kill women on their wedding night by a memory he can't quite recall which is funny because he designs wedding dresses for his fashion house.

There is much technical trickery from director/cinematographer Bava to be found in this little piece of brilliance. Lassander plays Helen Wood, a lovely little lass. John's got a secret hideaway place (and it's not his butt) decorated like a child's room. Aw, his mannequin make out sessions are just adorable. The crazy echo guitar and synths just kicked in! This delightfully sleepy film segues right into a séance and I couldn't be happier.

John's wife Mildred is played by the very odd Laura Betti (of Twitch of the Death Nerve). She talks to the spirit world while someone hums a lullaby. Oh silly Femi Benussi, don't tell your boss that you're getting married. He is totally going to kill you! But hey, John is killing because he needs to kill brides. The trippy camera tricks are so totally bitchin' like I can't like believe my eyes and stuff. Wait a second, shouldn't this be called Meat Cleaver for the Honeymoon?

I have to ask: "Um, if that cremator is so hot then how can he pull the tray out with his bare hands?"

LeEtta whispers: "Supah powahs!"

Mildred is just begging to get hit with his meat cleaver but mainly because she really hates grapes. Who hates grapes? While their flirtation blooms, Helen tells John that she likes to amuse herself by doing 'crazy' things! I can totally relate. The non-horror sections of the soundtrack are elevator drone frenzy. Hey look at that, John's watching a scene from Bava's Black Sabbath on TV and the dialogue has been changed to make it sound like a soap opera.

At she and John's mansion, Mildred wants some action but John can't give it to her. Ha ha, they've never made love. What a couple of idiots! People who have marital problems are all serial killers. Marital strife reaches a fever pitch as John is coming after Mildred with the meat cleaver. Hmm, I can't tell if she's scared, happy, or horny about it. I'm feeling all three of those things myself right now.

The cops show up for a little "Telltale Heart" action as Mildred's body is dripping blood from the top of the stairs. Why don't they just start tearing the goddamned mansion apart? Since when do Italian cops do things by the book? I wish I had a little doppelganger of my younger self hanging around me constantly. Cool and spooky moments abound as Mildred's spirit doesn't stay departed for long. Broads with loose morals are drawn to the dreamy lady-killer John like flies. There is a shape coming up the stairs getting more and more tangible as it gets closer to the room and John is paralyzed by fear. I'll say no more

GIALLO MELTDOWN

"I am a horse. Not a woman."

4:03 PM
My Wife Has a Body to Die For (1973)

I get off the phone with Brad (boo!) and put this movie on. This washed out print and warbly soundtrack is just what I need. The film opens with some very 'exciting' water skiing footage. Silvano Tranquilli plays Paolo, a middle aged politician with a hot younger wife named Simona (Antonella Murgia). At a studio, a sexy redhead photographer is talking down to her model. Simona shows up and has an obtuse conversation with the photographer. Did they used to be lovers or something? What's going on?

When Simona goes to pick up Paolo from work, she discovers that he had a meeting with Marco, her former lover. Paolo is less than ecstatic about that. Simona and Marco have drinks together and it's clear that he is still in love with her. There have been two J&B sightings in this film so far. Uh oh, Simona agrees to go on a little boat trip with Marco. And we just had another J&B sighting. What the heck?

Marco and Simona go to an island for some hanky panky but it seems like she's just leading the schmuck on. Now they're getting it on but who's driving the boat? So Paolo allowed Simona to go out and have her little fling with Marco because their marriage is awful. Simona is wearing some explosively bad denim outfit and- another J&B sighting! At a swanky nightclub that plays some righteous tunes, Paolo explains some of his theories on why their open marriage will work. Obviously, his wife-sharing is just a sick game that he's playing.

Simona bangs some guy she just met at a nightclub and it makes Paolo horny. That's nice. And now she's sleeping with the redhead photographer and a black guy. LeEtta asks the questions: "Are you sure this is a giallo?" I too am starting to have my doubts about this one. Simona goes to Marco's place so that he can feel her up and then she curses him out. Then she fucks two more random guys! Oh well, at least the music is good.

If this film had as many death scenes as sex scenes, it would have quite a body count but this sexy thriller has way more sex than thrills. I'll have to go back and figure out just who said this was a giallo. This isn't a giallo. Another J&B sighting does little to counter my disappointment. Someone just died! Finally! I dig the unexpected ending but this movie is a bust.

NAP TIME

My Wife Has a Body to Die For made me sleepy so I took a dang nap. It felt good to have my head on a pillow and our fat cat Sparkles sleeping beside me. Just kidding, she's not fat; Sparkles is all muscle!

"These tears spoil your beautiful eyes."

6:31 PM
Crimine a due (1964)

Man, this better be good. The film starts with a dude running from some shady characters. He ducks into a swanky nightclub where a singer belts out a fucking awesome song. I like this already. The guy on the run is Paolo (John Drew Barrymore) and he has amassed some gambling debts so he asks the girl who sings there to spot him some cash. But it's too late, the bad guys rough Paolo up and strongly encourage him to pay them back.

At the office where Paolo works, everyone is accusing him of stealing money, especially his boss David (Jean Claudio). Anna (Luisa Rivelli), David's wife, defends Paolo but even she seems to have her doubts. David hates Paolo and accuses Anna of sleeping with him. That is one slinky music score by Berto Pisano! Paolo's girlfriend Christina (Ombretta Colli of The Blancheville Monster) is trying to help him out but all he cares about is that she aborts their unborn kid. Nice guy!

David has two secrets: 1. he has a heart condition and 2. his poor brother Carlo, who is a mess of scar tissue. Carlo is in the care of a rather bitchy nurse named Elizabeth (Lisa Gastoni). Anna is trying to care for David but he's a stubborn idiot. They live in a badass castle which is filled with Carlo's screaming which Anna believes is a terrible omen.

This tawdry story gets more tense when, as David is about to call the cops on Paolo, he has a major heart attack. While he's being treated for his condition, they let Paolo mix his drugs for him. Of course, David croaks while disfigured Carlo just howls on and on. Anna finds out that David had a big life insurance policy and a will that requires her to stay in the old castle and take care of his freakish brother.

The detective that David tried to call on the night he died receives an anonymous letter asking him to look into David's death. Meanwhile, Paolo is happy to help Anna spend her newfound wealth by planning to build a swimming pool and tennis courts around the castle. In a very gothic horror moment, Anna nearly gets killed in the tunnels under the castle. After that, they decide to take the money and run, ignoring the will. But the cops are already suspicious and are building a case against them. Bitchy Elizabeth tells the cops that she thinks Paolo and Anna murdered David.

I am quite smitten with this film. And unless one of my crazy theories comes to pass, I have literally no idea how this is all going to end. My good friend Matt Torrence just called. He's going to stop by and have some awesome giallo times with us. I get back to the movie and hell yes, my crazy theory was correct. Damn yo, this movie is fun as shit.

*"Do you still think that I'm delusional?
Or that I'm crazy?"*

8:49 PM
The Girl Who Knew Too Much (1963)

We finally get to what is considered by some to be the very first giallo. The opening song is a fine slice of rock and roll. Thank you, Mr. Bava for the best TWA commercial ever. While flying to Rome to visit a sickly family friend, Nora (Letícia Román) mistakenly takes a pack of marijuana cigarettes from a stranger on the plane. Judging by her horrible snakeskin coat, she smokes them all the time. A young and strapping John Saxon (of Tenebre) plays Dr. Marcello Bassi who clearly has a thing for Nora.

That nightie you got there is hella sexy, Miss Nora. But not such a great job taking care of Ethel. She dies the first night you're there? Bava's black and white photography of Rome is razor sharp. After being knocked senseless by a purse-snatcher, Nora witnesses a murder. She passes out again and some helpful goofus gives her whiskey to help her wake up. Now the cop doesn't believe her story because he thinks she's a drunk.

I don't think I trust this weirdo named Laura (Valentina Cortese), who claims to be dead Ethyl's friend. Nora decides to accept Laura's offer to stay in her house. Now our heroine is alone and everything is getting wonderfully suspicious and creepy.

Nora is awesome! She's so obsessed with her murder mystery novels that she decides to treat this very dangerous situation like a game. Her complicated trap made with a maze of string and flour that she sets up to catch the killer is hilariously overdone. Poor love struck Marcello falls into the running joke (literally) by getting injured over and over again throughout the film.

An outstandingly eerie atmosphere creeps in at the deserted building with the swinging light fixtures. The voice guiding her through the building with the constantly shifting light is outstanding. Every clue leads to another twist of the story. But there's comedy to keep things light. When Nora gets too close to the truth, the game isn't so fun anymore.

"I'm not some cheap bitch!"

10:26 PM
The Flower with the Petals of Steel (1973)

Carroll Baker AND scuba diving? Great! This has Gianni Garko in it as a talented doctor named Andrea. Carroll Baker plays Evelyn, a lesbian hanging out with Daniela, a hot topless chick played by Paola Senatore (of

The Killer Reserved Nine Seats). You should Google Senatore with the safe search off. In the next scene, Andrea is a total dick while performing surgery. Apparently, browbeating a nurse is a lifesaving technique.

When the going gets tough, the subtitles just give up. Maybe it was just boring doctor stuff. In this stellar soundtrack, a badass drummer drives the funky business and it's all good. Composer Marcello Giombini, you are the man. Carroll Baker's perm is unfortunate; she looks like she was guest starring on "Dinah!" in 1977. Daniela is Andrea's lover and he's a dick to her too. He tells her to leave and shoves her across the room.

After chugging some J&B, Andrea notices that Daniela is dead, impaled on his stupid metal plant (is that the flower with petals of steel?). This uninvolving, emotionless film has segued into an unbearably tense thriller. Andrea uses his medical expertise to dissect Daniela's body. The filmmakers effectively keep things tame by leaving most of the gore to our imaginations. I wonder if Fulci ever saw this. He would have loved this morbid shit. Time to dispose of the body in a cement mixer!

Inspector Garrano (Ivano Staccioli of Death Walks at Midnight) shows up and starts questioning him. I feel bad for Garrano because his tiny office is wallpapered with puke. Andrea goes home where Baker (with a new hairstyle (Thank goodness!)) is waiting to harass him some more. It seems that Andrea was banging her too a long time ago. LeEtta says Baker's weird silk outfit makes her look like a Whirling Dervish. Andrea pisses Baker off by asking her to drop the missing persons report on her lesbian lover (who was also her step-sister?).

That night, Andrea goes out on his patio to think but the wind is causing a window to bang open and closed or is someone watching him? This is ominous as fuck. I shouldn't give two fucks about this jerk but I am scared for him. An engrossing story? No way! His sexy assistant (Pilar Velazquez) comes over to his apartment and they get it on. Poor thing is smitten with him. After the lovin', Andrea gets a package containing a piece of his metal plant. That kind of kills the mood.

After a mysterious phone call, Andrea goes wandering through Melted Doll Head Forest. Wait, what? The inspector is snooping around a mental institution based on a tip from Baker but I better not say anymore. You should seek out this movie. It's got day-for-night radness, pseudoscience, scuba diving sex (with a glaring continuity error), and THE VIBE.

SUNDAY

The alarm on my phone wipes any memories of my dreams away. I get up before I realize how tired I am and wash my face, brush my teeth, and get dressed. I had a bit of a rough night last night. There were a lot of onions in those potstickers and I suffered for them. In the living room, I leave the blinds shut and start a film before my senses catch up with me.

> *"You know in good families,*
> *girls don't have babies illegitimately."*

8:29 AM
Devil in the Brain (1972)

The strains of gorgeous and mournful score by Ennio Morricone and Bruno Nicholai let me know that I'm in for something good. A young man named Oscar (Keir Dullea), spots Sandra, an old acquaintance of his. When he tries to see her, her stuck-up family hides her away. Oscar rents an apartment overlooking their backyard just to get a chance to speak to her. The family are suspicious but Oscar might just be a dang psycho! He knew Sandra back before she married Fabrizio (Maurice Ronet) and had a child.

In a crushingly sad scene, when Oscar finally gets to talk to Sandra, he finds out that the death of her husband has driven the poor woman bonkers. She's regressed to an age before she ever got married or gave birth to her son, Ricky (Renato Cestiè of Damned in Venice). He enlists his friend, Dr. Emilio, to try and get Sandra some psychiatric help.

After Sandra cuts her wrists by breaking a window in front of Oscar and Emilio, Sandra's controlling mom, Claudia (Micheline Presle), finally agrees to get her some help. Mom says that Sandra can't face her memories. This film cuts wonderfully between the past and the present without patiently holding the hand of the viewer. This is very confident storytelling.

It's revealed that Sandra's son Ricky is not a normal boy. He is a little sociopath and it's not too surprising since his mom is a childlike basket case. Okay, this film is amazing. And that superb score is drifting right into my bones. Ricky is in a ward for troubled boys run by some nuns. When Emilio interviews him, he makes a shocking discovery. I won't tell you what that is. There's a J&B sighting. I'll tell you that much. Man, I am so emotionally drained. I feel like I need a hug and a lollipop and a promise that everything's gonna be okay. You need to find Devil in the Brain.

> *"People love and hate, kill and die,*
> *you can do nothing."*

10:22 AM
Death Occurred Last Night (1970)

This movie opens with a brassy and sultry song by Italian pop queen, Mina. Detective Lamberti (Frank Wolff) is talking to a man whose daughter, Donatella, is missing. The kicker is that she is a 25 year old woman with the brain of a 3 year old. The father, Mr. Berzagi (Raf Vallone), is a nervous wreck imagining what could have happened to her. Because of her mental state, he kept her locked up tight and one day she just vanished.

I really dig Frank Wolff. He makes a great sensitive sonofabitch detective (with sinus problems). He starts to gather some leads and employs a former pimp to infiltrate the local brothels in order to find Donatella. He runs into some really depraved hookers. There's a great montage with a jazzy and fun music score as he goes from brothel to brothel.

Lamberti enlists a black prostitute named Errera (Beryl Cunningham of The Weekend Murders) to help him track down the girl. She is a damaged soul who thinks she might have heard something about Donatella. Much to the chagrin of his wife, Lamberti lets Errera stay at their home while he utilizes her knowledge of the underworld. They catch a break when their pimp informant is offered Donatella out of the blue. A sting to get the bastards and rescue the girl goes completely awry.

Later, a hunter walking through a field finds the body of a woman burning in a fire pit that might be Donatella. Lamberti tells Mr. Berzagi and he nearly dies of a heart attack on the spot. They bring him to the morgue to identify the body and he confirms that it is his daughter. In a depressing scene, Lamberti helps Berzagi clean out all the reminders of Donatella. Next, the pimp who helped them gets shot for working with the cops.

This would make a great companion piece with What Have They Done to Your Daughters? and Enigma Rosso. I have no idea how this is going to end. In an amazing scene, the detective's wife tries to talk Errera out of committing suicide and the troubled hooker reveals a vital clue. Damn yo, this film is impossibly sad! That's two films in a row today that just rip your heart out and take a dump on your happy thoughts.

BREAK TIME

After having my soul ripped out by two depressing movies, I decided to clean out the catbox to cheer myself up. It turns out that the cold front has left just a beautiful day behind. I don't like to brag to my northerly friends who are no doubt freezing their asses off but Florida in January is pretty awesome. Once I give the cats a fresh place to crap and peepee, I go out for a cigar. Don't worry, I washed my hands! I smoke a Nub by Oliva. It's a quick smoke but I enjoy some nice giallo music and sip an Arizona iced tea. If only they would sponsor this book, I'd be a tea millionaire. Once inside, I have a lunch of deli meat and moldy cheese. Don't worry, I scraped the mold off!

"I'm your husband and I like you."

1:35 PM
Diary of an Erotic Murderess (1975)

At a beautiful estate, a young man named Mark (Juan Ribó) is having some kind of fit. His nurse, an old crone, quits because she can't deal with him. In the opening credits, we see Marisa Mell (oh baby!) cruising along in her little sports car while a seductive piece of music floats in. I dig this movie already. A fancy businessman named Alexander (Richard Conte) is thinking of hiring Gina (Mell) to look after Mark. He claims that the kid has been a mute and a rather violent one ever since he found his mother dead.

She gets the job but something is wrong here. Mark is a very frightening young man. He acts like a caveman but he seems fond of Gina the psychologist. The dad explains that Mark had an unhealthy attachment to his mother and ever since she died, her possessions have become sacred objects and he constantly plays her favorite music on the piano.

Marisa Mell running around the garden in a flowing nightgown and carrying some roses while the breathy music of the film's score melodramatically beats me to death. Thank you for the music, Carlo Savina. Did I mention that Gina is a dead ringer for Mark's mother? Of course, dad can't keep his hands off of her. While snooping around, she finds Mark's dead mother's diary and finds out lots of dirt on Alexander. Oh shit, Alexander and Gina (An Erotic Murderess) just got married.

LeEtta gets a little scared by how excited I get when Anthony Steffen shows up. I might be bouncing up and down in my seat. When Gina meets up with Richard (Steffen), he immediately starts smacking her around. We find out that she is a thief and only posing as a psychologist. Richard is her abusive husband and a professional thief. Gina (An Erotic Polyandrist) manipulates the situation to get what she wants. She uses poor Mark as a pawn and plans to kill Alexander. Richard may be next. Three words: jaw dropping ending. Even though I kind of saw it coming, the freeze frame is just mind blowing.

NAP TIME

After I fall asleep for the 25th time during Diary of Erotic Murderess, I decide to go lay down for a bit. It's not the movie itself, I just can't keep my dang eyes open. I crash out for an hour and then LeEtta comes to wake me up mere seconds after my alarm does it for me. She informs me that she has made dinner. Bowtie pasta with olives, spinach, and feta cheese.

"How strange, Marco. I sense fear and my head feels light."

5:08 PM
Delitto d'autore (1974)

I call up Brad so we can view this very rare flick together. The bootleg of Delitto D'Autore from Cinema de Bizarre is super scratchy but watchable. I'm very excited about this giallo that I know nothing about. Marco (Pier Paolo Capponi) is cruising around in his hot car with his hot wife, Milena (the luscious Sylva Koscina), who he's secretly married to! Now they're having sex. Marco is so hairy that just looking at him makes me grow hair in places that I didn't even know I had. This DVD has a warbly soundtrack and washed out colors and I feel like I'm getting away with something just by watching it. Hey, Krista Nell, wassup?

Marco and Milena are on a committee planning some kind of an art giveaway. Ah yes, of course, the Girosi prize! I'm sure you've heard of it. During their first meeting, a mysterious motherfucker calls up and threatens to kill whoever wins first prize. Cut to some skeet-shooting! The extremely badass Luigi Pistilli is here playing don Lino, a priest. Milena's aunt thinks that Marco is a loser and only married Milena for her family's money.

Milena confesses to don Lino that after nightclubbing the other night, she must have been drugged. When she woke up there were a pair of black gloves on the bed next to her. Pfft, happens to me all the time. She thinks someone is out to get her. In a very creepy scene, Milena goes to a Roman bath (presumably to wash her delicious boobs) in the creepiest subterranean grotto ever built. This place looks like a dang torture chamber. I love this scene. Even the music is awesome.

Uh oh, Milena just got kidnapped. Her auntie takes the call from the kidnapper and then someone bashes her fucking head in with a flashlight. And now Brad and I are totally lost. What in all that is holy and convoluted is going on in this friggin' movie? It all goes back to the shoe factory. There's an outrageous orgy scene but the damn fuzz breaks it up. Is it just me or does that ending (and the whole movie) feel rushed?

POOP INTERLUDE

There was some commotion coming from the living room. I can hear both LeEtta and Margie yelling. I decide to lay low unless my name is called. It turns out that Shadow the dog came in after his evening pee and just started scooting and just rubbing his butt on the carpet like there is no tomorrow. Yeah, it's a mess.

"I don't care what you smell like.
I smell like loneliness tonight."

8:57 PM
Thirsty for Love, Sex and, Murder (1972)

What better way to end a moviethon than with something truly exotic? I mean like really exotic. This piece of craziness is a remake (or a ripoff) of The Strange Vice of Mrs. Wardh. This is just all kinds of fucked up. Music queues feel like they are totally random and/or stolen from other films. This is a shot for shot remake and it is barely competent! I love this. Our main character is Mine and she is played by a terrible actress but she is thick-hipped. I like her!

Every frame of this is the most important thing ever filmed. I'm so happy right now. There are so many shots in this energetic schlock that just launch my brains at the ceiling. Is the editor a crackhead? Literally every scene is hacked away at with the care and loving touch of a drunken lumberjack. Even when the actors attempt to properly show emotion, the editor says "Boring! Fuck you! Next!"

I spoke too soon on the shot for shot remake bit, there is some slight differences but most of the key scenes are all here, only totally incompetently done. I want to see every Turkish film ever made right now. Are they all like this? And I think I just heard music from one of the Blind Dead movies. The best part about this whole clusterfuck? It's only an hour long!

CONCLUSION

Well, shit on a brick and call me 'Shirley', this moviethon is done! I haven't had a Giallo Meltdown end on a note quite this positive in a while. I pry myself out of the chair and head to the kitchen for a celebratory shot of J&B. The shot goes down hard, like poison. I think I'll be looking up some girly recipes to make this jumbo bottle go down easier next time. Wait, shhhh. Just let me bathe in the afterglow for a moment. Thank you.

The next morning, while heading to work, I feel tired but pretty happy with the whole weekend. I didn't get as many movies as I wanted but hey, I am physically and emotionally wiped out these days. It's called 'Life'.

I haven't felt this happy at the end of a moviethon in a while. I guess because I took it pretty easy, I am able to go to work Monday morning without even the slightest of moviethon hangovers. I think I'll be more organized next time when it comes to titles. There were so many choices that the title choosing just got out of control. See y'all next time!

GIALLO MELTDOWN 7:
THE CASE OF THE BLEEDING EYEHOLES

I like to read, I enjoy smoking cigars, I like playing guitar, and I like to obsessively arrange and rearrange my guitar pedals to get weird sounds. I really like cold drinks. But do you know what really gets me going? Friggin' moviethons! Ha, you already knew that! There's nothing more daunting than a big list of movies picked for a 3 day marathon. Many moviethons have been canceled due to illness or cowardice and sometimes I just know I can't do it. This is not one of those moviethons.

FRIDAY

The alarm goes off at 7:45am and I sit up on the edge of the bed feeling like my head is full of sand. I took the day off for this moviethon and I'm already regretting waking up so early. LeEtta and I head out to breakfast at Panera Bread where I make good use of their Mountain Dew. After bagel breakfast sandwiches, we go to the bank and then to AOE, an art supply store LeEtta likes. The weather is wonderfully overcast and it occurs to me for the millionth time how much I despise sunshine. We head up 56th Street where I discover that Cigar Castle doesn't open until 10. Fuck that noise, I'll go out for cigars tomorrow.

Back at the apartment, Margie's day of work is already in full swing. She works from home which makes me burn with jealousy. I spend a few minutes pulling titles from my stacks of bootleg DVDs, printing up a title list, and typing the paragraph that you're reading right now. I text with Brad about film choices and figuring out a time when we can watch Bay of Blood together over the phone. I make a quick silent prayer to God that the rash of tornadoes doesn't hit anywhere near my Kentucky friend.

"Do you wear long-johns or briefs?"

11:00 AM
Libido (1965)

A scratchy old black and white print shows us a quote from Frued and now a creepy Jiminy Cricket toy while a music box plays. A young boy hears a scream somewhere in the castle and goes looking for its source. He finds a blond woman lashed to a bed, screaming her head off. Carlo

Rustichelli provides the musical score for this one and it's both haunting and boisterously loud. The boy sees his father with a bleeding scratch on his hand. When his father leaves, he sees that the woman is dead, her wide eyes staring into his. Holy shit, I like this already.

The boy has grown into a handsome young man named Christian (Giancarlo Giannini). He, his wife Helene (Dominique Boschero), his family lawyer Paul (Luciano Pigozzi), and Paul's ditzy blonde wife named Bridgette (Mara Maryl), return to the castle many years after the death of his father. It's obvious that Christian is haunted by his past and is one bitter bastard. In three months, he will inherit the house and the fortune. His plan is to sell the castle and never look back.

LeEtta just got done with a job interview over the phone so we each get a shot of J&B to celebrate her kicking some ass. Ernesto Gastaldi, one of the most prolific screenwriters in Italian genre cinema, directed this flick. I'm liking the gothic feel of Libido so far. Paul and Brigitte start getting kinky in the bedroom where that woman was killed. While Pigozzi sits frustrated on the bed, his blond vixen does a striptease to some Hawaiian music. Christian sees all this and freaks out because of his psychosexual urges. He clutches his hands so tight that he scrapes the back of his hand with his own nails, just like daddy.

There are some revelations concerning the inheritance and the mysterious death of Christian's father. Is the old man really dead? Also, whenever that Jiminy Cricket music starts playing, shit gets creepy. Thanks to the internet, I just smacked my forehead over Dominique Boschero. She was in both Who Saw Her Die? and All the Colors of the Dark! Brigitte expresses her interest in banging Christian and it doesn't go over very well.

LeEtta brings out a tray of olives, feta cheese, pickled garlic cloves, and other goodies for us to snack on. She also has pate and goat cheese to spread on crackers. What a woman! I chow down while Christian and Helene are chasing what may or may not be the ghost of his father. So far my predictions for the twist have been way off and that is a good thing. Great ending! I highly recommend you check this one out.

"The harder you try... The deeper you fall into this world of shit."

12:49 PM
The Cat in Heat (1972)

The first copy I scored of La gatta in calore was pretty terrible, just pixelated and impossible to watch. The internet saved the day once again and I was able to burn another disc to replace it. The film opens with Antonio (Silvano Tranquilli) cruising the interstate, smoking, and thinking about his hot wife, Anna (Eva Czemerys). He gets home and discovers a dude's corpse in his front yard. The body is that of his new neighbor, Massimo, who just moved in recently. There's a trail of blood in the house and his wife is sitting in their kitchen, in shock.

After he covers up the body with leaves, Anna admits to being in love with Massimo and sleeping with him. The film flashes back to show how this mess got started. Poor Anna just wanted to get it on with Antonio but he fell asleep. Instead of just waking him up and jumping on his dong, she looks all dejected and crap. Duh, lady! If you tell a man you want sex, they will always comply. ALWAYS! The Silly screenplay says he's way older than Anna but I'm not convinced. That night, she sees their hunky neighbor fighting in his front yard with some bimbo and she is clearly intrigued.

Anna becomes so lonely that when Antonio is away at work, she obsesses over Massino and his lascivious exploits (like making out with some big-breasted chick in his front window). This film is shot beautifully by its cinematographer, Joe D'Amato. Back in the present, with the body only half-buried in the yard, it isn't long before someone nearly discovers the crime.

I don't know composer Gianfranco Plenizio's work at all but his dreamy music here is driven by female vocals. I love it. More flashbacks! Anna overhears a ruckus over at Massimo's house and checks it out. A couple of thugs have beaten him up in his own dining room. To heal his bloody and bruised body, Anna starts sleeping with him. Their affair includes walking on the beach, driving around, and getting it on in a barn. Massimo also enjoys shooting heroin and lame suicide attempts. Yeah, he's a degenerate fuckbag and he even violates Anna with a Pepsi bottle (thankfully not shown on screen) for the amusement of his drugged out bitches.

Finally, some J&B (even though it's being used as a candle holder)! Jeez, Anna is a walking doormat for Massimo. She goes back to him so he gives her LSD while her creepy friends watch and listen to scary opera music. This whole sequence is just insane. Finally, Anna gets the hint and starts to avoid this guy but it's too late. Stereotypically gay character alert! This guy is really annoying but the great ending makes up for it.

"I see those God damn eyes every night.
Why me? Why me?"

2:24 PM
Madness (1994)

Directed by Herik Montgomery, eh? This 1994 giallo from Bruno Mattei has some cool opening music but I bet it was lifted from something else. Here's something I've never seen in a giallo: mini-Formula One racing!

During a boring race (that the crowd is amusingly excited about), an annoying little girl gets bored and wanders away from the bleachers. Her babysitter follows her to a secluded garage where a maniac dressed all in black carves out the babysitter's eyes and shoves broken glass in the sockets. Nasty! I just caught myself enjoying this. Is this really you, Mattei?

At a press conference where everyone is yelling at the top of their lungs, we meet Giavanna Dei (Monica Seller) a comic book artist talking about her character named Dr. Dark. Lately, a serial killer is running around and copying his exploits. She and writer Nico (Gabriele Gori) are having a PR nightmare but their scumbag publisher, Marizio (Achille Brugnini), is happy about all the negative press. Some dickhead reporter named Lorenzo Calligari (Fausto Lombardi) is the most outspoken critic of Dr. Dark but Giavanna is VERY passionate about Dr. Dark.

That night, after a threatening call from the killer, Giavanna lounges around in her nightie and eats a sandwich. Then she discovers a pair of eyeballs on her drawing table. Giavanna and Nico cooperate with the cops and plan a vacation to get away from all the weirdness. Lorenzo the creepy reporter shows up with flowers to apologize but his shoes match the killer's (gasp!). Next, a babysitter wearing mom jeans is awkwardly making out with her handsy boyfriend. When he leaves, the killer injects the babysitter with a syringe full of something. Now the two dumbest/most annoying cops in giallo history are discussing the case.

Giavanna gets another threatening phone call and another pair of eyeballs in her house. Nico fights off the killer in the yard and the cops materialize from nowhere and shoot the bad guy though not fatally. It's Lorenzo! But wait a minute, there's a lot of movie left. Giavanna, Nico, Marizio, Marizio's secretary, and some guy named Massimo in very short jorts are hanging out on a yacht. Giavanna and Nico are an item now but they kiss and it is like two mannequins being bashed together.

Giavanna has a nightmare about Dr. Dark carving her eye out and she wakes up screaming. Nico calms her down by yelling right in her face. Oh goodie, more murders and more suspects! Considering this director's awful output, Madness could have been a lot worse. The staged suicide scene is so dumb that brain cells die of embarrassment. Highlight of the movie: Massimo sexily posing in his jorts while reading a Dr. Dark comic and lazily playing with his knife. I'll never forget that one!

NAPTIME AND 7-11

After an all too brief nap, I run out and get a hot dog at 7-11. As past moviethons have taught me, this is a terrible idea. I decide get creative. I call my creation the "Duder Dog" and it has chili, cheddar cheese, hot sauce, and sour cream on it. I expect it to be mentioned on my gravestone.

"You couldn't find your dick in a windstorm!"

6:09 PM
Knight Moves (1992)

I heard from a reliable source (Brad) that this was an American giallo, so I'm checking it out. The film opens very stylishly with an intense black and white chess tournament between two boys in 1972. One kid wins and then tries to stab the other kid to death with a pen. The psycho chess kid finds his mother dead, having slashed her own wrists.

Years later, Christopher Lambert (who terrifies and fascinates me) plays chess champion, Peter Sanderson. Nice! Peter just proved that all chess players get so laid. He screws a chick and she gets murdered. Enter a two cops: a Baldwin (it's Daniel, by the way) and Tom Skerritt. The killer slits the wrists of his victims and poses them to look like the kid's dead mother. This is all very stylish. Lambert has a weird ass accent in this film that I cannot place. He gets a mysterious phone call from someone threatening him, someone who wants to play a game. Queue the suspenseful music!

Skerritt and Baldwin call two psychologists, a weird looking one and a hot one (Diane Lane) to check out Peter, who looks guilty as hell. Oh snap, the killer wears gloves and just assaulted a light bulb a la Tenebre. They find another victim and all Peter cares about is his next chess match. LeEtta spots a very young Katharine Isabelle from Ginger Snaps as Peter's daughter. The cops reroute Peter's phone to an underground basement full of water pumps or whatever and I have no idea why. Forget Knight Moves being giallo-influenced, this is a dang giallo!

Of course, Diane Lane is the love interest (queue the sexophone music!) and whoa, she has nice tits. Even LeEtta is impressed. I actually say out loud: "I'd like to take a stroll down Diane Lane!" Peter looks even guiltier so she doesn't trust him now. We get some intense chess playing and yet another murder victim. Not sure what's worse: Lambert's voice and accent or the stinky cheese dialog he's spitting. Even though it stalls out for a bit, I am enjoying Knight Moves.

*"If you're not wearing sunglasses,
you're stark naked."*

8:10 PM
The Double (1971)

Ewa Aulin and Jean Sorel (as Lucia and Giovanni) in a film together with Silvano Tranquilli, Giacomo Rossi-Stuart, and Marilù Tolo! Shit y'all, I'm very excited about this. Jean Sorel parks his car, gets out, and gets shot in slow motion by some sweaty professor-looking guy. Now the film is jumping around like crazy. Giovanni and Lucia are swimming naked in the ocean and I swear I saw his cock. LeEtta is sorry that she missed it.

The soundtrack is achingly awesome and everything is edited in such a surreal way that I am suddenly very excited. Lucia just dropped the info that they are in Morocco or whatever. Their thermos is empty so Sorel goes over and gets some water from some friendly nomads. They meet some dang hippie by the beach named Eddie (Sergio Doria of Death Smiled at Murder). He's an American. Yucky Americans!

Some guy named Roger (Tranquilli) just offered everyone some J&B. This is going very well so far. Marilù Tolo plays Marie, Roger's wife, and she's hotter in this film than I've ever seen her. Giovanni gets all bent out of shape when Lucia's mother flies in to visit. He shouldn't be upset because she is such a MILF. Their pal Nora (Lucia Bosé) spills the beans that Lucia wants to marry Giovanni and he is like 'Let's all have some J&B!'

Giovanni is getting rather possessive with Lucia. Eddie just got a spear gun to the groin! And now everyone is out partying together. Wait, what? Giovanni nearly rapes Lucia and now he's going after Nora in a similarly rapey fashion. These are my least favorite scenes in trashy cinema. It's like motherfuckers didn't know how to write a film without a rape scene where the (always female) victim just accepts being raped. I hate hate HATE that.

Oh well, at least the editing is impressive as the films jumps all over the palce. Giovanni follows Nora back to Rome because he's obsessed with her after their little rape-adventure. Giacomo Rossi-Stuart shows up as a fast-talking character that I just can't keep up with. While Lucia is painting her face with green makeup, the phone rings, and Giovanni answers it. He tells the person on the other line that Lucia is cleaning the toilet. Okay, that was funny. This is a kickass flick but trust me, you will fucking hate Giovanni.

QUICK BREAK

I take a shower because I'm feeling pretty lousy. Gee, I wonder if that my 'Duder Dog' (patent pending) isn't to blame. Living 82 paces (Yes, I counted) from a 7-11 is what the industry calls 'A Renters' Terrible Mistake'. Other than feeling stomach sick and very tired, I'm ready for more.

"Stop shouting, you're disturbing little Ferdinand!"

10:50 PM
Bay of Blood (1971)

My preferred title for this film is Twitch of the Death Nerve. I love the reactions I get from people when I say it out loud. In a recent medical journal, scientists have actually located and have managed to isolate the 'death nerve' in the human body. Millions of lives have been spared.

I played this film for some friends once and it went over like a lead balloon. I can't really explain it. This fast paced giallo with a very high body count and gratuitous nudity bored them to tears. It was a very traumatic experience for me and is the sole reason why I'm the shut-in that I am today. Oh Stelvio Cipriani, you're soundtrack is so soothing especially with all of the carnage that director Mario Bava has in store for me. Poor old lady (Isa Miranda), someone should put her out of her misery soon. And here I thought all rich people were happy. Oh look, someone put her out of her misery. And now her killer has been killed. Everyone wants to inherit the bay (of blood) and will kill to get their hands on it.

Who wipes their nose on a squid? Did Simon (Claudio Camaso) actor improvise that or did Bava ask him to wipe his nose on that poor, defenseless squid? Paolo Fosatti (Leopoldo Trieste) is a great comic character. He chases bugs around. Oh goodie, a carload of fun-loving young people. Thank God, they are marked for death. Brunhilda (Brigitte Skay) is so hot that it breaks my mind. All is not right at this quaint decrepit villa on the bay. Someone is watching these scumbags with wild, evil eyes.

Laura Betti, the horny wife from Hatchet for the Honeymoon, is here as Paolo's drunk (and possibly horny) wife. She reminds LeEtta of Medusa (which I think was intentional). Brunhilda's death scene is completely awesome. She gets abandoned by her 'friends' and this makes her an easy target for the killer (or killers). Oh shit, machete to the face! I can dig that. Then the killer pins the lovers together with a spear and their death squirms look like they're still making love which is erotic, repulsive, and totally bitchin'. Man, dig that tacky décor.

Luigi Pistilli (from The Iguana with the Tongue of Fire) and Claudine Auger (Black Belly of the Tarantula) are also in this one. All the storylines are intersecting and characters coming into contact with one another invariably leads them to their death. Geez, every one of these scenes is so perfectly shot and lit that it makes my eyes dance. One thing I've learned from gialli is that all paths lead to Nicoletta Elmi.

SATURDAY

I really wanted to sleep in but LeEtta wakes me up around 7:40am. Barely awake, I get us some breakfast sandwiches from 7-11. After breakfast, we do chores. Then we go to the liquor store and the cigar store. We get more juices and things for mixing with alcohol than actual liquor because I believe there must be some way to make J&B go down easier. Tonight, there'll be a mixing party, you'll see. There is a chance that Nafa will be stopping by and an even better chance that Shelly will be coming over tonight for some giallo action. LeEtta agrees to do a shot of J&B with me and we toast to Rosalba Neri. She's a pro but my shot goes down really hard and I make all kinds of bizarre sounds and faces. Time to pick the first movie of the day.

> *"Their beef sandwiches are the best in town."*

10:56 AM
The Girl in Room 2A (1974)

This Italian/American coproduction starts with a woman exiting her apartment then getting chloroformed into submission and kidnapped. Next, her hands are bound by a rope from the ceiling and a long spike is poking her in the 'giant breasts' area. A mysterious figure in red gloves and a cape impales her on the spike and then her body is flung off a cliff.

We cut to Margaret (Daniela Giordano), a young lady just getting out of jail. After a stroll through a rather imposing courtyard, she misses her bus and then calls up Alicia (Rosalba Neri!), a social worker. Margaret checks into her apartment, the titular Room 2A, and already things are pretty hinky. This is probably one of those movies where everyone and everything is suspicious and creepy. I hate those kinds of movies! She's in the apartment for about 2 minutes before noticing a huge bloodstain on the floor.

After some sedative-laced tea with Mrs. Grant (Giovanna Galletti of Kill Baby, Kill), the creepy landlady, Margaret goes to bed and has a nightmare of men in red cloaks coming after her. In the next scene, some men are talking obtusely about a clandestine cult. A writer who wants to publish an article on the cult is captured and tortured until he jumps out a window. The cult members stuff his body in a car and roll it off a cliff. It explodes before it reaches the bottom. That's probably my favorite movie cliché.

Margaret meets Jack (John Scanlon), the brother of the girl who died at the beginning of the movie. He gets all the cringe-inducing dialog while looking for his sister. Of course, Jack and Margaret hook up. After we get a good look at Daniela Giordano's body double, the couple resumes sleuthing. Next, Margaret gets abducted and taken to the torture clubhouse. The day-for-night filters are working overtime so I can't see shit and the music is all over the place. Is this someone's fucking mixtape? LeEtta gets out yesterday's fancy leftovers for our lunch.

One thing about this film: it's not boring! I am loving Girl in Room 2A. Blonde bombshell, Karin Schubert, is in this and she just got killed! Her bloody visage won't be leaving my memory anytime soon. Jack and his pals finally show up at the cult's hideout for some sped up fighting. This truly is a stupid gem and there's even a hilarious reveal at the end. I highly fucking recommend this (especially if you enjoy clunky crap)! The utterly random music queues, tepid dubbing, and freaky mannequins patch over the rough spots. Girl in Room 2A has a real Al Adamson vibe.

"You're gonna get the same treatment as the cockerel!"

12:37 PM
Do You Like Hitchcok? (2005)

Ah, it's nice to have some Argento in a Meltdown even though I've been putting this one off. I know for a fact that I liked this better than the fucking Card Player last time I watched it. The films starts with a kid playing in the woods. He spots some sexy witches casting some spells and sacrificing chickens (off camera, thank you very much). Now the witches are chasing him through the woods and the credits start. It's nice to see that good old consistent Argento starts a Hitchcock tribute with a sequence that has absolutely nothing to do with Hitchcock.

So that nerdy peckerwood kid has grown up into a nerdy peckerwood grad student. His name is Giulio (Elio Germano) and he is a big Hitchcock fan writing a thesis on something film related. He likes to spy on his neighbors through binoculars like Cary Grant did in North by Northwest. His hot girlfriend Arianna (Cristina Brondo) comes over and they screw. Then she leaves and he goes to the video store where he meets Andrea (Iván Morales), the video nerd. The score of this film is pretty damn good and I like the ultra-Italian vibe which is excellent despite the fact that everyone speaks perfect English with British accents.

The first murder, a brutal bludgeoning, is very bloody and over the top. No complaints here. Someone just wacked one of Giulio's neighbors, the mother of Sasha (Elisabetta Rocchetti), some chick that he's spying on. Giulio suspects that two people may be switching murders so that they'll each have an alibi, just like in Hitchcock's famous film, The Birds. Next there is a parody of the famous shower scene from Hitchcock's Rebecca.

I really like the lighting in this and it's shot quite well. Woops, I was just asleep. What the hell? How long have I been out? I remember LeEtta waking me up and saying, "Richard, you're missing the movie." I think I said something like: "It's all right, this just isn't very good." And then I went back to sleep. Maybe you can explain this to me. Why is 1970s dubbing better than dubbing nowadays? Am I totally crazy? I just find the old stuff hokey in a charming way and sometimes really well done whereas I think the dubbing in millennial films is just terrible. So I slept through all but the very ending of the film. Maybe I don't like this one as much as I remembered but I think Argento's heart was certainly in the right place.

GIALLO MELTDOWN

"Everyone needs someone to love."

2:28 PM
Slaughter Hotel (1971)

A killer, dressed all in black, is skulking around a castle and breathing like an asthmatic. He/she then goes through a basement full of torture devices, grabs an axe, and enters the room of a naked girl. The camera is really, really focusing on this chick's pubic region. The killer is about to strike when a buzzer goes off. This film should have been called Killer, Interrupted. The credit sequence is a green-tinted dream. Rosalba Neri is back in the moviethon again today! And Mr. Klaus Kinski is here too.

Fernando Di Leo directs this wildly sleazy flick about a mental institution full of sexy ladies being stalked by a deranged mad-person. Sexy nurse Helen (Monica Strebel) is chatting with Mara, a sexy patient, and they are so totally into each other. Meanwhile, a jackhole is driving his fancy sportscar along a scenic route to bring his batty wife Ruth (Gioia Desideri) to this loony house. She grabs the wheel, attempting to kill them both. He drops her off and gets the fuck out of there. The moment she is on the grounds, she attempts to murder one of the doctors. I love her.

While the patients are out playing croquet on the lawn, one of my favorite pieces of music from a giallo starts playing. Kinski plays Dr. Clay and you can tell that he doesn't give a double donkey shit about being in this movie. Margaret Lee of Liz & Helen is in this! While a chauffeur (Fernando Cerulli of Watch Me When I Kill) is feather-dusting a fancy car, Rosalba Neri makes her grand entrance in the film. She plays Anne, a freakin' nymphomaniac! Is this nuthouse hiring? She takes the doctor's advice and takes a shower. It's a freaky sequence with lots of water and wild overdriven reverb and distorted human voices.

Anne is visited by her brother(?) who she blames for not being able to quench the urges in her loins. Speaking of quenching urges, nurse Helen is giving a massage to a buck naked and bootylicious Mara and things get naughty. I thank LeEtta for being very understanding while I watch pervy shit and she says, "It's okay, I'm a perv too." J&B sighting! A nurse with a huge beehive gets scythed. It's a lame beheading but I'm happy. Anne tries to screw the gardener but he slaps her around so she tries to get it on with two orderlies. The killer is about to plunge a dagger into a sleeping Ruth but decides to leave the blade in her hand instead. She wakes up and immediately tries to kill the killer. He really should've seen that coming.

That same night, the chauffeur sneaks around the lounge finishing everyone's drinks. Classy move, bro. The killer rewards him by throwing him into an iron maiden. Mara is taking a bubble bath and I predict that she will not be alone for long. After the editor does a line of coke and flashes back and forth between shit we've already seen, nurse Helen shows up to assist in the bathing. This scene goes on forever.

Next, Anne is writhing in around in her bed for what feels like 10 minutes then her body double plays with herself very, very explicitly! LeEtta are I are both of the 'yikes' opinion and agree that we really didn't need to see that. The killer agrees and takes an axe to Anne. More gooch assault as nurse Helen touches herself. I fast forward so that we can get to she and Mara's wicked dance number. They get it on and the killer just can't resist shooting Mara in the neck with an arrow.

The boring cops show up and they are understandably angry at the whole clusterfuck (emphasis on the "fuck") this situation has become. I'm definitely warming to this film but I still can't stand the over-gooch. I'm so glad that my dang mother-in-law wasn't in the room for this one. We're talking about serious anatomical details on display here. I suppose that any giallo with Kinski and his beautiful golden hair is worth giving a second chance. And the ending is totally manic and an incredible sight to behold.

BREAK TIME

Shelly is on her way so I run to 7-11 to get some drinks. I get the 2 for $2 deal for both Arizona Southern Style Sweet Tea and Mountain Dew. My head feels a little strange. Maybe it's just a headache but I suspect it has more do with that enormous inheritance I just got a letter about. I sure hope there aren't any killers around tonight. When I return home, I consult with Brad via text about the playlist for the evening.

Shelly arrives and we head out to the patio for smoking. I fire up my Oliva Nub which is a perfect size for a short smoke. The hot weather has given up a bit and it's very windy, reminding me Argento's Phenomena. Shelly and LeEtta smoke cloves cigarettes while we talk about gialli and SCTV. Afterwards, I order Chinese food, and watch "The Soup". The Chinese food arrives. I've got chicken teriyaki, egg drop soup, egg rolls, and crab rangoon. I'm in old school Chinese food heaven, y'all.

"Her body was so young, so pure. Her skin was hot from the sun, from desire."

6:41 PM
The Sweet Body of Deborah (1968)

A beautiful beachside scene reveals Carroll Baker in a fur coat and the fabulously handsome Jean Sorel starts kissing on her. I can't remember if I liked this one or not the first time I saw it but I'm thinking this time, it'll be good. You can't go wrong when the Martino brothers are producing and

Ernesto Gastaldi is writing. Hey, this is the same director as The Double. Nice. So Baker plays Deborah (the one with the sweet body) and Sorel play Marcel. These two fools just got married and they are headed back to Marcel's home town of Geneva. He gets there and he sees his old buddy Philip (Luigi Pistilli again!) who tells him that Suzanne, his old girlfriend, committed suicide. Philip blames Marcel for her death and calls him a murderer.

In a flashback, we see that the very rich Suzanne (Ida Galli) leant Marcel some money to save his ass from some (not) scary Swiss gangsters. Then he dumped her with the intention of making something of himself, returning, paying her back, and then marrying her. But along the way he fell for Deborah (and her sweet body) and never returned. So she offed herself. Nice going, fucko.

One thing about Carroll Baker: when not dubbed, her speaking voice is pretty nasal and her delivery of dialog is very robotic. This provides LeEtta, Shelly, and I with much amusement. Oh yeah, LeEtta is mixing drinks with J&B and made something Shelly named called 'The Giallo Ginger' AKA 'The Ginger Finger' which includes J&B, Canton liqueur, lemon juice, and ginger beer. I take a taste but it's a little too grown up for me. I'll tell you what, I find Carroll Baker very attractive in this movie. Weird.

George Hilton, you sneaky fuck! I totally forgot you were in this movie. He plays Robert, a crazy painter who lives next door to their honeymoon villa. Now it seems like someone is trying to get to Marcel by making him relive his memories of Suzanne. No time for that! Let's have some bad disco dancing in the tackiest nightclub with a comic book/space theme on Earth. It looks like Stan Lee threw up in here!

The next morning, there's a shocking moment. Marcel and Deborah are playing Twister in the backyard but that's not the shocking part. Carroll Baker is wearing a friggin' green onesy like she's The Riddler. They are twisting and grooving to the record while playing the game and we all die a little. To bring me back to life, LeEtta makes me a 'J&B Loudmouth Punch'. It's got grenadine, lime juice, pineapple juice, orange juice, and J&B. I'm going to call it 'The Bouchet'.

Deborah starts popping pills and things are getting ugly. Philip shows up in the middle of the night with a switchblade and tries to kill Deborah (by stabbing her in her sweet body). Marcel wrestles the knife away and stabs him to death. They decide to cover up the incident and the film gets really dreamy and weird. Is someone trying to drive Deborah crazy?! This is a fun film, y'all.

RICHARD GLENN SCHMIDT

"Even an oak tree is softer than you!"

8:27 PM
Trhauma (1980)

This giallo from 1980 opens with boys running through the woods; one is a bossy jerk who makes the other, a one-eyed kid, climb a tree. The one-eyed kid falls out of the tree and the bossy jerkwad makes fun of him. Then the opening credits kick in some totally boss disco music. Flash forward years later and that kid with one blind eye (I call him One-Eye) is all grown up, living in a cellar, playing with Legos, and beheading cats (hilariously fake, thank goodness). This movie has a vibe to it all its own already.

Some young, beautiful people are hanging out by a pool when Olga shows up. Jeez! Where the hell have you been, Olga? Paul has been waiting for you for hours. This has some serious atmosphere already and it's barely even trying. Did I just hear a Theremin? Lovely Lilly is mad at her husband Andrea (Gaetano Russo) for squandering their money on the house she and their friends are staying in. It's a cool house. She needs to chill. There's a busty MILF in this movie named Silvia. She's got a good attitude.

Paul is shooting photos of Olga in a clearing near the woods. She strips down in the buff to some breathy disco garbage but Paul is a pushy dickweed about her poses. The fat guy (Franco Diogene of Strip Nude for Your Killer) just showed up, stripped down to his boxers, and jumped into the pool without saying a word to anyone. Oh fuck, the theme from Play Motel is on the radio in this movie! Now Olga is being chased through the woods and the music has gotten very dark and moody. We see some sheep running through a field. When they leave, One-Eye is having his way with Olga's corpse! A dog attacks him so he kills it. One-Eye is a dick.

After his sexcapades with Olga's body, we follow One-Eye back to his lair where someone brings him more Legos. These dopes finally notice that Olga is missing and go looking for her. Lilly looks just delicious in her nightgown. Why the hell is she married to Andrea? More people start dropping dead as the night goes on. This movie is great!

We're all thrown for a loop by the super abrupt ending. I immediately call Brad to see what the hell is up. I'm a little drunk at this point but I know that I'm also very confused. Brad assures me that I'm okay and that Trhauma just has one of those endings. But it's a scuzzy little film that feels more like a trashy slasher than a true giallo. That makes me happy anyway.

SUNDAY

Last night, we started The House that Screamed but I was dozing immediately. We decided to start it over today. I had crazy dreams all night and apparently, I slept through a slightly torrential rain storm. I did wake up with acid reflux from my Chinese food feast. Acid reflux is fucking horrible and it's not to be taken lightly. Go see a doctor if you ever experience it. I'm serious. I might be dead right now. I know what you're thinking: "Wow, how ironic. This guy is so dead right now." Or you're like: "Just stop eating garbage tacos and drinking soda with every meal, idiot."

I set the alarm so LeEtta and I can get up early and go to Mimi's for breakfast before it gets too crowded. I step outside and almost immediately start dancing. We got a cold front overnight! It's been really hot the last few weeks so this surprise cold front is just brilliant. I actually do an elaborate dance for LeEtta to show her how excited I am. We go to Mimi's and during breakfast, LeEtta mentions how she can't wait to see the end of The House that Screamed. I truly love this woman.

"Teresa! I'm asking if your mother is a prostitute!"

10:05 AM
The House That Screamed (1969)

The credits for this feature music by composer Waldo de los Ríos. It is creepy as balls and very classy. Teresa (Cristina Galbó) is getting dumped at a school for girls by 'a friend' of her mother. The place is kind of run like a prison by Mrs. Fourneau (Lilli Palmer), the headmistress. Right from the get-go, something just ain't right at this school.

This film is so eerie. The jailbait chick, Isabelle (Maribel Martín), goes looking for Luis (John Moulder-Brown), the headmistress's son, in the very scary greenhouse but meets a killer instead. Her death is one of the most stylish and beautiful murders I've ever seen in this genre. It's a bloody montage of stabbing and pretty music that winds down like a dying record player. Even more disturbing than that, the girls are showering and they're forced to wash themselves WITH THEIR CLOTHES ON!

Oh cool, Victor Israel, the lazy-eyed duder from a bunch of Spanish horror, is in this. Luis is salaciously sneaking around in a vent to spy on the girls while they shower (because fully-clothed showering is so hawt) but he gets locked in. Ha, the stupid perverted idiot is going to suffocate and die because he's a stupid idiotic pervert idiot. Luis manages to get out and then there's a scene when one of the girls goes out to bang the woodsman. While she is getting her fill, the rest of the girls are in sewing class, imagining what's going on. It's just a superb moment.

The House that Screamed is a fine film and a gothic giallo masterpiece. How about a Bluray? So the lead bitchy bitch Irene (Mary Maude) is teasing Teresa by telling her that her mother is nothing more than a whore. This causes Teresa to sneak out in the middle of the night. On her way out, she stops to say goodbye to Luis. In a sweet gesture, he smashes open his piggybank to give her some traveling money. Teresa kisses him and she's off to try and escape the school. The terrifying atmosphere settles over the film like a creeping fog and I wish I watched this more often.

Holy shit. I won't say what just happened but it is certainly a shifting of one's expectations for this film's direction. Seek this film out, dear reader. You will very likely love it as I do. The Shout! Factory DVD with Elvira, Mistress of the Dark is a good place to start.

"Don't worry, be happy. She's mine."

11:23 AM
The Washing Machine (1993)

I've been avoiding this one for a while so I'm kind of grimacing when I hit play. The opening music is pretty cool so I calm down a bit. The film opens on a man named Yuri (Yorgo Voyagis) and a woman having an argument. She has huge tits and her name is Vida (Katarzyna Figura). Duder made a big mistake when he gave her a bracelet with another woman's name on it. She starts to forgive him while she's drinking milk with her boobs hanging out. Next thing you know, he's humping her in the open refrigerator while her sister Maria (Ilaria Borrelli) watches and plays a triangle. Meanwhile, the cat is eating a plate of food that got knocked out of the fridge from the two of them screwing. I am not making this up.

Wow. Just wow. The opening 8 minutes of this film are kind of indescribably insane. It culminates in the one sister seeing the dismembered body of Yuri in their washing machine. Director Ruggero Deodato is a maniac. The cops show up and there is no corpse. It's pretty suspicious though because all three sisters are crazy. The police inspector, Alexander (Philippe Caroit), gets too wrapped up in this crazy case immediately. Okay, Vida's breasts are really, really distracting. This movie could be about dog racing and her boobs would make it tolerable.

Maria is sneaking around Yuri's place with her blind friend hiding in an armoire and the inspector nearly shoots her. Jeez, this is a quirky flick. Vida is kind of like a cartoon version of Melanie Griffith in Something Wild. LeEtta and Margie get back from the drugstore just in time to see her rape the inspector on the stairs. Now the third (alcoholic) sister Ludmilla (Barbara Ricci) is hanging around outside Alex's apartment banging cymbals together to get his attention. Then she throws a salad at his crotch and wipes it off with her panties while he's on the phone with his girlfriend. Man, I watch some weird shit.

Is this a parody of the erotic thriller genre? Is this Hungary? How could Deodato do this to me? This could become a favorite. So all three sisters are trying to seduce Alex and I have a feeling that they are either going to kill him, ruin his life, or something in between. He reveals to his girlfriend that a) he's slept with at least one of the sisters and b) he has a secret stash of bondage gear (huh?). Now each of the sisters are relating their very different stories of what actually happened to Yuri. You need to see this.

"The clock just struck 12 and I don't see my ghost anywhere."

1:08 PM
The Man with Icy Eyes (1971)

A senator is shot in front of his home and some dorky guy with long hair runs away. Did he kill the senator? What happened to the briefcase he stole from the dead man? What is happening here? Should I care? Antonio Sabato is riding a motorcycle to the incredible opening music. Margie says it reminds her of the opening theme of "Mannix". Sabato plays Eddie Mills, a newspaper grunt who wants to get into writing his own articles for the paper. He's investigating the very fishy case of the senator's murder.

And now a dwarf is making him breakfast in a field overlooking the highway. So this takes place in New Mexico? Barbara Bouchet just got naked for her official entrance in the movie (and this moviethon). Victor Buono plays Eddie's boss and he's a total dick. While snooping around for information on the case, Eddie meets a man named Isaac (Corrado Gaipa of Crazy Desires of a Murderer) who claims to be able to see his future. He says that Eddie is in danger and that he should just let the whole thing go. Does Eddie listen? Nope!

Bouchet plays a stripper named Anne Saxe who claims that she saw the real killer that night. She says the one who blew the senator away was a man with 'icy eyes'. But what's really interesting is that at a theater in this movie has a double feature of Elvis: That's the Way It Is and Speedway on the marquee. The guy accused of murdering the senator has been convicted for the crime and now it's up to Eddie to prove his innocence. Unfortunately the duder is on death row and will die in 24 hours. Holy crow! Prolific character actor Keenan Wynn is in this as the owner of the newspaper.

This Isaac guy keeps showing up and his predictions for Eddie's fate are getting more specific. Now he says that Eddie will die at midnight. Even though it barely counts as a giallo, this film is slowly winning me over. An air of misfortune hangs over the whole thing and it's even funny in parts. There is a layer of cheese but it's a very nice mozzarella. At that same theater the next day, the marquee reads Marlon Brando in Burn playing with Sabato. WHAT?! The conclusion of The Man with Icy Eyes is a white knuckle ride and I am in it all the way, my friends!

CIGAR TIME

I cannot resist the beautiful weather any longer so I head out to smoke a VegaFina cigar and wash it down with Arizona Southern Style iced tea. The wind is blowing every which way and the temperature is just waiting for the sun to go down so it can drop like a stone. You know what? This is what I love to do. I love moviethons. So if you ever meet me in person, just know that this is what I love to do. If you already know me and I'm at your house, please don't be mad at me. I'm not having a good time at your barbeque because I would rather be watching movies. How dare you keep me from gialli!

"Watch out, Robert. I'd be a difficult corpse.
I'm not the kind you can bury in a grotto."

4:13 PM
The Murder Clinic (1966)

And we're back with a gothic giallo that opens with a black-gloved and black-cloaked killer walking around a library brandishing a straight razor. At a creepy medical clinic run by Dr. Robert Vance (William Berger), there's some scary shit going on. The killer goes after one of the patients, a poor mute girl, who attempts to run for her life but to no avail. The bald groundskeeper witnesses the crime and gives chase. Of course, the killer gets away. The next morning, Mary (Barbara Wilson), the new nurse, is being shown around by Sheena: Queen of the Jungle. No wait, it's just Sheena, the mean old matron played by Harriet Medin of many great Italian gothic classics like The Whip and the Body and The Ghost.

There are several crazy patients in this clinic but the good doctor is protecting one named Laura, whom he keeps locked on the upper floor. They don't show her face but her hands are horribly burned. It turns out that there was some accident involving his sister-in-law, Laura. Their marriage is kind of rocky because Lizabeth (Mary Young) blames him for what happened. Could she be the one locked upstairs? Later, Mary really shows her nursing skills when she talks a psychotic patient named Fred (Massimo Righi of Blood and Black Lace) down from murdering Gisele (Francoise Prevost). Who is Gisele, you ask? Well, she's some tramp that the doctor can't get rid of. She witnessed the doctor burying the body of the mute girl in a grotto.

Gisele meets up with the mysterious patient on the third floor and has the pants scared off by her ruined face. I comment on how scary this scene must have been in 1966 and Margie says how fake the makeup looks. Thanks for stealing my thunder, thunder stealer! Just as soon as Gisele decides to blackmail Dr. Vance, she gets slashed to death. After her body is discovered, the doctor confesses to Mary that the woman upstairs is indeed Laura but claims that he had nothing to do with the accident that caused her disfigurement.

Damn, this film is gorgeous! It was filmed by Marcello Masciocchi who worked on films like The Sweet Body of Deborah and The Big Racket. We get more suspense and some great reveals. While Robert is being honest, he decides to proclaim his love for Mary. He does this right in front of Lizabeth and she doesn't take it very well. What happens next? Well, duders, you'll just have to get you own copy to find out. One thing though, there is definitely something about Mary. Heh heh heh. Get it? The closing theme sounds a bit like "Stairway to Heaven" for a moment or two.

"Silence! Behold the purifying flame which draws nigh, sinners. Prepare yourselves!"

5:45 PM
5 Dolls for an August Moon (1970)

This wild and wacky film is a classic case of Mario Bava taking a shit script and turning it into gold. With interchangeable characters and a convoluted plot, there's almost nothing to it at all. Professor Farrell (William Berger (twice in a row!)) has a secret formula and everyone wants to buy it. When he won't sell, people start turning up dead. A few twists and then it's over. Goodnight, everyone!

I should probably stop doing my fake-out endings. Does anyone like them? Did I mention that the succulent Edwige Fenech is in this one? LeEtta asks me if that means she's relatively hearty in dry climates. I say yes and I truly mean it this time. There are love triangles, some straight and some lesbian. Too bad no dude on dude action; am I right, fellas? The sexy soundtrack by Piero Umiliani melts in your mouth like ribald candy.

LeEtta (to Edwige Fenech): "Put your dress on, lady."

Me: "No! Don't you EVER tell her to do that!"

I love that jaunty music playing while they are stashing the murder victims' bodies in the freezer. George (Teodoro Corrà), you suave son of a bitch, your wife only has eyes for the raging lesbian affections of Trudy (Ira von Fürstenberg of The Fifth Cord), who also happens to be the professor's wife. Okay Mr. Bava, is it day or is it night? Seriously, the whole movie seems to take place in this perpetual twilight. Has it been days or has it been hours since the murders started?

If you like characters that like to buy formulas for industrial resins and who may or may not be willing to kill for them, you'll love this film. I know I do! Those day-for-night filters aim to please. Don't fuck with Trudy because she will super-karate your ass! Jack (Howard Ross of New York Ripper and Werewolf Woman) is frightening but his underwear frightens us even more. We're all very happy when he puts some dang pants on.

Strange and unexplained things happen, murders even, and none of the characters gets all that bent out of shape about it. Industrial espionage and microfilm; they go together like chocolate and peanut butter. The big reveal at the end is astoundingly stupid but hella fun. 5 Dolls may be slumber inducing but I like it.

"He's left a great void in all of us."

7:23 PM
La bambola di satana (1969)

A castle in the distance and body being dragged along the ground start this one off. Two pushy people are giving a delivery boy grief for being late with the groceries. Cut to a couple cruising in a convertible toward the family castle. Okay, now the credits started. Wut? The credit sequence is all jazzy smoothness with tinted stills from things that are going to happen in the film. We go to a bar where some kids are dancing Charlie Brown-style to the jukebox. I think that maybe Charlie Brown might be too energetic for this crowd. We're just amazed at what passes for dancing with this gang. This reminds me of Deadly Inheritance except not interesting.

There's been a lot of plot-dumping in the beginning of this film and I'm kind of lost. The subtitles are small and fly by really fucking fast. Let me see if I can catch you up on things. Sir Ball Janon(?) died and left the castle and its grounds to his niece Elizabeth (the lovely Erna Schurer). There are conflicting reports as to what her uncle wanted to do with the place. I suspect that Carol, Elizabeth's cousin (or aunt or whatever) is up to something. She's a secret hottie when she lets her hair down and has a lover whose face we aren't being shown. Mr. Shinton, the family lawyer, is quickly murdered by a black-gloved killer and made to look as though he decided to leave town before giving Elizabeth the "very important document". I'm leaving out a lot of details because I want to live.

We meet another character in this mess and it is Claudine, the artist/undercover agent who takes breaks from painting to snoop around the castle with a Geiger counter and radio back to base. I wish the movie was about her. One interesting revelation is Jeanette, Sir Ball Janon's former secretary, believed to be dead but who is now an insane mute living in the castle. At night, there is a wolf howling and it's the same looped howl that you've heard in 900 movies. That's brilliant.

Ha ha! It looks like someone sneezed when they were air-brushing the evening sky behind the castle there. WTF? To sum up the next 10 hours of this movie: bad day-for-night scenes, Elizabeth has gothic nightmares, Uranium under the castle, torture devices, heavy petting, vague masturbation, ghostly nonsense, hooded figures, etc. This movie does pick up in the last 25 minutes but I really dislike it. I should have turned it off after the opening credit sequence. It's no surprise that this director didn't do anything else. When La Bambola di Satana ends, I will happily go to bed.

CONCLUSION

At work the next morning, I feel hungover in body and spirit. I want to blame La Bambola di Satana for ruining my evening but it wasn't that bad. In fact, a second viewing will probably do the trick. As usual, I got in over my head in this moviethon and made some poor dietary choices. Too much smoke and too much drink that probably did more damage to me than the number of films I tried to get through.

But hey, any moviethon longer than 5 movies is a successful one in my book. I'd say 17 out of 21 ain't too shabby. Besides, all the unwatched titles from this will just get lumped in for Meltdown number 8. Wow, this is the most frequently I've ever had moviethons. Doing one a month makes me feel like one intensely brilliant/stupid asshole. Thanks for sticking with me this long. I'll see all of you next time.

GIALLO MELTDOWN 8:
RUSTY STRAIGHT RAZOR DANCE PARTY

I can actually see the end of this project off somewhere in the distance and I feel a little weird about it. Now that I've managed to get seven of these moviethons under my belt, I feel like an expert on certain things. For instance, I now know not to fuck around with my list of movies. There was entirely too much title juggling in the last two meltdowns. I have chosen the order that these films will play in and I am going to stick to it. Between the DVDs I bought, the files I have downloaded, and the bootlegs I have acquired, I have 22 titles picked for this eighth installment.

THURSDAY NIGHT

On the way home from work, it's very hot and bright outside. We are rerouted on McKinley due to a spectacular car fire. The cops are on the scene but I immediately suspect foul play. Once we get home, I call in an order of Chinese food for Margie, LeEtta, and myself. I get the usual: egg rolls, chicken teriyaki, and crab Rangoon (probably the least healthy thing that Chinese God ever created). I write up the schedule and start to prepare myself mentally. First some Sudoku, then Scrabble, then a quick game of checkers with LeEtta. Then I work on the physical exercises: sit-ups, lunges, push-ups, hard squats, butt squeezies, and finally triceps-boppies. My fortune cookie says: "Hardly anyone knows how much is gained by ignoring the future." Amen, duder.

> *"Love is one thing and the heart is another.*
> *And I've never been inside a Rolls Royce."*

6:30 PM
Death Will Have Your Eyes (1974)

Oh shit, the DVD from Mya Communications is kind of unwatchable. It looks like a 9 millionth generation VHS copy. A guy pulls a Rolls Royce up to a cliff, I think. He takes a moped out of the backseat, maybe. Then he dumps the car into the ocean, probably. I really can't see a darn thing. After this prologue and the credit sequence (with some snappy Stelvio Cipriani music), the picture quality improves greatly. Phew! I didn't want to have to abandon this title. Marisa Mell, Farley Granger, and Helga Liné are all in this flick. Color me excited.

Marisa Mell plays Luisa and she's looking a little beaten up. She has a cryptic convo with her gal pal, Yvonne (Liné), over the phone. When she hangs up, she cries alone in the house and then decides to kill herself by turning on the gas and letting it fill up the apartment. The film flashes back to her riding a bus somewhere. There's a wonderful and enriching scene of Luisa looking for a job. When things look bleak on the job front, she meets Yvonne who suggests that she should use men to get what she wants.

Suddenly it seems that Luisa already has a wealthy doctor duder in the works. His name is Armando (Granger) and he drives a Rolls Royce. Armando swoops in and takes Luisa into the good life. Wait a minute, Luciano Pigozzi is their cook? Lucky fuckers! Hmm, Armando seems wrong somehow. And wow, Marisa Mell gets very, very naked in this movie. Oh I get it, he's supposed to be impotent.

At a fancy party, Luisa is rocking a gray poodle wig that LeEtta says makes her look like Marilyn Temple or Shirley Monroe. Luisa brings Yvonne to come and hang out with the rich crowd. She tells Yvonne that her marriage ain't so great. Next, she's having an affair with a hot dude in a fringe leather jacket named Stefano (Riccardo Salvino of Your Vice is a Locked Room and Only I Have the Key), a colleague of Armando's. Luisa just had another wig change, Susan Scott-style.

A blackmailer (Francisco Rabal of Pensione Paura) breaks in and wants to rob Luisa blind. The cops show up looking for a drug dealer or something. She talks them into moving on without searching the house. This sleazebag intends to stay with Luisa all night so that she can take her jewels out of the bank for him in the morning. And he just tried to rape Luisa. I was secretly hoping the film would skip that part. The blackmailer just combed his hair with a fork! I dig the ending. Yeah, this is an okay film but I got super lost a couple times. It jumps around in time A LOT.

*"I think I'll stay with you for a bit,
you don't smell of poverty."*

8:25 PM
Giochi erotici di una famiglia per bene (1975)

Two dull looking mofos are talking about divorce or some shit. I think this is Italian but everyone is speaking Spanish in this version. Either way, it's incompetently translated. I really can't follow what they're talking about. When the guys face each other, it's daytime but the shots from the backseat are at night. It goes from day to night and then night to day and back again. Outside our apartment, a thunderstorm is raging. This is going to be bad.

The main character, Riccardo (Donald O'Brien) walks home after his buddy drops him off. He passes a hooker (Erika Blanc) along the way. She teases him in an emasculating fashion. It's funny because I already don't like this fucking guy. When he gets home, it's daytime. He catches his wife Elisa (Italian bombshell Malisa Longo) in bed with her lover and her enormous and beautiful boobs. Before Riccardo can put a bullet in her lover, a mysterious figure slips out a sliding glass door. And it's nighttime yet again (continuity, anyone?). Wow, telegraph the plot twist much?

Riccardo and Elisa have some serious ass marital problems. They argue and she begs him to kill her and set her free. Yay, there's more divorce debate in the dialog. Is this a fucking Hallmark Channel movie? It's a good thing these peckerheads don't have kids. After drugging his wife, he drives her out to the middle of nowhere, and pretends like they're going to make love. Then he calls her a whore and she dies. He puts her in a burlap sack while a mysterious bearded figure watches from afar.

All of this is happening in broad daylight by the way and it hits me: some stupid asshole at the lab didn't apply the day for night filters like he was supposed to. I feel really bad for the director now. So Riccardo throws his wife with big breasts off the side of a cliff and drives home. He hasn't been home for more than 45 seconds before Elisa start's haunting him. He's cracking up already? The next scene, we see Riccardo drinking with Eva, the whore from earlier. Talk about your quick stages of grieving.

Eva owns a copy of In the Court of the Crimson King. That is one pretty amazing hooker. She brings Riccardo back to her place and dances for him in her Daisy Dukes. They make love and some chick is watching them and touching herself. Oh I get it, she's not actually in this scene at all and the editor just added her in just to spice things up. The camera is zooming in and out, Jess Franco style. Oh crap, Renato Polselli (the director of Delirium) wrote the screenplay? I'm so screwed.

Riccardo's niece Barbara shows up and he starts flirting with her. Boy, she is a little minx. It's like she doesn't want to make out with her uncle or something. Or wait, maybe she does want to. Now they are in love? Forget the camerawork, did Jess Franco freakin' direct this? He brings Barbara to the spot where he dumped Elisa's body and that bearded person is watching again. Shit, this is only the halfway mark of the dang movie!

FRIDAY

LeEtta leaves for work at the usual time while my genius ass stays in bed another hour and 45 minutes. When I get up, I get dressed, grab my mp3 player, and head out for a walk. It's not much, maybe just a half hour jaunt a few blocks down Armenia and then back. It is hot this morning but I stick to the shady side of the street with my giallo soundtrack making things very mellow indeed. I'm trying not to think about Giochi Erotici di Blah Blah. What a mess! At 7-11, the air conditioning blast is very welcoming. On my way back home, I kind of strut to the theme from Killer Nun with a Slurpee for Margie and a sausage, egg, and cheese on an English muffin for me.

> *"Send me half a pound of butter, detergent,*
> *a bottle of gin, and some salt."*

9:17 AM
The Glass Ceiling (1971)

I know absolutely nothing about this film other than Brad digs it. The camera pans around a quiet courtyard in the morning and there are figures moving in a window. This is building tension nicely. A wife named Marta (Carmen Sevilla) is helping her husband Charles pack for a business trip. She infers that she cheats on them with their cat and he suggests that she sleep with Richard the landlord so he might forget to collect the rent. Rosa (Emma Cohen), the hot milk delivery girl, shows up to deliver some milk. Richard (Dean Selmier) is a sweaty and manly sculptor. I bask in his musk and the sexual tension between him and young Rosa.

Marta offers the creepy grocery delivery guy a glass of wine. This is a tactical error. He makes a lascivious advance and she tells him to get the hell out. That night while watching TV with the cat, we find out that Marta can hear her neighbors milling about and she knows what everyone is doing just by the sound of their footsteps. The next morning, her neighbor Julie (Patty Shepard) stops by because her fridge is on the fritz. Julia's sick husband seems to have disappeared and Marta suspects that she's lying about something. Man, I love the dubbing in films from this era.

My favorite actor in this film is Phaedra the cat. This cat really nails her performance. Richard visits Rosa at the farm so she squirts him in the face with milk from a cow teat. He says he should spank her for being naughty and there's a split second fantasy sequence where Richard spanks her sweet ass right there in the cow pen. Um, wow. The sexual tension is boiling over like in a trashy romance novel.

Marta's annoying friend Rita shows up and she confides in her that she suspects that Julie may have killed her husband. Rita's ugly kid (who looks like a young me in a dress) spills the beans in an awkward moment when Julia stops by. So now if Julia has killed him, she knows they know. Nice going, you stupid fucking brat. Everyone in the apartment keeps smelling something dead and rotting nearby. Rosa comes to Richard's studio so that he can sculpt her bust. I know where this is going! He just sprayed her in the face with Lysol. Okay, maybe I don't know where this is going.

That night, Marta, in her very unflattering nightgown, goes outside with a flashlight to investigate the rotting smell. This movie is turning about to be pretty dang amazing. The following day, Marta walks up to the roof to hang up her laundry and catches Julia sunbathing in the nude. I get an unintentional laugh as Marta masturbates obtusely. The camera dances around while she rolls around in bed, clutching her breasts and sweating.

Martta goes out to the country with Richard. Don't worry, she's not cheating on her husband. She's just going horseback riding with the guy! After chatter about photography and cinema and how it's all a lie, he puts the moves on Martha. There's more paranoia as Julia seems even more suspicious and danger is lurking very close. We're treated to a wild dream sequence and some horrible images that might just be premonitions of bloody and violent things yet to come. You should seek out this film.

"For a while there, I went on a safe sex binge.
It was kind of stupid."

11:25 AM
Body Puzzle (1992)

Latter day Lambava (that's what Brad and I call Lamberto Bava) is just what the doctor ordered. Some very 90s looking duder is playing piano in his garage but then he has a flashback to when he witnessed the motorcycle crash that killed someone he cared about. This explains why he goes to a candy shop and kills the proprietor. The killer then spies on a chick named Tracy (Joanna Pacula) in her fancy house (with an indoor pool!). He sneaks into her house and leaves her a present in the fridge. Her St. Bernard named Bo tries to warn her but no one listens to dogs in horror movies.

Tracy doesn't notice the following morning that her orange juice has blood in it. When she goes to visit her husband's grave, the cemetery owner informs her that her husband's body has been stolen. When she finally finds the severed ear in her dang fridge, she freaks and calls the police. Detective Mike Levitt (Tomas Arana) encourages Tracy to leave the city and go out to her parents' mansion. I'm so glad that Raro Video put this out. The budget version of this film is significantly shorter. Oh wow! The Sambuca-drinking police chief is played by Gianni Garko (of Cold Eyes of Fear).

The killer just cut off some lady's hand in a restroom stall. I hope it wasn't her wiping hand. Giovanni Lombarde Radice is in this as some kind of flamboyant horseman. A photo reveals that the killer was Tracy's dead husband's lover. In a very ridiculous scene, the killer leaves an empty motorcycle jumpsuit and helmet on Tracy's bed. A cop finds a bloody suitcase in the fridge but before he can open it, the killer runs in with panty hose over his head, grabs the case, and splits. What the damn heck was that about?

Erika Blanc plays a psychiatrist in this and she looks great! Through incredible psychological profiling, she tells Levitt that the killer 'went crazy'. The killer executes a perfect dive and then kills a lifeguard. He puts the dude's cock in an envelope and drops it in Tracy's mail slot. Ha ha! In that time-honored movie cliché, the morgue doctor (named Mort) gets done with his autopsy of the lifeguard and then immediately digs into a sandwich. I wonder if screenwriters even know why they do this anymore.

Mike and Tracy get it on to some sweet sexophone music. I just spotted Bruno Corazzari of Seven Bloodstained Orchids. This is an all-star cast! Whoa, what the truck? Mort's freezer contains bags of body parts suspended from the ceiling in little baggies on chains. The real showstopper in this film is a death scene that takes place in a classroom full of blind children. Now is that sped up car chase supposed to be metaphor or is it just boring screenwriting? The final freeze frame doesn't make a lick of sense. Thanks to some surprising atmosphere and lots of ridiculousness, I enjoy this 1992 giallo quite a bit.

"It's just a boring old story of an inheritance; please don't worry about it."

1:26 PM
Fashion Crimes (1989)

After munching on my leftover Chinese food, I pour myself some Pepsi and put on Fashion Crimes. With this opening song, "Why don't you save the night for me?", I'm thinking this movie should be called Music Crimes. Fashion models stalked by a killer? I've never seen that before. My copy of this film has Japanese subtitles. That means that this film is Japanese, right? Fashion model Gloria gets off work and gets stranded in the middle of nowhere. She sees something horrible in an old house, screams, and then nearly gets run over by a truck. In the hospital, she starts to remember what she saw: a woman being struck repeatedly by a man and blood everywhere.

Commissioner Rizzo (Anthony Franciosa of Tenebre) is on the case. He's an avid fisherman (chasing a big pike he's nicknamed The General) and not really interested in his job. I'm glad Rizzo is here because the lead detective on the case is a mustachioed dullard that makes me depressed when I look at his dumb face. The cops find Gloria's car and the villa but no evidence of a murder. They think she's a looney but the real weirdo is her doctor, a bleach blonde creature that looks like Brigitte Lahaie (if she lived next door to a nuclear power plant). This film breaks tradition by having the color wear white gloves.

Gloria starts going to a Gianmarco (Miles O'Keeffe), a hypnotherapist who happens to be dating the weirdo doctor lady. He helps her to remember more details about that fateful night. She sees a woman and a man having an argument while some opera is blasting throughout the house. The man goes crazy and beats the woman to death with a club of some kind. Gloria recovers and goes back to fashion modeling. It isn't long before her model friend gets offed in her place.

I'm no opera expert but this piece of music she keeps hearing from that night sounds an awful lot like the piece that drove the killer in The Dead are Alive. Gloria goes back to the villa with Gianmarco to help her get over this shit. There are some cheesy revelations about inheritances and crimes committed in the past by the people who may or may not have known the original owners of the villa. Ugh, I'm getting sleepy.

This film does feel like a throwback to the 1970s gialli but it's so cheap. If this had been made in 1973, I probably wouldn't give the budget a second thought. The mixing of dubbed actors and live sound really annoys the piss out of me. The dubbing actors are pretty decent but the English speaking cast is so bad. I'm talking to you, Mumbles O'Keeffe. I'm just getting nitpicky. The part of the film that feels like the finale that isn't actually the finale is packed with some garish style so I already feel silly for being so judgmental. Hey, Fashion Crimes. Do you forgive me?

> *"Come on, boy. What did you say your name was? Super Dog?"*

3:48 PM
Death Knocks Twice (1969)

After a nap, I reach into the bootleg pile and pull out this little number from Cinema de Bizarre. Yarr, there be Greek subtitles ahead. A couple is frolicking on the beach at night while some lardass (spaghetti western regular, Mario Brega) in sweat pants watches them. Now they are making love and there's some other duder with a mustache and wearing a smoking jacket watching them too. The girl looks uneasy and I can't say I blame her. As they're lovemaking gets more and more violent, I realize the guy she's with is Fabio Testi. Woops, she's dead and there are two witnesses. The opening song just kicked on and my heart skips a beat.

At the Estrella beach resort, the sleazy guests are drunk and partying, totally unaware that a woman has been killed. Francisco (Testi) runs around in his underwear a lot, showing off his insanely tight body. I'm not gay but Fabio Testi is gonna turn me. His wife (Nadja Tiller) is a dumbass. She notices the scratches from the rough sex on his back and he tells her absolutely nothing as an excuse. And she accepts it! Yup, that's how married people act. An ascot-wearing detective named Bob Martin (Dean Reed) is called in to solve the case. He tells his fiancé Ellen (Ini Assmann (uh, real name?)) that their wedding will be postponed for this case so she does a judo throw on him. That's more like a real relationship.

Francisco isn't just a murderer, he also seems to be crazy. Werner Peters (the gay antiques dealer in The Bird with the Crystal Plumage) is in this as Charly, a wheeler dealer type that's in trouble with a gangster named The Professor (Adolfo Celi). Peters and his mustachioed friend (who witnessed the murder) want Francisco to kill The Professor's wife Sophia (Anita Ekberg) and frame The Professor for it. Have I mentioned Fritz the dog yet? No? Well, he's a pretty amazing German Shepherd.

I text Brad to let him know what I'm watching and he says that this film has a very convoluted plot. Frankly, he's right on the money. There's all kinds of action, intrigue, psychobabble, and murder going on in this extremely entertaining movie. Detective Bob suspects that Francisco has something to do with the murder so he sends Ellen out to get close to the raving lunatic. Great plan! But no worries, Ellen knows judo after all and can kick the guy's ass. This gives Anita Ekberg the chance to swoop in and get herself some Testi.

In my favorite moment in the whole film, Anita Ekberg brushes her hair provocatively and then throws her hairbrush across the room like a rockstar before making out with Francisco. Meanwhile, Bob has to do some sick ass driving to get away from The Professor. He jumps out of the car and rolls down a cliff but gets knocked unconscious for his efforts. Lucky for him, Fritz the dog comes to the rescue. Did I mention the stolen priceless diamond necklace? No? Well, don't worry about it.

"You must collaborate with me!"

5:39 PM
The Skin Under the Claws (1975)

LeEtta has come home from work and is making mung bean dal on rice with squash. I put on this film I downloaded that looks like a 900th generation copy. Let's hope there are lots of daytime scenes. There's a figure dressed in black in a cemetery digging up a corpse (or burying one, it's hard to see). The opening music is very nifty. Now a doctor is explaining to some other doctors how a rotting body works. Some cheap whores (only $10 a fuck) are standing by a hooker bonfire. A mysterious figure picks one of them up and cuts her up exposing her hooker guts!

This is going to be a sleazy one, I think. Some artists are sitting around talking and there are ornamental naked women that no one is paying attention to. The body of the hooker is found and there are traces of corpse on her, as in advanced decomposition corpse. Another woman turns up dead, hacked up in suitcases. There is some nice pseudoscience from some doctors about transplanting baboon brains. We get a low impact striptease and the cops think that a sex maniac is committing the crimes. The inspector (Ettore Ribotta) hates his job and actually spends some screen time complaining about being a cop. Nice!

While all of this is going on, we meet two doctors, Gianni and Silvia, who are having an affair. When their colleague Dr. Helmut (Gordon Mitchell) has a heart attack, they decide to steal his body because they want to attempt to transplant his brain into a living body. Well actually Silvia is just kind of going along with the plan and is freaking out. I can't believe this is turning into a Frankenstein giallo. They also start stealing body parts from people. Oh shit, the reels are out of order. Characters giving statements on their dead friend are suddenly wondering where their friend is. Also, Gianni and Silvia are just happy go lucky doctors in love again and not discussing reanimating their dead colleague. Holy shat.

This movie is odd even without the mixed up reels. A body of a woman is discovered and she has been dead for months but her eyes are from a corpse only hours old. Sounds kind of fishy to me. Now Silvia has gone missing. And there are three very sexy ladies wrasslin' resulting in panty shots aplenty. Then a mysterious figure shows up and tries to assault one of the girls. Now Sylvia is chained up in a dungeon. This is fucking insane.

"You read the postcard- I'm a killer!"

7:15 PM
Snapshot of a Crime (1975)

This one starts off with bold fuzz guitar and prog rock vocal stylings. At a lake, a sexy couple is speed-boating around and kissing dispassionately. They are Mirna (Erna Schurer) and Luca (Luis La Torre) and they're kind of strange. Or wait, she just broke up with a guy who looks just like Luca. Dang it, I shouldn't be this confused already. Okay, Luca is her ex-boyfriend and she's an expert shot and a pretty good rider of horses. This soundtrack is balls out rockin'. So Luca is kind of stalking Mirna now.

Luca decides to pick up some chicks to take his mind off Mirna for a while. This gives him more opportunities to run around in his Speedo. The girls think he's strange so they ditch him. Now he's kind of following them around. I think this guy might be a little dangerous. Then they are hanging out with him again. Chicks, man. But he's still obsessed with Mirna or something. Wait, something is wrong here. This is the eighth movie in this moviethon and not a single J&B sighting yet.

Twenty-five minutes of this movie have passed and I have to ask: what the fuck does anything we've seen have to do with anything? Luca starts to get it on with the one chick. It's making one of the girls, Claudia (Monica

Strebel of Slaughter Hotel), a little jealous. None of it matters because their pal Stefania has disappeared. I'm glad. Something needed to happen in this dang movie. It looks very bad for Luca. He got a little rough with Stefania on the beach while the camera was taking photo after photo. Now he's just turning into an even more dickish and paranoid version of himself.

This sun-bleached movie is getting more and more intense but to what aim, I don't know. Luca claims that he just choked her out until she fainted. When he went to look for help, she disappeared, along with the camera. All he could find of Stefania was a pool of blood on the beach. Claudia goes to the beach and finds the blood spot. So she believes Luca and admits that she loves him. I don't know why but I'm starting to dig this film.

"Idiots! A nation of idiots!"

8:39 PM
Closed Circuit (1978)

A group of people anxiously await the opening of the doors to the cinema. There's a spaghetti western playing. Sign me up! They gather in the darkened theater where some very strange Italian commercials are playing. Now the main feature has started and it looks like the most generic spaghetti western ever but I kind of want to watch it. There are some cool posters in the lobby of the theater. I just spotted one for Deep Red. Brad is very proud when I confirm that this is indeed a film he sent me.

While the tension is building in the film before a showdown, the tension in the theater is building. And then BAM! A guy gets shot in the theater. That was awesome. Now all these sleazy and suspicious characters are being held there for questioning. The inspector shows up and starts his investigation. He's got a nice stache, that's for sure. He looks like the unholy spawn of Robert De Niro and Richard Dreyfuss. FINALLY, I spot a bottle of J&B in the concession stand.

This film is from 1978 and is pretty damn cool. I've never seen Italian cinema culture portrayed this thoroughly before. I had no idea that someone gets murdered during every spaghetti western. What a country! After keeping these people locked up for hours, the inspector stages a reenactment and another person sitting in the same exact seat as the first guy is shot too. Chaos ensues. The cops know that the murderer is inside the theater so no one is allowed to leave. Everyone just starts to lose it.

When the truth comes out, you won't believe your eyes and your mind will be blown on multiple levels. Seriously. I won't spoil a thing. This is some thought provoking and very smart cinema. Note to self: Don't forget to mention the Dario Argento-looking duder in the cast.

SATURDAY

LeEtta and I sleep in for a change. We get up, go to the post office, the liquor store (J&B and a cigar for me, a bottle of Burgundy for LeEtta), and then we try a new place for breakfast: Brunchies. I guess Brunchies is pretty popular because it full and loud. I get a breakfast chicken quesadilla and Mello Yello to drink. LeEtta gets coffee, orange juice, grits, eggs, English muffin, and sausage. When her enormously full plate comes, her eyes get wide. Lucky for her, I'm in a sharing mood and take most of the sausage. Back home, Margie has started the chores so LeEtta and I finish them up.

"Watch out! She knows how to drive!"

11:37 AM
Too Beautiful to Die (1988)

The credit sequence for this is a giant pair of red lips and some terrible sexophone pop that segues into a Victoria's Secret style fashion shoot. Alex (Giovanni Tamberi) is a sleazebag agent who gives a model named Sylvia (Gioia Scola) to his old scumbag boss. Next, he plays a very rudimentary porno game called "Porno Game" on his computer. Now the models are bathing together and I can't tell if this is music video or what's actually happening in the movie. Sylvia gets raped in a hot tub by the old scumbag while her model friends hold her down. Thanks for nothing, bitches. Afterward, she fires Alex, steals his car, and takes off into the night.

Alex's pal David (François-Eric Gendron) is directing a music video called "Blades" (that looks like a cross between Red Sonja and Beyond Thunderdome). He had the prop department make very real custom murder weapons for the shoot. David is disappointed that Sylvia isn't there. A detective shows up to let Alex know that his car was totaled in an explosion. There was a body inside and everyone assumes that it's Sylvia. Alex visits David at his sleek industrial apartment to ask him what happened. I think this is how James Cameron lives.

Now that Sylvia is gone, David is bummed because he has lost his muse. Oh wait nevermind, he just found his new obsession dancing on the bar of a crap nightclub. Her name is Melanie Roberts (Florence Guérin). She's from New York and she's perfect! Leslie (one of Sylvia's frenemies) invites Melanie to come and live with her. She can use Sylvia's old room! Oh doctor, even the sequence where Melanie makes the bed is filmed like a dang music video. Meanwhile, the cops use a computer programmed skull reconstruction and discover a .22 caliber hole in Sylvia's temple.

There's a speedboat modeling shoot with Huey Lewis and the News blaring over it. Man, Huey Lewis is fucking ear poison nowadays. The inspector (François Marthouret) is really coming down on Alex and the girls about what happened to Sylvia after she left the party. There is a terrible 'accident' at the music video shoot the next day when Leslie gets stabbed in the throat with a spike in an iron maiden. Melanie and David have sex to one of the most hideous power ballads of all time. The old scumbag who raped Sylvia gets killed but it's off camera (lame).

Wow, the cinematographer on this film is one talented SOB. This film looks friggin' vibrant and is almost unbearably stylish. There are a couple of fantastic stalking scenes in this. I love it. Why is this film such an obscurity? Sure, it's corny as fuck but it's pretty decent. Speaking of corny, this movie ends on Toto's "I Won't Hold You Back" which is some kind of transcendent moment in my life or whatever. Come for the murders, stay for the cute kitten.

CIGAR BREAK

I grab my delicious Oliva cigar, a huge mug of Mountain Dew on ice, and my mp3 player for an afternoon smoke. It's hot as heck out on the patio but the occasional breeze and very kind clouds offer some relief from the Memorial Day weekend weather. I put an ailing wasp out of its misery to the score for The Black Belly of the Tarantula. The less said about this incident, the better. Once my cigar is a happy memory, I water the plants and switch out the laundry from the washer to the dryer. See, I'm a good husband. Back to the fucking movies.

> *"The only pleasure for a fat man is to always be surrounded by beauty."*

2:52 PM
Tropic of Cancer (1972)

If I see one more gialli set in Haiti, I'm gonna scream. I'll probably never scream. Anita Strindberg graces us with her presence yet again. She plays Grace and her husband, Fred (Gabriele Tinti), is a dick. They're traveling to Haiti for some reason. Grace is in Haiti for two seconds before she starts making sexy eyes at a strapping young Haitian lad. Lucky bastard! They meet up with Dr. Williams (Anthony Steffen!), an old friend of Fred's. Williams' colleague just died under very suspicious circumstances.

There's a freaky obese guy hanging out naked at the hotel pool. It's disturbing but don't worry, Umberto Raho plays the owner of the hotel. For you sensitive types (like me) out there, be warned: this film contains cockfighting. And I don't mean the full frontal ding dongs at the pool. This movie has those too!

Fred and Grace get into a little fender bender and Fred (who is a terrible racist) starts yelling at the driver and making a huge scene. I was hoping he'd get a machete to the face but Dr. Williams comes to their rescue. A little girl (or shrunken old woman) cryptically tells Anita that Williams is a voodoo witch doctor. That night at dinner with Fred and Grace, the doctor rambles about voodoo and it all sounds like bullshit from men's pulp magazines. Ugh, this fat guy is so obnoxious. His name is Peacock and somebody needs to cut off his supply of sweet breads.

Williams gets a phone call and discovers yet another corpse in the hotel but doesn't tell anyone about it. Next, they all go to a voodoo ritual featuring topless women and a bull gets sacrificed (for real). The topless ladies start fighting over the bull's severed penis. This is just good cinema. Back at the house, Williams gets roughed up by some thug who works for a sleazy dude. They want some secret formula (eye roll) that Williams developed. Oh goodie, slaughterhouse footage! So that's where hamburgers come from. The guy who beat up Dr. Williams is found hung upside down among the dead cows.

Strindberg is only in this movie to be the damsel in distress. Other than fantasizing about and lusting after Jean-Pierre (that hunky Haitian), her character just gets freaked out a lot. Williams has to rescue Grace from the scary marketplace in this 'oh so scary' country. Damn, this movie is racist as hell. The only meat to Grace's character comes when she gets drugged and we see her blurry and weird nightmare sequence. The psychology behind all of this is she's scared of black people and she wants to screw Jean-Pierre.

In the best stalking scene in the movie, somebody goes after that fat fuck Peacock with a spear gun. They should have brought a harpoon. Wait a second, did Grace just screw Dr. Williams after he rescued her from her hallucinogenic adventure? Um, that's dumb as shit. Despite all the odious problems with this movie, I still like it. It's extremely exploitative, sweaty, and trashy. This feels like one of Umberto Lenzi's classic era gialli, only less politically correct (if that's possible).

"And tell me, Phillip. Do you like cherries?"

4:39 PM
The Student Connection (1974)

An assassin blows up a plane and this Spanish-Italian co-production is off and running. Ray Milland plays Dr. Mann, the doctor at a boys' school. He paid the assassin to kill a specific person but not to blow up a dang plane! He bludgeons the bald bastard with a statuette but one of the boys witnesses his crime. Because the kid lost his shoes when he chased him, Mann suspects that he knows who the little boy is but he decides to bide his time and bury the body in the greenhouse. I don't think this guy should be allowed to work with children.

Mann takes a little boy named John to the funeral of his father where we meet his mother, Sonja (Sylva Koscina (Va va va voom!)). Back at the school, Mann is hooking each boy up to a blood pressure machine individually and paying special attention to the ones who have the shoe size of the boy he's looking for. This is a very inane and ludicrous way to discover the identity of the kid. Meanwhile, the cops are searching for the assassin who blew up the plane.

It turns out that Mann and Sonja are lovers and hired the bald duder to kill her husband. I think Sonja is playing this guy for a fool. He's old enough to be her father and their chemistry is nonexistent. Mann is torn up about the 140 people on the plane that blew up but she doesn't give a fuck. She just wants him to kill the little boy who witnessed the murder. Mann says that he can't kill a child. The kid who he suspects has a heart condition and will probably drop dead anyway. Lucky! Oh shit, Milland is really bad in this movie. He's acting like this is his first talkie.

Ha ha, he had the wrong kid. Now he's using a word association game with the kids to see if one of the boys will reveal that he witnessed the killing. Fuck, I am not into this at all. Can't there be some fashion models in peril or something? Now he thinks that Sonja's kid John is the one and she warns Mann not to harm the tyke. Okay, I guess I'm into this. It's definitely suspenseful but the whole 'kid in peril' thing is not handled well. There's a chase scene in the film that goes on for 1,834,546 minutes.

"I didn't mean to interfere with your penetrating experience."

6:12 PM
Shadows in an Empty Room (1976)

Ah yes, it's Dirty Harry giallo-style! This crime flick/giallo hybrid was filmed in Ottowa and directed by the great Alberto de Martino. Stuart Whitman plays badass police captain Tony Saitta. His sister Louise (Carole Laure) is having an affair with Dr. Tracer (Martin Landau) and she plays a practical joke on him, humiliating him in front of her friends. The joke is on her when she drops dead at the same party. The doc looks very guilty. Actually, every single character in this movie looks guilty too. Armando Trovajoli's score for this film is a tad aggressive. Okay, not a tad.

Tisa Farrow plays Julie, a blind girl and friend of Louise. Her performance is very Tisa Farrow-esque. She delivers the same inflection on every word that comes out of her mouth. I love her. So Dirty Tony is throwing his Magnum .44-toting weight around to solve his sister's murder.

John Saxon is here as Sargent Ned Matthews, the guy who is supposed to keep Tony in line. Some woman just got her head bashed in with a lead pipe and then her body thrown into a rock crusher thingie. Yum, lady chunks! Next, somebody tries to trick Blind Julie into accidentally walking out of an open window four stories up. Things get complicated when Dr. Tracer calls in his lawyer to handle the Captain Tony's allegations.

For some reason, Tony goes to question some drag queens and all hell breaks loose. They have a major brawl in a fancy apartment. Glass is broken, a straight razor is brandished menacingly, and a very hot hair curler is shoved up a dude's ass (implied). Oh I get it, the lady who got her head bashed in was a transvestite and was connected somehow to all of this. Shit, I don't care; I just love seeing those trannies beating up on Dirty Tony. A fancy and ugly necklace is the key to all of this but this is so entertaining that the details don't matter. And now they're interrogating a bald midget at a football game. What the heck?

There's a chase on foot and then a very impressive car chase. It turns out that Louise wasn't so innocent after all. Their entire case against Dr. Tracer falls apart so Matthews and Dirty Tony have to start all over again. The campus slut gets murdered in front of Blind Julie and then the killer hangs himself in order to avoid capture. Dirty Tony figures the suicide was bullshit. Now they are trying to catch the killer at the hospital where Julie is recovering from shock. I really dig this film, man. It's a good time flick.

"It's a sexual revolution. Don't you know that girls burn their bras these days?"

8:04 PM
Reflections in Black (1975)

After an amazing opening piece of music and terrible opening credits (the VHS company probably made them to avoid legal complications), this film goes right into the brutal slashing committed by a black gloved killer with a straight razor. John Richardson plays Inspector Lavina. He and his partner, Panto (Tano Cimarosa (who also directed this!), are on the case. Another woman is killed while her boyfriend is changing a flat tire. All the witnesses know is that the killer was wearing some sexy black lace. All I know is that this is one trashy flick.

One victim was a secretary that worked for Anselmo (Giacomo Rossi-Stuart) and his wife, Leonora (the always mesmerizing Dagmar Lassander). J&B sighting! (I pause the movie and take a big old shot of the stuff for myself.) Leonora leans a little to the not straight side. She is lying around and looking dejected when her hot maid comes in and offers her some lovin'. No, Leonora would rather look at photos and then daydream of some other girl she boffed. A chick who knows the victims calls to talk to the cops but they ignore it. She gets strangled in her apartment with one of her own stockings. In that all too familiar giallo trope, it takes two seconds to strangle her to death. Those Italian ladies and their weak ass necks.

A drug-dealing hairdresser named Sandro (Ninetto Davoli) is the key to all of these murders. The cops pick him up for questioning. During this scene, I feel the energy draining right out of me thanks to this soul-sucking character. Sandro's perm shimmies while he talks and I really wish one of the cops would beat him to death with a nightstick or a curling iron. His info leads them to Contessa Orselmo (Magda Konopka), who takes pictures of naked ladies and then makes out with them. While the cops are there, someone wearing black gloves grabs one of her models. It's the Contessa's son Marco, a batshit psycho junkie with a penchant for waving straight razors at helpless lesbians.

I can't keep these friggin' character names straight. Someone named Mario owns the hair salon. Why do I care? Now this chick who doesn't wear a bra is playing amateur detective. The sexy maid who offered her body to Leonora just got killed. Unfair! I kind of like this movie but there isn't much to recommend it. I sure wish there was a better copy out there somewhere. That could improve my opinion a little.

"So come now, this atmosphere surpasses us."

9:29 PM
An Open Tomb, An Empty Coffin (1972)

This little Spanish number starts off in a more than moderately morbid cemetery at a funeral with some gothic looking types standing around, moping. Loosen up, people, it's just a cemetery. OMG, I love this friggin' soundtrack. I had it for years before I ever got the film. The credit sequence shows a young couple in love, walking on the beach and then in a park. Oliver (José Antonio Amor) and Ruth (Daniela Giordano) are going to get married. He's bringing her back to his family home. Big mistake. Huge mistake. Really bad mistake. His whole family are a bunch of Bromfields. I think that's also their name too.

Oliver's stepmom Sara (Nuria Torray) is really creepy and beautiful; she looks like someone who'd be wielding a whip in a Jess Franco flick. Apparently, he brought Ruth home on the anniversary of his first wife Helen's death. Nice going, shit for brains. The one person who seems the most upset about dead Helen is Jenny (the beautiful Teresa Gimpera), Oliver's sister. Sara is totally in love with her stepson and can't believe he'd marry someone like Ruth. Only she understands "his weaknesses". This house is just crawling with tension and incestuousness.

Jenny likes to pin live moths and butterflies in her collection. Fucking moth-abusing bitch. Now I know where mothburgers come from. There's lots of cool and creepy lighting in the old house and angsty chicks smoking. The cuckoo clock on the wall contains a secret peephole for Sara to spy on Oliver while he makes love to his young bride. In a flashback, it's revealed that Helen (Gioia Desideri) was a manipulative beyatch who married Oliver and drove him to drink. Then she seduced his sister who is still hung up on her. In a blind rage, Oliver hit Helen and she fell over the railing of the second floor to her death.

The Bromfields' hot maid has the cutest little pussy cat. Someone tries to poison Ruth by spiking her milk with something. She spills the milk (but doesn't cry over it) and then the kitty drinks it and dies. Anyway, she gets Oliver and they find the kitty quite alive. LeEtta notices a funny continuity error: The kitty is in Oliver's hand, then it's on his shoulder, but then it's in his hand again in just a few seconds. That pussy gets around! If you were trying to quit smoking and you watched this movie, you'd be so fucked.

Ruth invites her Uncle Edmar (Osvaldo Genazzani) to the house. He's a portly middle aged gentleman (but still totally fuckable) but he's really a private eye that Ruth hired to investigate Helen's death. This subtitler made so many mistakes. There are giggle-inducing mistakes in every scene my favorite being: "You had always being blind!" Edmar's subterfuge lasted all of one minute of screen time and now he's snooping around the house and rummaging around with his little black gloves. He's going to find the truth. Nope, scratch that. Something just sliced his throat with a switchblade. There is a thinly veiled masturbation murder fantasy sequence. Bonus! By the way, this film is really fucking good.

SUNDAY

I got up this morning after dreams of ransacking VHS bins at thrift stores but not finding anything good. Thanks for nothing, dreams! I was craving Starbucks so LeEtta and I feed the animals and hit the road. The Starbucks on Dale Mabry and Linebaugh used to be a Long John Silvers. Knowing that is somehow comforting to me. The air conditioning and the surprisingly decent jazz music playing over the stereo is definitely comforting. I get a delicious iced vanilla latte with whipped cream and a pastry and LeEtta gets a coffee with cream only and a breakfast sandwich. I nearly run over a skinny tattooed jackass on a ten speed in the parking lot. This ass clown tried to pin himself between our car and another going the opposite direction. It makes me wonder: maybe punk rock really is bad for people. Or maybe the guy is a Juggalo. Who am I to judge?

"You are incurably crazy."

10:43 AM
Death Haunts Monica (1976)

I'm keeping the Spanish giallo vibe going with this trashy and melodramatic little flick from my birth year. The first thing we learn about Monica (other than the fact that death apparently haunts her) is that she likes to pop pills and have her maid bring her breakfast in bed. We can all relate to that. Her husband Federico (the great Jean Sorel) runs some kind of business called Eurozona where people talk really fast. Monica's fancy friend Elena (Karin Schubert) calls her up because she's got something important to tell her.

Jean Sorel's business partner Arturo (Arturo Fernández) is a real letch and a pretty funny character. Everywhere he goes, half naked women shout and throw things at him. So Elena shows up and tells Monica that she knows something about Federico. It seems that he's sleeping with a model named Eva and it's more than just a casual fling. Meanwhile (I should just start every sentence with "Meanwhile" from now on), an old pal of Federico's named Diego has gotten out of prison and has come to collect some debt that he feels he is owed.

Apparently, Federico was involved in contraband, drugs, and kidnapping back in the day and Diego did the jail time for it. He wants to be a partner in Federico's business but everything is tied up in the partners and it's not doing that well anyway. Federico gives Diego a check for what little he can spare but it's not enough, Diego promises that he will be back. Next we find out that Monica's friend Elena is a lesbian and is having an affair with Eva the model and they've got some kind of scheme going to take over Eurozona. This movie is dripping with melodramatic soap opera goodness.

Monica wants to leave Federico but she can't because she loves him too much. Federico decides to dump Eva and stay with Monica because he loves HER too much. Aw, ain't that sweet? The lighting in this film is achingly bright and the fashions are making me think a disco ball will drop in so everyone can do The Hustle. That night, while Federico is busy dumping Eva, a mysterious figure breaks in while Monica is alone. She pulls a gun from Federico's desk and plugs the fucker. But bullets have no effect on this ski mask wearing creature of the night and Monica is left unconscious while - Oops, I don't want to spoil the whole plot!

This is my second viewing of Death Haunts Monica and I like it even more this time. Attention perverts: There's a naked woman in nearly every scene of this film. But more importantly, there are lots of goofy scares while Monica is losing her darn mind. You know things are bad when Arturo the super sleaze is the voice of reason during all this.

RICHARD GLENN SCHMIDT

*"Never pay attention to the police;
they always complicate things."*

12:09 PM
Cross Current (1971)

Here's another film that I've been looking for but know absolutely nothing about. The opening music is a very warped pop song that sounds like a B side to the "Monster Mash". On a dark and stormy night, a man gets a gun out of a drawer and goes outside. And then speedboat racing! Marco (Philippe Leroy), a pipe-smoking and dickish rich guy likes to race boats. He has a car crash in his speedboat and gets injured in the brain area. His doctor (Franco Fantasia of Knife of Ice) must perform a risky operation on Marco to fix a blood clot in his brain.

Marco survives the surgery but he is left rather unstable. The doctor tells Marco's wife Monica (the lovely Elga Andersen) and associates that he must be allowed to do whatever he wants because any stress will cause him to go irreversibly insane or something. So far, the tree in his yard upsets him a lot. He gets a call from his former gardener who wants to meet him alone at the graveyard to talk blackmail and stuff. Marco sneaks out that night but we don't know if he actually went to the meeting.

Inspector Baldini (Julio Peña) shows up to report that the gardener got run over by a car. Oh look at that, Marco's car is fucked up. Marco's business partner Burt (Ivan Rassimov) is trying to encourage him to retake control over his business but he couldn't care less about it. He offers Burt power of attorney but insists that he give his chauffeur a job in the company with a big salary. That doesn't sound crazy or anything. J&B sighting! Later, Marco's sneaky boat-racing frenemy Tommy Brown (Franco Ressel) gets knifed to death and his guts spill out.

Friggin' speedboat racing footage almost ruins this film's fine atmosphere. There's always a pair of eyes watching from the shadows. Marco's friend Elaine (Rosanna Yanni) is starting to become more than a friend and Monica doesn't like it one bit. Look here, lady, Marco does whatever Marco wants. He takes Elaine to a nightclub where she grooves to some Crudence Crapwater Repoopal. During a schmaltzy slow dance, Monica shows up and shit gets real. Are these people still in high school? Since neither of these chicks will fuck him, Marco starts chugging J&B.

Back at the house, a catfight between these two lovelies breaks out which is a little confusing because they could be sisters. They go for the gun and -BLAM!- one of them is killed. Forget calling the cops, let's just get rid of the body. Really? Come on, Marco. The gardener's mother shows up to blackmail a little money. Pieces of a whole different subplot turn up as fragments of Marco's memory begin to return. There's enough J&B in this movie to make up for all the titles in this moviethon that didn't have any. The climax of this film is a slow motion death sequence that is off the chain, yo. Seek this one out. For the record: I'm sick of Greek subtitles!

"Not even a ghost could escape this place."

1:59 PM
The Corruption of Chris Miller (1973)

Speaking of films you need to seek out… A rich lady tries to throw her lover out of the house because her husband will soon return. Her lover is dressed and acts just like Charlie Chaplin until he stabs her with a pair of scissors. That's not Charlie Chaplin behavior. He robs the house of any cash he can find and disappears in the rain. Ruth (Jean Seberg) and her stepdaughter Chris (Marisol) aren't weathering the storm very well either. Ruth's father left them there alone in their big house long ago and they're both kind of losing it. Well, Chris is really fucking losing it, especially when it rains. She has strange flashbacks of a man lifting weights and herself in a ballerina outfit. Then she repeatedly stabs her pillow. Yikes.

The next morning, Ruth finds a young man asleep in her barn. His name is Barney and he claims that he got lost in the storm and just needed a place to sleep. Instead of kicking this guy out, she lets him make breakfast. Chris, who seems very childlike for her age, is running around on her own and horseback riding without a bra on. You know, chick stuff. While she's off gallivanting around, her stepmom totally bangs Barney. While Ruth is asleep, he starts looking for shit to steal. Great guy!

Chris comes home and finds the Barney chopping wood in the garden. Ruth tries to get the guy to leave but his kisses are just too powerful for her. So now he works for them, doing manly stuff around the house and lusting after Chris. At first, she doesn't like Barney but he begins to win her over, much to the chagrin of Ruth. Double standard! Strangely enough, Ruth tells Barney to go visit Chris sometime when it's storming outside. He thinks he'll be in for a sexy time but we know how Ruth gets when it rains.

LeEtta orders us a pizza with mushrooms, olives, and green peppers. We eat and life is good. The woman killed at the beginning of the film was some kind of famous singer. She was the seventh victim in a series of brutal murders and the cops are looking for anyone suspicious. One detective is particularly interested in Barney. Rabbit violence! Well, now I know where bunny burgers come from. Chris and Barney start getting hot and heavy but she has visions of the weightlifter again and has to tell him to stop. Margie is surprised by how easily Ruth and Chris get excited when Barney kissed them. She calls it "going into hyper-drive". Maybe he's hiding a purple dinosaur in his pants. That would drive any woman crazy.

Chris is in the basement when a storm rolls in and she starts to lose her shit. Barney goes to help her and nearly gets killed when she gets ahold of a sharp object. This scene is just frickin' brilliant as everything is coming to a head. When Chris doesn't kill Barney, Ruth is very angry and she kicks him out at gunpoint. Barney doesn't take it very well and says that he wants to vomit in Ruth's bed. A mysterious individual shows up in town wearing a black raincoat and carrying a scythe. It's all very I Know What You Did Last Summer. This guy slaughters an entire family and the cops are clueless. Could Barney the hunky drifter really be responsible for these crimes?

"There's a lot of crazy people out there."

4:18 PM

Interrabang (1969)

I pop a couple of ibuprofen because I can feel the seams on the inside of my skull. Lucky for me, this movie is real easy on the yes and easy on the brain. A photographer named Fabrizio is out cruising some islands with a trio of hot chicks on his yacht. Their conversation is vapid and angsty. There's Margerita, the ditzy model, and Anna, Fabrizio's girlfriend who puts up with him sleeping with Margerita to inspire his art. And last but not least, there's Valeria, Anna's bookish, smartass sister.

As beautiful and idyllic as all this is, there is dread in the air as a faulty carburetor leaves them stranded. There also just happens to be a murderous criminal on the loose. While Fabrizio is away getting a replacement part for the engine, Margerita meets a man on the island named Marco who claims to be a poet. Valeria finds a corpse of a policeman but doesn't tell anyone. Ugh, now Marco the "poet" is there, just hanging out with the girls until Fabrizio gets back. This isn't going to end well.

So these chicks are totally taken in by this guy. Why? I don't have a fucking clue. They learn much too late that he's a psychopath. In my version, they band together and rip this motherfucker limb from limb. Oh okay, this just jumped the shark pretty hard. The ending makes a tiny bit of sense if you use your imagination but it's still better than where I thought this was headed. I waited for this film for a long time to turn up and now that it did, I'm not sure I should be happy about it or not.

"I got drunk in five seconds!"

5:53 PM

Nel buio del terrore (1971)

I throw on this film which stars Marisa Mell. She walks to the edge of a cliff overlooking the beach. Just as she is considering taking a header off the side, a duder in a yellow jeep beeps at her and she decides not to jump. I kind of wish she had. She hooks up with Arthur (Stephen Boyd) the guy with the yellow jeep. He is an artist.

I took a chance on this film and now it feels like a huge mistake. Mell is Carla, a high-priced escort who gets involved with a rich duder named Luis (Fernando Rey). The rich guy's wife, named Lola, is played by Sylva Koscina. Parts of me feel very happy about her being in this film. This is definitely a pretty film but I can't imagine that any murders are going to take place with all this melodramatic intrigue going on.

Later, she bumps into Lola again at a hotel. Her friend is making a living by working as a maid in the fancy hotel. There is more to Lola and Carla's relationship than just friendliness. Lola pisses off Carla when she up and marries Luis, the rich duder. Then he bites the bucket. Wait, either I'm really tired or I missed a flashback or both.

So this really is a melodrama with a rich industrialist, a high priced escort, and some con men. Howard Ross, the duder from 5 Dolls for an August Moon and a million other things, is in this. Whoa Carla just got scammed. Was there a murder? Yes? I don't know about this one. I'm kind of glad I've seen it but not really very much giallo-ness to it. The opening music by Carlo Savina and a great cast were worth the price of admission.

"Are we being ironic, my sweet tyrant?"

7:52 PM
Anima persa (1977)

I'm now watching a film. I have taken my first 5 Hour Energy thingie. I feel awake. This film opens in beautiful Atlantis, the underwater city. We call it Venice but everyone knows the truth: All mermen learned to breathe in English but they speak Italian. Some duder named Tino (Danilo Mattei) is staying with his Aunt Sofia (Catherine Deneuve). His uncle Fabio (Vittorio Gassman) is a gas, man. No wait, he is a gas man. He's like the minister of gas or whatever. Fart joke. Fart joke. Fart joke. There, I got it out of my system. "Out of my system." Get it?

This has a nice gothic feel to it from the get go. While Sofia is showing Tino around the creepy house, he finds a staircase and asks where it leads. She tells him it goes nowhere, the stairs are rotten, and to never go up there. She's a little nutty and the whole house is a spook fest. At night, Tino hears footsteps above him. In the morning, he wakes up to find his uncle Fabio sitting in the room, just staring at him. Fabio and Sofia are so old-fashioned that when I realize that this takes place in the 1970s, I'm shocked.

Tino goes to art school and sees his first live nude girl (Anicée Alvina) She's a model for the art students and they hit it off. Tino notices that

Fabio has some crazy ideas and even more nonsensical things to talk about. He is verbally abusive and manipulative toward Sofia. They're both afraid of what lurks in the attic. Someone is playing piano in the night. When Tino asks the maid about the noises from upstairs, she just takes him up the stairs and lets him look through a peephole in the door. Inside the room is a crazy person. Holy shit, this is just creepy. What the fuck?

The longer Tino stays in the house, the weirder shit gets. Even Sofia is starting to crack. The crazy person in the attic is his uncle's brother who went barking mad. They let him have at it with a hooker every once in a while which just terrifies me. The more we learn about this family and how their lives work, the more this shit just spirals out of control. The atmosphere of Anima Persa is getting thicker and more disturbing by the minute. This is a dark poem; every line blacker than the one preceding it.

SHORT BREAK

In order to celebrate breaking a moviethon record, it's time for some J&B and a short speech. I've never watched 22 films in a single moviethon before and Death Walks in High Heels will be the 22nd title in Meltdown 8. So I grab my official J&B glass and pour myself a shot. I ask LeEtta if the shot is big enough. She mischievously says no so I proceed to pour myself three shots into one glass. My speech goes like this: "Um, thank you. Grown men have never attempted these things before so don't tell your children. Viva la giallo." I down this monstrous amount of liquor in one gulp, make a horrible face, and LeEtta laughs at me.

"I like you when you're all blacked up."

9:48 PM
Death Walks on High Heels (1971)

A man with a silly eye-patch and gray spray paint on his mustache is murdered on a train. His killer is The Man with Icy Eyes. No wait, that's a different movie. The killer is a ski-masked duder with painful blue contacts. Once the deed is done, he starts ransacking the dead duder's belongings and then freeze-frame-stares into the camera for the title of the film. And I burst out laughing. We cut to Simón Andreu and Susan Scott riding in a car together and acting like young lovers in love. The music is some of Stelvio Cipriani's most decadent delightfulness.

I've never been a huge fan of this film. Let's see how it goes for me this time. Nicole (Scott) is a cabaret performer and Michel (Andreu) is her asshole boyfriend. The Parisian cops are questioning Nicole because her father, eye-patch guy, was a jewel thief and a bunch of stolen jewels haven't been recovered. At the cabaret, Nicole gets a phone call from a weirdo that wants to meet with her. She blows him off, thinking he's just some pervert. Then some blackface happens with Susan Scott with dark makeup and an afro wig. This is, to be quite frank, insane and just vilely racist.

When Nicole gets done with that atrocity, she and Michel have sexy time in her dressing room. Then she's off to another nightclub to do a different, less racist act. After she's done shaking her groove thang, a guy named Dr. Robert Matthews (Frank Wolff) shows up in her dressing room. He's a fan of her naked body. Nothing creepy about that! Nicole gets another phone call. This time, the stranger threatens to kill her. On the way back to her apartment, someone in high heels is following her. Is it death? No, it's a fat prostitute. Michel is drunk when she gets home. He throws knives at her and calls her a whore. and I want to kill him.

Michel leaves and the guy in the ski-mask and blue contacts bursts in, threatening Nicole with a straight razor. He ties her torn dress around her head which renders her powerless. He threatens to slice her up if he doesn't get those damn jewels. She flees her apartment and runs into Robert again. He gives her his card and expresses interest in seeing her again. Instead, she goes to Michel's apartment where he's significantly less drunk than he was 2 minutes ago. Nicole stays the night but discovers blue contact lenses in his bathroom. Dun dun dun! She hauls ass out of there and goes to see Robert. She tells him that she'll do "anything" to get out of Paris. So off they go on a plane to England. That's where Robert spills the beans about his wife who he can't divorce because she has all the money.

They go to Robert's vacation home in a small village. We meet Hallory (Luciano Rossi) and Peggy. Hallory is Robert's servant with a false hand and an awesome cat. He is sweating and glaring at Nicole. Peggy is a bartender at the local pub and she is equally unfriendly. I love this scene. So Nicole and Robert are essentially having a honeymoon which includes sexy fish eating by the fireside. I am only 35 minutes into this movie! Someone is watching Nicole through the windows. George Rigaud shows up as Robert's friend, Captain Lenny. He's trying to sell Robert a yacht. Nicole freaks out when she hears the local priest using an electrolarynx (thanks, Wikipedia!) that makes him sound just like her attacker!

Every time that Robert leaves Nicole alone, weird shit happens. This time, a woman shows up with some stacks of cash and tries to pay her to leave town. The next morning, Robert returns and Nicole is gone. Not seeming all that upset about it, Robert goes to work where he does some nasty eye surgery on a dude. Someone shoots Robert during the operation. While Robert is on the operating table, we meet his wife Vanessa (Claudie Lange) and two police inspectors (Carlo Gentili and Fabrizio Moresco).

It's a little awkward when Robert is coming out of anesthesia and asking for Nicole. Michel shows up and he's drunk (of course). He leans out a window and pukes on a cop. This is one of the very few scenes of someone actually upchucking in a giallo. Historic! The plot continues to thicken and thicken and thicken. Is Nicole alive? Is she dead? What is happening? Who cares, I'm having a funeurism! I officially love this film.

CONCLUSION

Wow. I can't even look at the television right now. It's the following day and I feel this weird nausea in my soul. The thought of even watching a movie today makes me uneasy. I hope I captured last night's mania for you. The weird thing about those 5 Hour Energy drinks is that they trick you. You feel like you're wired and in complete control of yourself but the fact is you're still delirious from being tired but now you're extremely AWAKE, totally fearless, and babbling nonsensically. Okay, maybe these reactions are exclusive to me.

GIALLO MELTDOWN 9: PLANET GIALLO

Somehow, I really believed that the book would be done by now. To me at least, it seemed that I actually had a snowball's chance in hell of actually getting to a stopping point this summer. I couldn't have been more wrong! But I'm not worried about it because I fucking love this shit. I'm also making the case for the American giallo this moviethon. I have a nice selection of giallo-influenced flicks from the good old US of A all lined up for Saturday. Controversy!

FRIDAY

When work ends, LeEtta and I go out to Kobe, a Japanese steakhouse on Dale Mabry. We order vegetable egg rolls, a selection of sushi, and green tea tiramisu. It's nice. We head home in a wide-reaching but ultimately weak thunderstorm. It's gray everywhere and I'm so tired tonight that I feel agitated and confused. This feels like it's going to be a tough moviethon but I've already put it off once due to some crazy family emergency last month. Plus, tomorrow is my birthday so I better come correct.

> *"Poor frightened little thing. We're not thinking bad thoughts."*

7:07 PM
In the Eye of the Hurricane (1971)

In a strange animated title sequence, a swan is humping an art deco Leda to a silky smooth pop song. A lady named Ruth (Analía Gadé from Maniac Mansion) is putting on makeup but her husband Michel (Tony Kendall) is trying to make sweet love to her. She ain't having it! Inside their fabulous mansion, they're disaffectedly talking about their trial separation. Michel starts kissing Ruth's shoulders like he's taking big bites out of her. Nom nom nom! LeEtta is fascinated by the Swiss subtitles on this bootleg DVD. It's a nice change from the Greek one, that's for sure.

Ruth tells Michel that she's filed for divorce and then four seconds later, she introduces him to her new guy, Paul (Jean Sorel). Michel is cool about it. Now Paul and Ruth are making out and going waterskiing. They kiss for a very long time while Paul is hanging upside down in a tree and I am just laughing and laughing. Ruth runs topless in slow motion and finds a swan in her bathtub. Then she and Paul make the creepiest kissy faces at each other. I'm feeling very good about this film.

This annoyingly happy couple goes into town where they bump into Paul's friend, Roland (Maurizio Bonuglia of The Fifth Cord), who has a pedophile mustache. While they're hanging out and painting pottery, Ruth meditates on life and what she'll do when she grows old. Paul says, "You'll never grow old." Very subtle. Later, he takes her to a deserted nightclub for a little wining and dining. It is all very foreboding and creepy Roland is always hanging around. If these scenes weren't so obviously a setup for something sinister, I would swear that this was an extended commercial for a swinging couples' retreat.

Ruth almost buys the farm after someone cuts the brake lines on Paul's car while she was at the wheel. Is someone trying to kill her or him? Damn it, Jean Sorel, do I really need to see you in a skin tight wetsuit again? That's right, another giallo with a scuba diving scene. Now Ruth almost dies while scuba diving. Now a maid is chopping up a squid with a huge meat clever. In a very disconcerting scene, Paul is harassing a swan with a weird mask and a pool skimmer. What a fuckhead.

When Michel comes back to the house, Paul and his best bud Roland have a little game of target practice in the back yard. They're the most irresponsible idiots I've ever seen. Let's hope this all ends in bloodshed! I was just going to complain about the plot and how generic it is but the story took a little detour I didn't expect. This film is getting better as its conclusion draws near and the atmosphere is a nice blend of captivating (good tension) and cheesy (red herrings and suspicious glances). Did I mention the overuse of swan imagery?

"No living woman possesses your mysterious fascination or your sweet repose."

9:07 PM
The Embalmer (1965)

If you guessed that I'm beginning to scrape beneath the bottom of the barrel when I break out this flick then you guessed right. Here is this film's plot in once sentence: A madman in scuba gear is stalking the watery streets of Venice, drowning beautiful women, and then embalming them for his macabre collection. The display case this duder uses for his lady friends is a fucking travesty. One girl doesn't even fit in one of the cases and she has to stand sideways in it while the others are facing forward. Production design fail. That was funny but I worry that this film might be a total dud.

Andrea is a dashing newspaper guy assigned to report on this sensational scuba killer story. There are a couple of surly custodial workers who are pretty amazing. Every moment they're on screen is magical. While giving a tour to some lovely ladies around Venice, Andrea takes a liking to Marie, the teacher leading a group of 17 to 18 year old ladies (the killer's favorite). Either he is trying to predict where the killer will strike next or he's just a lecherous SOB who is easily distractible by anything in a skirt.

The cornball bullshit in this movie is going down very smooth with the gothic architecture chaser. All the scenes with the madman talking to his lovelies and brewing up embalming fluid are great! I'm very surprised at how much I am enjoying this film since I normally just sleep through it. At a snooty looking nightclub, the floor show is an Elvis lookalike who climbs out of a coffin to play acoustic guitar and sings cruddy songs. This character is easily trumped by the old lady doing The Twist with her nerdy scientist nephew. More of these two characters, please!

Speaking of that scientist, he gets a little too close to solving the mystery and gets a dagger in the heart for his troubles. There's a pervert hotel manager who watches the female guests in their rooms through a two way mirror while the goofy desk clerk is making a date with one of the sexy little vixens. I'm so damn tired right now. Whoever lit this movie is a damn genius. They had to cut some serious budgetary corners with this one but they didn't skimp on the fun. The killer's costume is definitely more krimi than giallo but it's awesome just the same. I'm now a fan of The Embalmer.

SATURDAY

After an exquisite night's sleep, LeEtta wakes me up and wishes me a happy birthday. I get up, walk the dog, and go to 7-11. I get a donut and a 5 Hour Energy drink for tomorrow night when I know I will need it most. After chores and breakfast, I open my presents from LeEtta and Margie. Margie got me a rolling cart for my amplifier. Nice mother-in-law. LeEtta got me a drum machine. Nice wife. Time to get back to the movies.

"Why don't you stick your head in one of your washing machines and clean up your mind?"

9:59 AM
Violent Midnight (1963)

I've heard that this is a giallo-influenced proto-slasher film. The black and white cinematography on this is amazing. I love when color film was readily available but low budget filmmakers went with black and white film stock to save money. The cinematograper of Violent Midnight definitely made the most of it. During a prologue, there is a hunting 'accident' where a duder gets blasted in the face with a double barreled shotgun. The killer is wearing black gloves!

Dolores (Kaye Elhardt), who has a great rack, is posing nude for an artist (and Korean War vet) named Elliot (Lee Philips) in his art studio. A slick attorney named Adrian (Shepperd Strudwick) shows ups. He manages Elliot's fortune and I trust him about as far as I could throw him. Adrian reminds Elliot that his younger half-sister is coming into town by train. Meanwhile, the black-gloved killer is lurking around the garden. Charlie (James Farentino) is Dolores's creep ex-boyfriend. He dresses like Brando in The Wild One and is a total peckerwood. He and Elliot get into a little scrap over Dolores at the local dive bar and Elliot kicks his ass with some rage-fueled karate chops.

Dolores admits to Elliot that she's pregnant but it couldn't be his kid because they slept together six months ago. And, as my mother-in-law Margie points out: "She don't look six months pregnant!" So yeah, it's Charlie's kid but she hints at blackmail. When that doesn't work, Dolores tells Elliot that she knows why he doesn't want any kids because insanity runs in his family. None of this matters because the killer makes quick work of Dolores with a big knife. Elliot's hot half-sister Lynn (Margot Hartman) shows up and he drives her to the girls' college in town.

We get introduced to a whole mess of college girls and that makes me very happy because they're all hot. Elliot bumps into Carol (Jean Hale), an old acquaintance who is now a teacher at the school. After getting questioned by the cops, Elliot goes to Dolores's funeral where her mother screams "Assassin murderer!" right in his face. Charlie has a weak alibi (courtesy of the town slut) for the night Dolores was murdered but the cops buy it. Carol gives Elliot a ktten and Charlie bangs a slut in the laundry room at the college. Plot!

Adrian questions Lynn about Elliot's mental state and I'm like um, wait a minute. She's a psychology major, duder. I don't think she can give her professional opinion just yet. Elliot tells Carol (who is now his new flame) that his father's death wasn't an accident. LeEtta points out that this is the perfect combination of a giallo and a Teen In Peril movie. The cast is full of surprisingly decent actors, really bad actors, and Dick Van Patten actors.

Charlie's slut just ratted him out to the cops because she thinks he's the killer. He rips her earrings out the hard way to teach her a lesson or something. Violent Midnight is great and just one look at the killer's getup says to me that it is very obviously influenced by the giallo. I highly recommend this one.

LUNCH

LeEtta and I head out to get some essential things from Target. And then we go to my chosen birthday lunch special place: Zaxby's. I gorge myself on fried wonderful and LeEtta insists we get birthday cake milkshakes. I cannot argue with that. We head home with a bag of lunch for Margie. For some reason, our apartment stinks when we get home. Ugh. Time for another movie.

"Death... is a sacred thing."

2:17 PM
Eyes of Laura Mars (1978)

Here is another giallo-inspired American film from the director of my two favorite gialli: The Empire Strikes Back and Robocop 2. This opens with a shot of Faye Dunaway's eyes and some douche-rock Barbra Streisand song. Old Babs was supposed to star in this? Thanks, IMDB. John Carpenter wrote this screenplay but the other writers did a number on it. Even so, I like this movie. There's a killer in NYC murdering models from the photographs of Laura Mars (Dunaway). Her work is provocative (read as: trashy) and important (read as: violent). Mars has a psychic connection to the killer so she gets to watch the murders of her friends as they happen! The killer likes to jab people's eyes out with an icepick.

This film has lots of primo quality disco music, glamorous fashion models, a midget, and Brad Dourif as Laura's driver, Tommy. Tommy Lee Jones plays Lt. Neville, a cop, and his unibrow plays his partner. During a wildly silly photo shoot, Laura witnesses another murder. This time it was her friend Elaine. Laura claims that she saw the crime happen. The cops don't believe her but they haul in Laura and her weird friends anyway.

While she is being questioned, Neville shows Laura some crime scene photos that she has recreated in her photographs. Faye Dunaway is just a wee bit over the top in this film. Her character is supposed to be glamorous but she just comes off as impossibly pretentious. The killer comes after Laura, so composer Artie Kane goes all Ennio Morricone on our asses.

Rene Auberjonis is the stereotypically gay Donald, Laura's manager. This is some weak ass shit here and I feel bad for him. If his character was any more flamboyant and unlikeable, this DVD would catch on fire. Raul Julia plays Michael, Laura's loser ex-husband. He was shacked up with her friend that got killed and he is now one of the many suspects. The sexy lesbian models get killed too. Now Brad Dourif is a suspect just because he has a rap sheet with a bunch of priors. I will say no more about it!

"What sort of men turn you on?"

5:07 PM
Dressed to Kill (1980)

For some reason, I used to really dislike Dressed to Kill. Now I feel like giving it another chance. There's no way those are Angie Dickinson's boobs. Dickinson plays Kate Miller, a frustrated housewife. She has a frightening shower-rape fantasy and then the film cuts to her husband's amazing lovemaking technique. Yikes, the duder is just pounding away and of course, he finishes way before she does. After that depressing spectacle, she has a little pow wow with her brilliant son, Peter (Keith Gordon), who is building some kind of binary processor doohickey or whatever.

Enter Michael Caine as Dr. Robert Elliott, her psychologist. He's trying to get her to stand up for herself and live her life the way she wants to. She goes to the museum and starts flirting with some duder in shades. It's a weird scene. She makes a pass and then he makes a pass and OH FOR CHRIST'S SAKE, CAN WE GET ON WITH THIS BRIAN DE PALMA!? Sorry. I'm sorry. I swear that I'm giving this movie another chance. Kate and Mr. Shades go back to his place where they get it on. She wakes up that night and while she's getting ready to leave her little one afternoon stand, she discovers- nope, too good to reveal here.

Kate splits but gets brutally murdered in the elevator by a woman armed with a straight razor. Nancy Allen plays Liz Blake, a hooker who tries to help Kate but is too late. The scene is perfectly staged and is one of the most harrowing sequences in American cinema. After his mother's death, Peter becomes an amateur dick. He eavesdrops while Dr. Elliott is being grilled by Detective Marino (Dennis Franz). Marino thinks that the killer might be one of his patients. This gives Peter the idea to set up a camera outside of Elliott's office and record everyone who comes and goes.

The killer is hot on Liz's heels and she is about to end up like Kate, when Peter rescues her at the last second. Man oh man, Nancy Allen is fantastic in this film. She is hot for sure but she also just lights up the screen. In a scheme that the term 'foolhardy' may be too generous for, Liz and Peter's amateur sleuthing gets them into a very dangerous situation. You've probably already seen this but I ain't gonna spoil nothin'. We heat up some leftover pizza. Life is good. Next movie, please.

"Don't be afraid. I want to help you. Take my hand."

7:00 PM
Silent Night, Bloody Night (1972)

As I put this movie on, a storm rolls in. Huge raindrops are falling and thunder is crackling across the sky. Shadow the dog is very upset. Merry Christmas (in August), everyone! This is a very quirky and atmospheric film that feels like it sprung out of the Earth somewhere. This is such a bizarre flick but has a lot to thank the giallo genre for. If you want to argue with me about including this in my book, you're too fucking late!

The opening narration from Mary Woronov tells us about a disturbed family, the Butlers. A lawyer named Carter (Patrick O'Neal) arrives in town with his hot little mistress to settle the Butler estate. He has to do business with the eccentric leaders of the town including a mute John Carradine. Jeffrey Butler, grandson of the dude that burned to death mysteriously in the prologue, is selling the Butler house and the land it sits on to the town for 50 grand. They offer Mr. Carter a hotel room for the night but he insists on staying at the old Butler house. He heads out to the old house with his sexy lady friend to get it on but they're not alone.

That night, the black-gloved killer storms in while they're making love and kills the living heck out of them with an axe. After the double homicide, the murderer calls the sheriff, pretending or maybe not pretending to be Mr. Butler. In a chilling, whispery voice, the killer talks him into coming out to the Butler house. When the line is disconnected, the killer then talks to Tess the switchboard operator and refers to him/herself as Maryanne Butler. It's all very threatening and freaky as hell.

The immensely attractive Mary Woronov plays Diane, daughter of the mayor. She runs into a hunky/ugly guy who also claims to be Jeffrey Butler (James Patterson) who needs to get into the Butler house. Diane and Jeffrey head out to the house where they find the sheriff's car abandoned, not knowing that the killer just beat him to death with a shovel. The two run all over the damn town trying to figure out what the heck is going on.

This is such a fantastic film and very creepy. There are more revelations about the disturbing history of the Butler family. The patriarch turned his house into an insane asylum at some point. Something terrible happened in the Butler house on Christmas of 1935. When Jefferey gets inside the house, you start to wonder about him. Is this bro really evil or what? A sepia flashback with even more weirdness and lots of Andy Warhol's Factory people happens. Even though this film is hampered by an obtuse storyline and a low budget, just wait for that badass ending. It's really great.

RICHARD GLENN SCHMIDT

"Luca! Stop it! It was just a joke! Stop it! It's a rubber toy!"

9:18 PM
Il mostro (1977)

Okay enough of this American bullshit. Time for some Italianz, gosh darn it. This music score is very strident and disarming. Hi there, Ennio Morricone! This is very familiar: a murder scene from Death Walks on High Heels. A guy named Valerio (Johnny Dorelli) and his son Luca are watching the movie at the theater. They leave and we find out that Valerio is the most opinionated bastard in Italy. He tells it like it is, has a hot ex-wife that hates his guts, and sometimes he keys people's cars. I like this dude.

Valerio is a writer of violent detective stories but his terrible day job is at a newspaper (where his desk is next to the toilet in the basement). I think he is supposed to be answering letters? He receives a typed letter that says: "I'm going to kill Grandpa Gustavo." The letter is signed "Il Mostro". Valerio takes it to his boss who couldn't care less and of course, the police do nothing. Valerio heads down to the TV studio where the kids' show "Grandpa Gustavo" is filmed.

The TV studio is dark and mysterious, surreal even. This has The Vibe big time. I'm already smitten with this movie. He finds the actor who plays Grandpa Gustavo but too late, someone has bashed his head in. The cops send Valerio's clothes to the lab to see if there's any blood on them and he has to wait in a cold office in his underwear. In order to avoid embarrassment, the cops decide not to acknowledge the letter Valerio received or his statement. Now Valerio just looks like a fool. But the killer is still out there.

The cops think the killer is a graphomaniac. (I had to look that one up.) Valerio is a total dick. His wife calls him a vulture and she's right but so is everyone else in this film. Il Mostro is a satire of the highest order. In a hilarious turn, Valerio becomes a celebrity because of his connection to the killer and everything spins out of control. He takes advantage of his newfound fame and shits on everyone. He even starts dating a pop singer who has a hit song about the killer. Oh shit, the ending is deadly serious. This would make an excellent double feature with Closed Circuit.

SUNDAY

LeEtta and I wake up well rested. I walk Shadow. He poops. I pick it up. When I get back, we go out for Dunkin Donuts. It's going to be another disgustingly hot day. We bring Margie her coffee and I take some time to do some last minute playlist adjustments. The morning is getting away from me. I feel strange today like something terrible is coming.

> *"Artist? Murderer? Slasher? Fiend?*
> *His art was killing."*

10:39 AM
Fatal Frames (1996)

I've been avoiding this film for a long, long time. I've never heard a good word about it. Fatal Frames opens stylishly enough with some black and white photography and a sweet keyboard heavy soundtrack. An old perverted freak is watching a snuff film in his study. Was that a The House with Laughing Windows reference just now? A little kid walks in and gets scared. The old man grabs him and forces him to watch the snuff film. The film segues seamlessly to color. In an alleyway, a typical giallo killer is chasing a chick in a unitard and slashing her with a machete.

Next, we cut to a hideous music video that even Gerardo would have been too embarrassed to appear in. Now two douchebags, Alex and his buddy, are on a couch talking about the hideous music video. His buddy is trying to convince Alex to go to Italy and direct the next music video for the pop singer chick of the hideous music video. Alex agrees to go because he needs to get away from the bloodstain on the floor where someone decapitated his wife, Rebecca. During the airport scene, LeEtta points out that Alex and his buddy have Highlander hair. There can be only two.

The camera is certainly very hyperactive in this. It zooms and zips all over the place. Some foreboding shit happens at the airport but then the limo driver looks like Fabio and the pop singer, Stefania Stella, looks like a female Gerardo. (I think "Rico Suave" had a profound effect on me as a kid.) The way she talks is freaky and she has hungry eyes. This dialog is terrible and the acting is worse. There's a lot of testosterone pumping through this flick. It's a good thing the cinematography and lighting is so good or else I'd be in big trouble. (Spoiler alert: I'm in big trouble.)

There's a dream sequence where Alex watches his dead wife get hacked up by the masked killer. It's hilariously overdone with slow motion, fog machines, poorly mixed sound, and more slow motion. Oh wait, this isn't a dream, Alex really did witness a murder. The killer sends a tape of the dead girl to the cops. David Warbeck is in this. He plays the inspector who slams his hands on tables a lot. I pity him. It dawns on me who Alex looks like: Lorenzo Llamas! I text Brad and inform him that he needs to watch this ASAP. The poor man has seen this before.

Stefania Stella, who plays herself and has top billing, is just so damn annoying. Whenever she speaks, I want to punch something and it only gets worse when she sings.) She takes Alex to a creepy castle filled with weirdos so he can take part in a séance. Shit, this movie is going to ruin séance sequences for me forever. Did I mention the running time is 2 hours and 5 minutes long? It totally is. It's partly due to all the damn music videos. I'm suddenly wishing that Italy had never discovered live sound.

The presence of Linnea Quigley makes things all better for about 5 seconds. Donald Pleasence is here as an FBI investigator and he's very, very old. They dubbed his voice. I wish they had dubbed everyone in this except for him. Now Stefania and Alex are having a sex scene for what feels like 30 minutes and it's traumatizing LeEtta, Margie, and I. This is easily the most intensely painful experience in the history of Giallo Meltdown. Alex starts cursing at Donald Pleasence and it's unbearably depressing. This fucking doucheknuckle doesn't deserve to lick Pleasence's boots.

Angus Schrimm has a cameo and he makes the most of it. Right after his great monologue, I predict that there is going to be another music video and BAM! there it is. It doesn't feel good to be right. Alida Valli and Linnea Quigley in the same scene together? There's your Creepozoids to Suspiria connection, for ya! Since Pleasence couldn't finish his scenes, they use a painfully obvious double and even play the theme from Halloween over his exit. I want to reveal the killer's identity so you won't watch this shite but I want you to suffer as I have. The ending is so overdone and shrill that I put the TV on mute so I won't vomit on myself. I hate gialli now.

*"I keep getting the feeling that
we're on another planet."*

1:45 PM
Maniac Mansion (1972)

You want to talk about night and day in terms of quality, entertainment, and intelligence? Go from Fatal Frames to Maniac Mansion (I prefer the Murder Mansion title). And I'm not watching the muddy public domain copy either. I got this widescreen and very vibrant version from my friend, The Internet. I shared it with my other friend, The Brad. The very short version of this story is that a group of strangers get stranded at a mansion in the middle of nowhere and there are some supernatural things going on. You like that? Oh, I wish it was that simple.

Brad and I tried to record a podcast episode on this Spanish/Italian co-production and we failed miserably. There are so many characters and so many twists in the plot that we just got lost in it all. That is not to say this film suffers from poor writing. Quite the opposite! Murder Mansion is excellent and a fine mix of gothic horror and giallo. The score by Marcello Giombini is perfect, as is the cinematography by Guglielmo Mancori (Spasmo, The Weekend Murders). I won't say anymore for fear of spoiling the shit out of this as well as getting bogged down in the machinations of the plot and the numerous characters. I give this great, great film my highest recommendation.

SHORT BREAK

LeEtta and I go out for a Taco Bell run. It's important to note that I order way too much food and an enormous Mountain Dew to wash it all down. LeEtta's cousin Kathleen and her daughter Mackenzie may stop by for a visit. I scramble to figure out what movie to put on next. Shit! Everything I have left is pretty disturbing in one way or another.

"I don't need your face so you may suffer greatly before facing your destiny."

4:25 PM
Eyes of Crystal (2004)

This film was one of the biggest surprises of the last decade for me. It was one of the first times I'd heard of a giallo not directed by Dario Argento coming out in the 2000s. It opens with two cops rescuing a woman from getting raped. They chase the rapist down and corner him in an alley. Inspector Giacomo Amaldi (Luigi Lo Cascio) shocks his partner, Nicola Frese (José Ángel Egido), when he intentionally shoots the suspect in the leg after he was in custody. His partner helps him cover up this act and now we see a squirrel getting an injection. Wait, what? The very strident musical score by Francesc Gener kicks in while the credits play over scenes of the taxidermitization (which is not actually a word) of said squirrel.

In a ship graveyard, a hunter is setting a trap for a bird. As he waits, he overhears a couple making love in the weeds. There's a pervert masturbating to their display. He shoots the old guy in the dick and then goes after the young lovers. He kills the man and then shoots the woman. When she falls to the ground, he bashes her to death with the rifle butt. The scene is breathtaking and horrifying. I'm so glad I'm watching this with my wife, her mother, and members of their family right now! Next, at the police station where Giacomo works, a woman is filing a complaint about a stalker who leaves threatening messages on her cassette recorder. She's a lovely college student named Giuditta (Lucía Jiménez) and Giaocomo takes an immediate interest in her case.

Giacomo and Nicola are called to the scene of the murder we just witnessed. With the evidence lying around the scene, they know they are looking for a hunter. What is strange is that the killer tried to patch up the woman's gunshot wound after she was dead and this disturbs Giacomo greatly. The killer starts having visions of the dead woman. She's all patched up from the autopsy table but she's been stuffed like one of his birds. This is all rather terrifying. Next, our dynamic duo visits Ajaccio (Simón Andreu (who's all grown up in this movie!)), a retired cop with cancer, in the hospital. While they are visiting him, he has a flashback to a fire at the orphanage when he was a boy. Giacomo visits Giuditta at school and causes a minor scene during her class. They talk about who her stalker might be and she rescues a kitten.

Meanwhile, a woman is offering to sell a very disturbing life-sized doll to someone. Could it be... the killer!??! In a very atmospheric (and Argento-esque) moment, the killer shows up to claim the doll and brutally stabs the lady to death. When Giacomo and company arrive, her body is left up for display a la Silence of the Lambs. The cops note that he steals body parts and leaves cryptic messages left in blood at the scene. We may have a serial killer on our hands here, people! More revelations arise about the character of Giacomo as well as how Ajaccio's past connects him with the killer. Throw in a dash of red herrings on top of all of this and man, you have one entertaining and dark film.

"I want to see you die. Do you understand, Rosy?"

6:19 PM
"The Telephone" Segment, Black Sabbath (1963)

I have to make this little pitstop. Boris Karloff introduces us to the world of Mario Bava. The first story in this trilogy of horror tales is "The Telephone". It features a crazy hot chick named Rosy (the mesmerizing French actress Michèle Mercier) being menaced by a mysterious caller. No matter what she does to hide from her stalker, he seems to know every step she takes, every move she makes. I'm channeling Gordon Sumner.

This creep makes it very clear that he ain't after her body for the sexy time, he wants to kill her. This claustrophobic little tale is so exquisitely shot. I love her tiny apartment with the lovely stucco walls. The hot and bright colors of Rosy's gaudy décor are set off perfectly by this cold white backdrop. There's that dang bed that Bava loved to use over and over again. It will be making numerous appearances in Giallo Meltdown. The caller reveals himself as Frank, Rosy's ex-boyfriend who's just busted out of jail.

Good thinking, Rosy, call your lesbian friend Mary (Lidia Alfonsi). She will help you and only be hella creepy about being alone with you in the process. Mary shows up in her shiny dress (that looks bulletproof) looking absolutely stunning. They settle in for the night and Mary offers Rosy a lesbian tranquilizer. Frank (Milo Quesada of The Girl Who Knew Too Much) shows up in the middle of the night with murder on his mind. This neat little number wraps up perfectly. Kathleen and Mackenzie take their leave of us. Hopefully, Eyes of Crystal wasn't too traumatizing for them.

"Please, don't punish me. I need your loving."

7:10 PM
The Weapon, The Hour, The Motive (1972)

In a convent somewhere in southern Italy, there is a sickly young kid named Ferruccio who is segregated from the other orphans. His mother(?) Orchidea (Bedy Moratti) keeps him there because she can't care for him. When she visits to give him an injection, he asks for her to bring him some gialli. The kid likes his mystery stories. He also likes to snoop around the church's attic, peeping through holes at the goings on.

Next, a handsome young priest named Don Giorgio (Maurizio Bonuglia) is getting a tuggy under the table from Orchidea while having lunch with some nuns and some dudes. Don Giorgio does some self-flagellation to make himself feel better but it doesn't work. He breaks it off with Orchidea so he can go back to being a real priest and not one that gets public handjobs. She doesn't take his decision well and flips out. Then Orchidea goes to have her fortune read by her friend Giulia (Eva Czemerys). Giulia just wants the priest for herself. She gets totally naked in front of him and is all like 'Do me, padre!' What a freakin' bitch!

Later, while Ferruccio is playing with his marbles, he witnesses something terrible through one of his spyholes. He accidentally drops a marble down the hole so the killer knows that he saw something. This is actually pretty spooky scene. Don Giorgio is found murdered and the cops come in to investigate. The no-nonsense police inspector named Buito (Renzo Montagnani) is a bearded, motorcycle riding bastard! He asks the hard questions and Mother Superior (Gina Mascetti) doesn't like it.

The surly groundskeeper who has done time for murder is a good suspect. Ugh, dumb cops! Inspector Buito takes Orchidea on a little date where she takes out her pack of Astor cigarettes. No J&B so far but at least there's something familiar. Now she's sleeping with him? Things continue to get more tense as Buito gets a little too wrapped up in this case. The superb score by Francesco De Masi is very ethereal.

I've just downed a 5 Hour Energy drink. Shit is about to get real. An extremely brutal slashing happens and our collective jaws hit the floor. I tip my hat to you, badass movie. This grisly scene is bumpered by topless nuns flagellating themselves. Fun! The case is starting to come together as more facts come to light. I have to hand it to the actor playing Buito, it's fun as hell watching him work. Once again, I have stumbled across another gem that would make a great double feature with Don't Torture a Duckling.

RICHARD GLENN SCHMIDT

"With all these traps, you'll roast yourself like a chicken."

9:12 PM
Smile Before Death (1972)

This film opens with a scream. A woman named Dorothy in a yellow nightgown has had her throat slashed. She dies and the cops examine the evidence, ruling the death a suicide. The opening credits have a seriously infectious pop jam over them. This is from Silvio Amado, the guy who directed Amuck! so you know it's gonna be trashy as heck. Teenaged Nancy (Jenny Tamburi of Fulci's The Psychic) is the daughter of the dead woman. She's coming to live with Gianna (Rosalba Neri), her dead mother's best friend, and her stepfather Marco (Silvano Tranquilli).

Nancy has been in the house for all of 5 minutes when Gianna asks her to strip in front of her. Oh boy, this is gonna get kinky. It's already hinted that she and Marco are after Nancy's inheritance. Man, this film doesn't waste any time at all. Gianna is a photographer and she encourages Nancy to do some modeling. I hope this doesn't turn into a naughty fashion shoot! Marco returns from a work trip and finds that his stepdaughter is totally hot! Every single line of dialog between Marco and Gianna is suspicious (and not subtle in any known universe).

On a boating trip out on the lake, Nancy falls in the water. Marco dives in to help her and it's obvious they're filming in a swimming pool for the close-ups. Nancy survives the accident and she tells Gianna that she had a dream about Marco laughing at her while she drowned. (Foreboding.) The maid confides in Nancy that Dorothy's death was no accident. In a flashback, we see an argument between Dorothy and Marco about their terrible marriage and money he needs for a land deal. Marco was banging Gianna at the time and Dorothy was sleeping with her young lover Paolo (Hiram Keller of Seven Deaths in the Cat's Eye).

I'm getting very uncomfortable here. Marco is getting too handsy with Nancy and Gianna doesn't like it. And this frickin' pop song just won't stop. I think they've played it in every scene. Rosalba Neri is so great. Her eyes, her face, and her whole manner just scream 'sexpot'. Nancy has sex with Marco and we see a flashback to what really happened to Dorothy. Whoa, someone just tried to blow Nancy away with a pistol! I like where this is going. Thank you, Silvio.

SHOWER TIME

I am alone. Margie and LeEtta have gone off to bed. For some extra energy, I hit the showers. I get creeped out and half expect a shadowy figure to be standing in the bathroom. Fuck, I should have locked the door. Right now, I only have one weapon against a black-gloved killer. No, not that! My best weapon against a crazed murderer is my ability to cry easily.

> *"You've gotta let her body be seen by as many people as you can."*
>
> 11:21 PM
> The Pyjama Girl Case (1977)

The sounds of the ocean and some lazy disco (sung by the sultry-voiced Amanda Lear) fade into a bright sunny day at the beach. A little girl with a plastic parasol is playing with her dolly. It's so cute until she finds the hideously disfigured corpse of a woman. The Pyjama Girl Case is another very sleazy flick that I've been putting off. Straight up, this late entry giallo (set in Sydney, Australia) is just depressing and not very entertaining. But for some reason, I dig this one.

An ancient Ray Milland plays retired police inspector Thompson. He hears about the case of the girl whose murdered corpse is almost identifiable due to severe burns on her face. Since retirement is driving him crazy, Thompson begs to be put on the case. He has a buddy on the force who supplies him with information but he's not officially on the case. Meanwhile, the film follows a woman named Glenda (Dalila Di Lazzaro of Argento's Phenomena). She is a gorgeous girl with two lovers, a rich older man and a younger blue collar duder. Oh and she's also seeing Antonio (Michele Placido), an Italian immigrant. Glenda misplaces her panties a lot.

Glenda pays the bills by working on a steamboat as a waitress. Hot blooded Antonio (Italian stereotype!) gets jealous because of how the male customers look at her while she's serving them. I really like Ray Milland in this one. He's a real son of a bitch. In one of the most grotesque and just plain wrong setpieces in the entire genre, the cops put the unidentified corpse of the girl in a glass case. Then they invite the public to come in and see if anyone can identify her. The scene of all these fucking losers from all walks of life glaring at the nude corpse is just insane.

I used to not like Riz Ortolani's score for this film. It seemed more akin to a zombie movie than a laid back murder mystery. Now I dig it. So Glenda marries Antonio and continues seeing her other lovers. Meanwhile, every Tom, Dick, and Harry is convinced that the dead girl is someone they know. Director Flavio Mogherini certainly knows how to make a stylish film. There are lots of beautiful moments with excellent lighting and the color yellow is everywhere.

The cops beat a confession out of a local pervert but Thompson thinks they have the wrong guy. While Glenda is pretty much separated from

Antonio, she finds out she is pregnant. Not knowing exactly who the father is, she bounces between the three men in her life like a pinball. Okay, I want to tell you how all of this comes together but I'd be spoiling everything. Just know this: It's friggin' intense and very sad. This may not rub everyone the right way but there's just something about this film.

SUNDAY

The plot of my dream never did come together but in it, an Italian couple made a new life for themselves in an exotic country. All of the interiors were filmed in Italy. The killer never showed up. I wake up a couple hours after LeEtta has gone to work. I feel very happy about taking the day off today. After walking the dog and having some waffles with syrup, it's Mountain Dew time! Sparkles and I curl up on the bed and fire up the Pajama Girl Case DVD for the last half hour or so that I was too tired to finish last night. All right, NEXT MOVIE!

*"It's crazy, absolutely crazy. It's so crazy,
it might work."*

11:32 PM
In the Devil's Garden (1971)

After a quick run to 7-11 for hotdogs and Cokes for Margie and I, it is time for a movie from my past. Technically, this is the first giallo (albeit a British one) I've ever seen. When I rented Dario Argento's Creepers (AKA Phenomena), the tape for this film, under its alternate title: The Creepers, was in the box. I watched the whole film waiting for anything resembling the box art to happen. It never did. The sound on this bootleg is atrocious but the Japanese subtitles are very easy to read. Suzy Kendall, welcome to the moviethon. She plays Julie West, an art teacher at a girls' school.

A girl is raped in the woods near the girls' school she attends. During the assault, she stares at the powerlines above her and the whole scene is deeply disturbing. The cops don't know who committed the rape but they suspect the next victim may be raped AND murdered. The rape victim, Tessa (Lesley-Anne Down), is practically a vegetable and can't identify her attacker or do much more than stare off into space. Another girl, this one named Susan, cuts through the woods and she ends up raped and very dead. This movie is pretty grim and surprisingly atmospheric.

While searching for Susan, Julie spots a mysterious figure standing over the body. She sees him through the back windshield of the car and his face is eerily distorted by the glass and the brake lights. I am not what you might call a Suzy Kendall fan but I sure do like her in this film. Of course, the cops don't believe her because she describes the man as looking "exactly like the devil". Her testimony goes over like a lead balloon at the inquest.

Julie gets a harebrained scheme to catch the killer by having the newspaper promise to reveal a portrait of the killer in the next edition (4 days away). The detective thinks it's a nutty idea but hey, why not? The school's administrator (Tony Beckley) is a terrible pervert. He spies on and gropes the girls whenever her can. His crusty old wife finds his stash of nekkid pictures and, because this is sourced from a Japanese VHS, the genitals have been blurred out digitally. Julie's plan turns out to be totally dumb and the killer eludes capture once again. But yeah, you gotta stick around for how this ends.

CONCLUSION

Well, I am feeling pretty good about this moviethon. It was crazy laid back but I watched some good shit (and one worthless pile of crap). Think of this as a primer for Giallo Meltdown 10 where I really pull out all the stops. I settle down with Sergio Martino's Torso on Blu-ray (Brad's birthday gift to me) and Sparkles who is purring away without a care in the world. I'm half watching, half dozing, and just waiting for LeEtta to get home so we can go get dinner. Life is okay.

GIALLO MELTDOWN 10: LAUGHTER IN A GLASS COFFIN

I imagined the tenth meltdown for this book to be a record breaker, something totally over the top. But honestly, it's been a while and I just want to see if I can still even do a moviethon. So please bear with me while I attempt to get back into the swing of things. I have picked 13 films that will (hopefully) satisfy all of my darkest desires.

FRIDAY

The weather is perfectly overcast with just a few random showers here and there. It's been a weird winter. Here it is the end of March and we're still waking up to cold mornings. And any Floridian who complains about that is a jackhole. I love it. It's the perfect weather for a moviethon.

After work, we get home and pick up the mail. I got a bunch of non-giallo movies in the mail. Boring! I walk Shadow the dog while LeEtta makes dinner: yellow rice with green beans and kielbasa. Very nice. The apartment smells like food now. Crisco the cat is sitting next to me. He has his paw on my leg because he doesn't have a subtle bone in his body. He wants me to pet him and I'm not giving in. Sorry homey, I have a schedule.

"What's happening to me? This damn thing is turning into an obsession."

5:45 PM
The Bird with the Crystal Plumage (1970)

If this film didn't exist then the giallo genre would not have become the sensation that it did. This is the game changer. The black-gloved, vinyl-jacketed killer is lavishing a little too much attention on his knife collection. A victim is chosen and killed off screen. Next up, we meet Sam Dalmas (Tony Musante). He's an American writer and a whiny dick to boot. If you're into that sort of thing, then you're in luck! He's like that through the whole movie.

Sam gets paid for writing a handbook on birds and shows nothing but indifference for the work and for the people who hired him. Even his friend, Carlo (Renato Romano of Seven Bloodstained Orchids), is shocked by his crappy attitude. On his way home, Sam stumbles onto an attempted murder at an art gallery. Trapped in the automatic locking window display, he has to watch a bleeding woman named Monica (Eva Renzi) plead for help while the killer escapes bout the back.

The cops come and save the day. There is a great moment where Inspector Morosini (Enrico Maria Salerno) and Sam exchange a look while he's trapped in the display. The cops take Sam into custody for questioning. Sam knows something is wrong with the crime he witnessed but he can't recall quite what it was. Morosini takes Sam's passport so that he doesn't leave town until the case is solved.

As Sam is walking home in the foggy early morning hours, the killer takes a swing at Sam's head with a meat cleaver. Luckily, the creepy old lady from Case of the Bloody Iris is there and warns him just in the nick of time. Back at his place, his girlfriend Julia is waiting for him in bed. She's played by Suzy Kendall. Yeah, I'm still not even remotely attracted to this actress. They have sex but the memory of what Sam witnessed keeps flashing through his mind. I would have my mind on other things too.

There's a funny scene where the cops stage a lineup of "ordinary" perverts but a tranny named Ursula Andress gets mixed up with them. Mild comedy ensues. I wish Argento had chosen that moment to do a cameo but what can you do? Interestingly enough, Morosini confesses how desperate he is to Sam and encourages him to conduct his own investigation. Sam starts by going to see Monica to talk to her about what happened but her husband (Umberto Raho) won't allow it.

Next, Sam goes to an antiques shop where the first victim used to work. He meets an aggressively stereotypical gay dude who hints that the girl who worked for him was a lesbian. But he's not judging her because he's "not a racist". Sam borrows a print of a painting that was sold on the same day of the first murder that depicts a woman being brutally stabbed in a snowy landscape. The killer strikes again and this time the victim is a full-breasted woman. First he takes her panties and then he takes her life.

Later, the killer calls Morosini at the police station to taunt him in a freaky, raspy voice. Sam goes to prison to talk to Garullo AKA Solong (Gildo Di Marco), the stuttering pimp of the second murder victim. More comedy ensues. That night, Sam's police protection is killed and he's chased by an armed assassin (the devilishly handsome Reggie Nalder). I used to hate this part but Ennio Morricone's tense music and the perfect editing has won me over. Sam survives and even ends up chasing his own assassin (yeah, that actually happens).

The killer calls Sam who records the call and finally, there is a clue: a strange sound in the background of the call. The police attempt to apply their ridiculous pseudoscience to determine the source of the sound but it doesn't work. Only Sam's friend Carlo thinks he might know what it is.

Meanwhile, Sam meets the artist who painted the grisly painting that may have inspired all this crazy shit in the first place. His name is Berto Consalvi and he is played wonderfully by Mario Adorf. The killer goes after Julia and Kendall overacts so much in this scene that it's embarrassing to watch. I dozed off for a bit at the end there but so what? I've only seen this movie like 90 fucking times.

"Go ahead, kill me! Kill me!"

7:40 PM
Giallo (1934)

After a quick run to 7-11 for a Coke/Pepsi from the fountain, I magically transport us to that magical year: 1934. I'm so happy to have tracked down this one. Could this be the oldest known giallo? The film starts with some people traveling on a train. A woman is accosted by a weirdo the moment her husband steps out for a second. The weirdo claims to have fallen in love with her after he saw her vacant expression three days ago. The woman gives in to his advances and so they jump off the train together! This is just a ridiculous play the main characters are watching.

We meet Henriette (Assia Noris). She is a beautiful young woman who is considering divorcing her husband Giorgio (Sandro Ruffini). Her lawyer Carlo (Giulio Gemmo) is trying to convince her not to go through with the divorce. For some reason, Giorgio only wants to spend time with his chickens and his bees. Things get even more odd when a young man named Amati (Elio Steiner) rescues Henriette from an imaginary robber. It's a little suspicious especially considering how curious Amati is about some land contract or whatever that Giorgio is involved in.

Man oh man, the quick cutting in this film is harsh. It feels like they used a rusty knife to cut this thing and then pasted the splices back together with snot or something. Henriette finds out her husband changed his name and that he was on the run after being accused of murder. Comedic misunderstandings and more goofiness ensue. The acting style in this is your typical 1930s style and even the mildest plot elements are overcooked for the dumb audience's amusement. I'm loving this.

Of course, Henriette and Amati are convinced that Giorgio is trying to kill them. Henriette becomes totally hysterical after nearly being crushed by a scaffolding that suddenly collapses. Giorgio slaps her to calm her down and she likes it! He must be the killer because some old newspaper they found tells them so. This has some haunting moments in it and I really like the dark and stormy night (just like the weather here in Tampa is headed). Just like the plot of this movie, I blame the mystery novels!

"I told you not to make a scene. I don't like the ill-mannered woman."

9:15 PM
A.A.A. Masseuse, Good-Looking, Offers Her Services (1972)

An inane mother-daughter convo starts this film until it breaks into a pretty cool credit sequence that introduces all the characters via freeze frame. I'm not sure why but I'm actually really excited about this film. Christina (Paola Senatore) is going into business as a masseuse and it's driving her parents (Jack Betts and Yvonne Sanson) crazy. Her father (who looks like Hugh Laurie in a bad disguise) can't stand that she's going out on her own. Her first client is a bodybuilder that needs a massage. Christina shows up and they have sex. Wait a minute! The masseuse thing is just a cover up. She's a frickin' hooker!

Here's something that I love in movies: horseracing! Snore. I recover quickly because Howard Ross (of New York Ripper and Werewolf Woman) is in this as Oskar the pimp. Duder has all the fixins: poofy hair, a trench coat, purple shirt, loud ass tie, and big sunglasses. This movie makes prostitution look fun and awesome. Oskar says he's not a pimp at all but an "administrator" as he's talking up Christina for potential employment.

Christina's next John is a creep who looks like he's in The Polyphonic Spree. He's played by Franco Ressel of Eye in the Labyrinth, and a hundred other awesome things. He puts Christina in a bubble bath and then he sprays her money with perfume before he gives it to her. I think I just saw another J&B bottle made into a lamp. The killer in yellow gloves takes out Christina's John with a practically bloodless throat slashing. Oskar sucks at billiards but he sure can kick ass when some mofos start talkin' shit.

Daddy shows up and tries to beg Christina to come back home. Gee Dad, the old backhand across the face just didn't do the trick? Parenting is so hard. Speaking of striking, Paola Senatore is so damn hot. LeEtta and I have been discussing the contours of her ass in her countless nude scenes in the film. Since running away from home to be a total fucking whore, Christina has been living with Paola (Simonetta Vitelli). Paola's boyfriend Franco shows up and he's a real peckerwood. This "half-crazy" idiot makes a "pubic relations" joke and LeEtta and I decide that we hate his guts.

There's a great stalking scene but it's kind of spoiled by another weak throat slashing. Aside from falling for her pimp and refusing to sleep with ugly clients, Christina is also a total dick to her only friend Paoloa. She brags to her about how much money she's making and what not. Cutty Sark sighting! Wait, that's not nearly as cool as a J&B sighting.

Since things are getting too hot in the city, the plan is for Christina to screw some rich industrialist and run off with Oskar. Oh wow, there was just an awesome slow motion reveal of the killer. This has a great ending with fake Jimi Hendrix playing over the closing credits. This needs a decent release on DVD, I would happily revisit this clunky-titled and fun movie again and again.

SATURDAY

I woke up just before 8am. I was dreaming that I was watching what I thought was a 70s TV thriller with Marjoe Gortner but then there was all this nudity. I even saw Little Marjoe (if you know what I mean). I can't remember who the leading lady was; someone Faye Dunaway-ish. Outside, it is wet and muggy. The rain has stopped for now but the clouds are looking pretty menacing. I walk the dog, get LeEtta and I breakfast at 7-11, and then we start chores.

After the apartment has been cleaned within an inch of its life, we head out to the storage unit and sort through LeEtta's mom's stuff. I guess now is as good a time as any to let you know that Margie died nearly two months ago. She lost her two and a half year struggle with cancer. Now LeEtta and I have her dog, an apartment full of her stuff, and a storage unit that is full of -you guessed it- more of her stuff.

It was just three years ago, that Margie moved in with us because she had fallen on hard times financially. When she landed a great job and things were just starting to look up again, she was diagnosed with leiomyosarcoma. After many rounds of chemo, radiation, and surgery, she suffered a massive stroke that took away her ability to communicate with us and live on her own without machines. Months later, she died.

About as atypical as a mother-in-law could get, Margie was always super supportive of me and my moviethon endeavors. She bought me quite a few of the films covered in this book and sat through some pretty outrageous titles with me. I'll never forget the rather awkward late night viewing of So Sweet, So Dead with her. Now that was odd. So now, LeEtta and I are just trying to get our lives back together and move on while honoring a very important lady. This moviethon is dedicated to the memory of 'Old Marge'.

"I've memorized all your old seductive tricks."

12:26 PM
The Killer is Among the Thirteen (1976)

A windy overcast day at a beautiful Spanish villa is how this movies starts. This already feels like an Italian giallo but these people are speakin' Spanish! Simón Andreu is in this as playboy Harry Stephen. Paul Naschy is here as well as Ernest the chauffer. A group of 13 people have been invited to this lovely villa by lovely Lisa (Patty Shepard of My Dear Killer and Glass Ceiling). Why are they here? Rumor has it that Lisa hasn't been socializing since her husband Carlos died in a plane crash. Harry immediately starts flirting with Elena the hot maid. Before I start listing the rest of these friggin' characters, let me just say that there are too many people in this damn movie. Jeez! These people seem to not like Lisa very much. Are they frenemies? So much shit talking!

Lisa is showing Harry around like he was her pet. At first I thought they were lovers but it turns out that Harry was her dead husband's best friend. Ernest is trying to make sexy with Elena but she is resisting. This never happened to Waldemar Daninsky! At dinner, Lisa announces that the reason she invited all these fucks to the villa is because she knows that one of them killed her husband and she intends to find out who. She starts ripping these people to shreds (figuratively) by exposing their various corruptions including infidelity and art fraud.

There's a little style in this and that's hardly surprising as this 1976 flick was directed by Javier Aguirre who did Count Dracula's Great Love and Hunchback of the Morgue. One of the guests just said to Harry she thinks she knows who the killer is but she'll talk about it later. So she just signed her own death certificate. Speaking of death, is anyone going to die in this movie yet? I might be talked to death by this fucking screenplay. The insane 70s fashions on the ladies might be the most violent thing in this film.

At 53 minutes, the black-gloved killer kills the telephone! Ernest looks mad about something. Maybe Naschy is just mad about agreeing to be in this movie. I'm pretty mad right now. My copy of this film has a low droning noise in the background just a little quieter than the dialog and it's making me nauseous. One lady just theorized that there may be some "interwoven stories" at play here and LeEtta pretty much just lost it.

At 61 minutes, we finally see our first kill and it is glorious (because I'm bored)! Our cat Sparkles is cleaning herself rather noisily and it's more interesting than this plot. Maybe if I wasn't taking notes I wouldn't be quite so hard on The Killer is Among the Thirteen. LeEtta calls bullshit on that because she's not taking notes and she hates this movie. There are more kills and more revelations but I don't care. I'm going to take a much deserved nap after this is over.

"Everyone makes mistakes, even we policemen."

3:33 PM
The Devil has Seven Faces (1971)

After an all too short nap, LeEtta wakes me up and orders pizza. I've never seen this film in widescreen. Thanks, Internet! The opening music for this has a helium-filled lady howling in pain over a jazz trio and strings. Carroll Baker is in this (and a terrible wig) but unfortunately, she's not dubbed. She plays Julie Harrison who, after a late night party with some friends, is chased through the streets. Her attacker corners her but only takes her photo. The next morning at work, she gets a phone call from her twin sister, Mary (played by Karol Bayker). Mary says that she's being threatened by someone. Suddenly, an Asian man in a gorilla mask and wielding a huge knife plays a prank on her.

Julie goes to see her lawyer friend, Dave Barton (Stephen Boyd) for some advice. George Hilton plays Tony, a friend of Barton's who is hanging around and acting pretty suspicious. He and Barton chase off some ruffians who try to kidnap Julie. Then the three of them go out to her house in the middle of nowhere for some tea and cigarettes. This is all very fabulous. They find footprints all over the house indicating that an intruder has been intruding but Julie refuses to leave because that's where the phone number she gave Mary is.

The next morning, Tony calls her from the race track. That's right, he races cars and I have to laugh. George Hilton is completely believable as a race car driver. After a day at the races, some goons are waiting for Julie back at her place. They get the best of Tony and want to know where "it" is. They find out about her twin sister and leave just as the cops show up randomly. There's a shootout and Tony punches a cop for some reason. Barton covers for Tony and we meet the inspector played by Franco Ressel. That's your second appearance in this moviethon, sir. Nice work. Tony and Julie get a little out of the way place to lay low for a while.

There is a great stalking scene where Julie (finally out of that damn wig) hears some strange sounds in the house. The camerawork, lighting, and sound design are all spot on in this scene. The full frame DVD of this film can eat a dick. You have to see this in widescreen to appreciate it. She finds the old lady who rented her the house dead in the attic. When she tries to show Tony, of course the body is gone.

Luciano Pigozzi shows up as an insurance man. He and his company believe that her sister Mary has stolen some million dollar jewel. Carroll Baker is weird looking. She's sickly pale (something I normally like) and her smile looks like she is about to spit on someone. At the beach, Burton meets up with her and she's wearing a blue wig that makes her look like she scalped a cosplayer. Let the really long and boring sped up car chase begin!

POTTY BREAK

After the movie, I walk the dog. The wind is nice and it makes the air considerably less muggy but the sound of it could be covering up the sound of footsteps. So many giallo-related deaths take place in broad daylight.

Somehow I survive long enough to pick up the crappy mail and put on the next movie.

"Those are fightin' words, old buddy buddy."

5:31 PM
The Killer with a Thousand Eyes (1974)

Oh yes, there will be Greek subtitles. A cop in Lisbon follows a drug dealer into a shitty nightclub and then chases him outside. He tries to get the guy to rat out his supplier. They fight and another chase is about to ensue when a man in a kabuki mask strangles the cop from behind. The opening music (by Marcello Giombini) is kind of crappy but I like it. Anthony Steffen plays Detective Lawrence, a dickhead cop with a crummy British accent. He busts in on some druggies and starts kicking the shit out of the human garbage. He is interrupted by the news that his cop buddy in Lisbon is dead.

Lawrence goes to Lisbon to identify the body. His orders are to leave immediately afterward but he'd rather stay behind and catch the bastard who killed his friend. The hard-assed police chief orders him to return the next morning. Yeah right! A mysterious Frenchman says he will give Lawrence the name of the killer if he can board the plane and make it look like he's left Lisbon. He sneaks off the plane before it takes off and goes to meet the Frenchman but someone kills the guy with a sniper rifle.

Raf Baldassarre, who played the idiot bus driver in Eyeball, is in this as a cop. Lawrence checks into a hotel with a raging gay stereotype for a desk clerk. Next, he questions a hooker who is not very sexy. There's a raspy-voiced weirdo following him around and threatening all of his potential leads. The score for this film is Synth-Fuckery 101 and someone dropped out before the final exam. There's a hilarious scene where Lawrence tries to cook himself a meal but it turns out that he's a hopeless loser.

He catches a woman snooping around in his flat. She's lovely and she needs his help because her husband was murdered. The sniper takes a shot at Lawrence but kills the woman instead. Shit, I liked her! Somehow he manages to sleep through her murder and now he is on the run. Eduardo Fajardo is in this and he plays a Brazilian smuggler. Lawrence and a cop with a gray poodle on his head for hair go to a party. There is a cockfight and the smuggler's blond wife is a sick bitch. She is really, really into the whole cockfighting scene. I mean like REALLY INTO IT.

One of the cops from earlier in the movie is at this party. He gets killed by a bush. Lawrence looks guilty so he has to flee the scene. Poodle hair cop throws a chick in the pool because gets in his face. It is misogylicious. People of the world, stay away from Detective Lawrence or you'll get fucking killed. Who is the killer? I want to know. White guy karate! This movie is great. It is definitely more of a cop flick than a giallo but I dig it.

> *"I can feel her poison in my brain."*

7:29 PM
Love and Death in the Garden of the Gods (1972)

A girl wanders into a house and finds Erika Blanc dead in the bath. The music (by Giancarlo Chiaramello) over the opening credits is classy classical-sounding stuff. I've always found that Blanc is interesting looking but not exactly sexy. Well, she's sexy in The Devi's Nightmare and A Dragonfly for Each Corpse and The Redheaded Corpse and- Fine, I take back my previous statement. Anyway, an eccentric professor (Franz von Treuberg) and bird expert is moving into a fancy house. He immediately takes to running around the garden and surrounding woods, recording the bird life with his reel to reel tape recorder.

While out on an excursion, he finds a pile of cassette tape in the woods. He brings it home, cleans it off, re-spools it, and begins to listen. On the tape is Azzura's (Blanc) session with her psychoanalyst recorded after a suicide attempt. Viola (Orchidea de Santis of Seven Murders for Scotland Yard), the girl at the beginning of the film, found her in time. Damn, I really like the way this is unfolding. It's smart and weird and the camerawork is great. Romano Scavolini shot this; he also filmed (and directed) Spirits of Death.

We see Azzura and her lover Timothy or maybe he's her husband (Rosario Borelli) make love in an old, forgotten part of the church and a monk spies on them. Later, a younger man named Manfredi (Peter Lee Lawrence) proclaims his love for Azzura but she blows him off. He leaves but then proceeds to call her up on the phone and call her a whore before hanging up on her. LeEtta is like "That's her brother" and I'm like "What?" Now I'm really confused. This movie is leaving a lot to the imagination and I have no idea who these morose freaks are anymore.

Martin, her psychoanalyst is played by an actor I really like. It's Ezio Marano from A Lizard in a Woman's Skin and Black Belly of the Tarantula. The guy is so cool looking. I wish I looked like him. Oh okay, so Timothy is her husband. He's a drunk and even worse, he's a pianist. He's afraid of Azzura and knows that he can never possess her.

So Viola is Manfredi's girlfriend. Damn, this movie really is in no rush to explain a damn thing. She and Azzura have a nice lesbifriends moment. Azzura sends her back to Manfredi with her love-stink all over her. She refuses to let Viola wash herself off after their lovin'. This bitch is cold and it kind of serves her right getting trapped in this hell that she made for herself. It seems that someone has orchestrated her 'suicide attempt' and the tapes of the past have tipped off the professor to an unsolved murder. This is an intricate little thriller.

> *"This is so exciting. A wounded elephant is so unpredictable!"*

9:14 PM
Human Cobras (1971)

I jump in the shower to wash the lesbian love-stink off and wake myself up before I start this one. The films begins. A hockey team wins a game and the coach is nearly killed by an assailant. You take the good, you take the bad, you take them both and then you have Human Cobras! A guy named Tony (George Ardisson) gets a note asking him to return to New York. The film jumps again to Erika Blanc on horseback in slow motion. Glad to see her back yet again! We find out that some gangsters forced Tony to leave America, warning him never to return. He's in New York for 2 seconds before some gangsters are on his tail but no worries, Tony is a pretty intimidating dude; I can't imagine anyone telling him to leave the country.

Tony tries to find his brother's wife Leslie (Blanc) but her apartment is empty and trashed. He gets a phone call from her and heads out to her shitty apartment in Brooklyn. She's hiding out there with some floozy. We find out that all the trouble started when Tony's brother was killed with a sniper rifle at a football game. Leslie blames a gangster named George (Alberto de Mendoza) for the killing. For some reason, the country of Kenya is related to the plot.

Tony goes around shaking people down for information but it all seems like a setup. There's lots of footage of NYC and Tony being awesome but this really just feels like an out and out gangster flick right now. Luciano Pigozzi is in this as Mortimer, a sniveling little fuckwad. Mortimer informs Tony that his brother found some precious gems and got a bullet in the head for his troubles. This information costs Mortimer his life in an awesome straight razor killing scene that is so giallo that it hurts.

Tony and Leslie fly out to Kenya to get the bottom of this shit. They're in the country for 2 seconds before they are being tailed by a smooth-looking black dude. The guy who murdered Mortimer is also in Kenya. What a coincidence! People are trying to kill Tony already. Who knew that snake-wrangling and venom collection could be so fascinating? Tony meets up with a woman named Clara. She is played by Janine Reynaud (of The Case of the Scorpion's Tail) who I frickin' love! The giallo elements return to the forefront as we see someone stalking Leslie. I could have done without that final chase scene but overall, I like this weird movie.

SUNDAY

I had lots of confusing sped up science fiction dreams all night. I wake up to an overcast and windy day. After I walked the dog, LeEtta and I went out to Mimi's for breakfast. I got French toast and an iced latte. LeEtta ordered something with poached eggs on it. After a trip to the nearly deserted grocery store, we come home to Shadow's neurosis. In the short time we were gone, he chewed bloody holes in his fur. I guess he's a little emotional these days. Time for the next movie. So gloomy today.

"Women go crazy for me."

10:10 AM
Pensione Paura (1977)

This film explodes with thunder and jumps right into some very threatening music. This is from Francesco Barilli, the director of Perfume of the Lady in Black, so I have pretty high hopes. We see a girl (Leonora Fani) guiding a boat through a swamp. She stops in a bombed out gazebo to write her father a letter. He's a pilot in the War to End All Wars Part 2. Does she have daddy issues? Yer damn right she does! Her name is Rosa and she helps her mother Marta (Lidia Bondi) run a hotel but she hates the place and the demanding tenants. The score by Adolfo Waitzman is eerie and instantly intriguing. I love it.

Luc Merenda is in this as Rodolfo, one of the tenants of the hotel. He has a nice rapist mustache and hits on Rosa. The subtitles disappear for several minutes and we miss out on an entire conversation between Rodolfo and Marta. There is another tenant (I didn't catch his name) who likes to sneak up on Rosa and scare her. He keeps whispering in her hair about his dead family. Yep, this is gonna be a weird one, folks.

Marta is an unhappy woman. She is trying to keep this failing hotel running for some damn reason. Their customers are boorish and immoral. During dinner, bombers fly over, shaking the whole place and the tension is unbearable. Marta is also hiding a deserter (Francisco Rabal) in one of the rooms. Feeding him and keeping him a secret is just more drudgery for her. Marta and Rosa have a good relationship despite their hardships. Oh shit! Is that a black dress with polka dots? That's not good! I've seen where outfits like that can lead you.

One dark and stormy night, a woman's scream rips through the hotel. Marta is found dead with a broken neck. My stomach is in knots from all the tension in this film. Rosa is all alone now. I bet those letters to her father are a bunch of bullcrap. The following night, Rosa assumes her mother's duties and I'm just depressed now. Rodolfo is such a freak! He thinks he knows Rosa's type. Yuck. This girl is clearly too sheltered and inexperienced to know what the hell this psycho wants from her. The local priest/storekeeper is a total assface that refuses to give Rosa the same line of credit that he did for her mother. Everyone in this movie is scum. I hope this fucking hotel burns down with all these fuckers inside it.

Rodolfo hits on Rosa AGAIN but this time in front of his sugar mama (Jole Fierro). This old bitch goes ballistic and threatens Rosa. Later, he tries to rape her in the kitchen. When that doesn't work out, he demands to be served first. She gets a little revenge by spitting in his food. Eat spit, dickweed! Dumbass Rodolfo is mixed up with two gangsters and plans to steal diamonds from his sugar mama in order to buy a passport to Sweden. Rodolfo catches her spying and the scene is so harrowing that I almost don't notice how wonderful the lighting is.

Things continue to deteriorate as Rodolfo makes even more advances on Rosa and Alfredo, their drunken waiter, and only servant left has gone missing, presumably murdered by someone. Sugar mama tricks Rosa into her room and locks the door so that Rodolfo can rape her. Someone is going to die for this. And then someone does! Okay, shit just got crazy but I'm keeping my lip zipped. I will say this: Pensione Paura movie is intense, dirty, and painful to watch during some miserable sequences but it's also beautifully made. I highly recommend it to brave cinema viewers.

"Do you always have to behave like an idiot?"

12:03 PM
Five Women for the Killer (1974)

Oh, I like the way this film starts. It's just footage of an airport but the super sentimental strains of music by Giorgio Gaslini playing over it makes me feel right at home. A writer named Giorgio (Francis Matthews) gets off a place and calls his wife Erica. She's pregnant and due at any time. He is freaking out because she is having contractions while no one is there with her. He rushes home with a local doctor. They're too late, the child is born but his wife is dead. Erica's physician, Dr. Lydia Franzi (Pascale Revault), got there in time to deliver the boy but there was nothing she could do to save Erica. At the funeral, a strange duder shows up. He's looking despondent and has an immense afro that makes him look top-heavy.

The child is now in the care of Dr. Betti (Giorgio Albertazzi). He's at the top of his field but he's a cynical jackoff. Lydia assures Giorgio that the kid will be fine. While he's waiting in her office, Giorgio notices a file on her desk with his name on it. He opens the file and discovers that according to Lydia's tests, he is unable to conceive a child. Ruh roh! Lydia reveals that she did some unethical shit to protect her friend Erica. So now Giorgio is feeling pretty shitty, knowing that the baby was never his in the first place. He is also haunted by the memories of his dead lady. Thanks, life!

On his way to clinic one evening, Giorgio sees a woman named Tiffany (Ilona Staller) nearly get run over by a car. She insists on taking him home with her. He pours some J&B, they get to talking, and then she offers herself to Giorgio. When Tiffany admits to being pregnant, his face darkens. Bam! Quick cut to a razor blade slashing her naked flesh. Bam! Cut to the cops investigating the crime. The killer brutally slayed this woman, slicing her from vagina to stomach, and left a mark resembling an ankh on her chest. Gold old Howard Ross is here as the police inspector. IMDB says his character's name is "Police Inspector".

Is Afro-guy the father of Erica's kid? Wow. Dr. Lydia's jerk husband Fabrizio (Alessandro Quasimodo) certainly seems to think so. At the newspaper where Giorgio works, Oriana (Catherine Diamant), his coworker turns down an assignment because she's pregnant. She tells their boss (Tom Felleghy) the news right in front of Giorgio so it's no surprise when she gets killed in the same manner as the first girl. When asked why an autographed copy of his book was in Tiffany's apartment, Giorgio lies to the inspector. He also has no alibi for when Oriana was killed.

Thanks to a sleazy sex scene, we find out that Dr. Betti is having an affair with Sophia (Gabriella Lepori), a girl from his office. After a post coital argument, he says degrading things about women. Then Sofia tells him that she's pregnant. We've had 2 or 3 bottles of J&B so far and a J&B ashtray. Classy! Sophia is trying to blackmail Dr. Betti and his wife is pissed! Well, it was nice knowing you, Sophia.

Lydia gets attacked by the killer but Giorgio arrives just in time. She is pretty jealous of Alda (Katia Christine), the cute young nanny caring for Giorgio's kid. She also takes care of Little Giorgio, if you know what I mean. Alda informs Giorgio that she is pregnant. (Are there fertility drugs in the friggin' water supply?) But wait a minute, Giorgio can't have kids! More suspects start popping up as some less than flattering revelations come to light. I'm digging on 5 Women for the Killer! It's definitely on the trashy side but there's a lot of style during the stalking scenes, some comedy relief, a fast moving plot, and the musical score delivers.

"Have you already forgotten Juan's Face?"

3:11 PM
A Hyena in the Safe (1968)

After a quick nap (my second during this moviethon!), I put on this movie that I know absolutely nothing about. After a crazy big party, there are all sorts of suspicious characters cavorting around, covered in confetti.

They congregate at a castle where everyone gives everyone else suspicious glances. The group is missing an important member: Boris. Where is Boris? A lady with flashy earrings enters with lots of fanfare, claiming to be Boris's wife. She informs them that he died of a viral infection. Oh I see. These people are all diamond thieves and they're all a little tense.

These criminal types have their ill-gotten loot hidden in a safe submerged under water that only their keys can open simultaneously. Albert the idiot (Alex Morrison) is a little twitchy because he has misplaced his key so no one can get the diamonds. The others go apeshit and start hassling Albert's fiancé Jeanine (Cristina Gaioni) because she MIGHT have the key hidden on her somewhere. So yeah, now they all have to stay in the old mansion together.

In order to get him to him crack, the others take Albert's drugs away. He starts going nuts due to his withdrawal symptoms and everyone is just staying up all night, waiting. The cinematography in this pop art insanity is sharp and everything is so brilliantly colorful and brightly lit that it looks awesome. Out of nowhere, Albert claims that he made a mold of the key. Did I mention that the whole design of this safe is utterly ridiculous? Did I mention that it's also radioactive? No? Then forget I said anything.

I know there are supposed to be some murders happening but so far this has just been a big anti-drug message movie. Someone please put Albert out of my misery! If his DT's continue, I'm going to start fast-forwarding. A murder mystery? I like those! Juan (Ben Salvador) used to be Dutch but is now Spanish thinks he's the smartest criminal in the group and tells everyone so. He and Jeanine get it on (presumably). Now some idiot in a helicopter is yelling at them through Albert's radio.

The obtuse nature of this film is reminding me of 5 Dolls for an August Moon. If there was a drinking game for this movie and squinty-eyed suspicious glances was a reason to take a shot, I'd be in the morgue and my liver on a little metal tray in minutes. Another one of these fools is knocked off and I suspect that no one's going to make it. Speaking of double and triple crosses, Boris's wife starts playing people against each other. Despite my whining, I like Hyena in the Safe. It features one of the longest death scenes ever but I won't say who gets it and how.

> *"Blood. Blood. I see blood everywhere. I can feel something bad is going to happen."*

4:51 PM
Nine Guests for a Crime (1977)

A vehicle stops by a beach and some men carrying shotguns climb out. They walk up to a couple making love on the beach. They scare the guy by cocking their guns. When he runs for it, they shoot him in the knees and then in the face. Then they bury him alive in the sand and leave. After they leave, his bloody hand rises out of the sand. After a freeze frame, the credits and the music kick in and oh wow, I am getting a serious grindhouse vibe from this shit. This film comes from director Ferdinando Baldi, who directed some great spaghetti westerns and co-wrote Mario Bava's The Whip and the Body.

The movie starts proper with a sailboat on the water and a wonderful piece of Theremin music. Hot damn, the score from Carlo Savina is just fantastic so far. Some people are cruising on the sailboat, headed for a villa on a small island. The patriarch of the lot is Uberto (Arthur Kennedy of Let Sleeping Corpses Lie) and he has a young wife named Giulia (Caroline Laurence). Jeez, he could be her frickin' great-great-grandfather!

Elisabetta (Dana Ghia of Smile Before Death), Uberto's sister wants her rifles "for hunting". Patrizia (Loretta Persichetti) says that her "voices" told her that she shouldn't have come on this trip. The little doomsayer predicts that there's a bad moon on the rise. The island is very picturesque and the wind is constantly blowing, giving everything a spooky atmosphere. There's also some marital strife (a giallo cliché?) between Lorenzo (John Richardson of Eyeball) and his very naked wife, Greta (Rita Silva). Lorenzo has daddy issues but if Arthur Kennedy was my father, I'd have them too.

There's a J&B sighting 11 minutes into the film so I'm feeling very comfortable right now. Patrizia is guzzling it down while wearing a see through (and very nipplicious) muumuu and white panties. Michele (Massimo Foschi) and his dumb wife Carla (Sofia Dionisio) are feeling the stress of this vacation too. She is paranoid and has been packing a pistol ever since she got mugged. Walter (Venantino Venantini of Seven Deaths in the Cat's Eye), Patrizia's husband, tries to get his gloomy lady to go scuba diving with the family but she's too freaked out by the cries of seagulls. He smacks the tumbler of J&B out of her hand like a boss.

Things get real when an assassin in a black scuba suit kills the crew of the yacht and sets it adrift. Oh wait, never mind, time for melodrama! Michele is macking on Giulia right in front of Uberto and Greta is very unsubtly seducing Walter. They make love and of course, Greta's husband sees them. Patrizia sees them and then jumps in the shower to touch herself. Good times! That night, everyone is very pissed off at everyone else. This doesn't stop Michele from fucking Giulia. You go, boy! The next day, Carla starts screaming for help in the ocean. When they go to rescue her, she's gone. Now the idiots notice that the yacht is gone AND someone has tampered with their motorboat. Yep, they're trapped on the island and worse that that... they have to depend on each other now.

Elisabetta is having a nightmare of the murder that occurred at the beginning of the film. She was the girl, 20 years ago, who was caught making love with that dude. While everyone is trying to calm her down, a killer in black gloves disposes of Uberto. Now everyone is getting all excited about who's going to inherit his money. Oh shit! Another murder just happened and it was amazing! Despite some pacing issues, this movie is really kicking into high gear! Paranoia and death are everywhere.

"Cookie! Cookie!"

6:33 PM

The Cat o' Nine Tails (1971)

Is this the first Blu-ray reviewed in Giallo Meltdown? Wow, I think it is! Thanks, Brad! Ennio Morricone and Bruno Nicolai rock this one and they do it with flutes. Actually, the opening music kind of gives it a spaghetti western feel. Weirdly enough, this is almost my favorite Argento. I know it's not his best but I find it to be one of his most watchable efforts. I definitely like it better than his directorial debut, The Bird with the Crystal Plumage. Karl Malden is pretty great in this but then again, I have always liked him (especially in One-Eyed Jacks). He plays Franco, the blind ex-reporter turned amateur detective. And James Franciscus (who is such a beautiful hunk of a man) plays Carlo, the non-blind and non-ex-reporter, also turned amateur detective.

Now that's a job for a blind man: typesetting a friggin' crossword puzzle. Ironic empowerment or subtle cruelty? The sexy French-born Catherine Spaak plays Anna Terzi: a beautiful woman with helmet head hair and not a lot of 'acting skills'. There's a lot of details to the mystery in this film. You know, small things that only a blind person would notice. There's a great scene in the barbershop with a barber who should probably retire soon. Hilarious. Argento's comedy used to be good. Does anyone remember that? Oh snap, a wallpaper debate just broke out. Is that supposed to be jellyfish or brains on Rada Rassimov's (Ivan's sister!) apartment walls? Bust out the XYY chromosomes, y'all. This entire plot gets going because of some silly pseudo-science because a certain combination of chromosomes will determine if you're a criminal or not.

When Carlo's friend, the photographer, gets killed, it's so brutal. He has one of those 'I'm too young to die' tears running down his face. Then the killer slashes up his face, post mortem, just to scare off Carlo and company. I feel band for Rada Rassimov in this movie. Just like Catherine Spaak, she too has helmet head hair. She gets killed pretty dang brutally too. The killer tries to take out Carlo with a syringe full of poison in his milk. In her pointless nude scene, Spaak has a look on her face like 'Sorry about my boobs, duder.' And then there's Gigi the Loser (Ugo Fangareggi), yet another bizarre comedy character in an early Argento flick. We meet him as he's winning an insult contest. He helps Carlo break into a doctor's house to get some clues.

The inspector is played by Pier Paolo Capponi of Seven Blood-Stained Orchids. The guy has one hell of a mug and a perfect head of shiny, black hair. Karl Malden is fucking awesome in this film but his relationship with Laurie (Cinzia De Carolis) is just a tad creepy. Her parents are dead so they just kind of "found each other"? Even more freaky, she calls him "Cookie". IMDB just blew my mind. The actress who plays Laurie was one of the vampire kids from Night of the Devils. Also of note, J&B is all over this dang movie.

The cemetery scene is one of my favorites in all of giallodom. Franco and Carlo go into Rassimov's grave to get a piece of evidence and all heck breaks loose. Holy shit! Ken Doll just got face-checked with a two by four. The film wraps up with a great fight sequence and an awesome (though abrupt) ending. I'm sure I could have said more about this but I am friggin' burnt. The Cat o' Nine Tails is an absolutely essential giallo and I think it's unfairly underrated by fans of the genre.

CONCLUSION

It's so nice to end on a high note. Thank you, Mr. Argento. It feels good to get back into the moviethon swing of things. I still have a long list of movies that need to be watched for this book. That makes me happy. I have to go back to work tomorrow. That doesn't make me happy.

GIALLO MELTDOWN 11:
YOU SHOULD HAVE KILLED ME
WHEN YOU HAD THE CHANCE

So it would appear that I have made it to the eleventh Giallo Meltdown. What the hell am I supposed to do to keep this fresh? I watch lots of movies and I talk all blah blah blah about them. How about this time I watch all the crap I've been avoiding for the last few years? It's true. I've been awfully good to myself by passing over an abundance of bullshit; softcore porno films disguised as gialli and rape-tacular garbage that I consider the bottom of the underside of the barrel. There are also a lot of titles that I'm wary of due to reputation or poor quality transfers. So what the hell? I'm the kind of guy who slums it around the fringes of cinema, aren't I? I've sat through over 50 Jess Franco films for God's sake!

I think about how none of these films would have happened had it not been for an overabundance of movie screens back in the day. It's like the straight-to-DVD (or straight-to-streaming) market nowadays except the films didn't suck as badly. How weird is that? I'm watching the 70s equivalent of straight-to-video. These films were churned out and many of them were meant to be forgotten. I'm a dang scavenger.

MONDAY

I decided to use some vacation time for this moviethon. LeEtta and I are moving next month so I wanted to get this in before the craziness starts. While my sweet wife is at work, she'll miss out on some of the trash. Lucky woman. When the alarm goes off, I almost can't get up, I'm so tired. I was dreaming of high school. I had gotten a job there as an assistant teacher. The place was just as I remembered it only bigger, more labyrinthine. Back in the real world, I feed the cats and the bird, go to 7-11, and get a Mountain Dew and a hot dog. The sun is bright as hell but there is a nice cool breeze. This has been a very nice May so far.

"You're a whore. Like our mother."

8:58 AM
The Sister of Ursula (1978)

This flick opens up innocently enough with a nice slice of 70s elevator music and some picturesque scenery. Dagmar (Stefania D'Amario of Zombi 2) and her sister Ursula (Barbara Magnolfi of Suspiria) show up at a cute little hotel on the seaside. Ursula is terrified of the black statues in the lobby. Poor thing! She and sis go up to the room where sis strips naked to some phasey wah wah guitar. The hotel manager Roberto (Vanni Materassi) tells sis about Stella Shining, the nightclub singer and how great she is. We'll see about that! The locations in Salerno, Italy are stunning and the filmmakers certainly made the most of them.

Stella Shining (Yvonne Harlow) is amazing! She's a busty blonde in silver disco dress who lip-syncs like she was on "Ru Paul's Drag Race". Marc Porel shows up as Filippo. The first shot we see with him contains a bottle of J&B and a J&B ashtray sitting on the bar. Ursula is wary of Filippo as though he were a black statue. Ursula splits the scene like a spoiled child with Dagmar in tow. Filippo is left alone with Stella Shining and we find out that they are having some relationship trouble.

Back at the room, Dagmar offers Ursula a sedative but in a very poorly translated moment, she offers the same tranquilizer right back to Dagmar, who immediately takes it. What the heck? While I've been typing this paragraph, some douchebag picked up an insanely voluptuous hooker and we see simulated fellatio, cunnilingus, intercourse, and un-simulated full frontal nudity. It turns out she was paid by someone hiding in the closet to have sex with the dude. When he leaves, the hooker is murdered by the hider with a giant cock or at least the shadow of one.

The next morning, Ursula faints when she hears the news about the dead hooker and is a mega-bitch to everyone when she comes to. She has decided to leave the hotel. While she's packing, she tells Dagmar that it's impossible for her to like people. Dagmar talks her into staying for a few more days. I really like the actress playing Ursula. She's got this doped up look on her face. Maybe she's on dope.

It's revealed that Ursula and Dagmar are living off their father's inheritance and their mother went missing years ago. Ursula gets that far off look in her eyes and talks about their father like he's still alive. Uh oh, that's not good. They go to a church where Ursula talks to the most disturbing sculpture of Jesus I've ever seen. When Dagmar tries to comfort her, she screams "Don't touch me!" hilariously. We find out Filippo is a junkie which is why he and Stella Shining are on the outs. This is pretty painful to watch knowing that Marc Porel's life was cut very short by his drug addiction. Was this his last movie? No, that was Killing of the Flesh. (We'll get to that one eventually.)

A very unsexy couple is knockin' boots in an old castle when the killer shows up and kills the guy with a big knife but, of course, saves the giant cock for the lady. There's a big dollop of melodrama dropped on this sleazy taco as we discover that Robert and his wife Vanessa (Anna Zinnemann), who owns the hotel, are having troubles. Okay sure, time for a scenic drive with Stella Shining so Vanessa can visit her lesbian lover. Filippo shows up and harasses Stella because he's a jealous junkie scuzbag. A dog watches them from a second story window. It's an awesome dog.

Dagmar masturbates with a gold chain and I suddenly remember why I've been avoiding this dang movie. And now the lesbian sex scene! Some chick named Jenny (Antiniska Nemour) was paid by an unseen stranger to get Vanessa in bed for a romp. After Vanessa leaves, the killer breaks out that giant dick and that's the last of Jenny. To this movie's credit, I am definitely enjoying my second viewing. That being said, this is still a softcore porn with a killer who specialized in genital mutilation (but only on the female victims) so it will always be an unpleasant watch.

"Keess keess, no more."

10:36 AM
Giallo (2009)

Oh Argento, you crazy guy. Welcome to 2009, everybody. Two Japanese girls are partying in Rome. One hooks up with a duder at a club and another takes a cab home. The one who took the cab is not so lucky. The freaky looking cab driver locks her in the cab and absconds with her. We're then quickly introduced to a model named Celine (Elsa Pataky) whose sister Linda (Emmanuelle Seigner) is flying in. We go back to the Japanese girl who is still alive. She's bound on the floor and the cabbie is taking her picture over and over again. There is another girl in the room strapped to the table but she's dead. Fun stuff!

Celine gets picked up by the same crazy cab driver. He sticks a hypodermic needle in her head and brings her to his lair. Linda is left hanging out in Celine's apartment, just worrying about her sister. The next morning, Linda goes to the cops and they're not sympathetic because her sister was pretty. She is told to follow the pizza boy who takes a pizza down to an eccentric police inspector's office in the basement. He's Inspector Enzo Avolfi and he's played by Adrien Brody. He's also a dickhead. Enzo is working on a string of homicides of beautiful girls.

The killer is a sick fuck who enjoys store bought inhalants and cutting the lips off of women. I can relate. Enzo has visions of a woman being stabbed in the throat by a bald dude. Later, he gets freaked out when he's being followed by a cab. It turns out to be Linda following him, hoping for more info on her sister. He tells Linda that her sister has likely been kidnapped by a serial killer but she might still be alive. My cat, Sparkles, is under the coffee table snoring while the killer is taking a clawhammer to the forehead of one of his victims. Nasty!

The flashback sequences where we see Enzo's mother get killed are filmed pretty amazingly. Everything is tinted yellow and the camera never stops moving like it was in high seas or something. This briefly feels like old Argento. I like that. They find the body of the Japanese girl. She is alive long enough to speak for a few minutes and then she's gone. She says a Buddhist prayer and the word "yellow".

Meanwhile, Celine does her best to piss off the killer. She calls him ugly so he cuts her finger off. He has a flashback to when he was a little jaundiced kid. His mother was a junkie whore and that's why he's yellow. Aw, poor baby. They almost catch the guy when he goes to get his meds. Enzo harasses a nurse into giving him the killer's address. They go to the killer's house and of course, it isn't his current address. Celine manages to get free and electrocute the killer with one of his big floodlights. In slasher cliché #107, she doesn't make sure she's dead, she just runs for it. So you know, she's still fucked. The manhunt is on!

This movie gets a bad rap and I think part of it is because of the killer. SPOILER ALERT? It's Adrien Brody in a lot of makeup and he should be ashamed of himself. He is wretched, over-the-top (not in a good way) and his performance as Enzo sucks too. Supposedly, he sued to stop the release of this movie because he never got paid (which is pretty funny). That being said, I like Giallo okay. I think it's saved by Enzo's backstory and the competent filmmaking. A lot of people expected more from Argento but come on, the guy is way, way past his prime. I'm surprised it was this good.

LUNCHTIME

I heat up some mac and cheese. I also have some hummus and pita bread. I am so full now. Normally, I would be taking Shadow for a walk right now but we had him put down last week. He was already senile and his hips were terrible when all of a sudden, he lost control of his bowels. It wasn't easy but we sent him on his way to go be with Margie. Brad texts me that Rosella Falk (of The Fifth Cord) passed away. That's sad. I liked her.

"I'm the cheese on your spaghetti. Fru fru."

12:38 PM
Bugie rosse (1993)

Tomas Arana of The Church is in this one. I like him but he scares me. In this, he plays Marco, a writer who is into some kinky shit according to his chatroom conversations! He goes out to the 'gay district' (that's what I'm calling it) to pick up a dude but he's too nervous. Meanwhile, some deranged pervert is watching him pick up a guy. He keeps leading these dudes on. Come on, duder. I want some action! What is your game? This movie has more gay frustration in it than that Wham!'s "Last Christmas". While Marco is getting mugged, the duder he almost picked up gets killed by a black-gloved killer wielding a mallet.

The cops suspect Marco because he looks guilty as fuck but his cop buddy covers for him. Marco sees the mugshot of the duder who robbed him but he pretends not to recognize the guy. Marco is a reporter and wants to get the scoop on the killer before anyone else. There are lots of awesome and very dated computer graphics in the chatroom scenes. The killer calls Marco with a threatening whispery voice. The music in this film sounds like Claudio Simonetti. It isn't but it sure does sound like him.

Marco goes back out looking for the killer and nearly gets burned alive by a gay-bashing Polish guy. Someone saves his life and his cop buddy tells him to be careful. Back at his work, there's a vampish lady reporter named Lucia (Natasha Hovey of Lamberto Bava's Demons) that's trying to rape-seduce Marco. It doesn't work. We cut to a hilarious sex scene where Marco's naked wife Adria (Gioia Scola) is lowering herself onto him like she's about to birth a baby on his lap. What the fuck am I looking at? And we're off to the gay bar for some denim grinding and a J&B sighting.

The next night Marco brings home a gorgeous guy named Andrea (Lorenzo Flaherty), you know, for research. While he's asleep, Andrea comes in and (presumably) blows Marco. Is that a dreamjob? Now Adria is trying to take an erotic bath with him but he can't get Andrea off his mind. Meanwhile, the can of pasta sauce is boiling over on the stove. All of this is going on while an unseen saxophone player tries to Kenny G us to death. What the heck is going on here? Andrea's red banana hammock ends up in the wash and turns all the whites pink. The way Adria stares incredulously at the red bikini underwear is truly hilarious.

The cinematographer on this is really good. He shot a bunch of good shit like The Bloodstained Shadow and Watch Me When I Kill. I feel so bad for Adria. She's really confused. So now Marco and Andrea are both trying to catch the killer. They go to a Roman bathhouse to scope out some possible suspects. There's a bitchy blond lady who acts as a pimp for this old duder who holds orgies and stuff. Marco has to show her a good time to get closer to the old guy. But she's a slapper and a pincher and I have to stare at the ceiling to get through this 'audition' scene.

You will need a shower after this tawdry movie that comes with all the kinky attachments from the back of the catalog. When Lucia lets her hair down, she looks like Sean Young. The bodies keep piling up as Marco keeps getting in deeper and deeper into this story. I'm surprised by this one. I was expecting the worst but somebody, very late in the game, tried to make a great and sleazy giallo and they did a pretty damn good job. And I just realized Alida Valli is in this!

"I can tell. You smart mammary glands. Welcome, honey. Pay for your sins!"

2:39 PM
Angel: Black Angel (1989)

While this chick named Arabella (Tini Cansino) is driving around, she takes a swig from a bottle of J&B and goes "Ah! Tasty!" A guy is following her and he complains about what a bitch she is. She stops at an old mansion with a bunch of perverts on the lawn. A Peter Criss lookalike tranny sitting on what I think is a penis shaped chair demands payment. She pays, goes in, and discovers all kinds of sex going on in every corner of every room. In fact, there's more sex in this scene then in the entire running time of Bugie Rosse. This is bargain basement sleaze, dubbed for your pleasure. The guy following Arabella is a photographer sneakily taking snap-shots of her.

Two hunky dudes start sexing her up but then they pull a knife on her, demanding that she become a hooker. The cops show up and bust up the party just as things are about to get violent. Arabella escapes but the lead detective, De Rosa (Carlo Mucari), captures her and rapes her against her car. He lets her go when he finishes but she leaves her friggin' purse at the scene. Of course, De Rosa finds it. I've already had it with this film.

Poor Arabella lives at home with her writer husband, Francesco (Francesco Casale), who's confined to a wheelchair and he's a total dickhead. She has memories of a happy time when they got married but those days are over ever since "the accident". On their wedding day, while she was giving him road-head, they crashed and he became paralyzed. I'm not making this up. His mom, Marta (Evelyn Stewart!), shows up and she takes care of Arabella and Francesco like they were children.

De Rosa shows up to blackmail Arabella for more sex. They go out to the garage so he can go down on her. She hits him on the head with a mallet, killing him just as Francesco rolls by and catches them. Next thing you know, a black gloved killer kills the photographer from earlier with a big pair of scissors (and apparently castrates him). From there we go to an amazing disco sequence and to get my blood moving, I get up and dance. A cowboy picks up Arabella at the disco and takes her home. She pours champagne all over herself and he mentions how he paid her $50. So she's a prostitute now? Arabella disappears and the cowboy ends up dead.

The other detective in this, named Scognamillo (Renato D'Amore), has a huge beard, eats ketchup-smothered hamburgers, and dresses like a slob. He's eating a hamburger at the crime scene! It seems that the cowboy has had his dick and balls cut off. Scognamillo works with a detective named Gina Fowler (Valentina Visconti) who has a weak stomach and hallucinates blood coming out of faucets. She likes to go out at night in see-through outfits to prowl around and taunt the killer. Oh wait, that was only a nightmare. Her lesbian lover Agnes (Rena Niehaus of Damned in Venice) is going to make it all better. Yep, I know what that means. No lesbian sex scene!? Okay, I guess I don't know anything about movies.

Gina told Agnes about how her mother castrated her father with a pair of scissors when she was a kid and how it has haunted her ever since. So Agnes freakin' tells the press about it to get some quick cash and gets her thrown off the case. What a beyatch! Scognamillo may be dumb but he's the only likeable character in this flick besides Gina. Don't worry, this has both male and female genital mutilation. Black Angel makes Strip Nude for Your Killer look like Bambi. I actually recommend this one. It's deliciously stupid and, if you can get past the sleaze, there's a fun flick here. Director Stelvio Massi: delivering the goods in 1989!

DINNER

LeEtta gets home and I run out to take out the trash and check the mail but there is none. I'll have to come out later. It's an astonishingly beautiful day outside. I make us a frozen pizza and it comes out great thanks to the extra cheese and seasoning I add. I'm a master chef, deal with it. LeEtta breaks out the tequila her dad picked up in Mexico and we both do a large shot. We're both surprised when it turns out to be a tequila liqueur that tastes like honey and licorice. Why can't J&B be this easy?

> *"Ghosts are everywhere. I don't know why but I feel them."*

5:22 PM
Sex of the Witch (1973)

This is my second viewing of this film. My first impression was pretty abysmal. Hopefully, a second time will prove to be a better experience. This opens with a catchy little tune while a priest drives along a windy road. The Hilton family is standing around their dying patriarch. Duder gives one hell of a final internal monologue. Meanwhile, the butler politely forces some chick to give him head in a crypt. Well, this movie starts off promising enough! Camille Keaton is in this and she is looking nice and sullen. I'm ever so slowly starting to find her attractive.

The Hilton family are a bunch of catty jerks. Ugh, I hope the killer gets here soon. One of the daughters, Ingrid goes and picks up a huge dog named Twinky. Now for the reading of the will. Nobody gets the money until they turn 30 and if anyone dies, the others get to split their money. Nice plan, dad. These losers are gonna start killing each other any second now. All the characters are pairing off in couples and getting it on. I hope that they're not all blood relatives! Other than boning, there's lots of suspicious glances thrown around all over the place.

The gang goes to an underground nightclub and for some reason the film is tinted in yellow, green, and other colors. There's a hippie band playing and naked ladies groovin'. The lyrics consist of a guy yelling "Yes, I know!" over and over again. The sequence goes on too long and I get pretty tired from my own hippie dancing. When one of the Hiltons arrives back at the house, he's bloodily bludgeoned to death with a mace.

I'm going to be honest with you: This film introduces a lot of characters and rather incompetently so it's kind of hard to keep track of who's who. Ingrid possesses a secret that would destroy mortal men and there's one chick who was injured as a child but her beautiful breasts look normal to me. Also, there are some fancy press-on nails from the Orient that I think are supposed to have supernatural powers.

We hit some major downtime in this movie while the two mustachioed cops (Donald O'Brien and Irio Fantini) are waiting for the killer to come back. There's an endless scene of somebody boning and my eyes are getting heavy. Even LeEtta is like "Um, has anyone even died yet?" Thankfully, the killer hears our pleas and kills again. He goes after Camille Keaton and starts to kill her but she gets all turned on and- Huh? We figure those fancy nails he's wearing hypnotize the person who gets cut by them. And I just woke up. Man, Sex of the Witch is a bad movie. It starts off so good and then just farts out. My advice to you: Skip this one.

*"The music holds a secret and
the secret means death."*

6:57 PM
Giallo napoletano (1979)

I tried to watch a longer cut of this film in Italian but the English subtitles were screwed up, so here I am with the shorter, dubbed version with Greek subs. The music over the credits sounds like an Abba breakdown with some vocoder thrown over the top. It's weird and I love it. This giallo comedy opens with workmen carrying posters of Alfred Hitchcock and Luis Buñuel. We're introduced to Raffaele (Marcello Mastroianni), a mandolin player who works at a small restaurant. He's a total goofball. A pretty girl gives Raffaele an odd look while he's playing and says something to her date. Then they both look at him suspiciously. This can't be good.

Raffaele's father owes debts to a gambling parlor. It's run by a vampish homosexual stereotype named Giardano who offers to tear up the check his father bounced (with Raffaele's forged signature) if he can pay with cash or sexual favors. Giardano then offers Raffaele some work to pay off the debts. He is to play a specific piece of music on a specified street corner at 5am. Raffaele agrees to do this. In the middle of his serenade, a man starts shooting at a woman with a shotgun from a balcony right over Raffaele's head. The woman is hurt but manages to escape in her VW Beetle before the man falls (or jumps) to the street below, dying instantly. Someone knocks Raffaele out, leaving him for the cops to find in the morning.

After giving his statement to the police, Raffaele is picked up by Victor (Michel Piccoli), a famous conductor and Elizabeth (Zeudi Araya Cristaldi), the opera singer. The man who died was Elizabeth's brother. Victor asks Raffaele to look into what happened and offers him a spot in his orchestra as a reward for solving the mystery. He goes to see Giardano to ask him who paid to have that piece of music played but someone throws the poor gay bastard off his balcony! Raffaele spots Lucia (Ornella Muti), the girl he spotted earlier at the restaurant. She flees the scene in the same VW Beetle. He follows her to a lunatic asylum where a pyromaniac tries to light him on fire. Lucia agrees (only after Raffaele threatens to go to the police) to meet up later and discuss what she knows about the crimes.

Back at home, a huge thug forces Raffaele to the roof of his building where a gangster named Bugsy is waiting for them. Bugsy threatens to have him thrown off the roof if he doesn't give up the case. Someone is being blackmailed, they are willing to kill to keep their secret, and that piece of music is at the heart of it all. Of course, police inspector Voghera (Renato Pozzetto) is incompetent and always one step behind Raffaele's own investigation. Do you like comedic cocaine use, comedic domestic violence, complicated plots, harrowing chase scenes, references to Deep Red, albinos, comedic cross-dressing, and Christmas parties at insane asylums? I do!

I'm really digging on this zany movie but the Greek subtitles are giving my eyes a hangover. It's a shame that I don't speak Italian because the widescreen print is really the best way to appreciate Luigi Kuveiller's cinematography. He shot Deep Red! Director Sergio Corbucci is very confident here (as always) and delivers a film that's stylish and very funny. As an added bonus, Riz Ortolani's score is really, really odd. Maybe he got into some of the comedic cocaine.

> *"I've been waiting for you through four cigarettes*
> *and a lot of Mozart."*

9:06 PM
Evil Eye (1975)

Yeah, this one is going to hurt. This supernatural pile of 1975 crap from director Mario Siciliano is sort of a giallo and I just want to get this over with. The score by Stelvio Cipriani is the only thing that I recall liking about it. This opens with a black magic ritual featuring a lot of naked people screaming. Peter Crane (Jorge Rivero), a suave playboy, wakes up from this dream (?) in a room full of people he doesn't know when a sexy lady calls him on the phone. Her poodle is very excited. LeEtta thinks that the dog is probably going to pee on the bed. He barely remembers the horrible nightmare that her call woke him up from.

Peter asks his butler Walter (Eduardo Fajardo) to go around waking up all of the strangers passed out in his apartment. Next, Peter dresses up like Travolta in Saturday Night Fever and goes driving around town to the soothing sounds of Cipriani. He calls on his girlfriend Elizabeth (Daniela Giordano) but she's busy having an ugly fashion show. Then he meets Yvonne (Lone Fleming), a weird lady that had a nightmare where someone told her that a man named Peter Crane would kill her.

Later that night, Peter runs into Yvonne again and she tells him that she's terrified that something bad is going to happen to her. He invites her into his home and they have some drinks. Of course, they hook up immediately. Peter Crane is dangerous, lady! He'll get into your panties. Peter remembers the dream while they're making out. Then he has a bout of telekinetic powers and uncontrollable rage which makes him strangle Yvonne to death. Isn't it wonderful when your dreams come true?

After a restful night's sleep, Peter wakes up to find everything is normal. No dead women here! Anthony Steffen shows up as Inspector Ranieri, the cop-type character. Ranieri carries around the evil eye on a keychain that his wife made him for protection. He's investigating Yvonne's murder. Meanwhile, Peter Crane and Elizabeth are brushing their teeth and kissing each other while showering together. So erotic.

Whoa, hold the phone. Luciano Pigozzi is in this too? What in the world? There's so many characters in this that I feel like it is a mashup of two unfinished films. Peter is wearing the most amazing Canadian tuxedo. LeEtta says it looks like it was acid-washed at a tar pit. For some reason, he murders Pigozzi and his wife in front of the ghost of their dead aunt and more telekinesis happens. Don't worry, I'm confused too. Peter goes to his doctor friend to have him run some tests to see what is going on. Pilar Velázquez is in this too? Dang! This is worth a watch just for the cast alone.

My favorite scene is when Ranieri is sitting for a portrait that his wife is painting. The painting is making me laugh no some reason. Now there's a party at Peter's place and it starts getting pretty fucking crazy with red lighting and insanity. Somebody just puked up a frog. Okay, this isn't a giallo with a black-gloved killer or an inheritance scheme giallo or any other kind of giallo. Damn it all to hell, I've come around on Evil Eye. This movie is so weird that you just have to see it for yourself.

TUESDAY

I got off to a very slow start this morning. I remember LeEtta going to work and then I just passed out again. Finally, a little after 8, I was able to pry myself off the bed and slowly get ready for the day. I step outside and I am struck once again by the beautiful weather. It's wild. I almost wish I was one of those people who had any use for the outdoors.

I just remembered something. Before I took my shower last night, I walked to the mailbox. It was dark, windy, cold, and not a cloud in the sky. The mailbox was jammed full with a ton of mail and a book for LeEtta so I had to pry it all out. As I walked back to our front door, I heard steps behind me. A chill went up my spine and I looked down the sidewalk. It was just a random woman walking to her apartment or maybe just pretending to. Could she have been the killer?

"I told you once and I'll tell you again, you're mine forever!"

9:28 AM
Giallo a Venezia (1979)

This movie is some repugnant stuff but it's not without its merits and certainly opens with a shock. We see a man being stabbed, a girl drowning in the water, and a guy waking up from a nightmare. Then the fabulous and yearning strains of the score by Berto Pisano comes drifting in like a happy dream. But there are still two dead bodies. The worst thing about this film is the kooky cop, DePaul (Jeff Blynn). He's eating hard-boiled eggs in every scene which means he definitely has stinky farts. His colleagues find drugs on the dead guy and postulate that it might be LSD.

The dead couple is Fabio (Gianni Dei), an architect, and Flavia (Leonora Fani), his wife. The cops discover that the girl had sex before she died but it wasn't rape. That's just crazy! The detective meets with Marzia (Mariangela Giordano), a woman who knew the victims. She reveals that they had a complicated sexual relationship. We see, in flashback, how Fabio was a sex addict and would coerce Flavia into some kinky and unsafe stuff. These two really needed a safety word. Man, this movie is just sad. You really feel all of Flavia's torment that Fabio, her demented monster of a husband, is putting her through. It's depressing but it saves the movie.

So why is this such a notorious title? The sex scenes are borderline hardcore and the violence is especially brutal. There's a sadistic killer in mirrored sunglasses on the loose in Venice. Marzia has a stalker that has been harassing her. Could they be the same man? The killer pays a hooker for sex but kills her instead. He stabs her with a knife right in the cooter.

That's not cool, man. Almost in PSA fashion, DePaul gets a lecture on addiction from a doctor. Then another flashback as Fabio rapes Flavia in their kitchen. If the point of this film was to destroy my soul then congratulations director Mario Landi, you did it. I feel like garbage now.

DePaul questions Bruno (Vassili Karis), Flavia's ex-boyfriend who she was with before she met Fabio. He tells the inspector how Flavia complained about how horrible her marriage to Fabio The Overfiend was. Bruno admits to the inspector that he offered to kill Fabio for her but that she wouldn't hear of it. I wish Fabio was still alive so I could fucking kill him. In a genuinely terrifying scene, the killer watches Marzia having some wild sex with a dude. The way he watches them is just inhuman and the music is really, really unnerving. When the guy leaves Marzia's place, the killer shoots him, douses him in gasoline, and sets him on fire. The poor sap burns to death and his screams make my stomach churn.

And the hits just keep on comin'! The killer goes after Marzia. He knocks her unconscious and ties her to her own kitchen table. Then he starts dismembering her with a hacksaw. Man oh man, this movie is brutal. When she passes out from the pain, the killer wakes her up so she doesn't miss out on any of the fun. The next day, the maid finds Marzia's corpse in the refrigerator. It's impossible not to be shocked by this film.

The killer gets caught and confesses almost immediately. But what did he have to do with Fabio and Flavia? They were on his list but someone else got them first. The mystery continues. DePaul brings the case back to Bruno who knows more than he's telling. They go back to the scene of the murder and find out that there was a witness on that fateful day. I'm not even kidding right now but I feel like crying.

"How different you look inside a box!"

11:09 AM
Tutti defunti... tranne i morti (1977)

This giallo comedy from Pupi Avati starts with a raspy voiced woman in a black shroud making a cryptic statement and then lightning strikes a tree. A publisher who likes to paint his nails red thinks he has a bestseller on his hands. The book is a version of an old manuscript that tells the tale of an old family and some mystery connected to them. A nerdy book salesman named Dante (Carlo Delle Piane) takes two copies to go out and sell. In a nice change of pace, the opening credits feature ragtime jazz.

The marquis living in an old mansion is dying but the servants think it's a joke. The soft focus gives everything a dreamy feel. In the next scene, someone kills the publisher and burns all of the books. Of course, Dante is in grave danger since he's carrying the only remaining copies. He shows up to the mansion to try and sell them the books. Ilaria (Francesca Marciano), the lovely daughter of the marquis, mistakes Dante for someone else and the butler Giulio (Giulio Pizzirani) is a total jerk to him.

More of the crazy Zanotti family shows up including a man named Donald who has to be handcuffed to keep him from masturbating constantly. Dante tries to leave but someone has stolen the steering wheel from his car. When Ilaria comes onto him, he insists on driving away anyway and immediately wrecks the car in the yard. It's funny as hell.

The scenes between Giuilio and the maid are freaking me out. They are just so weird and shrill that I'm having faux acid flashbacks. He wants to black-mail someone but she's against it so he forces her to write a letter (because he's illiterate), When she won't give him the letter, Giulio poisons her and cuts her hand off. The killer tries to take the book while Dante is distracted with Ilaria. The note from the butler arrives with the maid's severed hand still attached and all hell breaks loose.

At the funeral of the marquis, his widow shows up and she's clearly a man in drag. I'm starting to think that Pupi Avati might be mentally ill. The family buries the marquis but then discover that his body is still inside the house. They dig up the coffin and find that Giulio is in the coffin, dead with a stake in his heart. A private detective named Martini (Gianni Cavina) shows up to help solve the murders. Martini is the stupidest character so far so this should be pretty good.

With everyone locked in the house until the case is solved, the killer is taking them out one by one. The most unusual method is the gun hidden inside the hair dryer. Someone just got a stick of dynamite shoved in their mouth and blown up by the killer. This movie is friggin' great! There's a huge bottle of J&B featured prominently on a coffee table. Awesome. The deaths keep on getting weirder and the jokes keep on getting crazier. Then there's the Russian roulette scene that must be seen to believed. This movie has nearly 30 cast and crew members in common with Avati's classic The House with the Laughing Windows.

LUNCH BREAK & CIGAR TIME

LeEtta comes and gets me for lunch. Of course, I suggest Burger 21 since we haven't been there in a while. I get The Greek burger (which is a veggie patty with all the trimmings) and a smores shake which is incredible (they even toasted the marshmallows!). LeEtta gets the spicy Thai shrimp burger and we share the sweet potato fries. She drops me off at home on her way back to work and I am so full that I have to roll back into our apartment to finish the movie.

After the crazy comedy by Pupi Avati is over, I select a cigar that LeEtta's dad got me. They were rolled in Mexico with Honduran tobacco.

Very nice. I have a big can of Arizona Arnold Palmer Pink Lemonade & Sweet Tea. Also very nice. I give Brad a call and we shoot the shit about gialli for a while. Brad is such a good dude.

"This town should be blown up! Brick by brick!"

3:27 PM
The Flower in His Mouth (1975)

Jennifer O'Neill plays Elena, a young woman travelling by bus to a small town to work as a teacher. On the ride there, a guy hits on her and she brushes him off. When she arrives, she is shown to her small apartment by a little old dude and the town at night is gorgeous. The film so far is subtly beautiful and has lots of atmosphere. The next morning, the headmaster of the school tells her not to teach in her progressive style to these kids. Keep things nice and traditional. She meets a dashing colleague named Michele played by good old Franco Nero. Welcome back to the book, sir.

On her first day of teaching, Elena sees that her class is practically empty and the kids who are there have a huge chip on their shoulder. Michele takes her on a tour of the town and tells her the history of the place. This film was shot by Ennio Guarnieri and it's beautiful to behold. The score by Ennio Morricone is awesome as well. Elena explains to Michele that this is her eighth job in eight provinces because she has a problem with authority.

The music takes a sinister turn when she goes to meet Campo (James Mason), the surly and eccentric gentleman who owns her apartment, to discuss the terms of her rent (which is free?). Back in town, she gets hit on again by that idiot from the bus. She calls him a pig in front of everyone in the town square and complains about their "stinking town". That night, the guy's corpse is found shot five times and propped up in a chair in the center of the town with a flower in his mouth.

The cops haul in Elena since everyone saw her insult the guy. They believe that the flower in the mouth means that he insulted a woman and someone made him pay for it. The mafia holds a huge funeral for the guy and now Elena is being watched. The fun atmosphere of this has been replaced by a sinister one. Michele wants to help but he's trying to avoid being the subject of town gossip. She calls him a coward and they make love. I call that building the foundation of a great relationship.

Elena has lunch with Campo and he tells her a story of how sleazy the town is and that the list of suspects is as big as the town itself. A sniveling reporter is trying to get Elana to tell him all the juicy details of her story but he gets business end of her handbag instead. Everyone in the square sees it and you know this motherfucker is next. Sure enough, he gets the shit kicked out of him by two toughs in the street. The doctor asks him who did it but he won't squeal.

Elana manages to get some progress for the poor families of the town because the local government is scared of her. That night, a couple of psychos on a motorbike harass her on her way home, dragging her around the square by her hair. The two are found dead and tied together on their motorbike, still running in the square. The hothead police inspector (Orazio Orlando) flips out and makes a speech about how much he hates the town and how it should be destroyed.

This is a very unusual and very intelligent film. At school, every kid finally shows up for her class for the first time because their parents are scared of what will happen if they offend Elena. Things start looking up for a second so I know the worst is coming. Cop Hothead informs her that he's being transferred for being too nosy and he warns her to get out of town while she still can.

DINNER

LeEtta gets home from work and makes an awesome dinner: couscous, arugula, and goat cheese. I run out real quick and pick up Shadow's remains from the vet. His urn is very nice. Now he can sit next to Margie's ashes and her other pets' ashes. Man, that is weird. But it's been a weird year.

"It's not true you're frigid. You're a bitch on heat."

6:37 PM
Opera (1987)

I want to love this film but Opera continually rejects my loving advances. A bitchy opera singer flips out over the "bad direction" of a production of Verdi's Macbeth. Duh bitch, live ravens and laser beams have been around since Shakespeare! When opera bitch gets knocked down by a car, young Betty (Cristina Marsillach) gets her chance at the starring role. Betty doesn't think she's ready or good enough. Enter her friend and manager Mira (Daria Nicolodi) and a parade of theatre people to boost her confidence. Meanwhile, someone is watching Betty from the air vent in her room.

This production of Macbeth is pretty badass. I wish I could handle opera for more than five minutes at a time. The killer POV is back with a vengeance in this film. As the killer watches Betty perform, he fantasizes about a woman being assaulted while another woman is tied up, looking on. The killer is accosted by an usher and strikes out violently, killing the guy and knocking some lights over in the process. Much like the opera onstage,

Opera is total sensory overload. It is impossible not to get swept up in all of the gusto. Then a little girl, who is so poorly dubbed that it's on the level of Bob in House by the Cemetery, cheers Betty on from her bedroom while watching the Opera on PBS at home. This takes me right out of the movie.

We get a peek into the killer's twitching brain. It races around a beautiful old building. Next we see black gloved hands pulling the sheet off a woman sleeping in the nude. Then a woman's hands are bound and the killer strikes. A dream? A memory? Probably both. The killer watches Betty's performance on tape while preparing his tools for a murder. The first victim? Betty's costume! This killer tears at it with a knife while some angry ravens caged, conveniently in the same room, go ballistic. The ravens harass this poor murderer into killing a few of them. The night watchmen interrupts the killer at whatever task that was supposed to be.

Meanwhile, Betty is apologizing to her boyfriend and stage manager Stefano (William McNamara) for being a lousy lay. She has a hang-up about sex but doesn't know why. While Stefano is out making tea, the killer shows up, ties Betty to a pillar, and puts tape with needles on it under her eyes so she can't close them. She has to watch while the killer brutally (and I do mean BRUTALLY) stabs Stefano to death while some heavy metal plays over the soundtrack. I used to have a huge problem with the friggin' heavy metal on this soundtrack but I'm trying to come around to it.

The killer lets Betty go and she is rescued from wandering around in the rain by Marco (Ian Charleson), the director of the musical. Back at her place, she tells Marco about what happened to Stefano. One thing about this movie, there is some serious stereo porn going on. Betty has a crazy awesome sound system. Did I mention Santini (Urbano Barberini) the boring cop? Yeah, he introduces himself as a fan of Betty's but and the actor dubbing him fucking sucks. Coralina Cataldi-Tassoni plays Giulia, the kooky costume designer. I love her! While trying to repair Betty's costume, she discovers a clue in the armor plating. The killer shows up and murders her (while making Betty watch, of course). The damning piece of evidence falls down her throat and the killer retrieves it by doing some impromptu surgery. Queue the wildly distracting heavy metal!

After having watched two people murdered in front of her, Betty is going a little nuts. Her paranoia is growing understandably. Santini suggests that the curse of Vivaldi's Macbeth is coming down like a bloody bitch on this production. In a scene that is classic Argento, Betty is trapped inside her apartment with Daria Nicolodi while someone they think is the killer is posing as a policeman outside the door. I won't say what happens just in case someone reading this hasn't seen the film yet. It's jaw dropping.

Okay, I won't spoil anything else but what the hell happened to the ending? The last minute weirdness doesn't make up for the meandering and the whole vacation to the Swiss Alps (for a tenuous Phenomena reference) is just bad. The film winds things up so tight and then it just loses it but I'm starting to come around and appreciate Opera. Spanish actress Marsillach is part of what makes this so great. The last moments that show Betty's fate are just genius but the road that leads us there is a perilous one. LeEtta and I debate how we both have problems with the ending of this movie but for different reasons. That's marriage!

> *"Just imagining myself naked like a worm in front of someone would make my blood freeze!"*

8:55 PM
The Police are Blundering in the Dark (1975)

Now this is a bootleg and yet the garbled music and scratched up film make me feel very much at home. A bloody pair of scissors adorn the screen for a while and then we see an idiot laughing in a garden. Next, a woman gets a flat time and a man approaches to help her. Help her die, that is! He tries to stab her with a pair of scissors, tears her shirt open, and chases her through the woods. Her boobs flop painfully as she runs. Ouch! Finally, he catches up with her and kills her. Double ouch! Brad warned me this film was weird and I suspect that he was right.

A duder named Edmund picks up a sexy chick at a bus stop and they drive off in his beat-to-shit VW Bug. He's a photographer of naked ladies and she's the next victim- oops, I meant model! At their house out in the middle of buttfuck nowhere, Roberto the butler is a suspicious chap and the sexy maid doesn't like him at all. Sara the niece pushes her uncle with a huge afro around in a wheelchair and Eleonora the wife acts all bitchy and shit. What's her fucking problem?

A blond chick named Erica is stranded at a crappy bar and tries to call her boyfriend Giorgio but he's busy with a hot brunette. LeEtta would like me to mention that he's wearing a diaper. I think that it was the sheets draped around his junk for our protection but LeEtta says "No, that's a diaper." We'll wait and see if this "diaper" plays a key role in this murder mystery. Poo poo diaper baby wah wah wah! The tracking on this copy of the film just went haywire and it was beautiful.

Erica is warming her naked body by the fire and just calls out to whoever is there. The idiot we saw earlier shows up and he wants to touch her boobies but brings her dinner instead. He's their servant? After he leaves, she gets stabbed to death. The camera lingers on her naked and bloody body for a while. I think that's in pretty poor taste! Giorgio arrives, looking for Erica. He decides to hang out with these weirdos.

There's a very awkward dinner scene. But then again, everything about this movie is awkward. Big-eyed Sara is desperately trying to play footsy with Giorgio but his legs are pressed tighter together than something that is pressed tightly together. Someone presses a button on a remote control and a statue's left eye begins to glow. I don't know what that means.

Giorgio is invited to stay due to a horrible storm raging outside. He agrees and is shown to his room where the lusty maid is waiting for him on his bed. She strongly encourages him to come to her room later and promises him a good time. I trust this woman. Downstairs, Eleonora tells Edmund that she wants to leave him and he goes berserk. Sara sneaks into Giorgio's room and begs him to take her away with him. She reveals that Edmund is a madman and believes that he can photograph the human soul.

The next day, Giorgio leaves to visit his doctor pal, armed with the info he's learned. While he's there, Eleonora calls to say that Sara has disappeared. Meanwhile, the maid, who is pissed off and horny, decides to have sex with the idiot servant behind a tree on the property. I guess it doesn't go too well because she calls him a beast and takes a very gratuitous shower. Next, Edmund is in his lab working at a complicated looking machine with sound effects that make the speakers on my TV puke.

More crazy shit happens but I'll say no more about it. The acting in this is very off and scenes seem to go on longer than they should. The movie jumps around a lot and I can't keep track of the characters. Brad told me he thinks some reels are out of order but I think there's one missing. Maybe after filming, this was too short so they just repeated some shots to make up for it. Either way, the results are pure accidental genius and fascinating to behold. Look under the lettuce.

WEDNESDAY

I wake up slowly once again and head to 7-11 after feeding the animals. I get a Mountain Dew and a granola bar. I take my vitamins and finish watching The Police are Groping Around in the Dark. It is a very strange way to start the day.

"You know what? Playing detective excites me."

9:26 AM
Play Motel (1979)

Everything I know about this movie I learned from the promotional materials reprinted in Blood and Black Lace by Adrian Luther-Smith. I'm secretly hoping that this isn't the porno version. This movie starts with a hideous rock-ish disco song that is so upbeat and happy that it's just nightmarish. A guy goes to a bar and orders a J&B by name! He picks up a hooker and takes her to a hotel room. The Play Motel theme song kicks in and I am already in awe of this film. Here are the lyrics:

Stop on by at Play Motel
And have a lot of fun
Drink the flow there'll be no tell
The darkness meets the sun
I'm just an Easy Rider
Who was lookin' for a bed
I'll stay just for the night
So he said
If you're passin' by my way
Just stop and say hello
We can have a real good time
The motel has a show
You can pass the weekend
You can really get on down
At the Play Motel
Outside of town
There's always room at Play Motel
It's the place to be
When you're on the road
And nowhere to go

So while this song is playing, a guy named Cortesi (Enzo Fisichella) dresses up like a devil and the hooker dresses up like a nun. There is some sex and some outside of the mouth porno-kissing. Jeez! Is this a Jess Franco film? While these two are bonin' (in a non-simulated kind of a way), a hidden camera captures all the action. Later, Cortesi is at work when he receives an envelope full of the photos and a blackmail letter. The idiot ignores his lawyer's advice and pays up to avoid any scandal.

Cortesi's wife Luisa (Patrizia Behn) gets curious and sneaks a peek at the photos and the letter. She takes them to De Sanctis (Anthony Steffen), the cop. A fellow detective informs him that the girl in the photos is Loredana (Marina Hedman), a porno model for Shamrock Studios. De Sanctis goes there to question Loredana and it makes everybody at the studio nervous. De Sanctis used to be with the Vice Squad and was prone to seizing pornographic materials (for his private collection?).

The killer, hiding in the back of Loredana's car, bludgeons her with a heavy object. The next day, they find her car in a field and her dead body in the driver's seat. Luisa goes to Play Motel to snoop around. She discovers the hidden room and watches a guy dressed as Tarzan whip a hooker in a jungle girl outfit. They have some non-simulated genital manipulation while the killer sneaks up on Luisa and strangles her to death.

While the killer is disposing of Luisa's corpse, Roberto (Ray Lovelock) and his lady Patrizia (Anna Maria Rizzoli) are just finishing up at Play Motel. The couple go down to the parking garage and almost spot the killer, who watches them from the dark. It turns out that Patrizia just wanted a thrill by going to a naughty hotel. They discover Luisa's body in the trunk of their car. They call the cops from a phone booth but while they are gone, of course, the body has disappeared.

Luisa's body turns up the next day so, for some reason, De Sanctis asks Roberto and Patrizia (who insists on doing her civic duty!) to help with the investigation of Play Motel and Shamrock Studios. He's particularly interested in the owner, Max (Marino Masé). Roberto and Patrizia go undercover, he in a fake mustache and she in a black wig, to stake out Play Motel and investigate Max. Don't these two have jobs?

While they are there, Max shows up at Play Motel with Anna (Antonella Antinori), the voluptuous prostitute who wears more makeup on than Lon Chaney in Phantom of the Opera. He dresses like an archbishop for their sexy play and knowingly winks at whoever is taking pictures in the next room. After the photographer is done capturing some special moments, Roberto and Patrizia follow him to his studio. De Sanctis encourages the couple to keep going so she has this total stranger to take nude photos of her. Even for a giallo, this is all highly implausible.

After nearly getting raped by the photographer, Patrizia finds some evidence that Max is indeed blackmailing people. Because this movie hates me, there's a scene where some old executive likes to pee on women (yuck) and stick champagne bottles where they don't belong (barf). Anna is understandably upset when she finds out about being used as a tool for blackmail so she goes undercover too! De Sanctis is one lazy fucking cop and he's gonna get all these people killed.

The plot of this film makes The Case of the Bloody Iris look like a documentary. Play Motel is pretty hilarious but would be a lot more fun if not for the porn sequences. In spite of my better judgment, I'm digging on this crazy crap. The presence of Lovelock and Steffen as two of the most irresponsible 'heroes' ever written really saves the film.

"Some things... Take a bloody long time."

11:37 AM
The Killer is Still Among Us (1986)

A couple pulls over to do some smooching but they are rudely interrupted by a serial killer. He kills the guy first and then the girl when she tries to escape. He drags her body off and mutilates it in bizarre ways. Wow, this is fun! A phone call awakens Christina, a young criminology student.

It's her friend Chiara telling her about the murders. She travels to the scene of the crime and questions the criminologist (and father of Chiara) about the murders. While she's there, someone is watching from behind the barricade. The killer, perhaps?

Next, Christina goes to the morgue to look at the bodies and she nearly tosses her cookies looking at the body of the woman. She makes friends with the studly forensic surgeon named Alex and they go out for a drink afterward. She brings him home and they screw. Damn, Christina! After they get it on, he asks her to give up on this case for her own good but she is adamant about sticking with it for the sake of her thesis!

Christiana gets a mysterious phone call and she automatically assumes that the killer knows who she is. She goes to the cops and they tell her she's crazy. While there, she sees the cops questioning a suspect, a voyeur they caught peeping on couples in the woods. The guy is a gynecologist so Christiana goes to see him at his practice and starts to question him about his theories on the killer. He flips out and screams at her to leave. This chick might just be totally crazy.

To investigate further, Christina goes to a bar where the peeping doctor likes to hang out. When she walks in, the whole place goes crazy. The whole bar is full of perverts! She pays a woman to be her guide to where people like to get it on out in the woods. They get out there and there's a network of perverts including a guy with expensive listening devices at work while some couple is making out in their car. This is the weirdest scene I've ever seen. Now she suspects Alex could be the killer!

Man, this film is good at ratcheting up the tension. One night, while Christiana is waiting for Alex to come over so they can hit that crazy bar together (seriously?), she feels like someone is trying to get into her apartment. The scene is really intense. The mailman just knocked on my door and I jumped because I was so into the movie. Christiana and Alex go to the bar but her informant, the bartender, is dead, hanging from the ceiling. Her professor tries to warn her and suggests that she choose a different thesis. He also suggests the killer could be a witch. Holy shit. What?

After some of their friends are killed, Christan and Chiara go to a séance to see if the spirits can tell them anything about the killer. This movie is based on real events and that makes all of this even stranger. At the séance, they witness another murder of another couple making out. I love séances! Jeez Louise, genital mutilation is lovingly filmed in this movie! The ending is really interesting and self-reflexive!?! Despite its low budget, this one holds together pretty well but you're going to hate yourself in the morning.

*"Jesus Christ! You never change!
Don't break my balls!"*

2:45 PM
Slap the Monster on Page One (1972)

This is definitely more of a political thriller but I won't hold that against it. The film opens with riot and protest footage. It's communism versus socialism and everybody has gone friggin' crazy! This is why I fled the big city. Somewhere in Milan, a political office is vandalized by some protestors and the campaigners are making the most of the attack. They invite the press to come see all the "terrible" damage these hoodlums committed. Bizanti (Gian Maria Volonté), a greasy newspaper guy, calls up Montelli (John Steiner), a politician, to arrange a front page story on the whole thing.

But then a young girl's body is found near a trash heap in a park. The conservative newspaper takes this story and tries to put a spin on the tragedy to suit their needs. This isn't what you would call objective journalism. Bizanti is chastising one of his new writers named Roveda (Fabio Garriba) for making the story about a man who immolated himself and his five children too depressing. He tells him to rewrite it and play up how he the dead man was an immigrant.

The young girl who was raped and murdered turns out to be the daughter of a prominent family in Milan. When the father comes to identify the body, two cameramen are discussing how much money they'll get if they can get a shot of the corpse, double if it's nude. Is this the most cynical film ever made? The newspaper gets right to work exploiting this family and the poor girl's virginity which, of course, they're only speculating on. Meanwhile, Montelli is at the heart of a scandal. He and a few others have been secretly funding the fascist side of the protestors. He isn't alone but he's the one taking the fall. He and Bizanti strike up a way to improve his public image by having him take interest in the case of the murdered girl.

Enter Laura Betti (of Hatchet for the Honeymoon). She plays Rita, a very opinionated lady and something of a revolutionary. She curses a lot and likes to argue politics. Bizanti wants Rita to write something for the paper. She's a sad lady whose husband left her for girls with mini-skirts and he's playing her for a fool. She has an on-again, off-again thing with Mario, an anarchist guy half her age who was the last person to see the murdered girl alive. Thanks to Rita's tip-off, Mario gets busted and the newspaper publishes a photo of him resisting arrest and hints that he might be the murderer. Then the insanely cruel cops try to beat "the truth" out of Mario.

Rita is fucking pissed off and goes to Bizanti, saying that she'll deny everything she told him. Bizanti tells her that it's too late and no one will believe her anyway. He reads to her what Mario said about her in the police interview. This son of a bitch is reading from a blank piece of paper just to get her to sell out Mario even more! Then Bizanti sends Roveda in to go and talk to the protesters and defend the newspaper, hoping they'll beat the shit out of him. When they don't rough him up, a disappointed Bizanti has to destroy the headline that he's already printed about the protestors attacking a journalist.

Rita is pitted against her old friends and things get very ugly. At the crime scene, the cops hilariously reenact what happened while Mario curses them for being lying perverts. Roveda begins to question his role in all this and confronts Bizanti on what he feels is wrong. A new suspect (and probably the real killer!) has turned up but it's all too late. Oh boy. I know exactly where this is headed. Interesting film though not a favorite.

THURSDAY

Band practice runs a little late and I could try to sneak in another movie but I am beat. Once I'm home, I haul my gear into the apartment, and join LeEtta on the couch for the tail end of an episode of "Miss Marple". I decide to have her wake me up when she goes to work so I can get started on the last leg of this moviethon.

That was easier said than done! When the alarm goes off at six, I feel like shit. While LeEtta gets ready for work, I doze, knowing that eventually she'll want to make the bed and I'll be forced to get my ass up. It all comes true. I brush my teeth, wash my face, and get dressed. I walk my wife to the car and then I trudge over to 7-11. I get a Mountain Dew, a hot dog, and a 5 Hour Energy (grape flavored) and go home. After the hotdog, I wash my hands and start typing what you're reading right now.

"I'm sure you're used to people using your photos as Kleenex."

7:13 AM
Knife Under the Throat (1986)

It's hard for me to believe that the French ever made a proper giallo without Italian financing and yet here I am. A girl running through the streets of Paris wearing an overcoat, boots, a bra, and nothing else makes me think that everything is going to be okay. The cheap slasher music is awesome so far. The girls runs into the police station crying rape and everyone is laughing. The inspector comes out and asks her if crying rape twice a month is too much. This scene makes me uncomfortable.

The luscious Brigitte Lahaie plays Valérie. She and J.B., a surly guy with a club foot, are a photography duo doing a nude photo shoot in a gorgeous cemetery. While they're shooting some rather tasteless pictures among the gravestones, the caretaker is flipping out. The crew sells their photos to a tabloid as some kind of fake shock story and the caretaker is really losing his shit over it. He got paid on the sly to let them in so what is the fucking problem? Now he's stalking some random chick in the graveyard because she reminds him of one of the models.

The caretaker follows this girl out of the cemetery and runs her car off the road. When she runs through a field to get away from him, he rips open her blouse and then strangles her to death. He feels so bad about it that he throws himself under an oncoming truck. This is just like that NCIS episode! My favorite character so far is Annie, she lives with the models but has a burned face so she resents their beauty. When the girls come back from a shoot in NYC, Cathy (Florence Guérin), Annie's sister (?), gives her a bitchin' t-shirt that looks like a Duran Duran album cover. Annie tries it on but her scarred face makes her angry so she throws the sweater on the floor. This is my favorite scene so far today.

Meanwhile, Cathy, who has a lot of stuffed animals for a sexy grownup, gets an obscene phone call and goes berserk. She runs into the apartment of some neighbor dude named Nicholas and asks him to search her apartment for an unseen attacker. She really is nuts. J.B. and another model get home and they laugh about what a loony Cathy is. J.B. pours himself a huge glass of J&B like a boss. Later, J.B. bursts into Cathy's room and torments her, laughing the whole time. Then he terrorizes Florence, another model, and screams at her to smile while choking her. This guy is a class act.

Cathy has a creepy ex-boyfriend who likes to paw her in the phone booth which is located in the men's room. France is a crazy place. Somebody beats up Nicholas and Valérie takes him in. I guess she's gonna seduce this dude. Lucky bastard. They have a photo shoot at a train depot with comedic homeless guys and a big argument breaks out. That night, a black-gloved killer slices J.B.'s throat in his darkroom. Wait a minute! A character named J.B. who drinks J&B gets killed by a black-gloved maniac? If this scene had happened in Titanic then Titanic would be a giallo. This film ends with a freeze frame of Cathy screaming. I like that. This is just a baffling, trashy, and bizarre good time flick.

"All for one and one for all!"

8:57 AM
Sweets from a Stranger (1987)

Happy music that is vaguely bossa nova-like plays over the opening credits for the 1987 giallo. A fat guy picks up a hooker and, lucky for me, they don't show their sex scene. After he leaves, the girl discovers that the guy left his expensive gold watch on her coffee table. When she's out walking her dog, a car chases her around. She runs for it and gets away but a murderer with a straight razor catches her instead. After slashing her to death, the killer fires a weird air-powered gun into her abdomen.

Later, a hooker named Lena (Barbara De Rossi) is working the beat and gets picked up by some badass hookers led by Elisa who tell her to play by their rules or get off their turf. When Elisa gets home, she reads her daughter's diary and then harasses her for having human emotions and for wanting her own mother not be a hooker anymore. The next morning, Lena pays Elisa a percentage of her night's earnings and ends up chatting with Elisa's daughter. It's a sweet scene. See, hookers are people too! As expected, there is a hooker bonfire to keep them all nice and toasty.

Later that night, when Lena is arguing with a potential John, she discovers Bruna, a fellow hooker, slashed up and dying. She drives her to the hospital but it's too late. At Bruna's depressing funeral, the hookers get to talking. They're scared that one or all of them will be next. The cops are harassing the ladies of the night but are clueless about who the killer might be. In my favorite transition ever, a hooker is doing some odd exercises on bars mounted to the wall. This leads right into the next scene. Why?

The hooker conference scene is awesome. The hookers start to organize after a rousing speech from their leader. Now they're getting organized and this The Great Escape-esque military music kicks in. I pity this fucking guy if they ever find out who he is. In just about the craziest thing I've ever seen, the hookers -like 20 of them- line up along the outskirts of the park and do a sexy lineup dance in front of car headlights just in case the killer is watching them. Are they trying to lure him out or is this just a lascivious show of solidarity? I may love this film.

An old and slightly crazy hooker, who refuses to work with the other girls, gets slashed up. When the killer goes to shoot her, the gun misfires so he gives up and wipes the blood off his gloves with her wig. This movie has a serious yet schmaltzy message to it about the indignities that prostitutes suffer and how unfair the world is for them. I'm glad that prostitution only happens in Italy. Lena meets some potential business but he's a real creepo. She kicks him in the balls, repeatedly. You go girl!

The cops figure out that the gun the killer is using is one used by butchers use on cows. This changes the tone a bit. These chicks are out for blood. Better watch out, you murderous scumbag. The girls start beating up and assaulting their clients because they might be the killer. A hooker blows her rape whistle with one of those burning smokestacks in the background and the effect is such that she looks like she's breathing fire. This somewhat self-indulgent film is way smarter than it looks. There's a scene in this near the end that's like an electric charge through my eyeballs. Damn, I underestimated this one. It's 10 minutes too long but otherwise a great movie.

RICHARD GLENN SCHMIDT

"Frederick! I can't see you! I'm blind!"

10:41 AM
The Secret of Seagull Island (1981)

Ah yes, scuba-diving. It's the most amazingly dull thing you can pad your movie with. I'm not being judgmental here but seriously, who the fuck goes underwater to make out? Ha ha, stupid idiots got caught in an underwater avalanche! Those are pretty common. Barbara (Prunella Ransome) arrives in Rome to spend some time with her blind pianist sister, Mary Ann (Sherry Buchanan). The thing is, she's been missing for three weeks and the snooty teacher at the music school is offended that the girl missed rehearsal. The last person to see her alive was Lombardi (Gabriele Tinti), a studly boat captain who claims rather vehemently that he doesn't know where Mary Ann is. Holy shit, Paul Muller is in this as a cop! He's not the main inspector but I do like seeing a familiar face. And the inspector is Fabrizio Jovine (of Fulci's The Psychic)! Dang.

And this just got creepy. The cops have an unsolved case where a girl was found on the ocean floor, tied to a concrete block, and the fish had eaten her eyes. Or perhaps she was blind to begin with. They show the girl floating in a Jesus Christ pose and it's just eerie. Some fishermen find a blind girl adrift in a life-raft but it's not Mary Ann. One of the doctors is played by Umberto Raho! Barbara goes off to try and solve this mystery herself. Lombardi tells them about some rich duder named David who lives on -Dun dun dun!- Seagull Island!

Barbara goes to visit the blind girl that they found. She walks into the room just as someone plays a cassette tape of seagulls screaming. This sound causes the blind girl to burst out of bed and jump out the dang window. While Barbara is screaming, someone hits her on the back of the head. When she wakes up in the hospital, she has been temporarily blinded from the blow on the back of her head. Is blindness fucking contagious in this town or what?

In the next scene, Lombardi is driving a little submarine around underwater and I have to roll my eyes. Underwater cinematography is bullshit. I hate it. A boat comes by and someone aboard starts throwing underwater grenades at Lombardi. Back at the hospital, they reveal Barbara's clouded over eyeballs like she was the little girl from The Beyond. This is really good so far. While at a health spa, Barbara meets a man (Jeremy Brett) who claims to be the David they've been looking for. They have a drink and she agrees to come and see him on –Dun dun dun!- Seagull Island!

Due to a not so chance meeting, Barbara (who is now pretending to be blind), David takes her to the island. We are introduced to David's cousin Carol (Pamela Salem), who is just a little crazy. David likes to mumble about bizarre bullshit about a son named Frederick, some mangled face wacko. While Barbara is off exploring by herself, she hears a terrible scream and then she's attacked by the biggest seagull I've ever seen. David tries to get Barbara to hang out with Frederick who goes berserk. Strangely enough, this ugly sonofabitch has taken a liking to Barbara so they want her to stay and be friends with him.

Lombardi, who survived the grenade attack, shows up and wants to help Barbara find out what is going on. Wait, how does he not know what's going on? Bah! This film is very, very convoluted thanks in no small part to its origins as a TV mini-series. That's why this feels like three years of "Dark Shadows" condensed into a 100 minute movie but with more underwater photography. And no werewolves. Yet. Jeremy Brett chews on the scenery like it was the last piece of seagull jerky on the island.

NAP TIME

I give in to my sleepiness and take a nap, instead of downing a 5 Hour Energy drink, to keep going. An hour in bed with a cat named Sparkles (we're just friends) and I'm ready to call an end to this moviethon. Okay folks, here's the last movie for this damn meltdown…

"You can't accuse someone of murder just because he made love to a nymphomaniac."

1:41 PM
The Killer Wore Gloves (1974)

My bootleg of this has more hiss than I can handle right now but I've got to get through this. I know that Brad LOVES this one so I'm pretty excited. During some uninspired shots of an airplanes landing, the opening music sounds like something more akin to a crime flick. Inside the airport, two men with matching bags go to the men's room. One forces the other into a stall and slashes his throat with a straight razor. Well well well!

Somewhere in England, Peggy (Gillian Hills) is walking down the street and she sees her husband Michael drive by. Since he's been MIA for some time, she jumps in her car to chase him. After losing him, she meets her pal Jackie (Silvia Solar) at a coffee shop. Peggy admits to renting out a room in her flat so she won't lose the place. Jackie accuses her of just making that up so she can shack up with a new lover. Peggy's lecherous boss Ronald (Stelio Candelli of Tropic of Cancer) tells her that she needs to satisfy her "biological necessities" (meaning SEX!) and calls her a wench. She storms out and goes home where we meet her neighbor Mr. Lewis (Carlos Otero). He looks like Gay Dracula (Brad's term), takes his cat everywhere, and plays upright bass. I love this character. He's very relatable.

When Peggy gets back to her apartment, she strips out of her nearly all leather ensemble and throws her dirty panties into a Frankenstein head laundry bag. She dons a robe when her new tenant John (Bruno Corazzari) shows up. He creepily flirts with Peggy while she shows him around. The moment she leaves him alone, he starts rummaging around. Just then Peggy gets a phone call from Michael begging her to meet him at "the old hangar". She goes and while walking around this creepy placed filled with airplane parts, a black-gloved killer shoots at her with a pistol.

After narrowly escaping being shot to death, Peggy goes home and there's quite a commotion since someone jumped off the roof while she was out. Inspector Walton (Manuel Gas) comes to talk to Peggy about the suicide. Another guy named John (Ángel del Pozo) shows up to check out the room for rent. Uh oh, who the fuck was that other guy? Who cares, this John is way handsome! Peggy finds one of the black bags that we saw in the beginning of the film in her laundry bag. It's full of cash! That night someone is creeping around her apartment and there's a cat scare. I can never get enough of those!

So Ronald is fucking his secretary Shirley (the mouthwatering Orchidea de Santis) but she's busy fantasizing about her affair with Michael. The killer comes by after Ronald leaves and slashes her to death with a knife. Peggy sneaks the bag of cash out of her building (by pretending to be pregnant) and puts it in a safe deposit box at her bank. Mr. Lewis claims to know something about Michael but the killer pays him a visit too. For the sake of not ruining this whole movie and not typing myself into a coma, I'm skipping A LOT OF DETAILS. Between this great cast, a funky and infectious score by Marcello Giombini, confident direction by Juan Bosch, fun comedic moments, and some trashiness, I really like this movie. I really hope someone put out a copy of this with improved audio quality. All that hiss gave me an eargraine.

CONCLUSION

LeEtta comes home from work early and she catches me in the act, watching gialli! It's very hot and very bright outside as I help her carry in the groceries. Well gang, I got through a bunch of films during this moviethon that I had been avoiding and it all came out all right. Too bad my vacation is almost over and I have to go back to work tomorrow. I suddenly find it hilarious that I took four days off of work just to watch movies. I guess that's just the kind of person I am.

GIALLO MELTDOWN 12: PENULTIMATE RADIATION

The dread in my heart is growing. The war of potential titles for this moviethon was pretty epic. I'm getting very nervous that something important will be missed. I guess I just shouldn't worry about it. LeEtta asked me if the 13th Giallo Meltdown would be the last and I hesitantly agree. She tells me that I need to pick a stopping point and she's right. This book can't go on forever. I'm afraid of all this wonderfulness coming to an end but how much of that is encouraged by my fear of hard work (like editing)? Yikes, I'm terrified. The killer must be close.

FRIDAY

We get home from work and order a pizza. I take my time organizing DVDs and various files with the movies I've been gathering together for this adventure. I guess I should really try getting organized the night before the moviethon and not the night of the moviethon. Once that's done, I'm ready to grab the netbook and start typing this. I'm sitting here in our new apartment with my lovely wife. Both cats have joined us on the couch and I'm ready to rock and roll.

> *"She only wanted to make love in the bushes, she must have been crazy!"*

6:12 PM

Prostituzione (1974)

The opening credits say that this was produced by Angry Film. A name in the credits catches my eye and I know right where this is headed: Rino di Silvestri. Oh shit. The movie starts with some duder driving around surveying the land of hookers (and hooker bonfires). He chooses a ho named Giselle (Gabriella Lepori) and takes her to the woods where he screws her up against a tree while some old pervert (who might be Umberto Raho) watches. The guy takes all of 14 seconds to get off and the moment he's gone, Giselle is murdered (off camera). The cops have no leads because she wasn't one of the usual girls. Giselle was a loner, a rebel.

Dang, this voice-acting is some of the worst I've ever heard. The inspector and his assistant are voiced by a robot and a piece of wood. Giselle's fiancée Michele (Elio Zamuto) shows up at her flat where the cops inform him that she's dead. His alibi is lame and the cops add him to their list of suspects. A Sicilian hooker informs on her fellow whore named Primavera (Maria Fiore) and then gets picked up by a sleazeball. After she washes her vagina and is about to earn her paycheck, the movie cuts to Michele sexing some chick that isn't his dead fiancée. He rambles about a scam they're committing and the films cuts again to the cops questioning some hookers.

Another hooker is Benedetta (Orchidea de Santis of Seven Murders for Scotland Yard) and she's a real knockout. Her John wants to do it without a rubber and she calls bullshit on that. She tells him that she gets "caught" easily and the doctor says the next time she gets "caught" that she needs to just have the baby which is dangerous because she's anemic. He gets angry and kicks her out of his car but then he won't leave her alone. Then his motorcycle buddies show up and gang rape her. This horrible business is brief, thank goodness. They leave her unconscious out in the woods.

Next, Luciano Rossi enters the movie. He's playing a scumbag photographer who's blackmailing Umberto Raho with a photo of him with a hooker. The rapist guy and his motorcycle gang (of rapists) go for a little ride out in the middle of nowhere. He gets separated from them by some other bikers who corner him in a quarry. Apparently, these guys are friends of Benedetta. They grab him and start punching him in the cock. Then they bend him over and do something (off camera) to him that makes him scream in pain. That was pretty awesome. After that, dueling trannies! I will say no more because you need to see it for yourself.

Nearly every scene in this movie feels cut off and so brief that it's hard to follow what's going on. I know that the killings have something to do with hookers, a brothel/fashion house, and an old music box. There's a big bag of melodrama when Primavera discovers that her lover Antonio (Paolo Giusti) is sleeping with her daughter and intends to marry her. She flips out and picks up a young guy who goes wild when she accuses him of being a virgin. This movie is turning into one of my favorites. I hope it stays this brilliantly dumb all the way through. Spoiler alert: it did!

"If he lay a fingah on my sistah,
I kill the mothafuckah!"

7:29 PM
Dark Bar (1988)

This flick (from the guy who was assistant director on Play Motel!) looks very odd and stylish right out of the gate. Barbara Cupisti (from Michele Soavi's Stagefright) plays Elizabeth, a girl caught up in some shady business. She goes to a seedy club called Dark Bar where she gets harassed by one of her annoying friends. The bartender totally has a Hitler mustache and the people in the nightclub are moshing to some crap ass music. Elizabeth goes to the restroom and is immediately shot to death by a typical giallo villain. Next, we see Elizabeth's sister, Anna (Marina Suma), playing trombone in a hipster jazz bar. She and her band dress like extras from a Falco music video. Dark Bar is throwing me for a loop and I'm totally okay with that.

Anna is informed that her sister is missing so she goes to her apartment only to find it totally trashed. She listens to the messages on Elizabeth's machine and they only add to the mystery. The score for this film is really creepy. It makes up for the shitty maudlin songs they keep playing in between. LeEtta points out how poorly translated the subtitles are. I have the English dub of this but the dialog is so muddled that we have the subs on. Anna meets Marco (Richard Hatch), a dude that Elizabeth stood up the night she was killed. He works as a projectionist at a tiny theater and he wears a striped shirt, the kind that French artistic types wear.

Some creepy dudes in fedoras and trench coats show up and chase Anna around and beat Marco up. They want something from her but are being super vague about what it is. One of these creeps has the weirdest facial hair I've ever seen. It looks like he used hedge clippers to hack away at his poor face but did it on purpose. This movie's plot would be impossible without answering machines. Oh okay, now I see. Elizabeth was keeping a diary on the criminal types she was working for and everyone thinks that Anna has it. How Blood and Black Lace can you get?

Dark Bar is somebody's art school film project (and Argento fan letter) but it avoids tediousness by being entertaining and very, very quirky. Back at the nightclub, everyone has crazy makeup and hair. It looks like a Halloween party on some pretentious planet in a distant, flamboyant galaxy. Elizabeth's gal pal gets some bad heroin but manages to lay out the whole plot to Anna before she croaks. Back at Anna's place, she and Marco get it on while a sad trumpeter plays a sorrowful tune and the goons who've been chasing them wait impatiently outside. This film is certainly unique.

"You're a frozen fish!"

9:02 PM
Violent Blood Bath (1973)

The great Jorge Grau directed this and I think it's only the third film of his that I've seen. This opens with a delivery guy bringing a money order to an old woman. It's from her son named Jacques Morel who was executed 3 years ago. Next, a judge named Oscar (Fernando Rey) annoys his wife Patricia (Marisa Mell). If she wants to spread too much marmalade on her toast, it's her fucking business. Leave her alone! While the two of them are on their vacation, a murdered family is discovered in town and the judge knows where all the bodies are going to be. He tells the investigating officer that someone is recreating the murders of Morel, the man whom he had put to death 3 years ago.

A writer named Vargas (Espartaco Santoni) shows up to their hotel and he wants to write a book about the hypocrisy of the death penalty. He's thinking of calling it The Hypocrisy of the Death Penalty. Vargas also wants to fuck Patricia because they used to date. He's a real dickweed. Oscar, Vargas, and Patricia go to dinner together. Things are very tense and after Vargas insults him, Oscar bails. Back at the hotel room, Oscar wants to make love to Patricia but he's too obsessed with the dead bodies he saw that day to get very far. It seems that Oscar has OCD and it's driving Patricia crazy. Vargas, on the other hand, is obsessed with Oscar. Both of them are complete bastards to her.

At a fancy party at the hotel, an MC encourages everyone to adjourn to the patio where a bunch of bikini-clad ladies take part in an eating contest. While the cops are out trying to find out who the killer is, Oscar is haunted by a premonition that terrible crimes are going to be committed and that someone is targeting him. I gotta hand it to Fernando Rey. He's really good in this movie. I've seen him in a bunch of stuff but I never gave him much thought before tonight. Another murder, based on another case that the judge presided over, is committed at the hotel. It took place at a swimming pool at night. Oh baby, now I'm getting The Vibe. What a night I'm having!

SATURDAY

After a restful night's sleep, I get up with a spring in my step thanks to last night's trilogy of great flicks. LeEtta makes us coffee and I microwave some sausage biscuit sandwiches from the freezer. After years of toiling with ice cube trays, I finally live in an apartment with an icemaker. I'm all about the iced coffee now! After chores and a trip to Target in the rain, I finally settle down for some leftover pizza and a movie. Shit on a brick! I forgot to go to the post office. Damn it. Oh well, folks who paid for my zine will have to wait. Sorry, y'all.

"Oh my goodness! The prophecy! The prophecy!"

11:48 AM
Death on the Fourposter (1964)

Oh boy, my copy of this movie is in rough shape. This is going to be hard on the eyes. Hee hee, I said "hard on". Some catty young people are sitting around a table at an outdoor café being catty to each other. When their friend Ricky (Michel Lemoine) shows up, they drive to a castle while some swingin' jazz and rock music blasts over the credit sequence. They pull over long enough to pretend to throw one of the girls in a lake and then they jump back in their cars and take off again. I'll never understand kids these days. What the fuck? They pull over again to goof off some more and then off they go.

These weirdos finally arrive at the very gothic castle and Ricky is acting a tad suspicious. He tells everyone to enjoy themselves and then, like a game show host, he reveals what's being door number three. It's Catharine (Luisa Rivelli), his servant! While the girls are freshening themselves up, the men are talking about them. At the same time, the girls are talking about the guys. This whole sequence is intolerable. When Nicki (Maria Pia Conte) gets separated from the rest, she runs into Aldo (Giuseppe Fortis), the creepy caretaker. Ricky assures her that he's harmless.

A sexy and voluptuous woman named Serena (Antonella Lualdi) shows up with a duder named Anthony (John Drew Barrymore) and the party (and the movie as well) get lively. She does some sexy dancing to some brassy music with lots of bongos. Catharine really seems to enjoy her dance, like a whole lot. I don't know where this movie is going but I'm now totally entertained, especially when all the girls start dancing with Serena. After the dance, Serena suggests they play a game called "Shattering Illusions". This ain't Milton Bradley, kids! This is one of those adult games. Basically, you tell Serena what you care about most and then she seduces you into forfeiting it. Fun!

For a new game, Serena asks Anthony to demonstrate his psychic powers! He can sense psychic energy in objects and give details about the past. When asked if he can predict the future, Anthony conducts a séance. Now we're getting down to business! In a very cool séance sequence, that's chock full of foreboding; he warns them that terrible things are going to happen and that they should get out of the castle. Does anyone listen? Of course not. When that's over, we see Ricky taking off Catharine's stockings for her. That is so perverted. I'm blushing in shame! Why must movies always be so dirty?

The cinematographer on this shot both The Horrible Dr. Hichcock and The Ghost! That makes me wish this was in color, damn it. The party turns sour when the first body is discovered. Someone has been strangled to death on the four-poster bed and there are at least five suspects in this party. Oops, there's been another murder but where's the body? This is a little clunky and a little silly but I'm definitely enjoying myself. Was that a bottle of J&B? I would rewind to confirm it but this DVD is so murky that I know it won't help. Man, I hope a better copy of this turns up someday.

"We're all hunchbacks of one kind or another."

1:56 PM
The Possessed (1965)

Another black and white film? Boo! Naw, just joshin' ya. This 1965 flick opens with a writer named Bernard (Peter Baldwin) talking on the phone. He's speaking Spanish but I know this to be an Italian film. Good thing the subtitles are in English! This was co-directed by Luigi Bazzoni, director of The Fifth Cord and Footprints. Nice! Bernard is heading to his favorite hotel in a lakeside village to lay low now that his luck has turned sour. What is it? A layoff? A bad breakup? It seems that he has come to this hotel for a woman named Tilde; she worked at the hotel and he hopes to see her again.

This town that he's visiting is practically a ghost town during the winter. Out on the streets, he thinks he sees Tilde but it's not her. Bummed out, he decides to go and visit his hunchbacked friend, Francesco. LeEtta comments that there sure are a lot of hunchbacks in Italy. I tell it's because of all that pasta. That evening, at dinner, the owner of the hotel informs Bernard that Tilde is dead. She killed herself and no one knows why. I would take solace in one thing: Valentina Cortese plays the hotel owner's daughter. I would let her comfort me all the live long day. But Bernard has got it bad. He dreams of chasing Tilde (Virna Lisi) through the streets and seeing her in bed with a man.

He goes back to his friend Francesco who tells him that Tilde's death was very suspicious. They found poison in her mouth and stomach but the cause of death was actually from a stab wound. Francesco shows Bernard a photo of Tilde and it looks like she was pregnant at the time of her death. Francesco suspects someone in the town knocked her up and then killed her to protect his reputation. Bernard tells Francesco about seeing Tilde in bed with a man on the day he left. So that wasn't a dream!

I love the atmosphere of this one. It's very haunting. And much like Footprints, it's tough to know what is going on. This jumps from dream to fantasy to reality and back again enough to make your head spin. The cinematography is super sharp and lovely to behold. Man, this bootleg looks fantastic. The sickly wife of the butcher tries to pass Bernard a note but it vanishes before he can read it. That night, he tries to meet up with her by the lake but she keeps her distance. Now Bernard has come down with the flu. Right when he's recovering from his illness, the cops come to see him and ask him to identify a corpse. Jeez, this really is turning into a Kafka-esque nightmare.

"I have no allusions about your sex."

3:35 PM
The Sensuous Assassin (1970)

This film opens with a couple, Marina and Claude (played by Romy Schneider and Gabriele Tinti respectively), arguing. The woman enrages the man so he starts slapping her around. She pulls out a gun and fires it but misses. Once that's settled, he puts her in their little red car and they take off. Some groovy rock and roll kicks in over the credits. This sequence features some awesome stunt driving. At the end of the credits, the car goes over the edge of a cliff and into the ocean. Up on the rocks, the woman is watching in horror. Hey, how did she get out of the car? She jumped out! Duh! I looked up the Italian title for this movie and it translates to "The Corpse from the Claws of Steel".

Traumatized from the horrors of the accident, Marina goes to stay with Claude's brother Serge (Maurice Ronet), an architect. She has nightmares about engines running and hears gunshots in her sleep. She runs into Serge's monochromatic bedroom (his robe, sheets, walls, art, everything is all black, white, or gray) and he points a gun at her. When he pulls the trigger, music starts playing. Who the fuck owns a gun-shaped music box? The next morning, Marina meets Dorothy (Simone Bach). She is Serge's ex who won't go away. She's the info dumper but I missed it because of the dang subtitles. You'd think that I would be able to speak Italian by now.

The cinematographer, Jean Bourgoin, is on some serious pep pills. He follows the action like a dog follows a laser pointer. This film has some serious style. At a party full of jerks, Marina's purse falls open and Serge sees a pistol clip inside. When he questions her about it, she's happily evasive. This drives Serge nuts but Marina starts to seduce him. It works, Serge is seduced! He takes her on a little road trip to where Claude drove off the cliff. Serge drives wildly toward the edge, just as his brother did. When Marina doesn't jump out like in her version of what happened, he gets irate. You know, I just noticed how luxurious our cat Sparkles is. Seriously, she is like Bond villain stroke-worthy. Maybe we can rent her out to criminal masterminds. "Stroke-worthy" is a phrase that I need to remember to edit out of this book.

Continually obsessed, Serge rents some diving equipment and goes snooping around his dead brother's car. He finds a gun under the seat and looks hilariously surprised when he looks at it. That's good scuba acting right there! With every accusation that he makes, Marina has some story or excuse to explain it away. Serge starts to lose it. My favorite scene is when he's drunk and spitting on people in the street from his window. Then he gets eggs and starts chucking them at the people below. This mega-douche almost pegs a duder in a wheelchair! It seems that he and his bro were cut from the same cloth. LeEtta asks me if this even counts as a giallo. I can't comment on that or else this entire book falls apart!

Okay, I'm getting a little bored here. This movie's rock score has taken a very shitty turn. They keep playing some terrible song with awful lyrics. Of course, they're in English while rest of this film is in Italian. The best character is Dorothy but she's not on screen enough. The cops call Serge to come and identify a body that might be his brother. It's been in the water for 20 days so they can't positively say it's him or not. In the very next scene, a man who looks a whole lot like Claude starts chasing Marina around the rooftop of a department store. It's a good chase but I'm not sure if I care anymore.

FOOTBALL GAME BREAK?

So here is a moviethon first and last. We went to a football game! LeEtta's brother is an Iraq War veteran and they were honoring him at the first game of the season. It was pretty surreal, especially when LeEtta was down on the field with him and they had the whole family up on the Jumbotron. We stayed until a little after halftime. It was clear that USF was getting smeared all over the field. Did I mention that I fucking hate football? But at least now I have some theories about why I hate it that are too exciting to share here. Anyway, we got back and I finished the last 15 minutes of The Sensuous Assassin.

"They kill each others."

10:44 PM
Love and Death on the Edge of a Razor (1973)

Looks like we are heading to Venice for this one. This print is a little washed out but I am okay with that. Lidia (Erika Blanc) and Stefano (Peter Lee Lawrence) seem to have just had a 'love at first sight' thing. The schmaltzy music kicks in and there's a dog licking his private parts in the street. Stefano is making some grand romantic gesture to Lidia and such as laying a bed of flowers on the street and spraying it with perfume. She just looks confused but she takes his arm and the rest is history (or at least a credit sequence). They ride in a gondola, kiss, and then say goodbye when he drops her off at the train station. I guess that concludes the Venice section of the movie.

Sometime later, Stefano comes out to Florence or somewhere so he and Lidia can be together. They have more romantic silliness. They make their promises and Stefano goes back to work. One afternoon, Stefano's father comes to the office to bring him some bad news: Lidia died in a car accident. It's so abrupt that I have to laugh. While he's putting some flowers on Lidia's grave, the music goes all funny and it looks like Stefano may go mad. Before any real grieving can happen, Stefano is already in bed with a new sexy chick, Giovanna (Ivana Novak), the daughter of a rich guy.

Sigh. Stefano sees a girl who could be Lidia's twin (Erika Blanc again). Back at her grave, the tombstone is blank. He checks with the caretakers and they tell him she was never buried there. Next, he goes to the newspapers but they claim that they never printed a story about Lidia getting killed. Giovanna suspects that he's still pining over Lidia. Duh, lady. His parents insist that Stefano should get engaged to Giovanna but he refuses. He'd rather keep screwing her and having his little daydreams about Lidia. My copy of this film sucks. The audio is buzzing like a beehive.

Now shit gets weird. The chick that looks just like Lidia is a journalist that is canoodling with some jerkwater gangster who talks about himself in the third person. She is trying to avoid Stefano and I'm barely interested in what is going on here. This is more silly than intriguing. Silvano Traquili shows up, spies on the gangster with his binoculars, and then vanishes. Then a big shootout at a shipyard happens and I can't wait until bedtime. Dear reader, I don't give a sweet and salty unicorn-shaped shit about this lame ass movie. Lidia's twin gets mortally wounded and only Stefano's love can save her. This is easily the worst film I've watched in a decade.

SUNDAY

We wake up at ten until eight in the morning and my first thought is how much I fucking loathe Love and Death on the Edge of a Razor. I've seen some films for this book that weren't gialli-related enough for my tastes but that wasn't even movie-related. Walking through the parking lot to Brunchies, I feel hungover. My body really wanted more sleep but I wanted breakfast before everything gets too busy. If you want to be served breakfast in Tampa, you get your ass out of bed and out the door before 8:30 on the weekends or you're fucked. By 9:30 or 10:00, you better add at least an hour waiting time on to your breakfast because either you're going to wait in line to get a table or wait to be served once you're finally seated. Or both. That's life in the big city.

I get French toast and a side of bacon. LeEtta gets a skillet with eggs, spinach, sundried tomatoes, and bleu cheese. I get French vanilla iced coffee and start to feel human again. LeEtta likes her coffee with cream but no sugar. My boss and a couple of my other fellow coworkers come in and sit down. I really didn't want to think about work today but hey, Brunchies is an awesome place. They'll serve anybody, even librarians.

"My my, what a whore you are."

10:47 AM
Lay Your Hands on My Body (1970)

Lino Capolicchio stars in this one as Andrea, a wild and crazy kid (emphasis on crazy). I don't remember liking this film very much the first time but my opinion may change. Andrea, when he's not causing trouble and riding his motorcycle around with his eyes closed, he hangs out at the beach, internal monologuing this movie into the pretentious stratosphere. He imagines his mother beckoning to him (almost like a lover) and he remembers her on her deathbed, an event that greatly traumatized him.

The score for this film by Giorgio Gaslini is really beautiful, scrumptious even! Andrea likes to act like a little psycho but he enjoys torturing Mireille (Erna Schurer), his step-sister, the most. Gee, I wonder why. Could it be because he's in love with her? José Quaglio plays Andrea's father who he resents for remarrying and also for being an old jerk. Andrea also likes to toy with the maid (Pier Paola Bucchi), a simple yet sexy girl but she's just a minor distraction for this nut. Mirelle invites another distraction to their home: her friend Carole (Collette Descombes of Lenzi's Orgasmo).

Enter Dickbag, an arrogant cock-of-the-walk sonofabitch that is banging both Mirelle and Carole. He's not enough for Carole, she wants someone that interests her. And since she can't make heads or tails of Andrea, she sees him as a challenge. After a day at the beach, Andrea takes Carole to his room where Nivel, a black chick that Andrea crashed his father's party with, is waiting naked in bed. They perform some ritualistic free-form jazz dance with ridiculous religious and racist overtones. This might be why I didn't like the movie before. It's trying to shock or amuse me but I'm just annoyed. Carole freaks and leaves while Andrea laughs his ass off.

Mirelle tries to teach Andrea a lesson about women. She takes him to a party so he can see that Carole has already moved on and is back with Dickbag. Andrea flips out and chases Carole even more psychotically. I don't think this is going to end well. Andrea's little crazy games just got less playful and more deadly serious. His tenuous grasp on reality ain't helpin' matters none at all. No, sir. The vote is still out on this film.

"I hate myself."

12:30 PM
Evil Senses (1986)

This opens a very 1980s-looking naked chick getting out of bed, leaving her lover (or John) named Manuel (Gabriele Lavia of Deep Red) smoking and watching her go. Manuel is a hitman. He kills a guy by shooting him in the face and then an unimaginably bad song starts playing. I'm trying to block it out as best I can but it is aggressively awful. Lavia directed this one and I've heard it's very weird. Mimsy Farmer has a small part in this as Micol, a madam. Her shoulder pads have a very big part in this too. Manuel fucked up one of his hits and now everyone is out to get him. He gets on a subway train and there's a guy who looks exactly like Saddam Hussein. I think that may have been an inside joke from the filmmakers.

So far, this movie is very stylish and Manuel frowns a lot. He is told to lie low so he goes to stay with Micol in her high class brothel. They sleep together and Micol starts waxing nostalgic. This dialog is bad, full of clichés and a few zingers of the 'jokey' variety. Micol just hired a special new girl, Vittoria (Monica Guerritore), as a surprise for Manuel. She likes to talk like a naughty character in a shitty screenplay.

In one scene, Vittoria opens up a bunch of music boxes at once while the music score becomes nightmarish. Then she starts undulating in the nude as though she were turning into a werewolf. After they have sex, she tells Manuel that he was bad in bed and he tells her that he doesn't give a fuck. What a friggin' badass. Then he catches her masturbating in the bathroom and the music score gets pretty amazing; a great mix of eroticism and horror from Fabio Frizzi.

We find out that Vittoria is married to some crass old rich guy (Lewis E. Ciannelli). So she turns tricks for fun? Whatta gal! They continue to make slow motion love and talk in romance novel gobbledygook. She asks Manuel to kill her disgusting husband. When he refuses, she won't sleep with him anymore. Manuel actually gets jealous when Vittoria has another client. It turns out that her client is a hitman who's been following Manuel around. Ooh, intrigue! This movie has its head stuffed way up its own ass but I'm loving the style! It feels like what would have happened if Lucio Fulci and Jess Franco had collaborated on a screenplay together.

"I bet you screwed with tears in your eyes last night, didn't you?"

2:11 PM
Delitto carnale (1983)

This piece of trash should be a good time. The subtitles were going too fast so I futzed with VLC Media Player so they would appear -5 seconds ahead of time. In a J&B sighting of epic proportions, a sleazeball guy at a dumpy hotel pours himself a drink and then dumps the bottle in some chick's open mouth. Obviously, she gets wasted! Marc Porel shows up as Max the photographer and wow, he is lookin' harsh. Somebody's having a funeral party and everyone keeps saying how sorry they are and what a disgrace some old man's death was. What old man? Somebody's dad, maybe. LeEtta makes us Southern-style fried rice for an early dinner. Delicious! Let me just say that everyone in this movie has bad hair.

So frumpy underwear lesbian lady just undressed leotard lady. The porno-disco music just never stops and neither does the trashiness. The lesbian lovers stand in the shower and pour perfume over their naked bodies in order to get off. The music starts getting very discordant when someone mentions that there is a murderer nearby. Then more sex happens. Other than sleazy people being sleazy, I'm just confused. There is an inheritance involved, I think. LeEtta just explained the plot to me but I don't know how she knows.

On the disco floor, there is decadence aplenty and Leia the brunette keeps threatening to pull her panties down. When the party settles down, there are bodies on the dance floor. Unfortunately, they're all live ones. A topless lady discovers that Leia has been killed and stuffed into a pantry in the kitchen. The cops come and take the body away. The inspector insists that everyone must stay in the hotel during the investigation. They just showed the sign for the hotel, it said "Hotel Gemini 2". Oh I get it, this is the sequel to the other hotel. Elena the redhead is hanging out with the horses and they all make the same exact sampled horsey noise. I'm dying here. Max meets her in the stable and they have a literal roll in the hay. We're very amused as both Max and Elena's skin turns bright red from coming into contact with the hay.

Mike, the guy who looks kind of like a fat Benny Andersson, pretends to hang himself and no one finds it amusing except for him and me. I get a laugh out of it. Out of nowhere, someone strangles Elena to death. I'm going to miss her and her wild overacting. I shouldn't pick on her since everyone in this is equally terrible. This cut and paste synth score was done by someone named Mimi Uva. She also did the music for Sister of Ursula. Lady —I'm assuming you're a lady- no offense but your resume is AMAZING! Well, I'll be damned, I kind of like this film. Possible double feature with In the Folds of the Flesh sometime?

"Beaver scouting patrol leaves in 5 minutes!"

4:26 PM
Nightmare Beach (1989)

A biker gang waits solemnly outside a prison while a very cantankerous man named Eduardo Diablos is executed by way of the electric chair. He vows revenge on his accusers and then he's dead. Some brazen 80s garbage music kicks in and we're off to the beach for the credit sequence. Harry

Kirkpatrick directed this? I could have sworn it was Umberto Lenzi. It's Spring Break and Ronnie Rivera and his buddy Skip (the one who blew the big game) are there to party and to forget. John Saxon plays Strycher, the local sheriff, and he ain't happy about what's going on. Somebody dug up Eduardo's grave. The creepy preacher (Lance LeGault) reminds Strycher that Eduardo said he'd be back from the grave.

A mysterious biker picks up a teenage chick hitchhiking to Manatee Beach and electrocutes her with a special contraption on his bike. Man, this movie is friggin' overwhelming. I'm just drowning in 80s cheese. There's an un-subtle Jaws reference with the corrupt officials protecting their tourist town by any means necessary, taken to the extreme. Umberto Lenzi is aping Argento's use of heavy metal as the soundtrack to the murders. I also should note that I fucking love movies shot in Florida, especially when the filmmakers fail at making it look like a glamorous and fun place to visit.

If you enjoy Spring Break shenanigans (and I know you do!), you will not be disappointed with Nightmare Beach. There is a metric ton of it. Outside a bar, Ronnie and Skip run afoul of the bikers, which I just noticed are called the Demons (a Lamberto Bava reference?). Strycher breaks it up and bars the gang from beach. The acting in this scene, especially from the gang's leader, is fantastic. Inside the bar, Skip catches the eye of a pouty-faced bartendress named Gail (Sarah Buxton). She's impressed with his disdain of fun and frivolity. She finds it refreshing. Look at her face!

Meanwhile, a prostitute, posing as a college student, is working out a scheme to bang some old rich guy and take his money. Creepy Preacher's daughter doesn't want her old man telling her what to do even though she's been "drinking and acting lewd". Queue more Spring Break bullshit. There are some sad boobs on display. That night, Ronnie bumps into the Demons again and gets his ass kicked. When they take off, he gets electrocuted to death by our mysterious killer. Skip wants answers and starts investigating what happened to Ronnie against the wishes of Strycher. Gail joins his quest as more electro-charred bodies are piling up all over the beach. At the big beach party, musical sensation Kirsten performs her hit "Say the Word" and you will be dazzled. Seriously folks, you need to cover yourself in cocoa butter and watch the shit out of this movie. I promise you'll love it.

SHORT BREAK

I make a mad dash to the Hess station on the corner of Zambito and Bearss for some ice cream. Man, this place is a dump. The employees are aloof at best and the place is always in shambles. It's one of the very few things that I don't like about our new place. I miss the crew at our old 7-11 something fierce. Maybe I'll go see them tomorrow for no reason other than to get a Slurpee and say hello.

"I will destroy you for that, Harold!"

6:28 PM
The Perfect Crime (1978)

This copy is most definitely sourced from a Greek VHS tape. It has the washed out colors and the Greek subtitles to prove it. A guy on a tarmac slips some kind of bomb in a plane's fuel tank before it takes off. The plane explodes and it's fake as hell, even worse than the one in The Case of the Scorpion's Tail. The explosion looks like a poof of chalk dust. The Anglicized names for the Italian crew are awesome (directed by Aaron Leviathan?). The only proud motherfucker is composer Carlo Savina. He delivers another awesome score full of intrigue and menace.

So a duder on the plane was some kind of muckety muck big wig tycoon and the business has to choose who will be his successor. The candidates are Adolfo Celi, a very tired looking Joseph Cotten, and curly haired Leonard Mann as -I'm not kidding- Paul de Revere. His butler is Paul Muller! Janet Agren plays the rich, young, and pissed off wife of Adolfo Celi. LeEtta guesses that he married for money to further his business interests. I think that would be a big 'Heck yes!' Joseph Cotten is trying to get Polly (Gloria Guida), Adolfo Celi's mistress, to poison his competition. And he is very specific that she do it during his orgasm. What a weirdo.

Somebody has bought off Leonard Mann's butler. He cuts his brake lines and sends him out for a drive. His car goes off the cliff and explodes. Janet Agren has Celi by the balls. She has some incriminating evidence on him in a letter that will go to her lawyer's office if anything should happen to her. The cops are very suspicious of the events leading up to Paul de Revere's death. They announce publicly that the case is closed to put the murderer at ease, hoping he'll make a mistake. There's a J&B bottle sitting on a fancy tray. Why is no one drinking out of it? Someone who wears black gloves is keeping an eye on all the players with a pair of binoculars. I think I know who it is but I'm keeping my lips sealed.

Whoever is dubbing Joseph Cotten must have thought he was an ancient Chinese man. There are a lot of scenes at night in this movie and my eyes are getting shredded trying to see what is going on with this grubby old VHS dub. There's an awesome kill scene where the victim tries to cut their malfunctioning pacemaker out of their chest themselves. Genius! When lady and lord start throwing insults back and forth, Celi goes for the old infertility insult and that kills that little spat. It would be nice if there were some likeable characters in this. Alida Valli is Paul's aunt but she isn't in the movie enough for my tastes. I reserve my final judgment on this movie for when I finally see a decent copy of it (which I know exists).

GIALLO MELTDOWN

"It was a good fuck, wasn't it?"

8:16 PM
Trauma (1978)

My copy of this movie looks amazing! This comes from director León Klimovsky. Love that dude. This begins with some ugly bastard named Daniel (Heinrich Starhemberg (that is seriously his name)) driving his Fiat through the countryside. He arrives at his destination, a beautiful house with rooms for rent occupied by a beautiful woman and her husband. Her name is Veronica (Ágata Lys) and she is so cute. Her perm is not so cute but that's okay. Her husband, a cripple, is upstairs. He can't move about on his own and they aren't showing him at all. Uh oh, that's very suspicious.

A storm is rolling in and I am getting some nice feelings of dread from this film. Daniel catches a kid from the village spying on the house but he lets him go. When the storm hits, it is a sepia filter over the sky to indicate storm clouds. Cute. After Veronica feeds Daniel some fish for dinner, two hikers show up looking for food and lodging. Veronica treats them like shit. One of the hikers is Jess Franco regular, Antonio Mayans! Later, Veronica's invisible husband threatens to smack her around. He makes her strip for him and the accompanying crazy keyboard music is hilarious. She has fake boobs but they're nice. The female hiker does not have fake boobs.

A black gloved killer is snooping around the house and I cry out "Oh baby!" which causes LeEtta to give me a strange look. The killer makes quick work of the two hikers, slashing them with a straight razor. The bodies magically disappear and we're ready for some more guests. A sleazy guy and his busty lover (Isabel Pisano) get stuck nearby when his car breaks down. Daniel meets that little kid again while he's swimming around in the lake. Daniel helps him dry off and it's super creepy.

The trashy couple arrives at the house and the woman (a hooker) is so voluptuous that I'm just dumbfounded. LeEtta reminds me not to get too excited about her. Before they make love, the guy makes a reference to the Wolfman (Paul Naschy reference?). The killer liberates them both of the burden of keeping all that blood inside their bodies. Man oh man, this is a fun flick. Recommended if you can find it!

"You're just plain weird. Too weird."

9:41 PM
Eyes Behind the Wall (1977)

A serene train ride explodes into sexual violence when Arturo (John Philip Law) flips out and attempts to rape and murder a fellow female passenger. Next we meet a couple, wheelchair bound Ivano (Fernando Rey) and Olga (Olga Bisera). They're renting an apartment to Arturo and they're spying on him which is... odd. They have some very intricate snooping equipment and they use it to spy on him while he's acting very ordinary. He listens to progressive rock records and does push-ups naked. And I just saw John Philip Law's dangling balls. Wow. I'm in shock. Anyway, Ivano and Olga get off on spying on this dude.

José Quaglio (again in this moviethon!) plays Ottavio, the couple's peeping butler. I hope he doesn't do naked pushups. He's a terrible pervert with a life-sized tribute to Olga painted on the inside of his closet. He bows down before it and starts punching its groin with his fist. Now that's foreplay! Later, Olga catches Ottavio sniffing her hairs that he found in the drain after her bath. Arturo goes to a bar and there are at least 7 bottles of J&B in the cabinet. He catches the eye of, and is being followed by, a very cool looking black dude. On a bus, the black dude is making sexy eyes at Arturo. Holy crap!

The black guy is named Joe (Jho Jenkins) and he likes to go out for some serious disco dancing. He and Arturo smoke a doobie at the bar and then there's more disco dancing. This is one liberal nite club: you can smoke a doob at the bar and nudity on the dance floor is encouraged. When the party gets too much for Arturo, he and Joe go back to his place. They start drinking, fist-fighting, and then well um hey —how can I put this gently?- the black dude buggers Arturo in the bum. Olga, who's been watching this whole time, goes bananas. Ivano has known all along that this was Arturo's secret. Folks, I have NEVER seen gay sex (as in two dudes and not two lipstick lesbians) portrayed even remotely realistically in a giallo before (though this is definitely more of a psychosexual thriller).

The couple continue studying this man psychologically, trying to predict what he'll do. Ivano thinks he is on a path of self-destruction. Of course, that theory might be a little skewed. Homophobic, maybe? One round of sex with a stranger doesn't mean someone is going off the deep end. I think these two are in over their heads, especially since they don't know the guy is a dangerous motherfucker. Ivano sends Olga in to spend time with Arturo and encourages her to get intimate with him. Oh brother. Now Ottavio is getting some action from a girl he likes to smack around. Good for him? This movie is insanely grim and odd. Filmmakers in the late 70s really liked to stick it to the viewer. In the butt.

MONDAY

Last night in bed, I kept thinking of John Philip Balls. Okay, I'm just kidding. But my mind was in a strange place. I could feel my brain, happily simmering in moviethon juices. I should probably get a brain scan when I get like this and see what it would take to bottle and sell this feeling. So anyway, my brain is soaking in happy sauce when a stream of images shakes it loose from its reverie. My mind starts to spin faster and faster as images and memories from 12 moviethons go flying by. When it stops, I am left feeling afraid of the dark. I can hear my cat Crisco yowling at something but I'm too scared to open my eyes. Eventually, I fall asleep. Around nine in the morning, LeEtta wakes me up and the smell of coffee does the rest to get me out of bed. Another breakfast sandwich, vitamins, and caffeine. Let's get to work.

"Miscarriages of justice don't exist."

10:05 AM
Cadaveri eccellenti (1976)

Hello 1976, it's good to see you again. This film opens with the corpse of a saint and some brooding music from Piero Piccioni. An old man is walking around in the catacombs under the church. There are bodies of saints hang all over the walls. The camera lingers on their faces making this one of the most morbid opening sequences to a film I've ever seen. Outside, the old man stops to pick up a flower and he's shot to death by a man with a silenced revolver. He was Judge Vargas. The inspector, Rogas (Lino Ventura), is investigating his murder by talking to a really annoying old monk. Vargas's funeral is a debacle full of people honoring his struggle against the mafia and protestors saying that he was the mafia.

Another judge is found dead by the side of the road, his poor dog staying by his side and barking at passing cars. The judge murders continue and stories of their corruption rise to the surface. Rogas feels conflicted because he believes the killer might be a victim of a miscarriage of justice carried out by the victims. There are only three cases that these men had in common and only one judge, Judge Rasto (Alain Cuny), involved in those three cases is still alive. Rogas goes to meet up with the people who were convicted in these cases. They're not happy people.

The only one he can't locate is Cres, a chemist whose life and career was ruined by the judge's decision. Cres's wife (Maria Carta) accused him of trying to poison her and that was enough to destroy his reputation. A flashback makes her look like a crazy bitch who poisoned her own cat to get her husband accused of attempted murder. They show the cat getting poisoned but nothing cruel happened. The cat's death throes are clearly it playing on its back. Good cat acting though! Cres's friend, Dr. Maxia (Paolo Bonacelli), tells Rogas that Cres is now a recluse and hardly ever comes out of his house. All the photos of Cres have been destroyed. Very suspicious!

After two more murders, a wave of violence and unrest is sweeps across

Italy. Rogas is in trouble with his superiors for not solving the case already so they set him up with an organization that listens to phone calls and secretly videotapes supposed enemies of the state. The paranoia factor in this movie is hovering between orange and red. Other great people in this cast: the lovely Tina Aumont (of Torso), Luigi Pistilli, Fernando Rey, and not so lovely Ernesto Colli (also from Torso). This is an excellent film both classy and smart. Old Steppenwolf himself, Max von Sydow, is in this too!

LUNCH

LeEtta and I run out for a quick lunch pickup. I swing by the cigar store and get a couple of short cigars. There are rumors that Sam is going to come over and watch some movies with us. We try to go to the little Greek place called Little Greek but they are closed for the holiday. I'm annoyed as shit because I was craving some Greek food, darn it. We go to Publix and I get a ham and cheese sub. I also pick up a tomato to dice up and throw on top. LeEtta gets a salad. The place is crowded as fuck and everyone is driving like an idiot today. Time to go back home.

"Jeez, you really gave it to that whore!"

1:11 PM
Sleepless (2001)

I could've sworn that I covered this one for the book already but according to my master list, I have not! Seeing as I have the definitive edition (the Arrow Films disc) of this film, I better get on it! Want to see something funny? Google the original poster for this film. It's a boring piece of shit! Max von Sydow in two films in a row! He plays Moretti, a cop who, back in 1983, made a promise to a little boy that he would catch his mother's killer. We cut to the present day where a hooker with crazy fake tatas is refusing to fulfill a John's sick request. She leaves but not before accidentally stealing evidence that the John, whose face we don't see, is a serial killer. This hooker gets killed quite beautifully on a train.

So anyway, this is Argento's big comeback film after he royally fucked up The Phantom of the Opera. I really enjoyed this film and hoped that this was a sign of more good things to come. How did all that turn out? Well, let's just say it's been rocky to say the least. The soundtrack by Goblin is loud and kicks my ass all over town. The hooker's friend tries to meet her at the train station not knowing that the killer has already hacked her to death. She finds the blue folder (like a certain blue iris maybe?) containing the evidence of who the killer is. She goes right to the police, the killer is caught, and the movie ends. Just kidding, this chick doesn't even make it out of the fucking parking lot.

Years ago, a dwarf named Vincenzo was suspected of murdering a young boy's mother and Moretti went after him. The dwarf, a crime fiction writer, disappeared but his body washed up in the river, an apparent suicide. Case closed. Now the evidence seems to suggest that the dwarf is back and the killings are based on an old animal-themed nursery rhyme. The young boy, Giacomo, is all grown up now and he's played by Stefano Dionisi (but I call him Mr. Charisma). His friend called and told him about the new rash of crimes so he quits his shitty job at the Chinese restaurant and comes home. He meets up with Moretti and we flashback to his mother getting murdered with a French horn. It's one of the craziest gore setpieces ever.

Giacomo starts hanging out with his old friend Lorenzo. He is played by Roberto Zibetti. I am so glad that this guy dubs his own lines in this. The guy has a terrific voice. Giacomo is hitting on Gloria, his old friend, but she is dating some stupid asshole named Fausto. All of these people were from the same neighborhood and they all remember the dwarf and someone killing house pets back in the day. When Moretti and Giacomo go back to Vincenzo's old house, the figure of the dwarf is in the window. A little reference to Phenomena perhaps? The body count is growing and the murders are violent as hell and just really impressive. Keep your eye out for a small role played by Rosella Falk. This movie is still a little silly but I am a big fan of it. There's a lot to spoil here so I'll move on to the next film.

"My dear, I'd like you to meet Jackoff."

3:12 PM
Four Flies on Grey Velvet (1971)

My pal Sam arrives just in time for us to start this favorite of mine. After years of searching, I finally have a good copy of this film. Whoa, that creepy Kewpie doll mask! That is woefully disturbing to all three of us. Ladies and gentlemen, witness the supreme awesomeness of Mimsy Farmer. I get all kinds of stupid over this chick. Her presence gives me an urge to watch The Perfume of the Lady in Black (again). Though most reviewers (and probably Argento himself) think Michael Brandon doesn't work in the role of Roberto Tobias, I've got news for ya, people: He's playing a drummer. You ever hang out with a drummer? Exactly.

Poor Roberto has a lot of problems. You know, being blackmailed for stabbing a stranger and now he has visions of a beheading. Man, this movie (as well as the camera) is all over the place. This is my kind of Argento: beautiful and indulgent. Four Flies was to be Argento's "farewell" to the giallo. Everyone knows it wasn't but you can see the guy pulling out all the stops with this one. He's really challenging the genre here and giving it a surreal edge that makes me flip out every time.

God is played by Bud Spencer because Bud Spencer is God. He named his bird Jerkoff. That's nice. God damn it (sorry Godfrey), so many familiar faces in this! Hell, even Gildo Di Marco, who was Garullo the pimp in Birth with the Crystal Plumage, is back as the battered mailman. Then there's "The Professor" played by Oreste Lionello -the gay photographer from The Case of the Bloody Iris- and he is probably the coolest character ever.

Speaking of gay stereotypes, Jean-Pierre Marielle (of Sans Mobile Apparent) plays the hapless private eye, Gianni Arrosio. Ouch, vengeance of the gay stereotypes when Arrosio meets one of his own persuasion. We're all a little ashamed of ourselves now. LeEtta: "Oh my GOD, he had a fan and he was fanning himself with it like a Southern belle!" I have to admit that I laugh at this part. Sorry, everyone. I am succumbing to the style of this film. Four Flies is Argento firing on all cylinders. Hot damn!

The plot devolves into pseudoscience as images recorded on a corpse's eye help identify the killer. LeEtta: "What is this, the 17th century?" Oh but the ending is priceless. I want to tell you all about it but no, you must seek this film out as I did. Sam isn't overly impressed with this one. I try to explain to him why this movie is so important to me and the Holy Grail place it holds in the genre. I'm not sure if I've convinced him.

> *"Should I explain to you how to make love?*
> *Just lie down and act like a seductive woman!"*

5:32 PM
Who Killed the Prosecutor and Why? (1972)

We settle down with some fancy meat and cheeses for this film with an unpromising title. This opens with a picturesque montage of a model named Olga (Bebe Loncar) posing on the beach while a photographer named Carlo (Lou Castel) takes snapshots. They make love on the beach and see someone blowing up a car with an unconscious man inside it. Carlo gets some photos of this crime and develops them at home in his dark room. Olga wants to get laid but Carlo is too busy for her. There's a bottle of J&B hiding in the cabinet. Don't worry. It's the first of many in this film.

Carlo decides to take his photos to his wheelchair-bound Uncle Fifi (Massimo Serato of Bloodstained Shadow) to see if they can get some money for them. So apparently, Uncle Fifi is a pornographer. When they show up, he's directing a photo shoot of a Roman orgy. After seeing the blackmail pictures, he suggests that Carlo could get 20 million lira for them. Uncle Fifi tells him not to make a move until the police do. Oh Carlo, you greedy, ignorant fool. Don't listen to your Uncle Fifi!

Adolfo Celi is here as Inspector Vezzi. He's investigating the death of the man that Carlo and Olga witnessed and he sees through this staged accident immediately. The victim was a prominent prosecutor so Vezzi's boss has him under a lot of pressure to solve this so he decides to just grab a random suspect. Maybe I'm just burnt out from typing all this shit or maybe this movie is bad, but folks, I'm already sick of this plot. Carlo gets into hot water with the mafia and people start dropping like flies around him. Carla Brait of The Case of the Bloody Iris has a cameo in a nightclub. She gets nude because apparently, there was a camera with film in it nearby.

This film ended up being kind of a slog for all three of us even with the black-gloved assassin taking people out, decent music by Mario Bertolazzi, good suspense, and endless J&B sightings. I'm hoping to enjoy it more with a second viewing one day. Honestly, Lou Castel is kind of why I didn't enjoy it more. His portrayal of Carlo has absolutely no charm at all AND he's a dick. Once again, I'm trying to explain to Sam that he needs to come over when we're watching -insert classic giallo title here-. I'm definitely overthinking things because Sam says he's having a good time.

CIGAR BREAK

I have a little Rocky Patel cigar. It is dark as hell and very smooth. Sam takes his leave of us but he wishes us well on the rest of the moviethon. I'm so full of fancy cheese right now. LeEtta has been making me drinks with the little bit of J&B we have left. We call them Ginger Fingers: J&B, ginger beer, and lemon juice. Sometimes we add ginger liqueur but we are out of that. It is a grown up drink because I am not a little boy anymore. Time for the last movie of this meltdown.

"I do not want to be your lover! I want everything!"

8:01 PM
Macabre (1969)

A man with a scar on his face (Giacomo Rossi-Stuart) is driving through the rain. All we hear is the sound of the windshield wipers clicking back and forth when suddenly, the music kicks in and it is some tense piano driven by big percussion and a lovely chorus. He gets to his destination, a village in Spain. He walks into a store and buys an aspirin. He looks very suspicious in his sunglasses, hat, trenchcoat, and black gloves. He goes to the house of Denise (Teresa Gimpera), a lovely woman and an old flame perhaps? He's been to jail and wants her to help him out. When Denise's husband comes home, he leaves. I don't think it'll be the last we see of him.

When Old Scarface leaves, Denise assures her husband, John (Larry Ward), that he's the most important thing in her life. I'm loving the camerawork in this Spanish-Italian co-production. Old Scarface stops at a gas station and he sees a man who looks exactly like John. Meanwhile, Denise is acting like a bored and vindictive beyatch. John gets sick of the bullshit and leaves to go to the casino. When he's gone, she goes out to hang out with his twin brother Peter (Larry Ward again), an artist. Denise wants him to kill his own brother and take his place so that she can get at John's money.

Old Scarface calls up the twin to blackmail him so Denise and Peter decide to use this dirtbag to set their plan into motion. John has some kind of condition that requires him to take pills every four hours. They give him some knockout pills so that the evil twin can go and imitate his brother. Peter has some serious hatred for his brother. He resents him for having a beautiful wife. They can't let John die because if he dies, they won't get any money from his will. This is getting confusing.

Peter goes to see a girl that he's seeing and pretending to be John. He goes wild when she mentions Denise and then he half-rapes her so that she will think John is nuts. Now they're drugging John and making him think he's gone crazy. Then even get Old Scarface in on it too. They trick John into thinking that he killed a man. Now they're using electro shock therapy on him to confuse his mind even further. This is the most elaborate scheme to steal an inheritance ever conceived by humans. The interaction between the twins is handled very cleverly with camera tricks and editing, not special effects. Hi, thank you for that explanation, Dr. Pseudo-Science! With so many twists and turns, it is hard to dislike this film.

FINAL THOUGHTS

When Macabre ends, a feeling of pain mixed with relief washes over me. I immediately put on Lawrence Welk to come down. I feel spectacularly beaten, broken, and tired. While Mr. Welk is miserably failing at reading the teleprompter, I'm drifting along through my own mind and every corner of it is bleeding. I need a vacation. The last chapter of this is coming. I'm very sad about that. We're going out like champs so man, it better be good.

GIALLO MELTDOWN 13: THE LAST DEAD BODY (IS MINE)

This is sort of the worst thing ever. I really can't imagine what my life will be like when I don't have the next Giallo Meltdown to look forward to. If you haven't figured it out by now, I'm in love with the giallo. Putting a cap on this project terrifies me. Only 16 films stand between me and the end. What's really funny is that the scariest thing is me worrying about what titles are going to resurface now once I'm done. I couldn't find every giallo ever made and that is really fucking annoying.

FRIDAY NIGHT

The weather finally changed. Summer has been especially punishing this year. In fact just last week, right near the end of September, it was miserably hot. Just this morning however, the air was different. I don't think we'll be seeing any sweater weather in the next week or two but fall has definitely come to Tampa. Honestly though, it doesn't matter. I feel kind of shitty. Am I coming down with a cold? Do I have a migraine? I don't know. Either way, this is not an ideal way to begin a moviethon. The moment I get home from work, I immediately lay down to take a nap. After about 45 minutes, LeEtta wakes me up to let me know the pizza she ordered for us has arrived. Well, wish me luck. 16 movies or bust.

"Ah, but what do you know? You can't take advice from goats."

7:00 PM
The Seducers (1969)

The film opens with Rosalba Neri and the weird-looking Aldo (Maurizio Bonuglia) on a yacht, throwing sticks of dynamite over the bow. Paola (Neri) says that the explosions make her horny. They're all nearly killed when Aldo hands Tony, a mentally challenged guy, a lit stick of dynamite. Instead of throwing it overboard, Tony just drops it on the deck. Luckily, Tony's strident mother is there to get rid of the dynamite at the last second. This is a weird boat ride. These geniuses' idea is to get Tony laid to help him not be special anymore. Wait, what? It's hard to care because Rosalba Neri is wearing nothing but pasties, a bikini bottom, and jewelry.

So the craziest thing about this casting is that Neri is in this with Edwige Fenech. I've never seen them together in a film before! Fenech is playing Ulla, a prostitute that's supposed to sleep with Tony. But I think Aldo is having more fun with Ulla than anybody else. There are cameras in the whole boat but I think it's so that the captain can keep an eye on what's going on in the bedrooms. The voice acting in this could be better but now Rosalba Neri is naked. And now Edwige Fenech is naked. Neri and Fenech are naked together! LeEtta is trying to talk to me but I can't hear her. This is amazing, though it does remind me of Interrabang.

Somehow, Tony has managed to get off the boat and onto a nearby island, without getting wet. He meets a kindly shepherd girl named Beba that he falls in love with. Aldo and Ulla go to the island and something so insane happens, I dare not tell you about it. Okay, fine, you twisted my arm. They find a baby goat and Aldo urges her to get naked and play with it. Ulla gets naked and then the goat starts licking her, you know, down there. The goat pleasures her to orgasm and I feel like I've stepped into a wormhole (or a goathole).

Paola is a total psycho. Aside from playing with dynamite, she also enjoys slaughtering goats with a hunting rifle. The shepherd that lives on the island flips out over his dead goats but they buy him off. Aldo and Ulla see Tony with the shepherd girl and they realize she can bring him out of his shell. They bring Beba aboard the boat and start giving her champagne to get her to sleep with Tony. I think Rosalba Neri has to seduce the innocent in EVERY MOVIE! After a makeover scene, Ulla and Paola have sex with Beva. It is very rapey and creepy. Tony's mom interrupts and she sticks Beba in a room with Tony.

This is one of the most hilarious wannabe sleazy movies ever. All of the trashy stuff is done so halfassedly. Tony who isn't handicapped at all, just a total lunatic, is easily the best character. His interaction with innocent Beba is actually interesting. I predict (actually, I really hope) that death is coming for these evil pricks. Uh oh, Beba's husband just showed up on a little boat. Swarthy death is coming. Holy crap, this just got really good. Seek this movie out, my friends. It's unfairly obscure and definitely bizarre.

"Come on, ballet dancer, shoot at me!"

8:35 PM
Spirits of Death (1972)

This film opens with one of my favorite pieces of giallo music. A woman is sexing up her lover on a blanket on the grass. He's nude but she is wearing a white dress. A man arrives in a car and tells his daughter, Marielle, to stay in the car. The man proceeds to shoot the couple. The naked dude does this crazy flip in the air when he gets shot. Then the woman (Evelyn Stewart) gets blown the fuck away while little Marielle screams. Nafa just called. He's on his way to come and share the joy of this odd little film. Someone just put a little bird in a cage with a monkey and the monkey just killed the bird. That's not fucking cool.

Ivan Rassimov just showed up in his badass sports car. He plays Massimo. He asks a tramp sitting by the side of the road for directions. She doesn't respond. Whatta bitch! Wow, this film is gorgeous! Romano Scavolini shot and directed this. He also did the infamous Nightmares in a Damaged Brain! Massimo arrives at a beautiful house (is it the same one as Murder Obsession?) and he sees Marielle (Stewart again), all grown up now, in the garden. Does she recognize him? She seems freaked out and it's easy to see why; her husband Paolo (Luigi Pistilli) keeps her hopped up on pills. They're having a huge party at the old castle but Marielle is dead set against it. She thinks all of their friends are assholes and guess what… she's right!

The house is very creepy with dust everywhere and religious statues. A fake snake starts crawling up the leg of one of the party guest. She screams but Massimo shoots it off her leg! One dude tells them that snakes are "only poisonous if you die." The black chick is really freaking me out. I think she's supposed to be a nympho but she's acting more like she just dropped acid. My pal Nafa is here and everything is going to be okay. He arrived just in time for the orgy scene. The black chick has a strap-on that looks very painful. One duder is wearing a jacket that is supposed to be feathers but Nafa says it looks like it's made of bacon. LeEtta says this is a dinner party at an insane asylum. I say the butler looks like Danny Trejo. He surveys the mess after the party and he has this amazing 'fuck this' look on his face. Poor Mr. Bacon Jacket just got bludgeoned.

Nafa says Luigi Pistilli looks like Christopher Lloyd. Oh shit! I never noticed that before. There's a crazy brutal bludgeoning in the swimming pool at night. It's gorgeous! Speaking of gorgeous, the architecture of this house is wonderful. Then somebody gets eaten by dogs. I'm drinking Kraken rum with Pepsi and eating sweet and spicy Doritos Nafa brought. The film is a lot of style and not much else. Frankly, I love it. Massimo says "Who let the dogs out?" and we lose our shit. Genius.

"I am not crazy, schizophrenic, epileptic, or stoned."

10:10 PM

Phenomena (1985)

Ah yes, my second favorite horror movie of all time. I really fucking love the tits off of Phenomena. A tourist in Switzerland is left stranded by her tour bus. She goes to a nearby house to ask to use the telephone. A crazed killer tries to strangle her with chains and then goes after her with a pair of huge scissors. She runs and has her head cut off for her troubles. The scene is sublime. Next we meet Professor Wheelchair (Donald Pleasence) and his sweet little monkey. He's helping the police figure out how dead a dead body is and stuff because maggots. So many maggots.

We meet Jennifer Connelly and she plays Jennifer Corvino, a famous actor's daughter. Jennifer loves insects and insects love her. The scene where she in the car with a bee and Frau Brückner (Daria Nicolodi) is wonderful. She goes to a new private school while her father is in the Phillipines shooting Apocalypse Now. She meets her ditzy roommate and then goes sleepwalking. Iron Maiden's "Flash of the Blade" is played when some chick is being chased by the killer. Jennifer witnesses a murder while she's sleepwalking and then gets picked up by two Swiss rapists. She escapes by rolling down a hill and then meets the monkey who takes her to Professor Wheelchair. Then she makes the professor's bugs horny.

The next morning at school, the teacher, the headmistress, and the doctor give Jennifer an EKG and it makes her see flashes of last night's adventure. The bitchy schoolgirls find out that Jennifer talks to bugs and chant "We worship you" at her. It's my favorite scene. Jennifer falls down and we get a panty shot like we really needed that. LeEtta comments that it must be because Asia Argento wasn't on set so Dario couldn't exploit her. The wind! The wind is a freakin' character. Ew. Chimpanzees are so gross. Look at that damn engorged monkey butt.

Nafa says something interesting: What if this movie didn't have the inhuman elements like the monkey, the wind, and the fly as characters? It probably wouldn't be as interesting. I have to agree. This would be a clever little thriller but there's so much going on in this. When this monkey feels bad about Professor Wheelchair getting killed, the sound designers used the sound of a whimpering dog on the soundtrack. So stupid.

I love Daria Nicolodi in this movie. In fact, I love everything and everyone right now. The monstrous beauty of Phenomena is really doing a number on my mind. Some of the metal music in this film fails miserably. "Flash of the Blade" (used twice) is about duelists. There are no fucking duelists in this movie. This is me nitpicking as hard as I can because I'm like a kid on Christmas whenever this film is on. When it is over, Nafa bids us goodnight and LeEtta and I head for bed. What a great night!

SATURDAY

I'm so glad that I decided to sleep in this morning. That weird migrainey feeling has finally passed but I'm still really worn out. Chores are pretty easy but now I just feel off somehow. Standing in line to buy lottery tickets, I feel kind of swirly and strange. I buy a 5 Hour Energy Drink for tomorrow when things get really rough. When I get back home, the couch draws me like a magnet. I manage to get up, pick a movie, and then type this paragraph. In the immortal words of Bouncing Souls, "Here we go! Here we go! Here we go!"

"Close your eyes, Sylvia."

11:18 AM
The Perfume of the Lady in Black (1974)

Here is another favorite. I have been putting this off for as long as I could. Mimsy Farmer plays Sylvia, a scientist who works in a lab specializing in science-y stuff. When she gets off work, Sylvia goes to the cemetery to leave some flowers on her mother's grave. It seems that she goes there every day? The weirdness starts almost immediately as we get the sense that something is wrong. Her neighbor Signor Rosetti (Mario Scaccia) stops by for some sugar but the way he pushes his way into her apartment makes him not seem like the harmless eccentric like he portrays himself. Sylvia has a date with her boyfriend Roberto (Maurizio Bonuglia). They're visiting with some nice African folks who have some cryptic things to say about voodoo and human sacrifices. J&B sighting! The first of this moviethon?

Roberto is a total prick about her job when he drops her off. Sylvia has a work deadline but he flips out because she won't come and play tennis. Nice going, asshole. Next thing you know, it's 4pm the following day. Her ugly landlady wakes her up and the whole scene is just odd. How could she have lost so much time? That night, at Roberto's place, she sees a woman in black (who looks an awful lot like her mother) applying perfume and smiling at her like a freakazoid. She screams and then she and Roberto make love voraciously. Mimsy Farmer sure did like to get freaky on camera back in the day. My favorite Mimsy scene ever takes place at the tennis court the following day. She cuts her hand on a nail hidden in the handle of her tennis racket. The Afrcian dude (Jho Jhenkins) comes over and sucks some of her blood out. Then she goes into a trance and sees the ghost of her childhood self walking through a field next to the court.

Later, while she's home alone (with a bottle of J&B), she has a vision of her mother getting plowed by her sweaty stepfather. When he finishes with her mother, he approaches Sylvia. She cuts his face with a pair of scissors and we see her as a child doing the same thing. Yeah, I'd say that someone had a less than stellar childhood. At the zoo, she runs into Signor Rosetti again and he wants to take her picture. Damn, Mimsy Farmer is so beautiful in this scene. I'd take her picture too. Alice in Wonderland reference!

On the creepy scale, this film rates a supercalifragifuckingcreepy. There are suspicious characters everywhere watching Sylvia. Unexplainable things keep happening to her like roses wilting and mysterious gifts arriving. She visits a psychic who reads her mind and finds some dark things there. When her childhood self shows up in her apartment, all hell breaks loose. The score for this film by Nicola Piovani and it's classy, haunting, vibrant, and unbearably tense. Signor Rosetti is feeding his cats a plate of bloody meat and there's a human finger in it. The next day she finds out that her plucky friend Franchesca was found dead in her bathtub. They go to her cremation (do people really do that?) but Sylvia can't bear it and she leaves. That night, she finds a gift-wrapped box in her apartment full of ashes. Whoa.

This film is a train with no brakes and it's headed straight to hell. Sylvia sees the ghost of her mother again but this time on the ledge of her balcony. She walks over and pushes the happy bitch right over the side. It turns out that the guy watching her at the taxidermist's was her mother's horrible old boyfriend. He follows Silvia to her old home where he tries to rape her. I better not say anymore on the plot. Fact: this film won the Italian Oscar for 'Best Hallway in a Giallo'. The ending of this movie is a total mind-fuck. Some reviewers don't like it but I think they're crazy. If every movie fucked my mind the way the end of Perfume does, my brain would never be able to sit down again. This film is a classic.

"Let me introduce you to a new girl.
An original countryside yield."

1:05 PM
Corpse Mania (1981)

You want a Hong Kong giallo? You got it! A creepy dude moves in across the street from a nosy beyatch. He carries his wife in and everyone thinks she is sick. That night, the nosy neighbor sees him going to town on his sick wife. Um... I don't think she's sick, dude. I think he's sick because she's fucking dead, you idiots! When the smell of something dead starts to overpower the neighborhood noses, the cops are called to come in and investigate. Much to the surprise of everyone except me they find the worm-covered corpse of the guy's wife in the bedroom but he's nowhere to be found. The cops are on the case. Wow, I love the way this is filmed. The lighting is super stylish and perfect.

They go over a previous necrophilia case and we meet Li Hengyuan (Erik Chan Ka Kei), the corpse fucker, in a flashback. Let's all go to the brothel where chicks with "original countryside yield" are very popular. Thank you, subtitles. Madam Lan's (Ni Tien) most popular girl Hongmei is sick with cons-umption. Was she popular because she's coughing up blood all the time. Li shows up and he wants to take Hongmei off of Madam Lan's hands. He wears his sunglasses at night so he can, so he can have sex with the dead. Did you like my Corey Hart reference?

After Hongmei kicks the bucket, Li takes good care of her corpse, rubbing it down with lotion and fragrant powders. This is one disturbing movie! So many lingering shots of rotting flesh and worms. They go on and on. Did Fulci write this? Anyway, we see Li get arrested for his crime and it's back to the present day. They think Li has gotten out of the insane asylum and is running around, committing more crimes. One thing about this movie is that it is very methodically paced. I've never managed to get through this all the way and even now, I'm dozing to this dreamy business.

A mysterious character in sunglasses, a black hat, and a scarf wrapped over his face, has killed again. This time he killed a cop whose name translates to Beard Nine or Mustache Nine. We get more brutal murders and lots of blood that looks like paint. Nearly every frame of this movie is pretty to look at thanks to whoever lit this thing. It's so bright and clear that it looks way more recent than 1981. My only complaint, the characters are too thinly written and most of them are unlikable. The plot makes up for it.

"You can't go with me where I'm going."

2:38 PM
The House of the Blue Shadows (1986)

Here's yet another that I haven't seen before. This starts off in a beautiful house with a little girl playing piano for some bored housewives. Luca is playing hide and seek with his friend named Lola. She uses a kabuki devil mask to scare the heck out of the poor kid. The game ends when someone shoves Lola off the roof. So far this is incredibly stylish with lots of crazy camera angles and even a cat's POV. Very promising. Flash forward to the present day and Luca is all grown up. He and his wife have come to his family home. A mysterious woman who claims to know Luca shows up, says some mysterious things, and leaves.

There's a really creepy mannequin in the house. It's the size of a child and is shiny and black with blond hair. Jeez, I would burn that damn thing. Luca is haunted by his memories of Lola. A childhood friend of Luca's named Bruno shows up. So far, everyone in this is suspicious and creepy. My download of this movie keeps having tracking problems that I can do nothing to fix. At the market, Luca sees a girl that reminds him of Lola. He starts chasing her all over the dang place.

Luca is a weirdo and he has a beard. I guess that makes him a beardo. We see more flashes of his childhood and it looks like it was happy but full of strange moments. Lola was a weird little girl, probably a witch. He decides to shave off his beard and he gets even weirder. He chases Margit all over the house with a straight razor and she laughs about him pretending to cut her throat. The actor who plays Luca is kind of the worst thing about this movie. He has okay moments but overall, he's just really awkward, like he's in over his head with this role. A figure wearing the kabuki devil mask shows up and taunts Luca.

This isn't a great movie but I'm glad I tracked it down. Somebody is definitely trying to drive Luca crazy but they really didn't have to drive very far. He sees some children burning a doll and pretending it's a witch so he goes apeshit, burning his hands and face while trying to put it out. Someone in the kabuki devil mask attacks Margit and she barely gets away with her life. I feel like I know where this movie is going but I'm not laying my money down on the table just yet. It just started raining outside.

> *"I don't think he gives an Ecclesiastical fuck about the church."*

4:49 PM
Don't Look Now (1973)

After a short nap and a wet walk to the mailbox, I'm ready for another film. I think this weird film is responsible for Who Saw Her Die? I'm convinced that whoever wrote that classic giallo must have either seen Don't Look Now or read about it. There are so many parallels between the two films' plots. John Baxter (Donald Sutherland) and his wife Laura (Julie Christie) are sitting in their living room when he has a premonition that something is wrong. He runs outside to find his daughter has drowned to death. Later in Venice, John is working to restore some old buildings while they both are trying to recover from the tragedy.

The couple meet a pair of eccentric sisters Wendy and Heather (Clelia Matania and Hilary Mason, respectively). Heather is blind and very psychic. She tells Luara that she can see her daughter sitting between them, she is happy, and they shouldn't be sad. This causes Laura to faint in the restaurant. There are a string of murders being committed in the city but they are in the periphery of this plot (for now). Massimo Serato of Blood-stained Shadow and Autopsy is in this. And Leopoldo Trieste from Bay of Blood! Oh hey, there's a ridiculously long and gratuitous sex scene between John and Laura that the movie comes to a complete stop for.

John wants to keep Laura away from Heather and her sister. He thinks they're fakes. The psychic believes that John has a little of a psychic gift himself. There's a not subtle J&B sighting around 45 minutes. Speaking of not subtle, Heather starts rubbing her breasts and freaking out during an impromptu séance. She warns Laura that John is in grave danger.

Duder should really have left Venice. Trust me, nothing good ever happens there. Meanwhile, the police find another body in the water. He sees his wife on a boat with the sisters later on the same day that she left. Something is wrong. Very wrong. I won't spoil any of it for you. You need to see this and give it a couple viewings so everything can sink in. It's just a great movie.

CIGAR BREAK & DINNER

We pause Don't Look Now for a cigar break (I smoke a Wynwood cigar and it's delicious) and a trip out to pick up some Greek food. I get a Greek chicken pita with feta, tomatoes, and tzatziki sauce. It's amazing. LeEtta gets the spinach pie, potato salad, and dolmades. Shelly gets a gyro.

"Inspector, have him examined. He's impotent!"

8:29 PM
Blood and Black Lace (1964)

Much like Bird with the Crystal Plumage, the giallo genre just wouldn't be the same without this film. Blood and Black Lace is dripping with style, oozing with it. At a fashion house run by Miss Cristiana (Eva Bartok), a beautiful woman is murdered by a masked killer. Her name was Isobella and she was a fashion model. The number one killer of fashion models is killers. Damn, (pre-Toolbox Murders) Cameron Mitchell is smooth as fuck in this movie. Nobody seems to care that Isabella is dead except for Peggy, she was her friend. Isabella was dating Franco, a "famous antiques dealer". They shared something that lots of couples like to share: cocaine!

When someone finds out that Isabella kept a diary, the shit really hits the fan. I wonder if that dumb bitch knew that keeping a diary would eventually get EVERYONE KILLED! There are so many wonderful moments in this film. Just one of those is the scene in the antique shop. Nicole goes to bring Franco some drugs and the killer is waiting for her. The purple, blue, and green lighting is so brilliantly put together that it's jaw-dropping. The murders in this are amazing too. The killer is a sadistic motherfucker. It's nice to see Harriet Medin in this. I love her. And Luciano Pigozzi. I love him too.

Marco (Massimo Righi) is in love with Peggy but he's not well. He leaves her alone and we find out she's the one who stole Isabella's diary. She reads some nasty business about herself and also that Isabella was a wannabe blackmailer. She burns the diary but it's the too late, the killer shows up and smacks her around. The cops come but the killer drags Peggy out of her apartment to the basement for some more fun. Fun with a burning, red hot stove, that is.

The cops round up all the guys from the fashion house to detain and question them. I don't think Marco is going to be too good in a police lineup. The guy's too squirrelly. Oh, he's got epilepsy. That explains a few things. So epileptics act just like junkies? Okay, got it. While they're being held, another murder is committed. And another! This is such a sumptuously filmed and brilliantly designed movie. The only things I don't like about Blood and Black Lace are the little sped up moments. The editor must have been really impatient. Calm down, dumbass! We find out who the killer is and then oops, I can't say anymore. And we're done! Two words: timeless classic.

> *"If I wanted to be a whore, I'd have all the money and men that I wanted!"*

10:20 PM
Ring of Death (1969)

Shelly has left but she let us play her banjo before she went (that's not a euphemism). I don't know much about this movie from 1969 except it's on the Code Red DVD label and the trailer struck me as very giallo-ish. I do like the jazzy score and the camera work. Some duder gets shot to death in a hotel. Detective Belli (Franco Nero) is being hired by Adolfo Celi to get rid of some girl named Sandy that his son Mino (Maurizio Bonuglia) is dating. Not to kill her but to get her out of the country. He also wants him to investigate some people that his son wants to go into business with.

Belli goes to see Sandy (Delia Boccardo) to try and get her to stop seeing the duder's son. J&B sighting, with a pink label? That's different! She busts out her boobies so that he won't make her go. While following up a lead, he finds the body of the guy who got killed at the beginning of the film. The cops show up while he's there and the evidence collection scene is edited splendidly. They stick a thermometer up Romani's butt (!) to see how long he's been dead. Detective Belli discovers that Sandy had been at the dead guy's apartment and he goes totally bonkers while he's interrogating her. Duder thinks he's George C. Scott in this movie.

More J&B! Florinda Bolkan plays Adolfo Celi's wife. And she looks simply radiant. Belli meets up with Mino and beats the crap out of him. He finds out that Romani was just using him to get at his parents' money. Belli questions Florinda but doesn't beat the crap out of her. She was going to give Romani money. I like this film. It feels sort of Italian a lot. Next, we meet some bleach blond bimbo and I already forgot how she's involved. She definitely likes heroin.

A photograph of a nude woman with the face torn out of it is the key to all of this. Belli goes to see a photographer named Claude, he's that impotent dude from Torso. He beats the crap out of him too! Now he's figured out that the woman in the photo is Florinda Bolkan. But is it really her? Woo! This plot is convoluted. Franco Nero is so great in this. In a standout scene, he intimidates a witness into changing her story, right in front of a bunch of cops! Right after that, Belli takes Sandy for a ride. He drives insanely recklessly in order to scare her into spilling more information. It works! The score for this continues its jazzy and lounge-y vibe. I love it.

SUNDAY

I set the alarm for 8am so we could get up and get some breakfast at Brunchies. LeEtta gets eggs, potatoes, and grits. I get blueberry pancakes with granola on top and a side of duck bacon. I also get grapefruit juice and an iced coffee. Last night, I dreamed that aliens were invading the earth. They were like weird fish in bubbles and you had to fight them off or they would chew into your body and kill you from the inside. The attack started at a buffet lunch I was attending. There were alien eggs in all of the food and I was trying to crush them with a spoon so that the food would be safe to eat. I think I am now officially insane.

"I always dreamed of dining with a man like you."

9:18 AM
The Third Eye (1966)

Oh cool! The opening theme of this score is the same music from the music box in Riccardo Freda's The Ghost. Franco Nero is in this as Mino, the son of a bitchy old countess. He's in love with Laura (Erika Blanc) but the Countess (Olga Solbelli) is crazy and doesn't want him to get married. She and Marta the maid (who's freakishly possessive of Mino) decide that Laura should have a "nice little accident" to stop the marriage from happening. Theirs isn't the only madness in the family, Mino is a weird duder. He acts like a child and definitely has a mommy complex. And he's into taxidermy a la Psycho. If you're squeamish about bird guts then I suggest you avert your eyes when Mino goes to work on a pheasant.

Marta the maid, because she's a criminal mastermind, cuts the brake lines on Laura's car. She and the Countess are two of the most despicable characters I've seen on film in years. They are so broadly evil and needlessly catty that I want to punch holes in their faces with a hot poker. They're so rude to Laura that she leaves. Mino is pretty pissed off about it and goes after Laura in his car. Well, I didn't have to put up with the Countess for long. Marta the maid took care of that! Meanwhile, Laura is cruising down the dangerous roads when she loses control of the car and goes off the side of a cliff. Mino is on the scene and he sees Laura dead in the water. He goes home and finds out about his dead mother. Rough day for a son of a bitch.

Mino starts wearing all black and has night terrors of both Laura and his mother. He finally gets out of the house and goes to a smoky jazz club where a sexy stripper named Maria does her little number. Afterward, she goes back to Mino's place to get it on but I think he has other things on his mind. He strangles Maria to death. Marta the maid comes in and sees what he's done and also sees that he keeps Laura's corpse in his bed beside him. She suggests melting Maria's corpse down with acid in order to dispose of it. Oh yeah, this was remade by Joe D'Amato as Beyond the Darkness.

Mino kills again but Marta refuses to help him get rid of the body unless he marries her. Mino agrees. Things are going just great for about 20 seconds of movie time when Daniella (Blanc again), Laura's sister, shows up. She looks exactly like Laura and she's in town to give her sister a proper funeral. Aside from flirting with Mino, Daniella is also driving Marta the maid into a murderous rage. That doesn't matter because Mino's mind has fractured yet again. Now he thinks mother is still alive and that he's going to marry Laura in the morning. Oh boy.

Marta grabs a butcher knife from the kitchen and goes after Daniella in the middle of the night. Daniella tries to hide but finds her sister's corpse instead! Man, this is a fine film. I want to say more but I'd be doing you a disservice if you haven't tracked this down yet. Franco Nero is tearing up the screen for this role, cackling and scenery chewing. This is definitely the Italian version of Psycho with a twist.

"So many corpses. And every death... a mystery."

10:43 AM
Death Smiles at Murder (1973)

Here's another favorite. Joe D'Amato's gory and morbid little tale is a supernatural mystery film of the highest order. Luciano Rossi plays Franz. He loved his dead sister Greta (Ewa Aulin) a lot. A whole lot. Franz raped her while she was alive but luckily we're not forced to watch that spectacle. The next thing we know, there's a terrible carriage accident. The driver is killed but Greta survives and has amnesia. Wait a minute, she's supposed to be dead! Dr. Sturges is called (welcome back to the book, Sir Klaus Kinski). He examines Greta but can't find a heartbeat. She's wearing a medallion that has a formula on the back that interests him greatly. Sturges also sticks a needle into Greta's eyeball but she doesn't react.

The old house in this film is so beautiful. Its inhabitants are Walter von Ravensbrück (Sergio Doria) and his wife Eva (Angela Bo). They decide to let Greta stay until her memory returns. Poor Gertrude (the prolific Carla Mancini) the maid is being tormented by Franz. He appears, tortures her, and then disappears so she decides to get the fuck out of Dodge. While fleeing, someone blows her face off with a shotgun. It's gruesome! The gang go a-hunting and Walter takes a liking to Greta but Eva ain't too happy about that. It's 1909 but Walter has 1973 hair. The score by Berto Pisano is really pretty and he put a lot of love into it. Dr. Sturges is busy trying to figure out the formula on Greta's medallion. In his secret laboratory, he manages to reanimate a dead guy but someone sneaks up behind him and strangles him to death. This mystery killer also bashes in the brains of Sturges' assistant.

Eva tries to drown Greta in the bath but they have a good laugh about it. Eva confesses her love for Greta and they get it on. When Walter and Greta do it though, Eva is so jealous that she walls up Greta in the basement, Amantiallado style. Concerned that something terrible has happened to Greta but with no leads, the police inspector (the also prolific Attilio Dottesio) gives up. At a fancy party, Eva is having a gay old time but then Greta (who she knows to be dead (again)) shows up to spoil the fun. We get to see Greta transforming back and forth from beautiful to zombie. It's so hot. Eva does a header off the roof but it's probably for the best, you know? Walter is upset about it.

At the funeral, Walter's father, Dr. von Ravensbrück (Giacomo Rossi-Stuart) shows up and in a flashback, we see he was the guy who took Greta away from her incestuous brother. The plot, as dreamy and disconnected as it is, is thickening. At Eva's funeral, Dr. von Ravensbrück sees Greta hiding among the tombs of the cemetery. More supernatural insanity ensues and there's an excellent moment where Greta comes to seduce Walter, the night after Eva's funeral. Walter is clearly terrified of Greta. It's so damn good. The butler decides that he knows what is going on and tries to blackmail Greta. Bad idea, bro. If I wasn't already married, I would marry this movie.

"Fucking jerks, go away!"

12:15 PM
Without Trace (1975)

This opens with some fast tempo music with corny flute and a wild bass line. A bratty rich teenage girl named Fiorella is kidnapped or has run away and her parents are worried sick. Antonio Sabato plays Solmi, a crabby cop who really doesn't want to be involved with this case. The police chief is Enrico Maria Salerno of Bird with the Crstal Plumage! Luciana Paluzzi is in this too as a lady detective. Solmi hates the missing girls's father, Professor Icardi (Gabriele Ferzetti), because he reminds him of doctors and doctors remind him of when his wife died. Solmi is a totally dickweed. Anyway, he goes to the dog training cops to recruit some dogs to go looking for

Fiorella.

They find her body tied to her little scooter at the bottom of a lake. It seems that someone shot her in the back of the neck. But not until after the killer forced her to smoke marijuana. What? LeEtta and I are very confused. The autopsy doctor is Attilio Dottesio of Death Smiles at Murder! He determines that not only was Fiorella not a virgin, she was also three months pregnant. When the professor discovers that his daughter was not a virgin, he almost loses his dang mind. This movie has a whole class warfare vibe running through it. Everyone hates rich people and say it's their fault when bad things happen to them. I'm a billionaire so this shit hits close to home.

Their only information on who may have committed the murder comes from some total pervert who likes to watch couples get it on by the lake where the girl was found. One of Fiorella's frenemies gets picked up by a guy who drives a car that matches the description of the killer's. It's some pervert guy who likes to smack girls around. Apparently, her friend was involved in a teenage prostitution ring. They bust up the brothel and a pimp named Franz (Marino Masé) has a gun that is the same caliber as the one that killed Fiorella.

Somebody kills the shady gynecologist that knew Fiorella was pregnant with a straight razor. There's a very traditional giallo stalking and strangulation scene. The bodies are piling up and the cops are getting closer to their main suspect. We get a car chase, a shootout, and overall, I am very happy with this movie. It doesn't have an original bone in its body but I dig it. Nice job, Mya DVD!

"I warn you that the hate of woman can be very bad!"

3:06 PM
Delirium: Photos of Gioia (1987)

I've been saving this piece of wonderful for the final Giallo Meltdown. Every single time I made up a playlist and this tried to sneak it on there, I said no. This film is so incredibly dumb and over-the-top that I just couldn't bring myself to watch it until the time was right. This nonsense opens with a photo spread of Serena Grandi in various Playboy-esque pictures. In the English dub, her character is named Gloria not Gioia as the title suggests. But she doesn't have to get naked no more! You see, Gloria is the head of a magazine called Pussycat.

A creepy guy in a wheelchair named Mark (Karl Zinny) is watching Gloria from his window and making lewd comments to her over the phone. Daria Nicolodi is in this and she plays Evelyn, Glorida's assistant. This film has one of the most creative (and silly) uses of POV for the killer ever.

Everything starts flashing red and the killer sees his potential victims as monstrous creatures. The first girl looks like a giant eyeball where her head should be. I think Lamberto Bava (or Lambava, if you will) is trying to top Argento here and is just making something ludicrous. Serena Grandi is crazy hot in this movie. Her titanic breasts try to steal the whole movie.

Flora (Capucine), Gloria's former manager, shows up and she's a world class bitch. She's pissed off that Gloria won't sell the magazine to her. Their bitchy battle of barbs is very funny and is like something out of "Dynasty". The killer poses the victim in front of a poster of one of Gloria's famous photos and takes pictures in order taunt her. The cops come and the inspector (Lino Salemme) is a friggin' bore. The murder of the model is actually helping magazine sales and Flora is even more pissed off!

Tony (Vanni Corbellini), Gloria's brother, also works on the magazine. He takes her to a movie studio where he wants to stage a crazy naked lady photoshoot there. While she's wandering around she bumps into Alex, an old flame. Alex is played by George Eastman. He's as tall as her boobs are big. They talk about the old days and then go back to her place for some lovemaking. The scene where they get it on in the bathtub is what aliens think human sex is. Alex is humping Gloria's thigh as hard as he can. It's all in slow motion and the soap suds are flying!

The killer claims another victim. This time, the victim looks like a giant bee-headed girl. So, of course, the killer has this elaborate method of killing her with honey bees. It's poorly staged but they put A LOT of work into doing it wrong so it's perfect. Gloria decides to sell the magazine and go back into modeling, thinking that will stop the killings. While picking up clothes for her new career, there's a fun stalking scene in a deserted department store. Mark the wheelchair-bound creep shows up in Gloria's bedroom with a glow-in-the-dark dildo and starts terrorizing her. My mouth is agape. Between the drum machines, the huge shoulder pads, and the peach, white, and gold color scheme in Gloria's house, this flick is dated! But the campiness is as important to this movie as the trashy situations and the red herrings. Highly recommended for those with cheese in their veins.

"Pervert! Filthy, slimy pervert!"

4:40 PM
Tenebre (1982)

Okay, people. We are no longer fucking around. This is it. This is the shit. Bow down before the master. If you decided to only watch one giallo in your lifetime, then I'd say pick this one. This has all the style, blood, and baffling weirdness of the whole genre wrapped up into one film. Peter Neal (Anthony Franciosa) is biking down the freakin' freeway on his way to the airport. He's flying to Rome for a press tour and he likes to leave his baggage unattended. Dumbass move, homey. Meanwhile, in Rome, Elsa (Ania Pieroni) gets caught shoplifting because she's not a very talented shoplifter. She flirts with the store detective, promising him sex sometime. On her way home, she's assaulted by a horny hobo who gets a kick the balls for his efforts. Think Elsa's day can't get much worse? It can. A deranged killer stuffs pages from Tenebrae by Peter Neal into her mouth, slashes her throat, and then takes pictures of her corpse.

John Saxon plays Peter's agent Bullmer and he's awesome in this movie. The chemistry between he and Franciosa is genius. Daria Nicolodi plays his assistant Anne and she's just so dang cute. When they get to the hotel, Peter is met by detectives (Carola Stagnaro and Giuliano Gemma) who tell him about the murder and about the pages of his book in the girl's mouth. Detective Germani is pretty awesome. He only drinks alcohol when he's on duty. The killer calls while everyone is just shooting the shit. The cops run out after the killer they're too late. Germani complains to his partner about having a slow female detective. Nice going, asshole.

The killer is haunted by memories of a sexy chick (brought to life by the complex gender stylings of Eva Robins) who makes some boys hold a dude down while she stuffs the heel of her red leather pump into his screaming mouth. It's all played out with a haunting broken music box melody. Back in the real world, Peter Neal's harshest critic and good friend, Hilda (Mirella D'Angelo), is having relationship problems. Her busty girlfriend likes to fuck ugly dudes at their apartment. The killer has decided that lesbians are bad and pays them a little visit. A stalking scene happens that is so elaborate and pointless that only Argento would attempt it. The camera flies around their weird Lego house like it has wings while the music of three members of the legendary band, Goblin, blasts over the soundtrack.

I take one of those 5 Hour Energy shots and mix it with some Mountain Dew. It actually tastes really good until the nasty aftertaste kicks in. The autopsy doctor is played by Gianpaolo Saccarola (of Fulci's The Beyond) and one of my favorite Eurohorror stars, John Steiner, is here as a TV reporter with some pointed questions for Peter. Inspector Germani admits to Peter that he loves reading detective fiction but he can never guess who the killer is, ever. Another line of work, perhaps?

In what is probably one of the oddest sequences in all of the giallo genre, Maria (Lara Wendel), the daughter of the hotel manager where Peter is staying, gets into an argument with her boyfriend (Michele Soavi cameo!) and is left stranded in the middle of nowhere. She gets barked at by a dog so she taunts it with a big stick. Well, this super duper Dobie scales a fence and goes after her. It's delightfully dumb. The dog chases her right into the backyard of the killer! What luck! Before she can flee and go to the cops, the killer comes home, grabs an axe, and kills the living shit out of her.

Bullmer is thrilled with all the free publicity but Peter just wants to catch the killer. Fuck, I've already said too much. I can't put into words how important this film is. This will always be one of my favorites. Forever. The style, precision, and the sheer audacity of the bloodshed will knock you on your ass even after multiple viewings.

Crap. Okay, one more thing! Veronica Lario plays Jane, Peter Neal's vampish ex who follows him to Rome for nefarious reasons, is my favorite character in this movie. She's a cross between one of Andy Warhol's celebrity portraits and a Brian De Palma fever dream. If the whole movie was about her then this whole book would be about Tenebre. There. Done.

*"It's so nice to find two young people
not possessed by sex."*

6:24 PM
Murder Obsession (1981)

It took me two viewings before I realized that this film, even with its wild supernatural moments, is actually a giallo. While filming the final scene of a giallo, an actor named Michael (Stefano Patrizi) goes a little crazy and nearly kills his costar Beryl (Laura Gemser). He's so upset about it that he pours himself a big glass of J&B. In the next scene, Michael is playing guitar and singing badly. He stops to look at some photos of himself as a child and his lovely mother Glenda (Anita Strindberg in her final film role before retiring). He decides to get his girlfriend Deborah (Silvia Dionisio) and some movie friends together for a road trip back to his family home. This is a bad idea. Michael is really messed up about his crappy childhood. His father was a classical music conductor and some bad shit happened.

When they get to the old house, Oliver (John Richardson!) the butler is behaving very strangely. He tells Michael that he looks exactly like the dead maestro and that Glenda is very sick. Michael tells Oliver to keep Deborah's and his relationship a secret from his mom. Glenda wakes up and comes to see Michael, lavishing him with kisses that are not exactly motherly. He introduces Deborah to her as his secretary. What a coward! Deborah gets pretty pissed off and rightfully so. Michael has a memory of standing over his father with a bloody knife. Deborah forgives him and they have sex. I think this is the same shooting location as Spirits of Death.

Michael's friends show up including Beryl (boy, is she forgiving!), Shirley (Martine Brochard of Eyeball), and their director pal Hans (Henri Garcin), who's obsessed with death. That night, Oliver the butler does some astral projecting and his footprints magically appear around the house. It's pretty great. This Raro Video looks good and sounds good until the music kicks in. Fuck, why is the score so loud? I feel like my head is inside the piano.

The suspicious glances and overacting in this film are priceless. What isn't priceless is the damn giant rubber spider in Deborah's nightmare. In the same dream, she gets manhandled by a melty-faced monk and terrorized by fake bats. Shit gets crazy elaborate with a Satanic ritual in an underground cavern. The power of Satan is strong in this one.

LeEtta and I can't help but notice how perfectly pointy Silvia Dionisi's boobies are. As the story progresses, Micheal becomes more and more of a total prick to Deborah. They go off on a little woodsy adventure where Michael and Beryl hook up. After their bone parade, they fall asleep by the lake. When Michael wakes up, Beryl has been murdered. The morbid Hans gets a very morbid axe to the head when he tries to go to the police with some great secret that he witnessed (and possibly photographed). Shirley (who seems to be wearing a garbage bag) decides to develop Hans's roll of film. Don't do that. Please don't do that. The end of this film is out of control crazy and hauntingly beautiful. Riccardo Freda directed this one and I'm a better man because of that. This one has got The Vibe. Essential.

*"If you want to know the truth,
madmen fascinate me."*

8:11 PM
Deep Red (1975)

If you're going to go out, then go out with an Argento masterpiece. At a conference for the study of parapsychology, a psychic named Helga (Macha Méril) encounters the horrible thoughts of a murderer. Someone evil in the audience knows she knows their secret. Of course, Helga is dumb as balls and decides to go home first before she tells anyone about what she learned from reading the murderer's brain. Now everyone can die! Why are the psychic characters always the dumbest ones in a movie? The killer goes after her with a huge meat cleaver. No Psychic Friends Network for Helga! LeEtta makes me a Moutain Dew with whiskey and lime juice. She calls it a "Call It On The Mountain". I feel a wicked headache crawling up the back of my neck. In some ways, I'm grateful that this is almost over.

A jazz composer named Marc (David Hemmings) is walking home through the streets of the city when he finds his pianist friend, Carlo (Gabriele Lavia), drunk in the street. They hear a blood-curdling scream in the night. Carlo thinks that it's a virgin getting raped and he cheers her on. That's really not cool, you damn rummy. Marc leaves Carlo and witnesses Helga getting murdered in her window. He goes upstairs to her room, just missing the killer. The lead detective in this film is especially boorish and stupid. Marc knows he saw something but he can't put his finger on it. Something to do with a strange paintings in the psychic's apartment.

A sexy journalist named Gianna (Daria Nicolodi) bursts into the crime scene taking pictures. She assumes that Marc witnessed the crime and takes his picture. The cops take Marc down to the station to question him. They keep him for four hours. He gets out and finds Carlo still drinking in the street. Carlo might have seen the killer but he's too damn drunk to recall anything. What a fucking loser! Marc starts hanging out with Gianna, partly because she won't stop following him around and partly because her snapshot of Marc is making him a target for the killer and he needs her to help him get out of this mess.

The romantic bits between Marc and Gianna are really awesome. He's such a cocksure jerk and she deflates his massive ego at every turn, especially when they are in her piece of shit car which seems designed by the automotive industry to humiliate him. It's very playful and earnest and a real love letter to Daria Nicolodi. She owns this movie. The two hook up with Giordani (Glauco Mauri), a colleague of Helga's, to help solve her murder. No one even considers buying machine guns for this endeavor.

I love the Italian cut of this movie. It's over two hours and is so hypnotic with little details and strangeness. I've never been able to get very far in those other cuts. This is the one for me. This movie makes me paranoid. I feel like I'm being watched. Even the trailer for this film is creepy. The killer is a really deranged bastard. Killing someone by repeatedly shoving their head into scalding hot water. That's just fucked up. Marc reads about a house that is supposedly haunted. He decides to go there. It is the weirdest house on Earth. The caretaker says it's been abandoned because people are superstitious. The caretaker's daughter (Nicoletta Elmi) is adorable and she kills lizards for fun. Can't wait until she grows up!

Giordani finds an important clue but decides not to share it with anyone. Could mysteries even happen without this trope? The score when Marc goes inside the house is one of my favorite pieces of music ever recorded for film. It sounds like a synthesizer being melted in a microwave. Inside the house is an explosion of gothic and art nouveau textures and it's all just so beautiful. The killer makes short work of Giordani but not before scaring him half to death with a surprise that I'm sure inspired nightmares in generations of horror film fans. But what really chills my blood is what Marc finds behind the wall. His journey is far from over. But mine isn't.

CONCLUSION

Oh boy. I feel like garbage and poo poo with a dash of crap. My eyes are burning bullets and my stomach is churning. The braunschweiger sandwich I had for dinner was probably a poor choice. I think I regret that now. Why do I have to work tomorrow? That is not cool, man. Fuck. There is relief and a sense of accomplishment. I have watched 215 films for this damn book. Shit, I forgot about Formula for a Murder. Ha ha! I'm worried about one film being missed when countless other titles —Oh well!

My stomach is churning. Did I say that already? Leetta is done. She has gone off to bed. She is so lucky. I feel like shit! Did I say that already too? I want to stand atop the highest point in Rome in a white suit with a yellow tie and just cry out "Aiuto!". And the blood. You'll see it! The blood will pour from my eyes! Thank you, my friends. If you've made it all the way to this point, you're either the killer or a very clever amateur detective! Whatever the case may be, bless you and take care, my friend.

INDEX

A.A.A. Masseuse, Good Looking, Offers Her Services, 177
Adorf, Mario, 176
Agren, Janet, 92, 232
Aguirre, Javier, 179
Airoldi, Conchita, 28
Albertazzi, Giorgio, 185
Alfonsi, Lidia, 168
All the Colors of the Dark, 8
All the Souls... Except the Dead, 202
Amuck!, 47
Andreu, Simón, 22, 23, 154, 168, 178
Anima Persa, 153
Antinori, Antonella, 210
Arabella L'Angelo Nero, 196
Arana, Tomas, 136, 194
Ardisson, George, 183
Argento, Dario, 35, 39, 49, 50, 120, 175, 189, 193, 206, 236, 237, 244, 256, 258
Argento, Fiore, 36
Assmann, Ini, 138
Auger, Claudine, 118
Aulin, Ewa, 58, 76, 116, 252
Aumont, Tina, 236
Aured, Carlos, 76
Autopsy, 24
Avati, Pupi, 55, 202
Baal, Karina, 12
Bach, Barbara, 27, 46
Bach, Simone, 225
Baker, Carroll, 36, 65, 94, 105, 122, 180
Baldassarre, Raf, 181
Baldi, Ferdinando, 188
Baldwin, Daniel, 116
Baldwin, Peter, 224
Bambola di Satana, La, 130
Bambrilla, Pietro, 55
Barberini, Urbano, 206
Barrymore, John Drew, 223

Bartok, Eva, 249
Bava, Lamberto, 11, 69, 136, 255
Bava, Mario, 39, 118, 129, 168
Bay of Blood, 117
Beckley, Tony, 172
Behn, Patrizia, 209
Benussi, Femi, 9, 38, 71, 72, 73, 102
Berger, Senta, 22
Berger, William, 128, 129
Betti, Laura, 102, 118, 212
Betts, Jack, 177
Bianichi, Andrea, 9
Bido, Antonio, 5
Bird with the Crystal Plumage, The, 174
Birkin, Jane, 6
Bisera, Olga, 234
Black Belly of the Tarantula, The, 27
Black Sabbath (The Telephone), 168
Black Veil for Lisa, A, 62
Blade in the Dark, A, 11
Blanc, Erika, 14, 51, 86, 97, 134, 137, 182, 183, 226, 251
Blood and Black Lace, 249
Blood Link, 84
Bloodstained Butterfly, The, 79
Bloodstained Shadow, The, 5
Bloodsucker Leads the Dance, The, 72
Blue Eyes of the Broken Doll, 74
Blynn, Jeff, 201
Bo, Angela, 252
Boccardo, Delia, 250
Body Puzzle, 136
Bolkan, Florinda, 59, 83, 251
Bonacelli, Paolo, 235
Bondi, Lidia, 184
Bonuglia, Maurizio, 158, 169, 241, 245, 250
Borelli, Rosario, 182
Borrelli, Ilaria, 126
Boschero, Dominique, 16, 113

Bosé, Lucia, 117
Bouchet, Barbara, 13, 27, 47, 81, 82, 127
Bourgoin, Jean, 225
Boyd, Stephen, 153, 180
Brait, Carla, 9, 17, 19, 239
Brandon, Michael, 237
Brega, Mario, 138
Brochard, Martine, 10, 257
Brody, Adrien, 193
Brondo, Cristina, 120
Brugnini, Achille, 115
Bucchi, Pier Paola, 228
Buchanan, Sherry, 216
Bugie Rosse, 194
Buio del Terrore, Nel, 152
Buono, Victor, 127
Buxton, Sarah, 231
Cadaveri Eccellenti, 235
Calderon, Juan Carlos, 75
Calderoni, Rita, 29
Camaso, Claudio, 118
Candelli, Stelio, 99, 217
Cansino, Tini, 196
Capolicchio, Lino, 5, 55, 228
Capponi, Pier Paolo, 110, 190
Capucine, 255
Card Player, The, 35
Caroit, Philippe, 126
Carta, Maria, 235
Casale, Francisco, 196
Case of the Bloody Iris, The, 16
Case of the Scorpion's Tail, The, 17
Casini, Stefania, 5
Cassinelli, Claudio, 31, 32
Castel, Lou, 238
Castelnuovo, Nino, 9, 89
Cat in Heat, The, 113
Cat O' Nine Tails, The, 189
Cavina, Gianni, 56, 203
Celi, Adolfo, 65, 70, 139, 232, 238, 250
Cerulli, Fernando, 53, 121
Chan Ka Kei, Eric, 246
Charleston, Ian, 206
Chiaramello, Giancarlo, 182
Christie, Julie, 248

Christine, Katia, 186
Ciangottini, Valeria, 72
Ciannelli, Lewis E., 229
Cipriani, Stelvio, 6, 34, 61, 118, 132, 154, 200
Clery, Corinne, 26
Closed Circuit, 141
Cohen, Emma, 135
Cold Eyes of Fear, 67
Colli, Ernesto, 9, 25, 71, 236
Conte, Maria Pia, 41, 223
Corazzari, Bruno, 22, 137, 218
Corbinelli, Vanni, 255
Corbucci, Sergio, 199
Cord, Alex, 18
Corpse Mania, 246
Corrà, Teodoro, 129
Corruption of Chris Miller, The, 151
Cotten, Joseph, 232
Covello, Angela, 73
Cozzi, Luigi, 38, 49
Craig, Michael, 64
Crazy Desires of a Murder, 98
Crimes of the Black Cat, The, 43
Crimine a Due, 104
Crispino, Armando, 18, 25
Cristaldi, Zeudi Araya, 199
Cross Current, 150
Cunningham, Liam, 35
Cuny, Alain, 235
Cupisti, Barbara, 220
Czemerys, Eva, 93, 114, 169
Dallamano, Massimo, 13, 63
Dallesandro, Joe, 15
D'Amario, Stefania, 192
D'Amato, Joe, 61, 94, 114, 252
D'Angelo, Mirella, 256
Damon, Marc, 4
D'Amore, Renato, 196
Danning, Sybil, 14
Dark Bar, 220
De Angelis, 9, 11
de los Ríos, Waldo, 125
De Luca, Nando, 37
De Masi, Francesco, 66, 169
de Mendoza, Alberto, 18, 89, 183
De Palma, Brian, 162

De Rossi, Barbara, 215
de Santis, Orchidea, 42, 182
Death Falls Lightly, 99
Deadly Inheritance, 71
Deadly Sweet, 58
Death Carries a Cane, 23
Death Haunts Monica, 149
Death Knocks Twice, 138
Death Laid an Egg, 76
Death Occurred Last Night, 107
Death on the Fourposter, 222
Death Smiles at Murder, 252
Death Steps in the Dark, 88
Death Walks at Midnight, 30
Death Walks on High Heels, 154
Death Will Have Your Eyes, 132
Deep Red, 258
Dei, Gianni, 201
Del Pozo, Ángel, 218
Delirium, 29
Delirium: Photos of Gioia, 254
Delitto Carnale, 229
Delitto D'Autore, 110
Delle Piane, Carlo, 202
Deodato, Ruggero, 54, 126
Descombes, Collette, 228
Desideri, Gioia, 121, 148
Designated Victim, The, 25
Devil Has Seven Faces, The, 179
Devil in the Brain, 107
Dexter, Rosemary, 65
Diamant, Catherine, 186
Diary of an Erotic Murderess, 109
Diffring, Anton, 4
Di Lazzaro, Dalila, 171
Di Leo, Fernando, 121
Di Marco, Gildo, 175, 238
Dionisi, Stefano, 237
Dionisio, Sofia, 188
Dionisio, Silvia, 257
Diogene, Franco, 124
Do You Like Hitchcock?, 120
D'Obici, Valeria, 69
Don't Look Now, 248
Don't Torture a Duckling, 82
Door Into Darkness, 48
Doria, Sergio, 117, 252

Dottesio, Attilio, 253, 254
Double, The, 116
Down, Leslie-Anne, 172
Dragonfly for Each Corpse, A, 85
Dressed to Kill, 162
Eastman, George, 255
Ekberg, Anita, 15, 81, 139
Elmi, Nicoletta, 16, 60, 118, 259
Embalmer, The 158
Enigma Rosso, 90
Evil Eye, 199
Evil Senses, 228
Eye in the Labyrinth, 65
Eyeball, 10
Eyes Behind the Wall, 233
Eyes of Crystal, 167
Eyes of Laura Mars, 161
Fajardo, Eduardo, 36, 38, 84, 181, 200
Falk, Rosella, 12, 19, 27, 61, 237
Fangareggi, Ugo, 189
Fani, Leonora, 184, 201
Fantino, Irio, 198
Farmer, Mimsy, 24, 229, 237, 245
Fashion Crimes, 137
Fatal Frames, 165
Felleghy, Tom, 99, 186
Fenech, Edwige, 7, 8, 9, 17, 28, 54, 129, 242
Ferrio, Gianni, 79
Ferzetti, Gabriele, 253
Fierro, Jole, 185
Fifth Cord, The, 19
Figura, Katarzyna, 126
Fiore, Maria, 220
Fisichella, Enzo, 209
Five Dolls for an August Moon, 129
5 Women for the Killer, 185
Flaherty, Lorenzo, 195
Fleming, Lone, 200
Flower in His Mouth, The, 204
Flower with the Petals of Steel, 105
Footprints, 59
Forbidden Photos of a Lady Above Suspicion, 21
Forsyth, Stephen, 102
Fortis, Giuseppe, 223

Four Flies on Grey Velvet, 237
Fourth Victim, The, 64
Foschi, Massimo, 188
Frank, Horst, 65
Franciosa, Anthony, 137, 255
Franciscus, James, 189
Freda, Riccardo, 4, 39, 258
French Sex Murders, 81
Frightened Woman, The, 34
Fulci, Lucio, 39, 44, 64, 82
Gaioni, Cristina, 187
Gaipa, Corrado, 98, 127
Galbó, Cristina, 12, 38, 125
Galetti, Giovanna, 119
Garcin, Henri, 257
Garko, Gianni, 63, 67, 105, 136
Garrani, Ivo, 72
Garriba, Fabio, 212
Gas, Manuel, 218
Gaslini, Giorgio, 185, 228
Gemma, Giuliano, 256
Gemmo, Giulio, 176
Gemser, Laura, 257
Gendron, François-Eric, 142
Germano, Elio, 120
Ghia, Dana, 188
Giallo (1934), 176
Giallo (2009), 193
Giallo a Venezia, 201
Giallo Napoletano, 198
Giannini, Giancarlo, 27, 113
Gimpera, Teresa, 147, 239
Giochi Erotici di una Famiglia per Bene, 133
Giombini, Marcello, 37, 106, 166, 181, 218
Giordano, Daniela, 119, 147, 200
Giordano, Mariangela, 201
Girl in Room 2A, 119
Girl Who Knew Too Much, The, 105
Giusti, Paolo, 220
Glas, Uschi, 12
Glass Ceiling, The, 135
Goblin, 6, 236, 256
Gori, Gabriele, 115
Grandi, Serena, 255

Granger, Farley, 47, 73, 97, 133
Grau, Jorge, 221
Guarnieri, Ennio, 204
Guérin, Florence, 142, 214
Guerritore, Monica, 229
Guida, Gloria, 232
Hargitay, Mickey, 29
Harlow, Yvonne, 192
Hatch, Richard, 221
Hatchet for the Honeymoon, 101
Hemmings, David, 258
Heywood, Anne, 61
Hill, Craig, 5
Hills, Gillian, 217
Hilton, George, 8, 17, 28, 32, 37, 83, 123, 180
Hoffmann, Robert, 23, 41, 51, 62, 70
House of the Blue Shadows, The, 247
House that Screamed, The, 125
House with the Laughing Windows, 55
House with the Yellow Carpet, The, 87
Hovey, Natasha, 195
Human Cobras, 183
Hyena in the Safe, 186
Iguana with the Tongue of Fire, The, 4
In the Devil's Garden, 172
In the Eye of the Hurricane, 157
In the Folds of the Flesh, 51
Incontrera, Annabella, 27, 39, 43, 73
Interrabang, 152
Isabelle, Katherine, 116
Israel, Victor, 125
Jhenkins, Jho, 234, 245
Jovine, Fabrizio, 216
Karis, Vassili, 202
Karloff, Boris, 168
Kasche, Renate, 62
Keaton, Camille, 197
Keller, Hiram, 6, 170
Kendall, Suzy, 9, 41, 172, 175
Kennedy, Arthur, 188
Killer is Among the Thirteen, The, 178

Killer Reserved Nine Seats, The, 92
Killer is on the Phone, The, 61
Killer is Still Among Us, The, 210
Killer Must Kill Again, The, 37
Killer Nun, 15
Killer with a Thousand Eyes, The, 181
Killer Wore Gloves, The, 217
Kinski, Klaus, 39, 60, 121, 252
Klimovsky, Leon, 233
Knife of Ice, 36
Knife Under the Throat, 213
Knight Moves, 116
Koscina, Sylva, 43, 73, 110, 145, 153
La Torre, Luis, 140
Lado, Aldo, 16, 45
Lahaie, Brigitte, 213
Lambert, Christopher, 116
Lane, Diane, 116
Lario, Veronica, 257
Lasander, Dagmar, 4, 21, 34, 101, 146
Laurence, Caroline, 188
Lavia, Gabriele, 228, 258
Law, John Philip, 233
Lawrence, Peter Lee, 182, 226
Lay Your Hands on My Body, 228
Lazenby, George, 16
Lear, Amanda, 171
Lee, Margaret, 39, 121
LeGault, Lance, 231
Lemoine, Michel, 223
Lenzi, Umberto, 10, 12, 36, 40, 78, 93, 231
Leon, Eva, 75
Lepori, Gabriella, 186, 219
Leroy, Philippe, 35, 150
Libido, 112
Liné, Helga, 32, 133
Lionello, Oreste, 238
Lisi, Virna, 224
Liz & Helen, 39
Lollobrigida, Gina, 76
Lombardi, Fausto, 115
Loncar, Bebe, 238
Longo, Malisa, 134
Lorys, Diana, 75

Love and Death in the Garden of the Gods, 182
Love and Death on the Edge of a Razor, 226
Lovelock, Ray, 24, 78, 210
Lualdi, Antonella, 223
Lys, Ágata, 233
Macabre, 239
Maderna, Bruno, 76
Madness, 114
Magnolfi, Barbara, 192
Malco, Paolo, 69
Malden, Karl, 189
Malfatti, Marina, 8, 12, 13, 14, 64, 65
Man with Icy Eyes, The, 127
Mancini, Carla, 252
Mancori, Guglielmo, 66, 166
Maniac Mansion, 166
Mann, Leonard, 88, 232
Marciano, Francesca, 56, 203
Margheriti, Antonio, 4, 6
Marielle, Jean-Pierre, 238
Marignano, Renzo, 42
Marley, John, 18
Marchall, Isabelle, 98
Marsillach, Cristina, 205
Marthouret, François, 143
Martin, Eugenio, 65
Martín, Maribel, 125
Martino, Sergio, 7, 8, 17, 28, 31, 100
Mascetti, Gina, 169
Masciocchi, Marcello, 129
Masé, Marino, 14, 210, 254
Mason, Hilary, 248
Mason, James, 204
Mastroianni, Marcello, 198
Matania, Clelia, 248
Mateos, Julian, 68
Materassi, Vanni, 192
Mattei, Bruno, 114
Matthews, Francis, 185
Maude, Mary, 125
Mauri, Glauco, 259
Marano, Ezio, 182
McEnery, Peter, 60
McNamara, William, 206
Medin, Harriet, 128, 249

Mell, Marisa, 12, 44, 45, 109, 133, 152, 221
Mercier, Michèle, 168
Merenda, Luc, 9, 22, 184
Méril, Macha
Michelini, Luciano, 30
Milian, Tomas, 25, 83
Milland, Ray, 144, 171
Mills, John, 45
Miraglia, Emilio, 14
Miranda, Isa, 118
Mitchell, Cameron, 85, 249
Mitchell, Gordon, 140
Molnar, Stanko, 11
Montagnani, Renzo, 169
Morales, Ines, 75
Moratti, Bedy, 169
Morales, Iván, 120
Morricone, Ennio, 16, 20, 24, 27, 41, 46, 67, 85, 107, 164, 175, 189, 204
Morrison, Alex, 187
Mostro, Il, 164
Moulder-Brown, John, 125
Mozart is the Murderer, 100
Mucari, Carlo, 196
Muccino, Silvio, 36
Muller, Paul, 216, 232
Murder Clinic, The, 128
Murder Obsession, 257
Musante, Tony, 174
Muti, Ornella, 78, 199
My Dear Killer, 32
My Wife Has a Body to Die For, 103
Naked Girl Killed in the Park, 70
Naked You Die, 4
Nalder, Reggie, 175
Naschy, Paul, 42, 75, 85, 178
Nebbia, Franco, 7
Nell, Krista, 73, 97, 110
Nemour, Antiniska, 193
Neri, Rosalba, 47, 81, 119, 121, 170, 241
Nero, Franco, 19, 204, 250, 251
Nicolai, Bruno, 7, 10, 13, 15, 67, 189
Nicolodi, Daria, 205, 244, 254, 256, 259
Niehaus, Rena, 197

Night Evelyn Came Out of Her Grave, 14
Nightmare Beach, 230
Nine Guests for a Crime, 187
Noris, Assia, 176
Nothing Underneath, 17
Novak, Ivana, 97, 227
Oasis of Fear, 78
O'Brien, Donald, 134, 198
Occhipinti, Andrea, 11
O'Keeffe, Miles, 137
O'Neill, Jennifer, 63, 204
Open Tomb, An Empty Coffin, An, 147
Opera, 205
Orano, Alessio, 38
Ortolani, Riz, 45, 88, 90, 171, 199
Otero, Carlos, 217
Pacula, Joanna, 136
Pagliai, Ugo, 14
Palmer, Lilli, 125
Paluzzi, Luciana, 62, 83, 253
Papas, Irene, 79
Paranoia, 93
Pataky, Elsa, 193
Pensione Paura, 184
Patrizi, Stefano, 257
Perfect Crime, 232
Perfume of the Lady in Black, The, 245
Perschy, Maria, 75
Persichetti, Loretta, 188
Perversion Story, 44
Peters, Werner, 139
Phantom of Death, 54
Phenomena, 243
Piccioni, Piero, 97, 98, 235
Piccoli, Michel, 199
Piernoi, Ania, 256
Pigozzi, Luciano, 4, 6, 8, 17, 72, 113, 133, 180, 183, 200, 249
Piovani, Nicola, 60, 246
Pisano, Berto, 104, 201, 253
Pisano, Isabel, 233
Pistilli, Luigi, 4, 7, 18, 110, 118, 123, 236, 243
Pizzirani, Giulio, 55, 203

Placido, Michele, 26, 171
Play Motel, 208
Pleasence, Donald, 17, 54, 166, 244
Plenizio, Gianfranco, 114
Plot of Fear, 26
Police are Blundering the Dark, The, 207
Polselli, Renato, 134
Porel, Marc, 63, 83, 192, 229
Possessed, The, 224
Pozzetto, Renato, 199
Pregadio, Roberto, 23
Prevost, Francoise, 128
Primus, Bary, 24
Prostituzione, 219
Psychic, The, 63
Psychout for Murder, 89
Puzzle, 22
Pyjama Girl Case, The 171
Quaglio, José, 47, 228, 234
Quasimodo, Alessandro, 186
Quesada, Milo, 168
Rabal, Francisco, 133, 184
Raho, Umberto, 43, 48, 51, 79, 143, 175, 216, 219
Ralli, Giovanna, 31, 67
Ransome, Prunella, 216
Rassimov, Ivan, 7, 8, 28, 41, 150, 243
Rassimov, Rada, 189
Red Headed Corpse, The, 97
Red Queen Kills 7 Times, The, 13
Reed, Dean, 138
Reflections in Black, 146
Renzi, Eva, 175
Resino, Andrés, 42
Ressel, Franco, 70, 150, 177, 180
Revault, Pascale, 185
Rey, Fernando, 68, 84, 153, 221, 234, 236
Reynaud, Janine, 18, 183
Ribotta, Ettore, 140
Ricci, Barbara, 126
Richardson, John, 9, 146, 188, 257
Rigaud, George, 10, 36, 155
Righi, Massimo, 128, 249
Ring of Death, 250
Rivelli, Luisa, 223
Rivero, Jorge, 200
Rizzoli, Anna Maria, 210
Robins, Eva, 256
Rocca, Stefania, 35
Rocchetti, Elisabetta, 120
Romano, Renato, 4, 12, 19, 81, 174
Ronet, Maurice, 107, 225
Ross, Howard, 93, 130, 153, 177, 186
Rossi, Luciano, 24, 30, 73, 155, 220, 252
Rossi-Stuart, Giacomo, 14, 43, 72, 116, 146, 239, 253
Ruffini, Sandro, 176
Ruggieri, Osvaldo, 61
Russo, Gaetano, 98, 124
Sabato, Antonio, 12, 127, 253
Saccarola, Gianpaolo, 63, 69, 256
Saint-John, Antoine, 37
Salemme, Lino, 255
Salerno, Enrico Maria, 175, 253
Salvador, Ben, 187
Salvino, Riccardo, 50, 133
Sandrelli, Stefania, 27
Sanson, Yvonne, 177
Santoni, Espartaco, 222
Savalas, Telly, 61
Savina, Carlo, 109, 153, 188, 232
Saxon, John, 105, 146, 231, 256
Scaccia, Mario, 245
Scanlon, John, 119
Schanley, Tom, 17
Schneider, Romy, 225
Schubert, Karin, 67, 119, 149
Schurer, Erna, 130, 140, 228
Scola, Gioia, 142, 195
Scott, Susan, 8, 22, 23, 30, 73, 154
Secret of Seagull Island, The, 216
Seducers, The, 241
Seigner, Emmanuelle, 193
Seller, Monica, 115
Selmier, Dean, 135
Senatore, Paola, 92, 105, 177
Sensuous Assassin, The, 225
Serato, Massimo, 238, 248
Seven Blood-Stained Orchids, 12
Seven Deaths in the Cat's Eye, 6

7 Murders for Scotland Yard, 42
Sevilla, Carmen, 135
Sex of the Witch, 197
Shadows in an Empty Room, 145
Shepard, Patty, 32, 135, 179
Short Night of Glass Dolls, 45
Siciliano, Mario, 199
Silent Night, Bloody Night, 163
Silva, Rita, 188
Sister of Ursula, The, 191
Skay, Brigitte, 118
Skerritt, Tom, 26, 116
Skin Under the Claws, The, 139
Slap the Monster on Page One, 212
Slaughter Hotel, 121
Sleepless, 236
Smile Before Death, 170
Snapshot of a Crime, 140
So Sweet, So Dead, 73
Soavi, Michele, 11, 256
Solar, Siliva, 217
Solbelli, Olga 251
Sorel, Jean, 44, 45, 93, 116, 122, 149, 157
Spaak, Catherine, 189
Spasmo, 40
Spencer, Bud, 238
Spirits of Death, 242
Stagnaro, Carola, 256
Staller, Ilona, 186
Starhemberg, Heinrich, 233
Steffen, Anthony, 14, 43, 109, 143, 181, 200, 209
Steiner, Elio, 176
Steiner, John, 26, 212, 256
Stewart, Evelyn, 17, 36, 60, 64, 66, 80, 196, 243
Strange Vice of Mrs. Wardh, The, 28
Strebel, Monica, 121, 140
Strindberg, Anita, 7, 16, 18, 22, 143, 257
Strip Nude for Your Killer, 9
Student Connection, The, 144
Suma, Marina, 221
Sutherland, Donald, 248
Suspected Death of a Minor, The, 30
Sweet Body of Deborah, The, 122

Sweets From a Stranger, 214
Tamberi, Giovanni
Tarascio, Enzo, 14, 18, 26
Tenebre, 255
Testi, Fabio, 12, 90, 138
Third Eye, The, 251
Thirsty for Love, Sex, And Murder, 111
Tien, Ni, 246
Tiller, Nadja, 138
Tinti, Gabriele, 143, 216, 225
Tolo, Marilù, 32, 50, 91, 116
Too Beautiful to Die, 142
Torray, Nuria, 147
Torso, 8
Trauma, 233
Tranquilli, Silvano, 80, 103, 113, 116, 170, 227
Treviglio, Leonardo, 69
Trhauma, 124
Trieste, Leopoldo, 118, 248
Trintignant, Jean-Louis, 59, 76
Tropic of Cancer, 143
Trumpets of the Apocalypse, 91
Two Faces of Fear, 83
Umiliani, Piero, 64, 129
Valeriano, Leo, 72
Valli, Alida, 66, 166, 195, 232
van Ammelrooy, Willeke, 61
Vanzina, Carlo, 17
Velazquez, Pilar, 70, 106, 200
Venantini, Venantino, 97, 188
Ventura, Lino, 235
Violent Bloodbath, 221
Violent Midnight, 159
Viotti, Patrizia, 48, 99
Visconti, Valentina, 196
Vitelli, Simonetta, 177
Volonté, Gian Maria, 212
von Fürstenberg, Ira, 129
von Sydow, Max, 236
von Treuberg, Franz, 182
Voyagis, Yorgo, 126
Wallach, Eli, 26
Walter, Eugene, 27, 56
Ward, Larry, 239
Washing Machine, The, 126

Watch Me When I Kill, 53
Weapon, The Hour, The Motive, The, 169
Webley, Patrizia, 72
Weekend Murders, The, 66
Wendel, Lara, 69, 256
What Have They Done to Your Daughters, 31
What Have You Done to Solange?, 12
Who Killed the Prosecutor and Why?, 238
Who Saw Her Die?, 16
Wilson, Barbara, 128
Without Trace, 253
Wolff, Frank, 68, 107, 155
Wynn, Keenan, 127
You'll Die at Midnight, 69
Young, Mary, 128
Your Vice is a Locked Room and Only I Have the Key, 7
Zamuto, Elio, 220
Zibetti, Roberto, 237
Zinnemann, Anna, 192
Zinny, Karl, 254

ABOUT THE AUTHOR

Richard Glenn Schmidt is a writer, musician, and obsessive fan of horror and cult cinema. He is firmly dedicated to wasting his life by watching movies. In 2005, he started the horror movie review website, Doomed Moviethon. He also maintains the Cinema Somnambulist blog and is co-host of the podcast, Hello! This is the Doomed Show. Richard majored in English literature at the University of South Florida. He lives in Tampa, Florida with his wife, LeEtta, in an old house where they have a wall of DVDs and two cats. Despite what the evidence suggests, he is not the killer.

Made in the USA
Middletown, DE
08 January 2016